I0816609

# MARGINAL COMMUNITIES

*The Ethical Enterprise of the Followers of Jesus*

# MARGINAL COMMUNITIES

*The Ethical Enterprise of the Followers of Jesus*

Martin Walton

Pharos

**Kok Pharos Publishing House**
**Kampen - The Netherlands**

CIP-GEGEVENS KONINKLIJKE BIBLIOTHEEK, DEN HAAG


P.O. Box 5019, 8260 GA Kampen, The Netherlands
Cover Design by Rob Lucas
ISBN 90 390 0116 2

## TABLE OF CONTENTS

# I. PURPOSE AND PERSPECTIVE

## *The ethical enterprise and ecclesial integrity*

The present explorations in the realms of ethics and ecclesiology were prompted by modern discussions in theology and church on the *status confessionis*. The modern usage of the term dates from the early 1930's when Dietrich Bonhoeffer lifted the term out of its peculiar place in Lutheran dogmatic history and applied it in the context of his condemnation of the exclusion and persecution of Jews. The term has been more recently used to indicate a crisis of the church in the face of apartheid, nuclear weapons and world poverty. Whatever was being said and done by appealing to or refuting the *status confessionis*, something was being said and needed to be said about the relation between ethics and ecclesiology.

The first movement of this study (Part II) is to explicate and evaluate the discussions on the *status confessionis* in the hope of illuminating that relation. An excursion on ecclesiological aspects of the conciliar process for justice, peace and the integrity of creation (JPIC) is intended to serve the same purpose. The urgency of the task is underlined by its proximity to recent documents seeking to discern and define a *kairos* for the churches. The primary thrust of the present study is not an attempt to revitalize the *status confessionis* terminology (or the conciliar process, however legitimate such undertakings might be), but to use such recent histories as heuristic examples. They point to fundamental (and, as will be argued, inescapable) questions being put to the life of the church, questions that affect the identity and integrity of the church as church. In seeking to define the basic issues it will be seen how two key terms, catholicity and conciliarity, can serve both to undergird the (urgent) intent of the *status confessionis* and to provide direction for further consideration.

The church is not without resources for understanding and responding to the challenges it faces. Perhaps its most vital resource is the praxis and confession of exemplary communities and networks. However, that trajectory is not explored here explicitly. Instead the projects of several theologians who seek (or who have sought) to critically inform the life of the church are investigated. (Part III) The theologians treated in this second movement are: Dietrich Bonhoeffer, Paul Lehmann, Stanley Hauerwas, Enrique Dussel, Leonardo Boff, Elisabeth Schüssler Fiorenza, and Letty Russel. (Brief attention is also given to Rosemary Radford Ruether in connection with Schüssler Fiorenza.)

Whereas the review of the *status confessionis* may reflect my present European context, the choice of these particular theologians may to some extent indicate my (North) American biases. Their relevance will have to become apparent in the treatment afforded them. Their importance for the issues at hand lies in the explicit ways in which they have related ecclesiological and ethical issues. Of particular interest is their emphasis on community as a reality and subject of ethical praxis. As a result the understanding of the catholic and conciliar nature of the church can take on shape and substance. Consequently, a context and a climate can be engendered in which the concerns and convictions expressed in the *status confessionis* can become conceivable and compelling.

The third movement is an attempt to recapitulate and reformulate the substance of the *status confessionis* in new terms, particularly within the framework of catholicity and conciliarity. Under the heading of conciliarity basic perspectives and processes are indicated that follow from the history of the *status confessionis* and that are fundamental to the life of the church. Under the heading of catholicity several issues are defined that seem essential to the identity and integrity of the church. Whereas the first movement (Part II) is an attempt at analysis of the *status confessionis* debate and the second movement (Part III) a review of theological projects, the third movement (Part IV) is a constructive attempt to interpret the significance of the materials and perspectives thus gathered for what might be called an ecclesial ethic. This constructive enterprise is not an attempt at definition in an exclusive or exhaustive sense, but a proposal as to how (some) things might look like in a church responsive to the substance of the *status confessionis*.

The proposal is that just as the *status confessionis* needs to be understood and conceptualized in the context of ethics and ecclesiology and their interrelation, so also in reverse an ecclesiological approach to the *status confessionis* can prove illuminating for ethical and ecclesiological perceptions in a more general sense. The approach is neither descriptive (in the assumption that the church is as it should be) nor prescriptive (in the presumption that it is enough to say what the church should be), but ascriptive, in appealing to the identity and perspectives of the church as an inclusive ethical community. The approach requires at least some clarification of what it means to make theological claims on the church. (See e.g. III.8.1.)

Each chapter ends with a number of "considerations". The considerations are not primarily intended as a summary or set of conclusions, but as an attempt to lift several key issues and positions to the forefront. It is from the considerations in parts II and III that the materials and perspectives are drawn for the constructive efforts in part IV. The considerations in part IV serve to recapitulate the constructive proposals of each chapter.

In an epilogue an attempt is made to retrace the movement of the entire study as well as to relate the main concerns to the central ethical category of love.

# II. THE CHURCH PUT TO THE QUESTION

## *Status confessionis and the status of the church*

If the church today is indeed put to the question, why put the question in remote Latin? Why bother with an obscure theological phrase of uncertain meaning and application even in its particularistic Lutheran origins? What is a *status confessionis* and what is the question being put to the church?

Semantics do not help much. Not even our Latin is much improved by investigating the various translations that the term has undergone due to the intertwining of theological interest and historical interpretation with semantic intention. The interpretations vary from a situation demanding confession to a confessional stance itself, from the status quo of historical confessions to a state of resistance.[2]

What the terminological debate simultaneously conceals and reveals is that something essential seems to be at stake, something of the nature of the church, its confession and its life in the world. Something of what is at stake can already be ascertained by noting the contexts in which the term has been used. The modern origins of the *status confessionis* debate date from the church struggle in Nazi Germany. The flame has twice raged in relation to the nuclear question in Protestant Germany with later echoes in the Netherlands and the United States. The application of the term to apartheid in the South African context has resounded in ecumenical bodies. The question has been further raised with regard to world poverty. The World Council of Churches has responded with a document in which economy is labeled a confessional issue.

Clarification of the *status confessionis* in its modern significance can be sought by following those several discussions on the subject. The starting point and primary perspective is provided by Dietrich Bonhoeffer. It was he who introduced the term in its modern usage and who immediately related that usage to a concept and crisis of the church. He thus shaped the term to denote a situation in which the identity and integrity of the church are being undermined, and the gospel - for the gospel is the only fundament of the church - is being falsified.

It should be noted that whereas the term *status confessionis* suggests an understanding in terms of the confession and teaching of the church, the modern applications have their context in socio-political and ethical questions. Bonhoeffer suggests seeking a resolution in terms of ecclesiology. The present study arrives at the conclusion that a description of the *status confessionis* is problematic either in terms of heresy (confession) on the one hand or in terms of sin (ethics) on the other. Instead, a recognition of the *status confessionis* proves possible and imperative when viewed in terms of the nature of the church (ecclesiology), that is, its (ethical) self-understanding and delineation.

The *status confessionis* denotes, therefore, a crisis of the church and by intention not just any crisis, but a point at which the church would cease to be the (true) church. It is a crisis to which the church must respond, not due to an introspective self interest, but as a matter of faithfulness and obedience and, as will be indicated, as a matter of solidarity with the totality of the body of Christ with all its members. The response of the church requires a sort of redefinition (one might say confession) and perhaps a regrouping, not as a mere organization, but as the body of Christ and as followers of Jesus. That process of renewed definition does not incur the application of formal, isolatable criteria, but occurs in reflection upon the nature and praxis of the church in response to a specific challenge.

Crucial to the interpretation of the *status confessionis* is an understanding (confession) of the church as a catholic, that is, an inclusive, human, and, therefore, ethical community (expressed in the fellowship of the reconciled around the communion table of Jesus Christ). It is the threat to the catholic unity of the church, its integrity as an inclusive human fellowship, that is at stake in the present-day contexts of the *status confessionis*. The church is put to the question in the challenge to claim and recover its catholic character, its community and conciliarity, that is, its inclusive diversity. The point is made by Manas Buthelezi:

> We need a new confession - perhaps in certain regions of the church - which will clearly list criteria for the oneness of the church in relation to the crucial issues of our time, even to the extent of shaking the foundations of the pseudo unity in which we find ourselves.[3]

# II.1.

# CONFESSING CHURCH AND THE JEWS

## 1.1. *The German Church Struggle and the Aryan Paragraph*

In Germany, on April 1, 1933, Jews were boycotted and subjected to violence. On April 7 a "Law for the restoration of the professional civil service," the so called "Aryan Paragraph" directed primarily against Jewish civil servants, was introduced. Even before the civil law was instigated, the demand to introduce the Aryan paragraph in the German Evangelical Church was to be heard at the first rally of the so called "German Christians" on April 3-4. Other demands were made for a conformed national church with a national bishop. The political events quickly became inner church affairs.

The issue which in retrospect must be considered the central issue, namely, the non-Aryan question, was not the issue which attracted the most attention.

> Of the four catchwords with which the German Christians aroused unrest, reaction, and commotion in the Evangelical Church during the Spring of 1933, namely, [forced] accommodation, national church, *Führer*-principle, and racial purity (Aryan paragraph), the last caused initially the least disturbance among church officials and oppositional movements and received the least notice...The number of those who in March and April of 1933 immediately addressed the fourth complex, the so called non-Aryan question, can be counted on the fingers of one hand.[4]

This situation shifted somewhat when in the Fall of 1933, after the German Christians had in July captured a majority position in the churches, the Aryan paragraph was in fact introduced into the churches. On November 2 Martin Niemöller published his "Propositions on the Aryan question in the church" in which he wrote:

> Under these circumstances a church law that excludes non-Aryans or not full Aryans, to the extent that they belong to the Jewish people, from church offices is contrary to the confession, because it fundamentally negates the communion of saints as confessed in the third article; for precisely with regard to the converted Jews it must be seen if the church of Jesus Christ is serious about the communion which reaches beyond natural bonds.[5]

Despite this clear language it appears that Niemöller expected Jewish Christians to avoid offence and voluntarily abstain from positions of leadership.[6] Nevertheless, the pledge which members of the Pastors Emergency Union, founded by Niemöller, were to sign included as the last of four points the attestation that the introduction of the Aryan paragraph in the churches constituted a violation of the confession.[7] Included as well was a pledge of responsibility for the persecuted, that is, the Jewish-Christian colleagues.

The clarity on the Jewish question faded in the ensuing struggle. The membership cards of the fraternal councils of the Confessing Church made no mention of the matter.[8] Attention shifted from the Aryan paragraph to the struggle over church authority and order. Eberhard Bethge speaks of a tragic shift in priorities with respect to the *status confessionis*: from the Aryan paragraph in 1933 to the assault on the church in 1934 to questions of church rule and authority in 1935.[9] It need not be denied that the interference of the state in church affairs provoked a *status confessionis.* Nevertheless Bethge correctly understands the shift of attention away from the Aryan paragraph as tragic, even if it occurred under severe political and ecclesiastical pressure and persecution.[10] Furthermore, it should be noted that the primary concern in the churches was for the status of converted Jews, an internal matter. The status of the Jews in general was hardly an issue.

## 1.2. *Karl Barth*

*Theological Existence Today*

Karl Barth did not want to overhurriedly respond to the new developments. That is evident from his essay "Theological Existence Today!"[11], which he only published at the end of June 1933 at the insistence of several friends. Barth felt that his point of view should have been evident. He preferred to speak to the point (*zur Sache*) rather than to the situation (*zur Lage*). By that he meant that the task of the theologian was to practice theology and above all theology.[12] There the decisive and indispensable decisions were to be made. The external threat was primarily that the church might cease being the church by not attending to its own subject matter, its own internal necessity, namely, the word of God. Theological existence is theological identity. On the non-Aryan question Barth's position was clear enough.

> The community of those who belong to the church is not determined by blood, nor by race, but by the Holy Spirit and by baptism. If the German Evangelical Church should exclude Jewish Christians or treat them as second class Christians it would cease to be a Christian church.[13]

Nevertheless Bethge notes:

> If one looks closely, the decisive roles, even in Barth's so effective fanfare "Theological Existence Today" from the end of June, 1933, are played by accommodation, national church, and leader principle; the non-Aryan question receives almost no special attention.[14]

*Correspondence with Dietrich Bonhoeffer*

After the Aryan paragraph had been introduced in the church a few months later, Dietrich Bonhoeffer wrote Barth with reference only to the Aryan issue.[15] For Bonhoeffer the situation of which Barth had warned in that single statement had become a fact, provoking the *status confessionis*. Bonhoeffer asked Barth what the consequences would be for church membership, unity and politics.

Barth answered that he also was of the opinion that the *status confessionis* had arrived, even if the measures at that time only concerned church ministers and functionaries and not yet church membership in general. He advised Bonhoeffer to sound the protest (that the church had ceased being the church) again and again until either the offence or oneself had been expelled. "For the rest I am in fact for waiting. The schism, if it comes, must come from the other side." Barth advised continued protest and "a quite active, polemic waiting."[16] Disappointing for Bonhoeffer and his Jewish friend and colleague, Franz Hildebrandt,[17] was the following:

> Perhaps the heinous teaching now reigning in the church must first make way for other, even worse deviations and falsifications. ... It could well be that the collision will follow at an even more central point.[18]

Barth followed here the line indicated in "Theological Existence Today". A schism must not be forced by selfwilfulness and certainly not by violence. One must keep to the point and keep making the point until one is expelled.

*Barmen*

The theological declaration of Barmen, May 1934, of which Barth was the primary author, was a clear and courageous *actus confessionis* (act of confession) on the issues confronting the German church. It confronted the intervention of the state in church affairs and the conforming factions in the church. It did so by asserting Christ alone (*solus christus*) as the source of authority and proclamation in the church in the face of those who attributed religious significance to the rise of Hitler and the German nation. Despite divergent interpretations of Barmen, there is agreement that Barmen correctly formulated decisive confessional issues.

Missing, as has since been pointed out, is any mention of the Jewish question, either in specific reference to the Aryan paragraph or in more general terms. Pinchas Lapide has labeled this deficit a lack of compassion for the Jews.[19] According to Lapide the confession of "Christ alone" was to some extent responsible for the lack of solidarity with the Jews and perhaps for some of the hostility towards them as well.

Bethge considers it astonishing that Barth did not include the Jewish question, in light of his position in "Theological Existence Today". At a Free Reformed synod in January of 1934 Barth had similarly rejected the restriction of church membership and ministry to persons of a particular race.[20] It is likewise surprising that Barth's practical and diaconal solidarity with presecuted Jews did not lead to more direct theological reflection and confessional expression.[21] That only came later. Bethge points to an example in a lecture from December 1938.

> (In the persecution and extermination of Israel) the Christian church is attacked at its very roots in an attempt to kill it. ... What would we be, what are we without Israel? Whoever rejects and persecutes the Jews, rejects and persecutes him who died for the sins of the Jews and in so doing all the more for our sins as well. Whoever is fundamentally an enemy of the Jews, exposes himself ... fundamentally as an enemy of Jesus Christ. Anti-Semitism is a sin against the Holy Spirit. For antiSemitism means rejection of the grace of God. Where is Jesus Christ himself under attack, if not here?[22]

I note here how Barth expressed an indebtedness to and a solidarity with the Jews without surrendering the concentration on Jesus Christ alone.

*Confession of guilt*

In 1967, after reading Bethge's biography of Bonhoeffer, Barth made a confession in a letter to Bethge.

> New for me was above all the fact that Bonhoeffer in 1933 and following was the first and almost only one to focus so centrally and energetically on the Jewish question and to take it on. For some time now I perceive it to be my guilt that in the church struggle I did not, at least openly (e.g. in either of the Barmen declarations of 1934 that I authored) assert it just as decisively. A text in which I would have done so would not, of course, in 1934, in view of the mental constitution at that time, even among the confessors, have been acceptable either in the reformed or general synod. But that does not excuse the fact that I did not at that time - because of a different interest - at least formally engage in battle on that issue.[23]

No hubris of retrospect[24] is appropriate. Barth spoke, as one of very few, in clear, decisive and confessional language. Barmen was erected as a dam against the powers, even if it was eventually inundated. Nevertheless it is necessary to see the other side as well. Barth's theological interest concerned primarily the purity and singular right of the word of God in the church. He spoke clearly to the question of Jews in the community of the church, but the matter could not claim his central attention. A more general, theological understanding of the relation of the church to Israel received development at a later time. In view of the alternatives of church politics and theology, as formulated in "Theological Existence Today", much is to be said for Barth. The question is whether the alternatives are adequately chosen. For as became clear for Bonhoeffer, the question of solidarity with the Jews was crucially situated between theology and (church) politics.

### 1.3. *Dietrich Bonhoeffer*

*The church and the Jewish question*

As early as the beginning of April 1933 Bonhoeffer responded to the so-called Jewish question in a lecture, soon published as an essay, "The Church and the Jewish Question".[25] There the issue was immediately and decisively formulated, as by a voice crying in the wildernis. The question that Bonhoeffer put forth is twofold and concerned not only baptized Jews in the church, but also the church's response to the doings of government. Both questions, Bonhoeffer asserted, could only be answered from the perspective of a proper concept of the church. Both issues provoked a *status confessionis* for the church. In both instances the existence (identity, integrity) of both church and state were at stake.

Bonhoeffer framed the issue in terms of the Lutheran teaching on the two regiments of church and state. He granted the state its own responsibility to regulate the Jewish question (although it is not clear what Bonhoeffer meant by this dubious formulation). The church is not to meddle with affairs of the state, but, on the other hand, should inquire into the legitimacy of the actions of government, into law and order, especially in the Jewish question. The church is compelled to speak both by too much law and order as well as by too little law and order. There is a lack of law and order when groups of people are deprived of justice and protection. There is an excess of law and order when government interferes in church affairs. In both instances the state negates itself.

According to Bonhoeffer three modes of action were (are) available to the church with respect to the state. First there is speaking out to question the legitimacy of the state's actions. In the second place there is assistance to aid the victims of the state's actions. "The third possibility is not just to bandage the victims under the wheel, but to jam a spoke in the wheel itself." Bonhoeffer proposed political resistance. The first two possibilities were for him in April of 1933 already "the compelling demands of the hour". The third mode of direct political action could only be decided upon by a church council.

Consequently Bonhoeffer turned to the special relation of the church to the Jews. In doing so he employed several statements regarding a curse upon the Jews or their need of conversion that have unavoidably been subject to criticism in more recent years.[26] But again the hubris of retrospect must be avoided, as Lapide has pointed out.[27] In addition it is important to note that the focus of Bonhoeffer's argument lay elsewhere. The seemingly anti-Semitic remarks are placed in a context of "to be sure...but...", that issues in an affirmation of God's faithfulness to Israel and of the fraternal bond between Christians and Jews. The church knows

> that no state in the world can be done with this enigmatic people, because God is not yet done with it. Every new attempt to 'solve' the 'Jewish question' will founder on the significance of this people in salvation history. The church's knowledge of the curse that burdens this people, lifts her far beyond any cheap moralization. Rather, at the sight of that rejected people she knows that she too is humbled as the church that is ever again unfaithful to her Lord. And she looks full of hope to those of the people of Israel who have returned, those who have come to faith in the one true God in Christ, and she feels united with them as brothers.[28]

It seems not without irony when Bonhoeffer points out that those who introduce racial purity as a condition of church membership are guilty of a modern vision of Judaistic Christianity by demanding adherence to a law in addition to faith.[29] Clearly, expulsion of Jews was unacceptable.

> Rather it is the task of Christian proclamation to say: here, where Jew and German stand together under the word of God, is the church; here is to be verified whether the church is still the church or not.[30]

Bonhoeffer considered it imperative to state this in all clarity without immediately moving to expel those who thought differently. But whoever refused fellowship with baptized Jews, withdrew himself from the church. It remained to be seen if such division need be viewed as a tolerable schism.

*Theological development*

In August of 1933 Bonhoeffer and his friend, Franz Hildebrandt produced a pamphlet with the title "The Aryan Paragraph in the Church."[31] Their position was clear: "The exclusion of Jewish-Christians from church community destroys the substance of the church of Christ" in that the reconciliation between Jew and Gentile (Ephesians 2) is undone and a new law is established as a condition for membership.[32] "The church would no longer be the church."[33] It must be clear "that the substance of the church and of the ministry, i.e., the confession, is under attack."[34]

In the Fall of 1933 Bonhoeffer worked with several others on the Bethel Confession.[35] Although the final text with its alterations and mitigations did not meet Bonhoeffer's approval,[36] God's continuing faithfulness to Israel was confirmed in the paragraph about the church and the Jews.

> God abundantly shows his faithfulness by still keeping faith with Israel according to the flesh, from whom was born Christ according to the flesh, despite all their unfaithfulness, even after the crucifixion of Christ.[37]

Alongside unfortunate statements on the disinheritance of Israel by the church, on mission to the Jews, etc., is found a confession of the God of Israel and of God's faithfulness to Israel. Missing in the later redactions is the important sentence:

> It is the task of Christians who come from the Gentile world to expose themselves to persecution rather than to surrender, willingly or unwillingly, even in one single respect, their brotherhood with Jewish Christians in the church, founded on Word and Sacrament.[38]

Here solidarity and actual consequences were linked directly to confession. It is probably not the case that Bonhoeffer felt called to fundamentally rethink and reformulate the relation of Jews and Christians or of Israel and the church. Increasingly he sought solidarity, rather than new formulations. Nevertheless Bethge has sketched matters which indicate a theological development,[39] a development that consisted not in the least in an intensified interest in the Old Testament.[40] Bonhoeffer distanced himself from the idea of a curse resting upon the Jews,[41] from mission to the Jews,[42] and from the idea that the church had replaced and disinherited Israel. Bethge comments: "The critique of Israel turns now into a critique of the church, which has betrayed its task of preparing the way for the Messiah."[43] Of concern to Bonhoeffer was not only the attitude towards Jews, but also the fundamental bond with the Jews. "This is where it is likely to be decided whether we are still the church of Jesus Christ: the Jewish question!"[44]

> The actual church of the Messiah of Israel can for Bonhoeffer now only exist together with Israel in its persecution, and she can never have nor think to have Christ without the "irrevocable solidarity" (Eichholz) with Israel, that in its own suffering points to the suffering of Christ.[45]

The church, Bonhoeffer would write, "is guilty of the deaths of the weakest and most defenseless brothers of Jesus Christ."[46]

*Solidarity and resistance*

Bonhoeffer continued to adhere to the fraternity with the Jews, which he mentioned as early as 1933 (The Church and the Jewish Question) as well as to the resulting demand for solidarity with oppressed Jews.

> In the evaluation of later confessional synods it was his criterium, whether their stance was not limited to the baptized non-Aryans. ...in the daily struggles of the Confessing Church he found it again and again necessary to give a reminder that the protest in the synod declarations against state intervention was only legitimate when not just the maintenance of full, including social, relations to baptized non-Aryans was intended, but when the church also raised her voice for the Jews as Jews.[47]

"Open your mouth for the dumb," (Proverbs 31:8) was a word that Bonhoeffer repeatedly emphasized.[48] At the same time there was another side to solidarity.

> If today the synagogues burn, then tomorrow the churches will be set on fire.[49] An expulsion of the Jews from the West must result in the expulsion of Christ, for Jesus Christ was a Jew.[50]

Substance and fate, existence and identity of the church were for Bonhoeffer essentially and ultimately linked to the fate of Israel. This solidarity eventually led to his participation in the conspiracy against Hitler. As a lone prophet in the church on this issue, Bonhoeffer chose the path of political resistance, the third of three possibilities which he had proposed in 1933, but without the support of his church or of a church council as he had then considered necessary.

## 1.4. *Germany after the war: confessing guilt*

*Stuttgart (1945): critique by Eberhard Bethge*

In October of 1945 the executive council of the newly formed Evangelical Church in Germany (EKD) met with ecumenical representatives.[51] With a view to the (church) struggle in the face of the Nazi regime of violence it was declared:

> We accuse ourselves that we did not confess more courageously, did not pray more faithfully, did not believe more joyfully, and did not love more ardently.

Guilt was confessed, but there was no explicit word on the Aryan paragraph. There was no mention of the discrimination and murder of the Jews, though the issue did receive condemnation in an accompanying letter to Christians in other countries that had suffered under German warfare and occupation.

Eberhard Bethge has pointed out that the confession of Stuttgart was directed towards interference by the state in church affairs, the excess of law and order, the accommodation of the church. The lack of law and order, the lawlessness and violence of the Nazi terror against Jews and others, was hardly seen. The conclusion of Bethge (and of others, but I take Bethge as an example due to his proximity to Bonhoeffer) is as follows:

> Viewed in this manner the guilt of not holding out on the *status confessionis* was only partially confessed in Stuttgart. There existed no clarity and probably ... no agreement with a view to the particularities of the guilt of the decades of the thirties and fourties. But does not a confession of guilt only serve the renewal of the body of Christ when it designates the guilt at a particular time, by particular bearers and inflicted upon particular victims, just as the *status confessionis* is demanded for Christ's sake at quite particular points and requiring quite particular consequences? Otherwise confession of guilt degenerates into an alibi, and closes by its agreeableness the door to renewal, which a confession of guilt is intended to open.[52]

*Suppression and concretization: Werner Krusche*

The confession of guilt in Stuttgart needed concretization. Instead, according to Werner Krusche, former bishop of Magdeburg, suppression of guilt occured.[53] Krusche pointed to the "Word of Darmstadt" (1950), issued by a fraternal council seeking to continue the confessing church tradition in post-war Germany, as an example of clear theological and political concretization of guilt.[54] The errant ways of German chauvinism and reactionary anti-communist conservatism were explicitly confessed and refuted, but the "Word of Darmstadt" did not become an official church document.

Two years previously the fraternal council had already spoken to the Jewish question.[55] In 1950 the synod of the Evangelical Church did follow that example.[56] Stuttgart received, even if with some delay, concretization. More delay was involved before a study in 1965 recognized the atrocities regarding Poland. A statement on the relation to the Soviet Union did not follow until another couple of years after Krusche's reflections on the matter.[57] And what of gypsies, the handicapped, the Jehovah's Witnesses, homosexuals, communists, and other political dissidents? Recognition and confession of guilt proved slow in coming.

It was Krusche's contention that the severe sufferings of the Germans in the last months of the war and under the occupational powers deferred attention of Christians from their own guilt to the guilt of others. One's own misery was more concrete than one's own guilt.[58] Krusche concurred with Bonhoeffer's conviction that "Confession of guilt must occur without a glance to those who share guilt. It is strictly exclusive in that it assumes all guilt for oneself."[59] Krusche concluded:

> The Evangelical Church and the German people did not pass through the door which had been opened by the Confession of Stuttgart and did not reach the open air of a truly new beginning.[60]

*Status confessionis and confession of guilt*

Of importance for the present study is not a further evaluation of the developments within the Evangelical Churches of Germany since the Second World War. Of importance is rather the connection between the defaulted *status confessionis*, whether by lack of perseverance or by total neglect, on the one hand and specific confession of guilt on the other. If the *status confessionis* marks the point at which the church would cease to be the church, how can the integrity of the church be restored when the defaulted *status confessionis* is not or only partially confessed?

> The free confession of guilt is not something which can be done or left undone, rather it is the breakthrough of the form and figure of Jesus Christ in the church, which the church must allow to occur or otherwise cease to be the church of Christ.[61]

With these words Bonhoeffer was referring to the failure of the church, including the Confessing Church, in relation to both the excess and lack of law and order in Germany of the 1930's. Guilt, as Krusche underlined, can only be confessed concretely and historically.[62]

## 1.5. *Barmen revisited*

The deficit of Barmen in not mentioning the Jews has already been cited, along with Barth's later reflections on that deficit and his "other interest" at the time. In that light it is interesting to review the results of a conference fifty years later, "Barmen 1934-1984."[63] There an attempt was made to reflect on the relation between Israel and the church on the basis of the first thesis of Barmen regarding the sole authority of Christ.

In a declaration it was put forth that the "one word of God" (Barmen I) is none other than the Jew Jesus as "attested for us in holy Scripture" (Barmen I) of both Old and New Testament. As the messiah of Israel he is also the reconciler of the world. He cannot be separated from his people and the church does not disinherit Israel. God remains faithful. "Whoever rejects Israel, rejects the faithfulness of God."[64]

In a lecture at the conference entitled "Barmen I and the Jews" Berthold Klappert proposed that a new theology of Israel could be gained precisely from Jesus Christ as attested to in the whole of Scripture.[65] In no sense does Barmen I, the *solus christus*, exclude the Jews.

> Barmen I must in light of the Bible texts John 14:6; 19:9 be understood exclusively against the German Christians, but in light of John 4:22, "salvation comes from the Jews", inclusively with regard to the self testimony of Judaism.
> The exclusiveness of Barmen - formulated against the paganism of the German Christians - is precisely the precondition of the recognition and appreciation of an inclusiveness: the peculiar significance and self-testimony of Judaism as the enduring chosen people of God.[66]

The "other interest" to which Barth referred, is in Klappert's view, the challenge of natural theology and revelation. The "more central point" is the freedom of the word of God.[67] The deficit of Barmen and the direction which the majority of the Barmen confessors took is tragic. But for Klappert (and, in his interpretation, for Barth) it is that "other interest" and that "more central point" that offer a position and a perspective for the struggle against anti-Semitism. I take two examples cited by Klappert. In a sermon from December of 1933 Barth indicated his inclusiveness of Israel.[68] In a lecture in 1938 on "The Church and the Political Question Today" Barth summoned Christians in Germany to political resistance in the context of the *status confessionis*, "with the motivation that anti-Semitism is the decisive and sufficient sign of the anti-church and of a politically lawless state."[69]

The point in reviewing Klappert on these matters is not to defend Barth, as if that were necessary, but to further investigate what Christian confession with regard to Israel might entail. The consequence for Klappert is that

> the decisive task of the ecumenical church is to theologically advocate the native right of Jewish Christians in the gentile church, to realize the admission of Judaism, the community of God as a people, into the ecumenical movement (abstenance from mission to Jews) and to guarantee and secure the socio-political right to existence of Judaism among the peoples (the struggle against all forms of Christian anti-Judaism and anti-Semitism).[70]

Characteristic for Klappert's position is the reversal of the usual Christian position, a reversal that he illustrates in a quotation of H.J. Kraus. "More dangerous than the blindness of Judaism towards Christ is the blindness of Christians towards Jews."[71]

## 1.6. *Dutch intermezzo*

At this point one further excursion can be made in order to note two moments with regard to the confession of the church and the relation of the church to Israel. The setting is the Netherlands.

*Confessing in the face of anti-Semitism*

In 1941, in the face of German occupation, three Dutch theologians drew up a statement under the title of "What we do and what we do not believe."[72] The theses of J. Koopmans, K.H. Miskotte and K.H. Kroon bore a kinship with the theological declaration of Barmen, for example, in the concentration on Jesus Christ, but the Dutch document was more extensive and included a paragraph on Israel. Although not ratified by a synod as was the Barmen declaration, it was a confession that included Israel. It affirmed the election of Israel as an act of God's free grace.

> Therefore we believe that whoever sets one's face against Israel, has resisted the God of Israel. ... Therefore we consider anti-Semitism to be much more serious than an inhuman ideology of race. We consider it to be one of the most obstinate and fatal forms of resistance against the holy and merciful God, whose name we confess.

*Confessing in the face of neutrality*

In 1973, in the wake of the Yom Kippur war, six Netherlands Reformed theologians published a declaration under the title "No neutrality" in response to the silence of official church bodies and as a reaction to the summons by various church diaconal institutions to help the victims of "both parties".[73] The declaration sought to carry the understanding of God's continuing faithfulness to the people of Israel a step further.

> Under the present circumstances Israel can live in its land only within its own state. In our time, therefore, that state is an essential part of the sign of faithfulness that God has given to Israel in its return. Whoever infringes upon the right of existence of the Jewish state, runs the risk of infringing upon God himself ... as if the promise of the land for the Jews had no more meaning.

The right of existence of the Jewish state, combined with the land promise, was understood to be an essential element of the church's confession in the contemporary historical constellation. And it was understood to be a confession that required action.

> Because the church of Jesus Christ can only live by God's grace, she knows that she is bound to the faithfulness of the same God. Because in our time the right of existence of the Jewish state is at stake, we ask the members of the Netherlands Reformed Church to choose with us the side of the existence of this state, for only then can our preaching of reconciliation sound clearly and only then is our help for victims of both parties veracious. Church bodies in their "neutrality" on the right of existence of the state of Israel contradict the confession to which the church is now called. As long as they persevere in this standpoint, they are not entitled to act on behalf of the church.

Although no specific consequences for church fellowship were indicated, the suggestion was thus made that certain church bodies had ceased to be (representative of) the church. In a later reflection on the declaration A.A. Spijkerboer commented that the six theologians, of which he was one, had given too little consideration to the fact that the Palestinian question demanded a certain compliancy on the part of Israel.[74] Not clear from this later comment is how the need of such compliancy should affect the demanded confessional stance with regard to the state of Israel.

## *Considerations*

### *Perspectives on Israel*

It is not the intention of this study to provide an extensive discussion of Christian theology on Israel and/or the relation of church and synagogue, Tenach (Jewish scripture) and the gospel. Nevertheless a few basic perspectives that have been indicated in the context of the *status confessionis* debate can be noted here.

1. To confess the Lord of Israel, the Father of Jesus Christ, is to confess God's enduring faithfulness to Israel as people of God. (Klappert)
2. To confess God's enduring faithfulness to Israel is to reject the disinheritance of Israel by the church and to seek dialogue with Jews rather than their conversion. (Bonhoeffer, Klappert)
3. Anti-Semitism and anti-Judaism are affronts to the one God whom Jews and Christians commonly worship, denials of Jesus the Jew, and sins against the spirit of God. (Bonhoeffer, Miskotte et al, Klappert)
4. The first task is not to understand Israel and its scriptures in terms of Jesus, but Jesus in terms of Israel and its scriptures. The church is to recognize the priority of Israel in its own life and confession. (Bonhoeffer, Klappert, Kraus)

5. The community of Jews and Christians cannot be defined in terms of baptized Jews, but in terms of an ecumenical relation between Israel and the church. (Klappert)
6. Community with Israel means solidarity. Solidarity with Israel means solidarity with Israel's right to existence in peace (shalom). (Bonhoeffer, Klappert)
7. The essential relation between Israel as a people and the land and state of Israel raises the question of the political nature of solidarity with Israel. The strife within Israel, especially concerning the Palestinians, intensifies the issue of political solidarity in terms of the question of political justice in relation to peace.

*The task of confession*

8. Bonhoeffer argued that the response of the church to the political challenge is to be formulated in terms of a proper conception of the church. He ascribes to the nature of the church external, political significance. The church as a "church for others", as he would later formulate, seems implicit in this understanding.
9. Bonhoeffer's understanding of the *status confessionis* as a response to an excess and lack of law and order needs further clarification with regards to the significance of the state for Christian confession. The significance of the state of Israel provides a particular perspective in attempting to define matters.
10. Framing the discussion not only in terms of the church's relation to the Jews but in terms of political law and order broadens the scope of solidarity to include all victims. From here a line can be drawn to Miskotte's understanding of humanity in the Torah as inclusive humanity. The implication is that solidarity is an essential mark of the church.
11. There is no real renewal, no true life in the church without confession of guilt, historically, concretely, specifically. The integrity of the church is dependent on the quality of its confession of its failure. (Bonhoeffer, Bethge, Krusche)
12. Church membership is based on baptism and the Spirit alone. Any attempt to raise other criteria must be rejected as discriminatory and contrary to the calling of the gospel and the life of the church. (Barth, Bonhoeffer)

## II.2.

## APARTHEID

In South Africa things have changed. And change continues. In what manner and to what extent remains to be seen. The example of the United States shows that the acquisition of civil rights in itself, however important, is not enough to engender social equality and wholesome race relations. Poverty and social disorder remain. Violence remains. Justice remains unfulfilled. All too many churches remain within the color boundaries. Therefore, even as the situation in South Africa is changing, it is important to reflect on the heritage of apartheid. Moreover, the problem in South Africa was and is not simply that of racism. Even mainline white South African churches have rejected racism in name. The question is whether the policy and ideology of apartheid as were developed and practiced and theologically advocated in church and society constituted for the churches a *status confessionis*, that is, whether in the context of apartheid the integrity of the church was (is) at stake.

The discussion of the *status confessionis* with regard to apartheid has two main focuses. There is in the first place the manifold struggle in South Africa itself, the question of the need for a confessing church, the arisal of a confessing movement, and the arrival at confessional statements such as that of Belhar and the Kairos document. Of importance, in the second place, are the positions taken and procedures followed by two large ecumenical bodies, namely, the Lutheran World Federation and the World Alliance of Reformed Churches. From a review of those developments at two different levels I hope to arrive at an understanding of the meaning of the *status confessionis* in the context of apartheid. A consequent question (third level) is to what extent the situation in South Africa is a microcosm of world relations.

### 2.1. *Cottesloe and the World Council of Churches*

In the series of church statements on apartheid in South (or more generally in Southern) Africa, the statement of the Cottesloe Consultation, held in 1961 under the auspices of the World Council of Churches provides a good starting point.[75]

> No one who believes in Jesus Christ may be excluded from any Church on the grounds of his colour or race. The spiritual unity among all men who are in Christ must find visible expression in acts of common worship and

witness, and in fellowship and consultation on matters of common concern.

While the strongest language was directed, as in the above quotation, to matters of church fellowship, the consultation also directed its attention to political, social, and economic problems on the basis that

> the Church must proclaim that the final criterion of all social and political action is the principles of Scripture regarding the realization of all men of a life worthy of their God-given vocation.

## 2.2. *"The Time For a Confessing Church Has Come"*

It was Beyers Naudé who first confronted apartheid in confessional terms in an article entitled "The Time For a Confessing Church Has Come," published in 1965.[76] Beyers Naudé indicated several parallels between the situation in South Africa at that time and in Germany of the Third Reich: "racism; a false unity between church and *volk*; ideological pressure on, intimidation of, and an attack on the church; and a sinful silence in the face of injustice." By the description "confessing church" Naudé did not mean a new denomination but "a confessing movement within the churches, binding together in faith, study, and action those who sought to be obedient to Jesus Christ within apartheid society."

In and around the Christian Institute and the South African Council of Churches (SACC) the question of a confessing church remained a matter of discussion for a decade. In 1968 the SACC issued "A Message to the People of South Africa."[77] Although not a confession in a formal sense, the document conveys a confessional tone. I quote three passages.

> There are alarming signs that this doctrine of separation has become, for many, a false faith, a novel Gospel. (...) It presents separate development of our race-groups as a way for the people of South Africa to save themselves. Such a claim inevitably conflicts with the Christian Gospel which offers salvation, both social and individual, through faith in Christ alone.
> According to the Christian Gospel, we find our identity in association with Christ and with each other. Apartheid is a view of life and a view of man which insists that we find our identity in dissociation and in distinction from each other. A policy of separate development which is based on this concept therefore involves a rejection of central beliefs of the Christian Gospel.
> If we seek to reconcile Christianity with the so-called 'South African way-of-life' (or any other way of life), we shall find that we have allowed

> an idol to take the place of Christ. Where the Church thus abandons its obedience to Christ, it ceases to be the Church; it breaks the links between itself and the Kingdom of God. We confess, therefore, that we are under an obligation to live in accordance with the Christian understanding of man and community, even if this be contrary to some of the customs and laws of this country.

In 1973, following a visit to South Africa, Eberhard Bethge wrote that the question of a confessing church was still very much alive, that, however, the preformed name and model created somewhat of a burden, in that the thing itself had not yet taken shape.[78] In addition the denominational plurality, i.e., the fact of any number of various confessional churches, constituted an obstacle for arriving at a confessional body.[79] Theologically Bethge concluded that whereas in Germany of the 1930's the *solus christus* was at stake, in South Africa the issue was the *unitas* of the body of Christ,[80] the *unum* of baptism, as Bethge would later formulate.[81]

The German church struggle was and remained a church struggle. Bethge noted that the struggle in South Africa for a multi-racial church was linked to the struggle for a multi-racial society. There was an awareness of the political dimension of the Christian confession of the *unitas*, that is, an appreciation of the common human responsibility for the *humanum*.[82]

In the years that followed, the discussion shifted from the question of a confessing church to that of a confessional situation, that is, the *status confessionis*. The basic issue, however, remained the same. At stake was the integrity of the church as church and the political dimensions of ecclesiology.

## 2.3 *The Lutheran World Federation*

*Evian: On racial division in church and society*

I now turn my attention more specifically to the Lutheran World Federation (LWF). At the seventh general assembly of the LWF at Evian in 1970 a declaration on the race issue was approved which included the following two principles.[83]

1. In the Lutheran churches the members of all races should at any time be willing to take communion together.
2. The Lutheran churches should oppose the principles and exercise of racial discrimination and racial separation.

The principles were intended to provide a basis for talks with member churches for which the race issue was a particular problem, primarily the white Lutheran churches in southern Africa. It is important for what follows to note that both the ecclesial and the political aspects of the race issue are indicated.

*Swakopmund: Those who exclude themselves*

At an annual meeting of the Federation of Evangelical-Lutheran Churches in Southern Africa (FELCSA) in February of 1975, there was issued "An appeal to Lutheran Christians in Southern Africa for the unity and witness of Lutheran churches and their members in Southern Africa."[84] The appeal stated

> that those who allow racial divisions to be governing principles in the life and organization of our churches and who approve of the deprivation of human rights, of the dignity and worth of humans created according to the likeness of God, exclude themselves from the community of believers.

Again it is to be noted how both ecclesial and political dimensions are envisioned. An additional step is made in stating that those who advocate racial division or approve of the violation of human integrity exclude themselves from the Christian community.

*Dar es Salaam: status confessionis*

The statements of Evian and Swakopmund form the background for the declaration of the sixth general assembly of the LWF at Dar es Salaam in June of 1977 on "confessional integrity" in Southern Africa.[85]

> The Lutheran churches are confessional churches. Their unity and mutual recognition are based upon the acknowledgement of the Word of God and therefore of the fundamental Lutheran confessional writings, particularly the Augsburg Confession, as normative.
>
> Confessional subscription is more than a formal acknowledgement of doctrine. Churches which have signed the confessions of the church thereby commit themselves to show through their daily witness and service that the gospel has empowered them to live as the people of God. They also commit themselves to accept in their worship and at the table of the Lord the brothers and sisters who belong to other churches that accept the same confessions. Confessional subscription should lead to concrete manifestations in unity in worship and in working together at the common tasks of the church.
>
> Under normal circumstances Christians may have different opinions in political questions. However, political and social systems may become so perverted and oppressive that it is consistent with the confession to reject them and to work for changes. We especially appeal to our white member churches in Southern Africa to recognize that the situation in Southern Africa constitutes a *status confessionis*. This means that, on the basis of

faith and in order to manifest the unity of the church, churches would publicly and unequivocally reject the existing apartheid system.

Immediately following the declaration the discussion began on what had and had not been said.[86] Was the concern primarily a church affair? To what extent and in what manner was the declaration to be understood politically? What is the intended meaning of *status confessionis*? Would a political application be acceptable?

Without seeking to answer all the questions and short of a detailed analysis of the in some points ambiguous text, I ascertain that the first paragraph deals with Lutheran identity. The second paragraph deals with church fellowship and hospitality and insists that the unity of the church be manifested concretely. The third paragraph confronts the political challenge. In that context the *status confessionis* is postulated. That in referring to the "situation in Southern Africa" the ecclesial situation is also intended, does not detract from the political scope of the text of the declaration.

*From Harare to Budapest: Suspension as discipline*

In preparation for the seventh assembly of the LWF (Budapest 1984) the All African Lutheran Consultation met in Harare in December 1983. A resolution was approved suggesting that on the basis of the Dar es Salaam statement the white member churches of the LWF in Southern Africa be suspended until which time they did openly and unambiguously reject apartheid and seek unity with the other member churches in Southern Africa. To be sure, the white Lutheran churches in Southern Africa had declared their rejection of the system of apartheid and racism as well as their intention of attaining unity with the black Lutheran churches.[87] The white Lutheran churches, in line with the English speaking churches of South Africa, had advocated no theological basis for the system of apartheid or separate development as had the white Reformed churches in South Africa. The conclusion would seem to be that the white Lutheran churches were judged not only on the basis of their words and declarations, but on the basis of their praxis and policy. At issue were not only theology and (verbal) confession, but also church order and practice.

The general assembly in Budapest complied with the request of Harare, emphasizing that the white member churches in Southern Africa had excluded themselves from the common confessional fellowship. The intention of the suspension, in keeping with the practice of church discipline in Africa, was not to break fellowship but to strengthen its quality. Rights were withdrawn, but not all contacts were severed.[88]

## 2.4. *The World Alliance of Reformed Churches*

*The white Reformed churches in South Africa*

Apartheid has a long history, inseparably linked to the history of the white Reformed churches in South Africa. I do not intend to reproduce either that history or the biblical and theological underpinnings of apartheid. Such matters have been documented elsewhere.[89] I find it sufficient for the present study to note the following:

1. The history of apartheid and of the white Reformed churches is characterized by an entanglement of politics, theology, and racist ideology.
2. The white Reformed churches have advocated cultural segregation and racial separation as theologically desirable and imperative. Such separation has also been reflected in church policy.
3. The separation policies have proven to be discriminatory, oppressive, exploitive, violent, and humanly degrading.
4. The white Reformed churches have repeatedly and obstinately rejected all appeals for a fundamental change of course (conversion).

I do not intend to argue these observations. I assume them. And I note that two and four are sufficient for what follows.

*"Apartheid is a heresy"*

In 1981 the Alliance of Black Reformed Christians in Southern Africa was formed. Its charter asserted the Lordship of Christ and rejected the subservience of the Word of God to cultural claims and racist ideology.[90]

> The unity of the Church must be visibly manifest in the one people of God. The indivisibility of the body of Christ demands that the barriers of race, culture, ethnicity, language, and sex be transcended.

The Alliance committed itself to an authentic and relevant articulation of the faith.

> We begin doing so by declaring unequivocally that apartheid is a sin and that the moral and theological justification of it is a travesty of the Gospel, a betrayal of the Reformed tradition, and a heresy.

This proclamation provided the backdrop for an incident at the meeting of the General Council of the WARC in Ottawa in 1982. Eleven South Africans refused to participate in the celebration of Holy Communion, not primarily as a protest or boycott, but rather as a confession of faith. The Lord's Supper is a common meal intended to give expression to the unity of Christians. If common celebration were not possible in South Africa, then it should not be pretended outside the country.[91] The action, which provided a depiction of the actual situation in South Africa, moved the General Council to issue a declaration under the title "Racism and South Africa." I present several excerpts at length.

> God in Jesus Christ has affirmed human dignity. Through his life, death and resurrection he has reconciled people to God and to themselves. He has broken down the wall of partition and enmity and has become our peace. He is the Lord of his Church who has brought us together in the one Lord, one faith, one baptism, one God who is the father of us all (Eph. 4:5,6).
> The Gospel of Jesus Christ demands, therefore, a community of believers which transcends all barriers of race - a community in which the love for Christ and for one another has overcome divisions of race and colour.
> The Gospel confronts racism, which is in its very essence a form of idolatry. Racism fosters a false sense of supremacy, it denies the common humanity of believers, and it denies Christ's reconciling, humanizing work. It systematizes oppression, domination, and injustice. (...)
> Apartheid (or 'separate development') poses a unique challenge to the Church, especially the Churches in the Reformed tradition. The white Afrikaans Reformed Churches of South Africa have worked out in considerable detail both the policy itself and the theological and moral justification for the system. Apartheid ('separate development') is therefore a pseudo-religious ideology as well as a political policy. (...) This leads to the division of Christians at the table of the Lord as a matter of practice and policy.

The statement recalled earlier declarations in which racism had been labeled a "betrayal of the Gospel" and "idolatry" with the conclusion that the "Church that by doctrine and/or practice affirms segregation of peoples (e.g. racial segregation) as a law for its life cannot be regarded as an authentic member of the body of Christ." Past warnings having gone unheeded, the General Council felt compelled to conclude:

> The Nederduitse Gereformeerde Kerk and the Nederduitsch Hervormde Kerk, in not only accepting, but actively justifying the apartheid system by misusing the Gospel and the Reformed confession, contradict in doctrine and in action the promise which they profess to believe.
> Therefore, the General Council declares that this situation constitutes a *status confessionis* for our Churches, which means that we regard this as an issue on which it is not possible to differ without seriously jeopardizing the integrity of our common confession as Reformed Churches.

> We declare with black Reformed Christians of South Africa that apartheid ('separate development') is a sin, and that the moral and theological justification of it is a travesty of the Gospel and, in its persistent disobedience to the Word of God, a theological heresy.

The Council pleaded afresh with the NGK and the NHK to respond and repent, but felt compelled to suspend both churches from the privileges of membership until which time:

> (a) Black Christians are no longer excluded from church services, especially from Holy Communion;
> (b) Concrete support in word and deed is given to those who suffer under the system of apartheid ('separate development');
> (c) Unequivocal synod resolutions are made which reject apartheid and commit the Church to dismantling this system in both Church and politics.

Whereas the confessional portion of the statement of Ottawa has the church as its primary focus, the three conditions for rehabilitation make clear that the political dimension was likewise intended, both in terms of political struggle and support for the victims.

*WARC and LWF in concurrence*

I draw several conclusions from a comparison of the LWF and WARC statements on the *status confessionis* in the context of apartheid in South Africa.

1. Both statements related the *status confessionis* to both church fellowship and the socio-political system.
2. The judgement on the targeted churches concerned both their teaching and theology on the one hand and their order, life, and practice on the other. The WARC more explicitly spoke of heresy, idolatry, etc., with reference to both morality and theology.
3. The churches involved had in fact already excluded themselves from the body of Christ.
4. The suspension of the accused churches was nevertheless intended as a disciplinary measure and ultimate appeal, not as an act of excommunication. Whereas the LWF allowed an interval of several years between declaring the *status confessionis* and taking disciplinary measures, the WARC, on the basis of previous warnings, took both actions at the same time.

It might be asked if suspension was not a rather mild measure, but then again LWF and WARC do not understand themselves as churches but as ecumenical, confessional organizations. In addition, any definitive severance might better occur in the region of conflict.

## 2.5. *The Confession of Belhar*

The (black) Dutch Reformed Mission Church in South Africa responded positively to the theological challenge of Ottawa. At a synod meeting the same year in Belhar a declaration and confession were presented.[92] The second article emphasized the unity of the church.

> We believe in one holy, universal Christian Church, the communion of the saints from the entire human family. We believe:
> - that Christ's work of reconciliation is made manifest in the Church as the community of believers who have been reconciled with God and with one another;
> - that unity is, therefore, both a gift and an obligation for the Church of Jesus Christ; that through the working of God's Holy Spirit it is a binding force, yet simultaneously a reality which must be earnestly pursued and sought: one which the people of God must continually be built up to attain;
> - that this unity must become visible so that the world may believe; that separation, enmity and hatred between people and groups is sin which Christ has already conquered, and that accordingly anything which threatens this unity has no place in the Church and must be resisted; (...)
> - that ... the variety of spiritual gifts, opportunities, backgrounds, convictions, as well as the various languages and cultures, are, by virtue of the reconciliation in Christ, opportunities for mutual service and enrichment within the one visible people of God;
> - that the true faith in Jesus Christ is the only condition for membership of this Church.

The basic criticism of apartheid and of its theological justification is that it denies the reconciling and humanizing work of Christ. Separation and segregation, distinction and irreconcilability are made fundamental principles in church and society. Consequently it is not the belief in the one, holy, catholic church and in the communion of the saints which shapes the life and confession of the church, but the secular gospel of apartheid. It is to this that the accusation of theological heresy and idolatry is directed.

A positive vision of what the church is to be is also provided: a fellowship of the reconciled, in which plurality and diversity provide the opportunity for mutual service and enrichment within the one visible people of God. It is the unity which is to be confessed as normative, not the diversity. At the same time that unity and diversity are understood in a critical way. J. de Gruchy has pointed out how the Belhar confession in the light of its rejection of apartheid came to a commitment to the poor and to the cause of justice and liberation.[93] Article four of the confession is a claim that the church must stand with Christ against injustice and with the wronged and must stand by people in any form of suffering and need.

E. Bethge has made a similar point by way of comparison with Barmen. The confession of Belhar not only protested against the accommodation of the church as did Barmen, but also stood up for the victims of that accommodation in which Barmen was weak.[94] Bethge was again able to point to the example of Bonhoeffer.[95]

> Bonhoeffer said it in all clarity in an essay in April of 1933: There is no confession of Christ without confession against the violation of the body of Christ by the state, without a confession for those who are subjected to violence and persecution by that state. In that way the political aspect is directly addressed: a confession, that speaks up for human beings, that does not stop at church borders, but has especially those in mind who do not even belong to the church, like the Jews then. ... The first time I was in South Africa, I considered it to be a great advantage, that there was an awareness on a much broader scale, that there is no confession of Christ without confession for the persecuted groups, because that would be a betrayal of Christ.

De Gruchy and Bethge have indicated a subtle, but fundamental emphasis in the understanding of political witness and confession. The primary political relation for the church is not to the state or government, but to the poor and the victimized, to real human beings. Related to this in the comments of Bethge is the church's relation to itself. Immediate care is necessary in the formulations that are employed, for the victims may be, but need not be, members of the church; but whether inside or outside the church, they are not outside of the scope of the church's confession and concern. Crucial for the relation between the church and the poor, between the church and the victims, will be the extent to which the poor and the victims are understood to be subjects of their own struggle for justice and to be subjects of the life of the church, that is, the extent to which they constitute the substance of the life of the church.

## 2.6. *Kairos*

It is, in a formal sense, a departure from the *status confessionis*, to turn to *The Kairos Document*.[96] However, although the precise terminology is not employed, the document reflects upon the same crisis of the church in terms of heresy, blasphemy, and idolatry and upon the same crisis of the body politic in terms of injustice, persecution, and violence. The document arose out of crisis, in particular the heat of the summer of 1985, and purports to be, according to the undertitles, a "Challenge to the Church" and "A Theological Comment on the Political Crisis in South Africa". It reflects not only conflict and oppression, but also the division among Christians.

> Both oppressor and oppressed claim loyalty to the same Church. They are both baptized in the same baptism and participate together in the breaking of the same bread, the same body and blood of Christ. There we sit in the same church while outside Christian policemen and soldiers are beating up and killing Christian children or torturing Christian prisoners to death while yet other Christians stand by and weakly plead for peace. The Church is divided against itself and its day of judgement has come.[97]

The division of the church is confronted by dealing with three "theologies". "State theology" and "church theology" are subjected to criticism while a plea is made for "prophetic theology".

State theology, which is primarily to be found in the white Reformed churches, denotes the attempt to theologically justify apartheid. That attempt is labeled heresy and blasphemy. The god of the South African state is described not only as an idol, but also as the anti-christ. Fundamental theological categories are used to sweep aside the theological ideology and idolatry of apartheid. One must choose for or against. There is no middle ground.

The necessity of choosing sides is clarified in the discussion of church theology, found primarily in the so called white English speaking churches. Although church theology is cautiously critical of apartheid, its uncritical appeal to traditional Christians values such as reconciliation and peace, justice, and non-violence, effectively support the status quo of injustice and institutional violence. Its lack of real social analysis and its otherworldly spirituality prevent it from transcending the perspective of the dominant.

Prophetic theology seeks to appropriate the perspective of the dominated, to side with the suffering and the poor. Solidarity and liberation are the demands of the hour (*kairos*). The church must be converted and society transformed. The struggle is one of life and death, but under the sign of hope.

## 2.7. *"Church theology" and the status confessionis*

The recognition and declaration of the *status confessionis* in the context of apartheid and the subsequent disciplinary measures did not go unchallenged. It seems to me that the challenges to the *status confessionis* can well be understood as expressions of church theology. In that sense the *Kairos Document* provided an incisive analysis of the context of the *status confessionis* in South Africa. I do not propose to provide an account of the various responses and challenges, but simply to discuss a few of the key issues.

*Politics in the church and the church in politics*

The NHK countered the WARC declaration with a declaration of its own in which the legitimacy of the WARC decision was refuted.[98] Rules on membership were to be considered as practical measures and not matters of doctrine. Separate development was not contrary to scripture. Rather it was the WARC that had abandoned the basis of scripture and faith by opting for a theology "that politicizes and socializes the person and work of Christ in a biased manner." Such criticism that WARC and LWF confused politics and faith sounded from various quarters, perhaps more within the LWF due to the heritage of the Lutheran doctrine of two regiments. And, it should be noted, the criticism came also from those who unambiguously rejected apartheid.

Without engaging at this point in a general discussion of the relation between faith and politics, I would point out that such criticism sounds peculiar with regards to apartheid and the churches in South Africa. It can hardly be said that a political problem had been imported into the churches. Apartheid, as ideology and policy, has its roots in church and theology in South Africa. It was exported from there into the political realm.

Might it still be asked whether it is suitable to apply theological terms to political situations? A term like 'heresy', however burdened historically, is specifically applied to the theological justification of apartheid and refers to the ecclesial situation.[99] Applying the term *status confessionis* to both theological justification and social reality suggests more. The *status confessionis* then indicates that the identity and integrity of the church are also and equally at stake when Jews are victimized and when Christian (and non-Christian) children and prisoners are beaten and killed by Christian policemen and soldiers. Community with the poor and the suffering and the marginalized is understood to be of the very substance of the life of the church. The recognition follows that the practice of reconciliation and righteousness is at the heart of the gospel.

*Communion and coffee*

The declarations of both LWF and WARC pointed to fellowship at the Lord's table as a symbol of the unity of the body of Christ. There the unity of reconciliation is to become visible and manifest. It is noteworthy that the history of apartheid in the churches has its roots in sacramental questions. There was at an early stage hesitance among Reformed whites to baptize blacks for that would have required their acceptance into both the body of Christ and the body politic.[100] Also, the beginnings of the history of systematic apartheid can be marked by the introduction of separate communion.[101] The NGK asserted in response to the WARC decision that no rule against racially mixed celebrations existed, as if that made a difference. For it was made clear that the church was racially open neither in policy nor practice.

Yet the problem should not be too quickly reduced to the matter of common communion. (Excuse the redundancy.) Mana Buthelezi has characterized the problem by pointing out that not only celebrating communion together is rejected, but even drinking a cup of coffee together.[102] To cite another example: Common worship is legal, but hospitality in the form of providing an overnight stay for a minister of a different skin color is not.[103]

The table of the Lord becomes an exception and an excuse for exclusion rather than a reality of reconciliation if not embedded in human fellowship and social sharing, or at least in the (political) struggle to attain them. Christian community and holy communion are ridiculed and robbed of their meaning and power when idealized or viewed in isolation. To recognize this is to attribute to Christian community and holy communion an extrovert character. They are to provide an experiment, a measuring stick for human fellowship and interaction.[104] To put it more theologically, the celebration of communion is a missionary and eschatological endeavor, that is, for the sake of the world and the future.

*The life of the church*

One of the suspended Lutheran churches in South Africa, the Cape Church, rejected the judgment of the LWF and the fact that conditions were set for the repeal of suspension.[105] Church community is to be decided on the basis of common confession, on the purity of word and sacrament, not on any additional conditions, not on any good (or bad) works. The suggestion was that it was the LWF that violated the confessional community and the unity of the church by imposing principles alien to the Gospel. Unity is given by God and not grounded in any structure or organization.

The difficulties in responding to such a reaction are manifold. The response to the LWF declaration is not direct but via theological circumlocution that fails to confront and clarify what the specific differences are in understandings of confession, community, the nature of good works, etcetera. It does not at all become clear what the content of the word in pure form is nor what the meaning of the sacraments and their proper administration are.

The LWF declaration (together with that of the WARC) indicates that true unity is visibly manifested unity, that is, community. G. Krusche has demonstrated how the LWF declaration on the *status confessionis* is in line with ecclesiological thinking within the LWF. Both the practice of community and world responsibility (service) are to be understood as essential to the identity of the church. They are criteria for the church being the church.[106] A condition of confessional integrity is the corporality of the church. The context of confession is creation itself, the world, as the location for human and ecclesial responsibility.

Calvinists, like those associated in the WARC, might easily point to discipline as a third mark of the church *(nota ecclesiae)* alongside word and sacrament. The comments of Krusche, in interpreting the LWF, seem to point in the same direction. The life of the church as community and social movement define the church as church. Confession has a social content, a concrete reference in praxis. What becomes clear is that a disciplinary measure such as suspension motivated by an understanding of the practical nature of Christian community makes theological sense. Contrary to "church theology" there is an awareness that the spirituality of the church is to be visibly manifested and practiced in community and society, that reconciliation and justice also refer to social reality.

If it be asked what the criteria for community and social praxis are, then it may be admitted that they need to be further clarified and specified. However, a clear direction has been indicated above in terms of the priority of the poor and the pursuit of justice as essential to the identity of the church. It must also be asked if there are any clearer criteria for the purity of the word and the right administration of the sacraments. Is it not so that it is precisely the nature of community and the quality of witness and service that render word and sacrament their intelligibility and thus their meaning and purity and propriety?

> Ordinary Christians in our congregations need no Latin phrases to understand that it goes against the fundamentals of Christ's message and mission when some people are regarded as inferior because of race. Most Christians with elementary knowledge will hold that it revolts against all biblically based understanding of the unity of the church as the body of Christ, when some Christians because of the colour of their skin are not accepted at the communion table to receive the body and blood of Christ "given for all."[107]

*The quality of Christian unity*

What is the nature of the unity that has been asserted and confessed in the face of apartheid? What underlies the *unitas* of the body of Christ, on the basis of the *unum* of baptism, to use Bethge's terms? Four aspects seem common to the various confessional statements, especially those of Belhar and *Kairos*, LWF and WARC.

In the first place the term unity is used to indicate more than mere co-existence. Unity indicates exchange and, therefore, a visible unity that is to be practiced and confessed, believed and manifested. Unity is understood as a necessity and norm of community.

In the second place the suggestion is that Christian unity seeks both to reconcile and to respect diversity. Over against apartheid which would make of diversity fundamental difference, reconciliation has been fully emphasized. At the same time true reconciliation should engender mutual respect and equality in diversity.

In the third place a unity is conceived that attributes priority to the poor. Christian community reflects the praxis of Jesus in his proximity to the poor, the weak, the marginalized, and the suffering. It entails a commitment to justice and liberation. It involves the church in social searchings and political struggles.

In the fourth place the unity advocated is not a unity for its own sake, but an extrovert unity. It is envisioned as a way of living out the hope for the reconciliation of mankind.

## 2.8. *The question of a confessing church revisited*

A confessing church did not arise in South Africa. The various confessional and denominational divisions were a great barrier as was the financial dependence of some black churches. And even where confession was made, such as in Belhar, that spirit of confession still had and has to wage battle in the hearts and minds of even black Christians and their ministers.[108] No confessional church, but some sort of confessional movement arose, somewhere between the existence of lonely confessors and a confessing church.[109] The *Belydende Kring* (Confessing Circle) came about and let its voice be heard before its eventual financial demise. It made its point that there need be a recognition of and rallying around "contextual confessional issues" such as racial discrimination and cultural segregation. The *status confessionis* leads to a new type of confessional ecumenism.[110]

This contextualizing of confession means that it need not be counted as loss if in the heat of shifting social and political constellations the issue of the *status confessionis* receded. It is a recognition that the political struggle can at times take priority above the ecclesial strife. It would only be a loss if therewith the enduring challenge to the church were to suffer neglect, if Christians were to fail to practice community and seek unity. And it remains true that the crisis of the church in South Africa, like the political crisis, remains to be resolved. Our fear must be that the ecclesial crisis will take even longer to resolve than that in the political arena. Parallel to the question whether South African society will undergo fundamental change or relative reform is the question whether the churches will be transformed or simply find new ways of accommodating.

## 2.9. *Why South Africa and why apartheid?*

*Microcosm: The sign character*

Is the particular attention that South Africa has received justified? Such a question is ethically inadmissible if the intention is to exonerate South Africa by pointing to injustice elsewhere. Such a question is understandable if the attention for South Africa might obscure injustice and racial oppression elsewhere.

Two factors caused apartheid to constitute a particular challenge. One is the systematic and ideological form which 'separate development' took in South Africa. That flagrant situation had to be directly addressed. The struggle against apartheid became a spearhead and a symbol of a greater struggle against racism and political oppression.

A second factor is the history of apartheid itself and the complicity of churches and theologies in its development. The flagrant ideological misuse of theological argument and ecclesial power required specific rebuttal and resistance. That follows from the understanding of apartheid in terms of heresy and idolatry.

The most compelling reason for confirming the *status confessionis* in the context of apartheid in South Africa was ultimately quite simple. Such confirmation by declaration and discipline was requested by Christians involved in the struggles of that country and its churches. If in fact the identity and integrity of the church(es) was discerned to be at stake, then the *status confessionis* had to be asserted, for the sake of the gospel and the sake of the church, for the sake of human beings and human society.

*Macrocosm: Confessing complicity*

If it be asserted that the struggle against apartheid in South Africa bears a sign character, what is being said about racism and oppression elsewhere, what is being said about international relations? First of all, international complicity, particulary that of the Western world, must be recognized. The ties have been not only historical and political, but economic and ecumenical as well. That history, the ineffectiveness of international politics and economic boycotts, hardly need be rehearsed, but it does, according to U. Duchrow, have its consequences.

> We are in fact entangled in a unity with the South African state. And the gravity of the situation is that the mechanisms of death in which we factually participate are legitimized by theology and the doctrine of apartheid.[111]

Manas Buthelezi has pointed to the particular challenge of racism and its power to split the churches and destroy their unity. It is even worse than classical heresies in that it can maintain the appearance of accepting the confessions and symbols of the true church while undermining its substance. The challenge to racism must be met everywhere.[112] The issue is thus not limited to South Africa nor to the problem of racism, as Duchrow has pointed out.

> For racism is in almost all cases connected today with economic exploitation and political tyranny. The apartheid system in Southern Africa is only the microcosm of the world system and is deeply implicated in that system in various ways. When, therefore, the Lutheran World Federation

> in Dar es Salaam declared that the situation in Southern Africa constituted a status confessionis, it de facto declared the North-South situation a confessional issue. It is all-important that the one, holy, catholic and apostolic Church of Jesus Christ should declare this in a truly committed way and begin to act accordingly.[113]

This aspect will need further examination with regards to the *status confessionis* in the context of world poverty as Duchrow has put forward. (See II.4.) What the assertion does indicate is that while Christians and non-Christians are fussing about church and politics, economics may be winning the day.

### *Considerations*[114]

*On the unity and identity of the church*

1. Whereas in the German church struggle the confession of Christ alone was perceived to be the central issue, in the South African struggle against apartheid the unity of the church stood central. In retrospect and with a view to Jews and other victims, it could be asked if the same confession of unity could not have been meaningfully asserted in the German context.
2. The unity of the church is understood to be expressed sacramentally in one baptism and one table of the reconciled. The sacraments become a test case for the life of the church in the world.
3. The life of the church, conversely, lends to the sacraments and to the words of the church, their intelligibility and meaning. The life and praxis of the church are to be understood in terms of the marks of the church and theologically explicated.
4. The identity of the church expressed in its unity and praxis, its words and sacraments, is extrovert. It entails responsibility for humankind and the world.
5. The unity of the church is intended to be visibly manifested and practiced in worship and works.
6. The conceived unity seeks both to reconcile and to respect diversity.
7. The unity of the church attributes priority to the poor, the marginalized and the suffering.
8. The primary political relation of the church is not the state but the poor, the marginalized, and the suffering.

*On the status confessionis*

9. The *status confessionis* has both a political and ecclesial reference.
10. The *status confessionis* has reference both to teaching and practice, theology and policy, doctrine and ethics.

11. The *status confessionis* is not excommunication but an appeal, eventually leading to a disciplinary measure, to call back those who have in effect excluded themselves from the true unity of the church.
12. The response to the *status confessionis* need not take the form of a new organization but can be expressed by confessional ecumenism around contextual issues. In accordance with the context, priority may be attributed to either the political or ecclesial struggle.
13. The sense in which the *status confessionis* in the context of apartheid in South Africa implicates other churches in other places needs further clarification.

# II.3.

# INSTRUMENTS OF MASS ANNIHILATION

## 3.1. *A new answer to a new dilemma?*

> In exactly the same sense in which atomic weapons affect the entire earth and are therefore qualitatively different from all previous weapons of only limited significance, so do all decisions which are made with respect to these weapons affect the entire earth and distinguish themselves qualitatively from all previous decisions that were likewise limited in significance and did not determine the entire course of history.[115]

The nature of modern warfare has changed the very character of war. The nature of modern weapons has, as Helmut Theilicke indicated in 1958 in the above quotation, changed the very character of modern existence and politics. We speak of a nuclear age, but the weapons of mass destruction, the means of mass annihilation, include biological and chemical as well as atomic weapons, A.B.C. weapons. But the ABC of modern warfare includes also the saturation bombings of Dresden in 1945, defoliation and scatter bombings in Viet Nam and Central America, and high tech massacre in Iraq. And what of the malformations and suffering inflicted by nuclear testing and wastes? When in the following there is reference to nuclear, atomic or other weapons of mass destruction, I suggest that included by implication should be all such weapons and strategies, threats and consequences, which can be labeled instruments of mass annihilation. (IMA) The new dilemma is that these IMA threaten the very existence not just of armies and politicians, not only of nations and cultures and peoples, but of the earth itself, of creation and all creatures, of human civilization.

The discussion in the following pages dates from cold war days. The nuclear threat seems to have receded from intense public attention. It remains to be seen what the heritage of cold war armament spirals will be. It is at least clear that the new world order resembles the old world order in that modern warfare continues. The international arms trade continues. Nuclear proliferation continues. It is yet to be seen if and to what extent the discussion in the following pages is dated.

How are Christians to respond? Is the just war theory outdated, as some have suggested, or is it acutely relevant in that its criteria would necessarily lead to a thorough rejection of modern warfare? If war and human existence have changed, has something changed for the church as well? Are qualitatively new responses needed? Would a confessional stance contribute to the necessary quality? What does it mean to internationalize the *status confessionis* in the context of a world threatened with annihilation? Is the integrity of the church as the ecumenical body of Christ at stake?

The *status confessionis* debate does not focus on pacifism, although pacifist arguments do enter the discussion. Similarly the just war theory is not a central topic, although it echoes more in the discussions than does pacifism. Nor is the primary issue weapons and warfare in general, although it has become practically impossible to separate the question of war from the IMA. Nevertheless, the *status confessionis* debate has focused particularly on nuclear weapons and included any form or use (planning, production, possession, threat, employment, deployment, etcetera) of them. Can the IMA be tolerated by the body of Christ? May Christians as members of an ecumenical body in any manner participate in, support or tolerate any use of such means of destruction?

The similarity between the arms race and the *status confessionis* debate is that of the stockpiles of questions and declarations, arguments and accusations. Again I will be selective in wading through the confusion. The debate began and faded in the late fifties during the "nuclearization" of West Germany. It was later influenced by developments in the Netherlands Reformed Church resulting in a pastoral letter in 1980. Minds and hearts were refired in 1983 by a declaration by the moderating board of Reformed churches in West Germany. From there various echoes were to be heard in East and West. The echoes resounded in the World Council of Churches as well, especially in the peace component of the Conciliar Process for Justice, Peace and the Integrity of Creation (JPIC).

### 3.2. *The Bruderschaften: Confessing Christ in an atomic age*

*The church is always a confessing church*

The confessional controversy on nuclear weapons was opened in 1958 in the midst of the political debate on the nuclearization of West Germany. The initiative came from the *kirchliche Bruderschaften* ('church fellowships') that sought to continue the tradition of the Confessing Church in post-war Germany. The *Bruderschaften* directed a petition to the synod of the Evangelical Church in (West) Germany (EKD).[116] In the petition the *Bruderschaften* rejected the testing, production, deployment and employment of atomic weapons as well as their inclusion in political planning. Such weapons were seen to be contrary to the legitimate use of violence by the state as defined in article V of Barmen, for they would betray and destroy the very freedom and peace that they are supposed to defend. They would also be contrary to the principles of just war such as discrimination between combattants and non-combattants, reasonable prospect of future peace, proportionality of means to ends, etc.[117] Any participation by Christians in the use or preparation of atomic weapons under any circumstances was labeled sinful and unacceptable. "In our perception there is for the church in this matter a *status confessionis*." A series of ten theses (written by Karl Barth as was later revealed) concluded with the assertion:

> 10. A contrary or neutral standpoint in this question cannot be adhered to by a Christian. Both positions signify the denial of all three articles of Christian faith.

The *Bruderschaften* were accused of misusing the gospel for political purposes and of endangering the precarious unity of the Evangelical Church.[118] Ernst Wolf (and others) replied in *Confessing Christ in an Atomic Age*.[119] Wolf insisted that there can be no political decision for a Christian except as an act of obedience and faith. The unity of the church is not a matter of institutional self-preservation (which would amount to a political conception of the church), but always the unity of faith and obedience that is a gift of the Lord.[120]

> The church is always a confessing church or else she ceases to be the church. From time to time that "standing and confessing" can become condensed in an evident *status confessionis* for the church, i.e., in an inescapable entreaty to take an unambiguous and explicit position on a particular matter. (...) This is required first of all there where a Christian becomes aware that the faith of the Christian church is put in question, whether from within or from the world, by disbelief, superstition and heresy and that a positive protest of faith must be raised. (...) A confessional stance is also required, i.e., the *status confessionis* occurs or can occur, there where a Christian or a church faces a situation or problem in the world, in which the peril of human existence in this world, in which humanity itself, is at stake, whereby at the same time the recognition or denial of God is at stake.[121]

The debate became heated and emotional. Curiously, opponents of politics in the church often made the most use of political arguments by appealing to the "logic" of deterrence or to the communist threat or to the Lutheran doctrine of two regiments in order to defend the policy of nuclearization.[122] Sloganing entered the debate. "Better dead than a slave," to which was replied "Better dead than a mass murderer."[123] (The latter is at least more in keeping with the early Christian standpoint that it is better to suffer injustice than to inflict it.) An attempt was made to justify the use of atomic weapons as being a punishing rod in the hand of God,[124] although it might be asked which side if not both sides should be punished. Further: "Even these terrible means of mass annihilation could enter the service of the love of neighbor."[125] The question arises: Who is my neighbor?

The point in citing such sloganing and theological somersaults is to indicate the passion of the debate. And although both sides accused the other of mixing theology and politics, the controversy was, it seems to me, not only one of method, i.e. how theology and politics are to be related responsibly, but also a clash of basic positions and interests.

*Complementarity or consensus?*

The synod of the Evangelical Church in Germany, which in April of 1958 discussed the petition of the *Bruderschaften*, provided no real answer. The synod came no further than ascertaining the deep differences and concluded:

> We remain together under the Gospel and take efforts to overcome these differences. We pray to God that he will lead us through his Word to common insight and decision.[126]

The vice of the inability to decide one way or another was turned into the virtue of a complementary principle formulated in the "Heidelberger Theses" the following year.[127] Although not an official church document the theses offered a semi-official compromise. The common foundation of all Christian decisions on peace was said to be the goal of avoiding nuclear war and restoring world peace. In light of that both of the following were to be accepted:

> VII. The church must recognize abstinence from weapons as a Christian mode of action.
>
> VIII. The church must recognize participation in the attempt to secure peace and freedom by the presence of atomic weapons as a Christian mode of action still possible today.

The suggestion was made that the two modes of action were dependent on each other. By the use of the term "complementary" the Heidelberg theses legitimized the differences rather than overcoming them in common insight and decision as the synod declaration of 1958 had hoped. Complementarity meant a rejection of the *status confessionis* as well. One slight imbalance is to be noted in the addition in thesis VIII of the words "still possible today" ("*heute noch möglich*"). The suggestion is that there might be a temporal limit to the toleration of atomic weapons.

Although the theses received wide acceptance, the *Bruderschaften* rejected the complementarity idea. H. Vogel rejected the use of a term from physics in the realm of ethics. He considered the existing differences to constitute a deficiency, not a complementarity.[128] Wolf had already insisted that confession seeks consensus.[129] The total, confessional rejection of atomic weapons was still to be advocated.

> The very possibility that a human could do to humankind what the means of mass annihilation have within them, is a radical threat to the humanity of humans, even if that possibility were never to become reality.[130]

Creating the possibility of annihilating humankind, even considering it, was inadmissible, according to H.J. Iwand. How can a Christian say "Yes" to the manufacture of atomic bombs and thereby say "Yes" to their eventual employment?[131]

How was it to be made clear that the recognition of the *status confessionis* and the rejection of contrary or neutral positions was not intended as a threat to church unity or a denigration of other believers, but as an "invitation to belief in the promise of the Gospel" and "a summons not to separate oneself from the unity of the church"? How was it to be communicated that the *status confessionis* is not a threat of excommmunication, but a binding call to confession and decision, to faith and obedience?[132] Fundamental to this understanding is the awareness that the *status confessionis* cannot be created or declared. Rather the church may find itself from time to time placed in the *status confessionis* and must then recognize, confirm (state) and answer it.

### 3.3. *The Netherlands Reformed Church: A "No" and no "Yes"*

*Saying "No" and seeking dialogue*

In a pastoral message "The Question of Nuclear Weapons" (1962)[133] the synod of the Netherlands Reformed Church stated that nuclear weapons were unusable for any goal for which legitimate force might be employed and that Christians could not by conscience justify their participation in a war with nuclear weapons, even if the government should demand it of them. The synod was not as unambiguous on the issue of possession of nuclear weapons. There was no support of their use as deterrent, but there was the realization that nuclear disarmament would be a complicated affair. The synod suggested that the "community of fear" (mutual deterrence) might be taken as a God-given chance to search for a way out, It was a "No" to use without a "Yes" to possession, but allowing a respite.[134]

In 1980 following a church-wide discussion of the matter, the synod issued another pastoral letter[135] on the basis of the affirmation that "Christ is our peace." The conclusion was made that the period of respite had not borne fruit, that on the contrary the danger and threat of nuclear war had increased. The time had come to say "No" to the possession of nuclear weapons as well as to their use. Inasmuch as bilateral disarmament had not proven possible, unilateral steps should be undertaken. The synod recommended the denuclearization of the Netherlands. No illusions were nurtured with regard to the threat of other political systems.

> But confessing[136] we may say: we can live with our Lord no matter what the political system might be. In no case does the defence of our freedoms justify basing our security on the possible destruction of everything dear to us and to our opponents and on an assault on creation.

An appeal was made for continued dialogue which might touch the deepest motives of all those both in agreement and disagreement with the synod letter. "We are aware that we cannot speak in the name of all of you, but we wish to speak to you and thus with you." Despite this appeal some of the military who were members of the church questioned whether they were still welcome in the church if they were to persist in their different opinion on the matter. They were assured by the moderating board of the synod that their exclusion was not intended.

*Prophecy and wisdom*

This last point is in keeping with an incident related by the theologian H. Berkhof, a discussion he had with Christian members of parliament on the earlier pastoral message of 1962.[137] Several parlementarians suggested that it could become their Christian duty to take responsibility for an atomic attack on Moscow. Berkhof replied, with a reference to Bonhoeffer, that they were then "ethical heretics" in the eyes of the church and would do good to leave the church. The members of the synod moderating board who were present were terrified by Berkhof's reply and assured the listeners that the intention of the pastoral message was only to stimulate a serious discussion on the matter.

It is quite intriguing to note that Berkhof did not confer the same confessional status to the pastoral letter of 1980. In his view the "No" to use, stated in 1962, was a prophetic word which allowed no further discussion. Excommunication could be a possible consequence. The second "No" to possession, added in 1980, was to be seen as a combination of prophetic and wisdom traditions. The element of wisdom is one that allows for discussion and argumentation. It is a process that seeks communication.

Certainly the letter of 1980 which condemned possession expressed a deep desire for further communication and dialogue. And there was a realization that the "no without any yes" could only be realized in a gradual process. On the other hand it was declared that other directions, including that of unilateral steps, had to be pursued. And the text of the letter does not seem to support a differentiation between the two "No's".

> So, first of all, we must repeat our "No" of 1962 and then in all clarity state that this "No" also holds without qualification for the possession of all nuclear weapons.[138]

In the ensuing church politics the appeals for dialogue continued and confessional language was avoided, relegating the statements of both 1962 and 1980 to the wisdom tradition. There were certainly no excommunications, although there were some who sought refuge in another church. The church-wide debate (a sort of conciliar process) which preceeded the pastoral letter of 1980 failed to provide a basis for a further dialogue on the "deepest motives" thereafter. Wisdom was apparently lacking.

*On distinguishing use and possession*

It seems necessary to investigate the validity of the distinction between use and possession more closely. H. Thielicke, who was previously quoted, rejected absolutely the use of atomic weapons in actual warfare, but advocated their use as deterrent. He insisted that threatening or deterring the enemy with atomic weapons did not necessarily and logically imply their actual use. Their use as deterrent was in fact necessary in order to prevent the principle of "might makes right" from prevailing in the world. Thielicke sought to offer a possible (but in my view not evidently probable) psychological scenario in which both enemies would be convinced that the other dare not use the weapons.[139]

Two sorts of reply can be made to this position, one with regards to its logic and one with regard to its historic veracity. Opponents of atomic weapons have insisted that the credibility of deterrence implies the willingness to use the weapons. "It is nonsense to pretend that you do not intend to do what is the means you take to your chosen end."[140] Daniel Ellsburg and others have documented that the political willingness to engage in a nuclear attack has in fact been present in crisis situations of the cold war. Later generations of nuclear weapons were specifically designed, not for deterrence, but for targeted use. Thus distinction between use and possession has become increasingly incredible and irresponsible.

Did deterrence succeed or were nuclear weapons not employed despite themselves? There are too many other complicating factors to prove anything one way or another. But the sensitivities regarding even limited unilateral steps were seemingly exaggerated in a situation of gross overkill which continues even today. Two questions remain. What is the relation of means to ends? And is the preparation for atomic war, even if the proclaimed intention is deterrence, equivalent to atomic war and in what sense (politically? ethically? confessionally?)?

## 3.4. *Confession to Christ and responsibility for peace*

*"The peace question is a confessional question"*

In 1982 the moderating board of the Reformed Alliance of West Germany (Moderamen des Reformierten Bundes, henceforth MRB) issued a declaration entitled "Confession to Jesus Christ and the Church's Responsibility for Peace."[141] Intended as a preparatory paper for the general council of the World Alliance of Reformed Churches meeting in Ottawa of the same year, the document enflamed the theological fires of West Germany. The MRB chose the same guiding confession as in the Dutch letter: "Jesus Christ is our peace." Its tone was emphatically confessional and it stated unequivocally that:

> The question of peace is a confessional question. It entails for us the *status confessionis*, because in our position on the means of mass destruction our confession or denial of the Gospel is at stake.
> This confession of our faith is incompatible with the development, preparation or use of means of mass destruction that can exterminate the human being whom God loves and has chosen as a covenant partner and that can devastate creation.

This declaration of the MRB was a challenge to reaffirmations of the complementary principle of the Heidelberg theses.[142] Those theses had failed to provide a common ground, and the hope of the 1958 synod that differences could be overcome in common insight and decision remained unfulfilled. Such was the conclusion of the "Society for Evangelical Theology" that had reiterated the 1958 declaration of the *Bruderschaften* in February of 1981.[143] The declaration of the MRB can likewise be understood as a renewal of that call to decision. The Dutch pastoral letter had also made its influence known over the border. The MRB explicitly appealed to it and apparently attributed more prophetic quality to it than did Dutch church officials.[144]

*Double jeopardy, or: what is the issue?*

Eduard Lohse, at that time chairman of the executive council of the EKD, responded by stating that the *status confessionis* was the severest alarm that could be sounded within the church. He considered it irresponsible to endanger the fellowship of the EKD with "short-circuited, steeped theological declarations."[145] Immediately the question of unity and the nature of unity was again being addressed.

The MRB had attempted to anticipate such objections. The declaration stated that there was no intention of viewing those of a different political or theological mind with hostility. In a confessional issue, especially on matters of life and death, such contrary and exclusive positions can hardly coexist in the same church. But the "No" to a particular position does not suspend the "Yes" to persons. Therefore, the recognition of the *status confessionis* did not mean excommunication and threat of schism, but an invitation to faith and a call to the binding decision of confession. There was no intention to lord over the faith and conscience of those who thought differently, but the conviction that protest and warning needed to sound in the call to loyalty and responsibility to Jesus Christ.

In this position there is a tension, or perhaps a dialectic, between decisiveness and tolerance, between challenge and invitation. It would seem incorrect (and unfair) to label it an ambiguity. It is rather an unavoidable dilemma whenever imperative positions and relations to persons (or institutions) conflict. It is a sort of double jeopardy but one that does not in itself lessen the validity or necessity of taking a particular position. It is a risk, a tension, and a burden that must under given circumstances be borne.

Whatever the risk, it should not distract from the task of clarifying criteria for the *status confessionis* and illuminating the situation in question. Any *status confessionis* is rooted in the context, and its criteria become recognizable in the context. It remains important that sober analysis and theological discussion not be short-circuited by immediately pointing to the consequences for church (institutional) unity. The *status confessionis* is to be evaluated on its own merits. It must first be seen what kind of unity is at stake and whether the circumstances are worth the consequences or not.

The *status confessionis* has shown that it can loosen the theological tongues and enliven the polemical pens. It is not feasible to deal with all the various arsenals of theology that have been thrown into the battle. (I am no advocate of doing theology as warfare. I employ military language at times simply to mirror what in my perception often takes place.) More positively formulated, it is to be noted how in the debate on the *status confessionis* many foundational questions on ethics and the church have been raised and need to be confronted. An attempt must be made to select a limited number of issues that serve clarification.

*Confusion over confession*

The executive council of the United Evangelical-Lutheran Church of Germany (VELKD) also responded to the MRB declaration.[146] The VELKD executive could not concur with the presupposition of the Reformed declaration that there be only one conceivable political path for preserving peace, namely, unilateral steps of disarmament. Furthermore:

> We cannot consent to the appeal of the Reformed board to declare political decisions - even those on life and death - to be confessional questions of the church. The church stands and falls with her confession of Jesus Christ, the crucified, risen, and coming Lord attested to by Holy Scripture. Only by faith in him is the redemption or irredemption of humans decided.

Similarly the executive council of the EKD responded:

> The confession of Jesus Christ is misused when it is applied to decisions of open political paths. Responsibly thinking and acting Christians become

> distressed in their conscience. Questions of innerworldly survival, as important as they are, may not be taken for questions of faith and made into confessional questions.[147]

Confession is confession of Jesus Christ, human answer to the works of God. All parties agree on that. But what then? Is there a tension between a more traditional (Lutheran?) understanding of confession in terms of adherence to historic creeds and confessions on the one hand and on the other hand a more actualizing, renewing (Reformed?) understanding?[148] What of confession of sin? What of confession and denial of Jesus in times of decision? (Cf. Mt. 10:32f.)

A biblical excursion might prove helpful, but it must be recognized that the very formulation *status confessionis* indicates that each of the various uses of the term 'confession' is itself a theological statement and neither necessarily nor directly a biblical reference. If there is no consensus on what confession is about (historical or actual, exclusive or inclusive, etc.), what is being argued? The theological terms need to be clearly defined if they are to serve rather than circumvent communication.

It should be noted, for the above responses do not account for it, that the declaration of the MRB was not intended as a political confession. Its purpose was not to declare, create, confuse, etcetera. Its intention was to recognize how a political issue affected the church and its confession in a crucial way. The MRB felt itself likewise in a crisis of conscience and felt compelled to share the crisis. (If a crisis does exist, should it not affect the consciences?) The MRB sought to confess theologically on a crucial political matter.

*The political competence of faith*

The underlying issue would seem to be that of the relation and relevance of faith with respect to human life. The EKD also stated that the direction of Christian ethics pointed only to peace and not to war, for war meant the failure of politics, and the threat of war was irresponsible politics. On what basis, it could be asked, are such judgements made and is war denounced, once innerworldy survival has been so clearly distinguished from faith and confession? Is Christian ethics no part of Christian faith? How are ethical and political decisions to be decided by Christians if not in faith? Is the focus of faith exclusively otherworldly? The VELKD and EKD statements do not seem reconcilable with the interpretations of the LWF and WARC declarations on the *status confessionis* in the context of apartheid.

It seems to be a long standing dispute with little prospects of being settled? Who bears the burden of the proof, those who deny that such questions are questions of faith and confession or those who would affirm that? Might the critique of "church theology" be repeated by pointing out how terms of faith such as reconciliation and peace also refer to human and therefore to social and political reality? Is it desirable in this German Reformed-Lutheran context to engage in general reflections on the Lutheran doctrine of two regiments (including the autonomy of the political sphere) and Barth's teaching on the Lordship of Christ? That, however, does not really provide a solution to the problem, but is simply another way of stating it.

The matter that calls for clarification is the relation of statements of faith (and confession) on the one hand and political analysis and human reason on the other. (It should be superfluous to point to the need for proper analysis in accordance with human reason, although reason may have already been long overwhelmed by IMA.) It is important to realize that politics is not just a product of analysis, i.e., not simply a matter of reasoned consideration and estimation, but that politics is also and perhaps most importantly an art and responsibility of shaping decisions and social processes. (Force can be a means of politics but is a weak means, for the strength of artful politics is its ability to shape consensus and participation.) No decisions are purely "political", i.e., political processes are always formed and informed by other factors. Politics does not of itself require faith, but it requires more than political science and need not preclude faith.

A life of faith, on the other hand, seems hardly conceivable without the use of political and reasoned analysis. Not disregarding the powers of intuition, a decision of faith need be informed. Otherwise it cannot be known what is being decided and, consequently, if a responsible decision is being made. Decision is not a substitute for analysis, nor does analysis preempt the decision made from the perspective of faith. Analysis and the weighing of all considerations provide raw material. A decision must then be formed and shaped by the biblical story and the dynamics of faith. H.J. Iwand has pointed out that faith is never simply establishing the facts, but is a decision where "reality" is to be sought.[149] (I do not pretend that analysis and the perspective of faith can be cleanly separated. In fact our values and concerns affect the very way we see things and guide us in choosing models and paradigms for our analysis of reality. I simply point to two aspects of a process.)

This would seem to be the way things work in Christian ethical reflection and political decision making, although it is apparently not obvious when it is stated that innerworldly questions are not to be confused with questions of faith. The acceptability of various political options to which the EKD appeals is precisely the point in question. Confession, including ethics, seeks consensus, and that consensus can in a Christian sense only be a decision of faith, having heard the facts.

> To declare that the question of peace is a confessional question is nothing else than to radically validate the competence of faith in a critical, untenable situation. Because in Luther's understanding all of our action is confession ("tota nostra operatio est confessio"), our current confession can and must "attach" itself at a particular point in our actions. Thus, in

Christian confession "an utmost concentration on the confession of Christ is joined to an utmost breadth of thematic horizon." (W. Huber)[150]

*"There is no way to peace. Peace is the way."*

The direction of Christian ethics is peace. Not uncommon is the harmonizing comment that "In view of the goal to preserve peace we are in agreement. One must, however, distinguish between the goal and the political paths to it."[151] Yet to claim that everyone wants peace, whether it is true or not, is to veil the fact that it is precisely the question of means that is being disputed.

> For we know that certain means are evil more clearly than we know that certain ends are good, and when we do evil that good may come, we are much more certain of the evil we do than the good we hope for. If we are told that a certain policy or course of action involves genocide, murder, or torture, or enslavement, we should not ask: "And what good will it do?" We should have nothing further to do with it. (A. Kenny)
>
> As a student of ethics, I must confess that it is morally better to save lives rather than to lose lives, other things being equal. At the same time, we should recognize that the moral obligation to save lives is not the highest grade of moral obligation: the obligation to save lives is not nearly so powerful, for example, as the obligation not to kill people. (D.P. Lackey)[152]

The means must serve the ends, must lead to the goal, and not overwhelm it. From that perspective the question of means would seem to be more a test of faith and value than the question of ends, however important. That is reflected in the assertion that there is no way to peace, but that peace is the way. Peace, in Christian confession, is in God's hands. Humans possess (or dispossess) only the means.

Is this the same as to distinguish between God's peace and human peace as T. Rendtorff has emphasized?

> The rudiments of Christian confession demand that a clear and unequivocal distinction be made between witness to peace as the confession of God's own action for humankind in Jesus Christ and the endeavors of humans towards political peace. The human as well as the political endeavors for peace never have the quality of being a path to eternal, God-given peace. Every assertion in that direction is a false, unevangelical teaching.[153]

To or against whom Rendtorff was directing these comments is unclear. The declaration of the MRB makes more or less the same distinction while, however, insisting that human endeavors be in keeping with God's peace.[154] Again the question must be raised what the content of human confession to Christ is and what it's relation to social reality might be? In addition, it is ethically speaking not irrelevant which interests such distinctions serve: political inertia, support of the status quo, or sober, responsible endeavor.

To be sure, divine peace (the kingdom of God) is not just a product of human endeavor. It could also be true, as some churches have asserted, that the thirty or forty years of relative peace in Europe was not a product of deterrence, but due to God's prevenient grace. (One can only wonder what that relative peace looked like from the point of view of many other regions of the world.) It follows from such assertions that all peace that is worthy of the name is God's peace and that any violation of peace is violation of God's peace. At the same time a political concept like the "kingdom of God" seems to indicate that divine peace is intended to initiate peace in human, social, and political relations and calls for participation in the divine project of peace. In that sense confession of Jesus Christ entails witness to the kingdom and following Jesus on the paths of peace. Consequenstly faithfulness and responsibility with regard to means become ways for Christians to participate in the peace of God.

*The reality of reconciliation*

The second thesis of the declaration of the MRB, similar to the confession of Belhar, emphasized the reality of God's reconciliation. Faith in that reality is understood to be incompatible with ideological hostility and threatening portrayals of an enemy. Reconciliation in Christ includes the enemy and excludes his possible destruction by means of mass annihilation.[155]

Such emphasis on the reconciliation in Christ does not go so far as advocating pacifism, although it tends in that direction.[156] It is at any rate the converse of legitimizing nuclear weapons by an appeal to the sinfulness and fallenness of the world, as if sin justified sin.[157] The basic confession of reconciliation, of Christ as peace, would seem to meet the insistence by Rendtorff that any "No" of protest be preceded by and reflect the basic affirmation of faith, God's "Yes". The reality of reconciliation, not the factuality of sin and hostility, must provide the focus and orientation for Christian faith and life.

*Processus confessionis*

In order to counter the confusion that the *status confessionis* implied excommunication, U. Möller proposed a distinction between *status confessionis* and *status separationis*.[158] Another way of emphasizing the communicative intention was the proposal of W. Huber and U. Duchrow to speak of *processus confessionis*. Such a term admits on the one hand that the recognition of the *status confessionis* requires a process of dialogue and learning (and patience).[159] The term also expresses that not only the recognition and declaration of the *status confessionis* is needed, but also a clarification of the consequences in a "process of the church's confession." Ecumenical dialogue and an interactive conciliar process are needed.[160]

These terminological proposals were not intended to lessen the confessional intensity but to strengthen the communicative intent of the MRB declaration. To the extent that they serve such purposes and do not just supplement our Latin, they could prove helpful. What such terminological discussions reveal is the difficulty of defining and confronting the actual issues. That is perhaps the crucial downfall of the whole *status confessionis* phenomenon. Is there a term that will serve to clarify rather than complicate the intended issues, or are the issues and the crises doomed to debate whatever the terminology? Will the issues themselves cause factions in the church to grow away from each other in a *processus separationis*.

### 3.5. *Reception of the status confessionis*

The *status confessionis* was not generally accepted in the West German churches. The Ottawa assembly of the WARC, which confirmed the *status confessionis* on apartheid and to which the MRB declaration was directed, spoke strongly on the nuclear issue but did not apply the *status confessionis* to it. What was to be the further fate of the term?

*Ecumenical renunciation*

Two years prior to the MRB declaration a representative of the Evangelical Church in the German Democratic Republic (East Germany) had spoken of the *status confessionis* at the Amsterdam hearings of the World Council of Churches. G. Krusche included in his statement:

> In this connection the question to be put to the ecumenical movement is whether it should sharpen the conscience of the WCC member churches by declaring the use of nuclear weapons a *status confessionis* in the same way that apartheid was outlawed by the Lutheran World Federation at its assembly in Dar es Salaam in 1977. The identity of the church is really at stake in the question of whether it is permissible, for political ends, to sacrifice the lives of countless innocent people and even the future of our planet.[161]

Noteworthy here is that the question of the identity of the church is raised in connection with the *status confessionis* and political ends.

Previously (at Nairobi 1975) the WCC had urged the member churches to seek disarmament and express their readiness to live without the protection of armaments. The Amsterdam hearings concluded:

> We believe the time has come when the churches must unequivocally declare that the production and deployment as well as the use of nuclear weapons are a crime against humanity and that such activities must be condemned on ethical and theological grounds. The nuclear weapons issue is, in its import and threat to humanity, a question of Christian discipline and faithfulness to the Gospel.[162]

This position (later adopted in Vancouver 1983) was clear. The *status confessionis* terminology was not adopted, the difficulty being that many of the member churches were not familiar with it. It was recognized, however, that the term "indicates that an issue has ultimate moral significance" and "can be an instrument for sharpening the consciousness of Christians."[163]

What did occur at Vancouver, at the initiative of the delegation from East Germany, was the proposal for a Conciliar Process for Justice, Peace and the Integrity of Creation (JPIC). The peace component was the heart of the original proposal, in the hope that an ecumenical council of churches could speak a definitive word. I will return to that matter later.

The Evangelical Church of East Germany also deliberated the adoption of the *status confessionis*. One of the members of the federal synod, L. Grosse, stated:

> I consider it to be a question of the *status confessionis* that Christians, who in the ecumenical movement, pray together, deliberate together, worship together, and take communion into their bodies and into their blood, could or should kill each other for reasons of saving oil or national honor in order to preserve their social system. For me the answer is clear: No![164]

Grosse's emphasis on the identity and integrity of the church is reminiscent of Bonhoeffer's words: "Christians cannot direct weapons at each other, because they know that they then direct the weapons at Christ himself."[165]

The Evangelical Church in the GDR stated its position in terms of a "renunciation of the spirit, logic, and praxis of deterrence."[166] The *status confessionis* was not adopted because it was felt that the term did not clarify the issues. The precise political provocation, the mode of realization, and the consequences were all considered to be uncertain.[167]

*Ecumenical echoes*

I know of no churches who formally adopted the *status confessionis* on the nuclear issue. The Presbyterian Church in the U.S.A. considered the term in the context of its call to peacemaking.[168] It was noted that no churches had carried the notion to its logical consequence and that it was not clear if it should be. The Lutheran Peace Fellowship (U.S.A.) drafted "A Stand of Confession."[169] The strength of the one page statement, besides its simplicity and directness, was its expression of solidarity with a tradition of confessors (Confessing Church in Germany, the confessing movement in South Africa), with the peace movement, and with the entire body of Christ. "We oppose our weapons because they are aimed at members of our own body as well as at all of creation." Confession and commitment were understood to be a common thing.

The list could be furthered with other examples of covenanting and commitment to confront idolatry (the New Abolitionist Covenant which drew a parallel to the struggle against slavery), of references to the solidarity of the body of Christ (U.S. Catholic bishops), and of categorical rejections of nuclear weapons. Churches in the South Pacific as victims of the nuclear testing also raised their voices. That proliferation of voices was itself a significant step in the public witness of churches. Two points are to be noted.[170] First is the way in which many statements were concerned not only to appeal to public opinion and advise political officials, but also to focus on the fidelity of the church. Similarly, the reconciliation in Christ was asserted as contrary to the ideological hostility and political enmity at the root of the arms race. The issue of IMA was understood as a spiritual problem. Thus a relation between political responsibility and Christian spirituality, between identity and public witness, was assumed. What remains for further consideration is the meaning and adequacy of the *status confessionis* terminology with respect to instruments of mass annihilation.

### 3.6. *The significance of the status confessionis*

*Heresy demands clarity*

The debate on the *status confessionis* in the context of nuclear overkill did not produce a consensus, not even within Reformed and Lutheran churches familiar with the term. No precision or clarity was agreed to. The same might be said for other descriptions as well: idolatry, crime against humanity, renunciation of spirit, logic and praxis, etc. What is it precisely that is being rejected? For if heresy is being rejected, then the heresy must be clarified. E. Bethge has formulated it well.

> With which specific adulteration of the Gospel are we confronted in this status confessionis, that is to be rejected as an heretical falsification? (...) Which central aspect of the Gospel is now to be positively articulated in *confessio*, terse like *solus* in 1934 and *unum* in 1977, a word of theological clarity that immediately reveals its controversial character, that directly indicates the ethical-political implications, and that makes it possible to again carry out and to bear the eventual regrouping and division? (...) We are waiting for a new and decisive formulation, why the *status confessionis* now?[171]

Can the challenge that Bethge formulated be met with respect to the nuclear threat? It is clear that many are for peace. It is clear that many consider the IMA terrible, diabolic, frightening, unthinkable. It is clear that serious discussion is needed. But whoever wants serious, faithful discussion can do so without resorting to the *status confessionis*. Such was the ambiguity encountered in the position of the Netherlands Reformed Church. Was the intention to be serious or definitive? Similarly the Dutch organization "Kerk en Vrede" (Church and Peace) stated:

> Whoever thinks that nuclear weapons need not be categorically rejected, that we can still live with them for a while, has no reason for speaking confessionally. A discussion with someone who is of this opinion must deal with the seriousness of the situation, not with confessing.[172]

While one must agree that the situation is serious, it would seem insufficient to relate the *status confessionis* to a degree of seriousness. (Who would deny the seriousness of the matter?) If the *status confessionis* is to possess precision and decisiveness, it should be understood not simply in terms of the seriousness of the matter or as an extreme (exceptional) situation, but in terms of the very nature of the problem. The problem with the IMA must then be seen not just as a situation that has gotten out of hand, but as representing a threat to the life of the church in principle.

*The body of Christ divided*

The words (quoted above) of L. Grosse, an East German in a then divided Germany, indicate a way of understanding the nature of the crisis, namely, that the church has become divided against itself. How can those who pray, deliberate, worship, and celebrate communion together tolerate that such weapons are directed at each other? U. Duchrow, a West German in a then divided Germany, stated:

> Do I see correctly that in recent discussion the aspect of "the community of brothers and sisters" (Barmen III) has not or hardly at all been brought into play and made fruitful for confessing Jesus Christ against the means of mass annihilation? One could defend the view, that when our first loyalty is Jesus Christ and his body, we, as the community of Christ, must for that simple reason exclude armed service against each other. From that point of view the argument of the peace churches for categorical refusal to bear arms is conceivable and probably even consistent. In the case of means of mass annihilation, the case seems to me to be unequivocally clear, apart from categorical pacifism. How can I threaten my brothers or sisters in the churches of the GDR [East Germany] or the Soviet Union or other Eastern European country with mass murder? When even the diabolical possibility

of an unimaginable chaos for God's creation due to atomic war waged by me is wantonness, so also it is like a sin against the Holy Spirit, when I even think of rending apart the body of Christ, not even to mention the actual use of the means of mass annihilation between Christians.[173]

I recall how in the heat of the arms race local congregations in Eastern and Western Europe sought partner relations with each other, how Christians became godparents for each others children across the dividing lines of ideology. In that face to face of Christian community around the Lord's table and at the baptismal font, it became unacceptable to support and/or tolerate policies and missiles aimed at the annihilation of brothers and sisters. One could not share the life in Christ with them and willfully think their death. One could not pray for a godchild and conceive the abortion of his or her future.

Might it be argued that the annihilation of the other was not intended, only deterrence and therefore his/her safety? Yet the risk of death and annihilation was intended. The facts of the weapons and the risks of the strategies of hostility would seem to overwhelm any good intention. The annihilation of brothers and sisters, of fellow humans in mass, was willfully thought. The weapons and the strategies were (and are still) willed. In the spiritual-bodily reality (the body of Christ) which the church is, such thought, such threat, is already a rupture in the fellowship, a violation of community, a division of Christ against himself. Christ is divided, as if the eye were to say to the hand, "I have no need of you!" or the head to the feet, "I have no need of you!" (1 Cor. 1:13; 12:21) It would at any rate be more ethically responsible, if one may say so, to reckon with one's own annihilation, than to conceive of the annihilation of a brother or sister. The very unity of the church, the very body of Christ as a bodily and spiritual reality is at stake.

*The unity of the church as parable*

J. Moltmann contrasted the confessional issues of 1984 with those of 1934 (Barmen).

> One could say: in 1934 there were "errors" that "destroyed" the Evangelical Church in Germany and "broke up" her unity, as is stated in the introduction to the Barmen declaration. Since 1945 we are confronted with "errors" that "break up" the unity of mankind, which God created and wills.[174]

Moltmann's inclusion of creation and the unity of mankind provides a catholic and ecumenical perspective. Such an emphasis runs parallel to the argument that the God-given unity of the church is likewise at stake in the question of IMA. Understanding that unity in terms of the unity of the church makes it possible to comprehend the threat of IMA in a manner parallel to the exclusion of the Jews in 1934 and to the ideology of apartheid in South Africa. The international dimensions of nuclear hostility draw added attention to the ecumenical, catholic quality of the solidarity of the body of Christ. The unity of the church is then understood as a parable of the God-willed unity of mankind, the community of the reconciled as a parable of the God-willed reconciliation of all humans, including God's enemies.

Such a unity is one of solidarity. It has been argued that the weakness of the *status confessionis* with regard to IMA is that it has no particular reference to victims or persons persecuted. That argument sounds strange in consideration of those who have been subjected to nuclear testing and those who are captured in fear. Must more victims first be made? Must one wait until it is too late, as if it were not already so? Direct involvement has been inflicted on us all. And meanwhile our tolerant times seem to equally tolerate acceptance and resistance, false gospel and true gospel, and so render the gospel irrelevant. The complementary thesis was seductive in that it allowed mutually exclusive positions to tolerate each other. It mystified disunity. In so doing the question of real church unity was forsaken and the unity of mankind was endangered.

*Catholicity as a mark of the church*

Bethge has himself attempted to formulate the specific points of crisis for the church.[175] He has differentiated the various crucial moments in the German Church struggle: in 1933 the *unum* of baptism with regard to the exclusion of Jews; in 1934 the *solus* of Christ alone as norm for revelation; in 1935 the *libertas ecclesiae* as there arose differences among the confessors on church arrangements and organization. And further: in 1958 the *creatio dei* in the nuclearization of Germany; in 1977 again the *unum* of baptism in the face of apartheid; in 1982 the *vita hominis et creationis* in the face of nuclear overkill.

The Dutch theologian G.H. ter Schegget has classified the contemporary challenge of the *status confessionis* in terms of the one, holy, catholic and apostolic church.[176] He analyzes apartheid as a threat to the unity of the church. The sanctity of the church, the quality of communion between rich and poor, is at stake in the current world economic situation. Under the head of sanctity the integrity of our natural surroundings is also treated. Catholicity is to be asserted in the face of the threat of nuclear annihilation. Unity, sanctity and catholicity together give shape to the apostolic quality of the church which is expressed in the church's witness to the world. It is the apostolicity which is the primary and essential criterion of the church.

Both Bethge and Ter Schegget provide a differentiated interpretation of the *status confessionis*. Both include, albeit in different ways, the integrity of creation. Bethge emphasizes from an historical view a variety of perspectives on the *status confessionis*. Ter Schegget summarizes the contemporary challenge in terms of the apostolic confession on the church. His perspective is that of ecclesiology, but it is particularly the notion of sanctity that provides new perspectives.

An understanding of the *status confessionis* derived from Bonhoeffer's ecclesiological interpretation can be conceived in terms of the catholic quality of the church. Catholicity as an expression of fullness, of the whole,[177] indicates both community (unity) and diversity.[178] A less abstract description is simply: the body of Christ. (Cf. Duchrow) In each of the situations considered, it was seen how the integrity of the body of Christ had been violated and the confession of the catholic quality of the church had been at stake. Some members of the body, some category of people, whether Jews, blacks or the masses (under either communism or capitalism), were excluded or considered expendable.

The *status confessionis* has been perceived as a threat to the unity of the church, the question being asked whether nuclear weapons were worth a schism in the church. Conversely the *status confessionis* can be understood precisely as a defense of the unity and catholicity of the church. It serves as a signal that division and schism already exist when Jews are executed, when blacks are excluded, and the masses are expendable. The only unity that can be threatened by the *status confessionis* is institutional unity, which need not be degraded, but which is subservient to the unity of confession and communion.

From this point of view the catholic quality is equivalent to an essential mark and sign of the church. Catholicity, understood in terms of the body of Christ, that is, in a corporal as well as spiritual sense, is the flesh and blood reality of human community in the name of Jesus Christ. The signs of the church such as word, sacraments and the disciplined life stand in service to that reality of the communion of the saints. The reality of the body of Christ, both spiritual and corporal, combines confession and community, dogmatics and ethics, praxis and reflection. That leads to a recognition of catholicity as an ethical dimension and orientation of the church. The praxis of human community in diversity is ethics and politics and confession. The praxis of human community is, in Christian terms, nothing less than the praxis of peace.

## *Considerations*

*On the politics of peace*

1. The confession of Christ as our peace is the fundamental affirmation of the reality of reconciliation. God's love of God's enemies includes both oneself and one's enemies in that one reality. Reconciliation, and no hostility, ideology or other sinfulness, is the orientation and foundation of Christian praxis.
2. Distinquishing the peace and politics (kingdom) of God from the politics of humans can only serve to heighten the urgency of concrete participation in the peace of God.

3. Faithfulness and responsibility with regard to means is a way for Christians to participate in the peace of God. Means are, more than ends, a decisive test of faith. (There is no way to peace. Peace is the way.)
4. Solidarity in the body of Christ should preclude Christians from taking up arms against each other.
5. The political competence of faith is expressed in the processes of discernment and decision making amidst the complexities of human analysis and existence.
6. The peaceableness of the kingdom has priority above the unity of the church.

*On the status confessionis*

7. The *status confessionis* is not a threat to unity, but precisely its defense in the assertion of the inclusive character of the catholic church.
8. The confession of the catholic church is the confession of diverse human community in Jesus' name as a spiritual and corporeal reality. It is the confession of the body of Christ as an ethical reality and praxis.
9. The *status confessionis* must be precisely formulated in order to clarify the critical nature of the challenge to the church. Although timing and urgencies of the situation may play a role in recognizing the *status confessionis*, crucial is not only the seriousness of the concern, but specifically the nature of the crisis.
10. The *status confessionis* must be recognized, argued, and/or refuted on the merits of the direct concern and not short-circuited. In all confession it is necessary to clarify the real life reference and the concrete context if the confession is to convey meaning.
11. The *status confessionis* is not a threat of excommunication but a dialectic of invitation and challenge. In what manner the *status confessionis* is to be related to prophecy is not clear, for the dialectic of prophecy and wisdom, of decisiveness and deliberation, needs further consideration.
12. Clear is that the *status confessionis* must be imbedded in a *processus confessionis* of learning, dialogue, and discerning the consequences. The *status confessionis* is not "declared", but rather is to be recognized and confirmed, stated, and answered.
13. On the way to consensus tolerance is required, but a concept of complementarity, which mystifies rather than clarifies essential and exclusive differences, serves to frustrate rather than facilitate the *processus confessionis*.

# II.4.

# MECHANISMS OF MASS IMPOVERISHMENT

## 4.1. *When love is not enough*

The problem, or rather the catastrophe, is that tens of millions of humans are dying yearly from starvation. How many million others are victims of economically motivated oppression and unemployment and impoverishment? Since we are told that there is enough food, distribution being the problem, this situation represents an affront to humanity. What is the need for theological reflection? Is not the instruction to "Love your neighbor as yourself!" enough to realize that my neighbor has the same basic needs as I do? Is not any distraction from the simple imperative to feed the hungry an exercise in self-justification like that of a certain lawyer (ethicist) who asked, "Who is my neighbor?" (Luke 10:29) Or does the command to give to the poor only sadden the rich among us like it did a certain ruler? (Luke 18:23) If the failure to help a brother or sister in need betrays a lack of love (1 John 3:17) and a worthless faith (James 2:15,16), what need have we of theological reflection? Is not the *status charitatis* more crucial for the church than the *status confessionis*? Nevertheless, what if love is not enough? May I ask again, what is the church?

## 4.2. *W.A. Visser 't Hooft: Heresy and responsibility*

> It must become clear that church members who deny in fact their responsibility for the needy in any part of the world are just as much guilty of heresy as those who deny this or that article of faith.[179]

These words were spoken by W.A. Visser 't Hooft at the Uppsala assembly of the World Council of Churches in the context of his address on the task of the ecumenical movement. The sentence above has often been interpreted in terms of "ethical heresy." Of course, the ethical imperative was intended, but at the same time it is clear from the context that the proposition was not a form of moralizing. The task of the ecumenical movement is tied to the question of the unity of the church. It is at the same time a challenge to the church world-wide to be the church in its life and praxis. Visser 't Hooft desired to uphold the original conviction of the ecumenical movement that the true mark of the people of God is to live as a reconciled and united family and to show in witness to the world the image of a new humanity living without dividing walls.

Parallel to that, Visser 't Hooft pointed to the need to "first recover in theology, in our teaching, and in our preaching, the clear biblical doctrine of the unity of mankind." The unity of humankind is not something inherent or producible. "Mankind is one as the object of God's love and saving action. Mankind is one because of its common calling." It is scripture; it is revelation which concretely proclaims the unity of humankind. Doctrine is intended and not "just" ethics. That is further evident when Visser 't Hooft states that the failure to assume responsibility for the common life of humanity is a denial of the incarnation, of God's love for the world in Christ. The question of the very meaning of the church's common life is raised.

Solidarity and sympathy are certainly needed but are not radical enough, according to Visser 't Hooft, for they do not in themselves lead to the necessary changes in economic structures and to the essential acceptance of responsibility for the economically deprived. Needed is a new understanding of the humanity and of the unity of humankind. Needed is a new understanding of the unity of the church as a task for the sake of humanity. I note how the task and unity and identity of the church are here understood in terms of responsibility and justice. The denial of responsibility and of the imperative of justice is not simply an ethical shortcoming, but a denial of the doctrine of the unity of man and of the unity of the church.

### 4.3. *H. de Lange: "You are the man!"*

"The time has come to declare the poverty problem a *status confessionis.*" So stated the Dutch economist, H. de Lange, at a meeting of the central committee of the WCC in Geneva in 1980[180] in direct reference to Visser 't Hooft. Such a declaration would entail, according to De Lange, a struggle against political and economic powers as well as against church and mission organizations that contribute to the present situation.

> If people suffer from hunger and misery, then in most cases there are other people who are responsible for it. Our appeal should go to them. Coming from Europe this immediately reminds us of the famous words Nathan spoke to King David: "You are the man!"

The poor are to be their own protagonists, but what is the responsibility of the rich?

> What would, what could, what should be the consequences, if the churches, particularly in rich societies of the Northern hemisphere, were to become confessing churches regarding the world poverty problem? (...) Is it true to state that the good news for the poor always is bad news for the

rich? I doubt this, because what is morally good for one person cannot be bad for another, even if he/she has to share his/her wealth. How to build a spirituality for combat in the light of Luke 16:25, "And besides all this, between us and you a great chasm has been fixed, in order that those who would pass from here to you may not be able, and none may cross from there to us." In the ecumenical movement we confess that a church only is a catholic church where rich and poor are in communication with each other. But more important is that the poor recognize Christ in this church. Rich Christians in rich countries and also in poor societies have to make up their minds and to question themselves: How is it possible to live in solidarity with the poor? To speak for them and how to speak for them. To share their struggle for justice. To change our institutional and personal lives.

### 4.4. *The presence of Christ in the eucharist and the poor*

As part of a theological conference in Wuppertal-Barmen in 1984, the world economic system and mass poverty were put to the light of the third thesis of the Barmen declaration on the community of brothers and sisters.[181] In the portion of the concluding statement devoted to ecumenism and the world economic order a brief description of the economic system and its consequences (unemployment, oppression, and starvation) is joined to a call to solidarity and practical initiatives. Prior to that is a paragraph on the biblical and ecumenical basis for confronting the economic powers.

> In the Lord's supper Jesus Christ gives himself to us and in the poor he awaits us. Therefore, his eucharistic communion is not to be separated from community with the least of his brothers and sisters (Mt. 25:31-46; 1 Cor. 11:17-34). Thesis III of the Barmen theological declaration directs us today to the ecumenical community of all Christians and to ecumenical solidarity with the poor and hungry of the earth.[182]

The community of the church, centrally expressed in eucharistic communion, is thus not only a parable of the community of humankind, but has a critical focus in community with the poor.

### 4.5. *U. Duchrow: World economics and the confessing church*

It was U. Duchrow who addressed the conference mentioned above on matters of mass poverty. He published that address along with several other papers and reflections in a substantial study bearing the question "World economy today: A field for a confessing church?"[183]

*Luther on the body of Christ*

The common discernment of Christ in holy communion and in the poor is traced by Duchrow in a discussion by Martin Luther of the Lord's supper.[184] To participate in the Lord's supper is to partake in the body of Christ, with Christ as head and the saints as members. The reference is to visible bodiliness of concrete people in historically structured community. The sacrament of the Lord's supper as a sacrament of love, both received and practiced, means resisting all dishonor of Christ, all misery and suffering of injustice in the universal body of Christ wherever in the world.

Alleviation of misery and injustice is thus integral to the significance of the Lord's supper and is thus constitutive of the church. A similar conclusion is to be found, according to Duchrow, in Luther's understanding of the second tablet of the ten commandments as notae ecclesiae (signs of the church). In the context of the commandment "You shall not steal," Luther reflects upon the economic questions of his day, including his severe criticism of early capitalist developments.[185]

Duchrow points to a parallel in the theology of Bonhoeffer, for example the understanding (in *Ethics*) that humanity is united in the body of Christ.[186] Of the two, Luther was more explicit and concrete on the economic issues of his day. He rejected specific (capitalistic) economic practices such as extraction of interest, monopolies, price manipulation, etc. Theological reflection thus confronted economic issues. The ecclesiological context demonstrates the scandal of the coexistence of "active robbers, passive beneficiaries, and the robbed" in one universal body of Christ.[187] Ernst Lange is quoted.

> If it be true that the "Christ of the eucharist" is the same as the "Christ of the poor," then in the correlation between views of the sacrament and sacramental praxis on the one hand and the principle of social justice as a norm beyond discussion for the formation of the church and it's activity in the world on the other hand, the church as church is at stake, and not just the extent of its credibility. And as far as racism in the church is concerned, the Judaism problem in the New Testament is without doubt an earlier form of the problem, and, as is known, Paul judged that in that matter gospel and false gospel were at issue, salvation and doom.[188]

*The demonization of the world economic system*

The problem of the world economic system would seem to be as complicated as it is massive. Along with the armaments race it has served to renew interest in the New Testament understanding of the powers and principalities. The machinery of the economic order is seen as the beast of

Revelation 13 and as a Moloch swallowing its victims. The Vancouver assembly of the World Council of Churches spoke of idolatry and the work of satanic powers.[189] Richard Barnet has labeled undernourishment mass murder because it is avoidable. And because it is avoidable it is just as much an indictment of the present generation as Hitler's mass murder against the previous one.[190]

It is not only the magnitude and the seriousness of the situation which are being indicated by such descriptions - and many more could be added - but also a sense of futility and powerlessness, a sense of being inescapably complicit. There are as well the experiences of absolute poverty and of the face of death. It is essential that these experiences and emotions are seen and heard and reckoned with.

It seems to me that a description of world economics and its consequences in terms of idolatry and powers and principalities is fitting and discerning from the standpoint of faith. I hope that I do not distract from the existential darkness by suggesting that such description is more a conclusion than an argument. It is apparently not evident to everyone. And how can complicity in such complicated matters be proven? How can idolatry be localized? Any discernment of the demons will need be well informed. The words and descriptions used will need to open communication rather than short-circuit it.[191] It is important that the theological challenge and the ecclesiological crisis be formulated in a manner that will serve to clarify the issue and mobilize the church.

*Economic error or theological heresy?*

Heresy demands clarity. What is the precise heresy or theological error at issue in the world economic system? What constitutes the *status confessionis* in the context of world poverty? Duchrow points to the assumed or asserted autonomy of the modern economic order.[192] Freedom is defined as market freedom. The victims of the system are natural consequences of economic necessities. The economy is not made for man, but man becomes subservient to the economy. The measure of the economy is neither human life in general or the fate of the poor in particular but the functioning of the market.

Is this really heresy or is it "just" disastrous economic theory? Are there sufficient examples of theological justification of market freedom to speak of heresy? Duchrow points to a couple of examples.[193] Duchrow's assertion that the autonomy of the economic sphere is incompatible with the confession of the sole lordship of Christ (Barmen I and II) would seem correct.[194] However, is autonomy being confessed? Or is its practice enough to indict us? Or must we see the focus on autonomy as the complement to Duchrow's refutation of the modern Lutheran interpretation of the doctrine of two regiments which assigns to political and economic spheres their own rules and laws and self-determination (autonomy)?[195]

The question has been put to Duchrow to indicate what and/or who must be held responsible.[196] Another difficulty is the complicity of churches and most anyone with any amount of say or money.[197] What does it then mean to assert the *status confessionis* Is it self-indictment? With what consequences? What does our inclusion in the system, with all of its social, moral and theological dimensions, mean for confession and praxis? These questions must be answered with or without the *status confessionis*, but do not in and of themselves clarify the *status confessionis*.

The extremes of the economic calamity are easily identified. Crucial is whether such extremes are considered exceptions and by-products or are recognized for their heuristic function in evaluating the whole. The world economic system has many faces, not all of which appear demonic or defy humanizing regulation. The free market does not exist only in the extremes of its logical (idolatrous) consequences. As a result the bulk of those (Christians) profiting from the system will hardly recognize themselves in the assertions of idolatry or heresy. Although they may participate with uneasy consciences, what alternatives do they have?

Duchrow's judgement seems to fall upon the system as a whole and its deathly consequences. True, the system seems inescapable, but complicity that is not renounced and resisted is errancy and irresponsibility. The ideology of the free market can be recognized as an ideological form of death and rejected. The system can be resisted despite its seeming inescapability and thoroughgoing complicity. There remain sufficient channels of resistance such as alternative investments, economic sharing, increasing economic literacy, ecclesial and political networks, lobbying, etcetera.

*Responsibility*

Inherent to the present system, as Duchrow describes it, is that no one feels responsible. The system is so complex, includes so many actors and factors and is so interdependent that it seems to defy political and ethical regulation. No ill intention is needed to allow the game to follow its own rules. The system leads its own life and frustrates humanization and ethical responsibility.[198]

Similar to Visser 't Hooft Duchrow emphasizes the necessity of taking responsibility. The present economic disorder is no fate, but a (partially willed, partially unwilled) historic development and a product of human interaction. There are concrete alternatives. There is a possibility of a better economy. Active and passive participants must assume responsibility for change.[199]

Complicity implies guilt and responsibility requires the recognition of guilt.[200] And the *status confessionis* has always been joined to the confession of guilt. Crucial are not the feelings of guilt but the sober realization of guilt (being responsible) which can provide a basis for change and transformation. In the present question the notion of social or collective guilt would seem indispensible, as unclear as the concept might be. Although the inescapable complicity precludes pointing fingers, the system and its (rotten) fruits are to be judged.

What is the responsibility of the churches? They can confess their complicity as concretely as possible. They can seek to clean their own records and investments. They can support alternatives and seek justice. They can renounce the spirit, logic and praxis of the free market. Should they also state that the challenge of the world economic order requires the recognition of the *status confessionis*? Of what meaning would that be in a large institution? Or should confession be rooted in local communities where it can be concretely tied to commitment and discipleship, as L.A. Hoedemaker has suggested?[201] Duchrow has himself pointed to the role that discipleship groups and communities can play in exemplifying alternatives and trying out new paths.[202] What is then the form of ecumenical solidarity? These questions need further clarification, but the nature of the challenge to the church can be stated.

### 4.6. *Equality and catholicity in the church*

There have been innumerable statements by churches on economic issues.[203] The World Council of Churches has been particularly active and in 1992 produced a study document entitled *Christian Faith and the World Economy Today*. A preparatory paper (for the Central Committee in 1991) concluded with a quotation from the fifth general assembly in Nairobi (1975).

> Economic structures may also obscure the confession of Christ. Thus while we confess a Christ who frees and unites, the economic structures in which we live tend to enslave to wealth and divide.

"In this sense," it was concluded, "economic issues are confessional issues; economy is a matter of faith."[204] This statment follows careful analysis of the economic situation and explication of the theological motives for commenting on the economy. Nevertheless, it must be noted that the "confessional" emphasis is not argued, but serves as a conclusion. In the final study document it is not to be found. There the emphasis falls on God's preferential option for the poor and relating worship and economics.[205]

For the present purposes attention has been limited to the *status confessionis* debate on economics. That means that much relevant material on the theological evalutation of economics is left unused. There is one perspective, however, that seems peculiarly seldom mentioned in the material. That is Paul's admonition to economic sharing between churches.

> I do not mean that others should be eased and you burdened, but that as a matter of equality your abundance at the present time should supply their want, so that their abundance may supply your want, that there may be equality. (2 Corinthians 8:9)

Quite naturally most of the literature focuses on the fact that we live in a world of rich and poor people and rich and poor countries. Paul's admonitions serve as a reminder that we also live with the fact of rich and poor churches. To be sure, very many resources have been shared, for better and for worse, but the scandal of coexistent rich and poor churches has hardly been confronted. Mutual sharing is practiced but equalization, as Paul suggests, has hardly been defined as a goal, much less translated into policy. The question is, of course, complicated with divergent economic sub-systems (living costs) and diverse socio-cultural needs, but approximation would itself be a radical change. The principle of equalization implies that we cannot demand for ourselves what we in fact deny others. Equalization is, in Paul's view, a factor of the unity of the church.

The failure of the (Western) churches to approximate equalization and exemplify the unity of the church by economic sharing takes on life and death proportions as a reflection of the world situation. Humans and masses are wasted, bodily, of course, but culturally and spiritually as well. In the case of nuclear armaments it was seen that where the masses are expendable the church is suffering harm and division, that the body of Christ is being violated. The loss in the the face of world poverty is likewise both physical and spiritual.

Of further concern as well is the environmental damage that modern economic and technological practices have inflicted upon the earth and its inhabitants. The integrity of creation is also at stake, as the World Council of Churches has recognized.[206] Humans are creatures in body and spirit. Their identity and integrity are tied to that of all creation. It can be asked whether the biblical doctrine of the unity of humankind can be recovered without the biblical vision of the integrity of creation. Human life and culture are dependent upon the integrity of creation. Can there be good news of Jesus Christ without the good creation of God? The catholicity of the church assumes the catholicity of creation. The spirituality of the church is one of sharing with the poor and celebrating creation.

## *Considerations*

*On the catholic calling of the church*

1. Recognizing the presence of Jesus both in the celebration of the eucharist and among the poor correlates the practice of the sacrament to the pursuit of justice.
2. The integrity of the body of Christ is violated when human life is wasted by impoverishment and oppression.
3. The recovery of the unity of the church is correlated to the recovery of the vision of the unity of humankind and to the response of churches to the calling to responsibility and justice.

4. To that end churches need to formulate and instigate policies in the direction of economic equalization.
5. The vision of the unity of humankind and of the church assumes the integrity and catholicity of creation.

*On the status confessionis in economics*

6. The world economic order or disorder seems almost too complicated and too diffuse to assert the *status confessionis*. It is not clear what the specific criteria should be, given the inescapable complicity. It is not clear what commitment and praxis is specifically required in confessing Christ amidst the economic powers.
7. Churches need nevertheless to confess their complicity in the system as a whole.
8. Churches need to formulate their renunciation of the spirit, logic, and praxis of the free market with respect to its autonomous character and its deathly consequences.
9. Churches need to formulate and practice ways of resisting the economic evils and of seeking just alternatives, including equalization of resources among churches.
10. It may be that local communities and particular movements can lead the way by formulating specific commitments and enabling economic discipline.
11. If churches should take steps such as the above, they may engender a parting of spirits in such a manner that the economic issue will become a *status confessionis*.

## II.5.

## THE STATUS OF THE CHURCH

### 5.1. *The challenge to the church*

Thus far an understanding of the *status confessionis* has been explored in terms of Bonhoeffer's ecclesiological interpretation and the solidarity of the body of Christ. Various descriptions have emerged such as eucharistic community, catholicity as unity and diversity, conciliarity, and so forth. Such descriptions need to be examined more closely, not just in reference to their meaning, but also in reference to their context. What is the significance of the catholicity of the church in the context of radically divided churches in a radically divided world? It cannot be stated bluntly enough, as E. Lange has emphasized, that whatever divides the world, divides the churches as well. The churches even add to and aggravate those divisions, and theologians might be found guilty of disturbance of the peace. Lange even asks if the church's best contribution to the peace and unity of humanity would not be to dissolve itself. Is it not an inherent danger that the church necessarily distinguishes itself from the world?[207]

Lange suggests as well the question that will be considered in this chapter: What is the identity of the church in the midst of human community and dividedness? How is the church a sign or parable of the coming unity of humankind?[208] Or to put it another way: What will be the form and direction of the church as the body of Christ in this wayward and wanton world of God?

In seeking answers to these questions several resources present themselves: a discussion on the need for a confessing church in the United States; documents from third world theologians of liberation asserting a *kairos*, a moment of truth, for the church; a conciliar process for justice, peace, and the integrity of creation; as well as more general reflections on the ecumenical task of the church and its conciliar character. The material is in fact immense. A selection is made by focusing on those discussions and documents which seem to derive their impetus more or less directly from the confessional challenges explicated in the previous chapters.

The questions raised by Dietrich Bonhoeffer are again encountered. What is the nature of a confessing church? Can the church speak to the problems of the world in an ecumenical council? What is the ecclesial character of the ecumenical movement? Can the ecumenical movement be a confessing movement? For Bonhoeffer all of these questions were tied to the fundamental question of the church: Who is Jesus Christ for us today?

The present chapter thus comprises a further direction of thought derived from Bonhoeffer. It is a question situated between the specific question of the *status confessionis* (Part II) and the more general question of the theological relation between ecclesiology and ethics (Part III). It relates to the church in both its local and ecumenical dimensions. It is concerned with the relations between confession and conciliarity, catholicity and *kairos*.

### 5.2. *A confessing church today in the USA?*

Not only in Germany, but also in the United States, the fiftieth anniversary of Barmen received attention. Of particular interest is a brief but intensive discussion published in *Katallagete* on the need of a confessing church in the USA.[209] The discussion was initiated in an article by George Hunsinger entitled "Barth, Barmen and the Confessing Church Today" in 1985. In 1987 the responses of a host of theologians and Christian writers were published (along with Hunsinger's responses to the responses).

The principal focal points for Hunsinger's challenge seem to have been the nuclear threat and U.S. interventionist policies in Central America, but the crisis was understood to run deeper. It involved as well the accomodation of the church to "American ideals" and accompanying utilitarian notions of religion. Hunsinger's proposal was that of a doctrinal renewal in terms of christological concentration combined with prayer and political resistance. Crucial to the entire project would be the social novelty of the church as a church of reconciliation, non-conformity, and the cross.

The responses covered practically the entire breadth of theology, stimulated as the respondents were by Hunsinger's adherence to the line of Barmen and Barth. I will pay attention to two sorts of questions. In the first place, can a specific threat to the confession of the church in the U.S. be located and formulated? In the second place, whether confessional or not, what form should the response of the church to the contemporary challenges take?

One can point to the phenomenon of civil religion in the U.S., to the segregation of churches, to the aquiescence to government policy and American culture, and so forth, but is it possible to speak of a particular political and theological ideology which would require of churches a confessional response?[210] Hunsinger responded that even if no direct, literal parallel to the situation of Barmen might be demonstrated, nevertheless a functional equivalent of heresy did in fact exist. The pathology of nationalism veiled the compromised character of the church, but the heresies could be named: American exceptionalism, anticommunism, and nuclearism. "Nuclear weapons and crimes against humanity, to the extent that they elicit our consent, place us in as much of a *status confessionis* as we are ever likely to see."[211]

Such a response does locate specific dangers. I question whether it satisfies those who hesitate on the question. The comprehensive case which Hunsinger seeks to make for a confessing church is impressive in its accumulated weight, but at the same time tends to turn the matter into a theological project rather than incisively and concisively sound a call to confession.

Whether or not they agreed with Hunsinger's confessional case and theological terms, any number of respondents sought to collaborate on the calling of the church in contemporary America (USA). J.H. Yoder felt that Barmen was ecclesiologically flawed. A confessing church requires particular and accountable community structures as a locus for prayer and resistance.[212] (Is this an elaboration, one could ask, of the community of brothers and sisters as stated in Barmen III?) S. Hauerwas suggested that the "crucial issue is how we develop discriminating categories from our Christological commitments that will allow us to read the ambiguities of living in America."[213]

P. Lehmann indicated a basic orientation by reference to Bonhoeffer.

> A Confessing Church is a community of believers in Jesus Christ (baptized or not yet baptized) for whom Bonhoeffer's question "Who is Jesus Christ for us today?" is central, formative and determinative for faith and practice.[214]

R. Osborn, although questioning the specific confessional challenge, elaborated on that perspective in terms of the community of brothers and sisters in Jesus Christ as stated in Barmen III.

> The Church, the local Church as a member of the ecumenical Church, includes Israel as its presupposition and the world as its promise. The love in which the Christian community has its reality is grounded in its faith in the God of Israel and in His Messiah Jesus and is sustained and given its life by its hopeful participation in the universal community whose redemption is promised with the coming of Christ. In community with Israel, the Church has its faith; in community with the world it expresses its hope; sustained by this faith and hope it finds itself as a community of love.
>
> Barmen is political...because the Church as the community in which Jesus Christ acts as Lord cannot abstract itself from the Jews who always seem to be so much a part of this world and its politics, even though perhaps the least among its brothers and sisters, and because it belongs to the human community, the body politic, to whom Christ promises to bring God's kingdom.[215]

Osborn thus provided a christological concentration in no narrow sense, but rather as an orientation for inclusive community.

Daniel Berrigan agreed with Hunsinger that when the church has become normalized in an absolutely unnormal situation there is an obvious political crisis for the church. But why does Hunsinger question the possibility of a confessing church? "The qualities he seeks - resisting, resilient, repentant, and remnant - I believe are already present. These communities and congregations are among us and have been for years." And Berrigan pointed, just as Hunsinger had done, to the black churches, to the anti-Vietnam war movement, to the anti-nuclear and sanctuary movements.[216] Berrigan was sceptical of the usefulness of declarations or confessions.

> I submit the task is to strengthen the confessing quality, the depth of faith of the already existing communities. Our effort should be to deepen our confession both in private prayer, in worship, and in public witness. Let the main-line churches and society do what they want. The sign of the Church, the sign of the Kingdom is present regardless.[217]

Berrigan felt that theology, in accord with the pattern of base communities and liberation movements in Latin America, would come later. Similarly Monika Hedwig attached theological significance to the fact that movements are broader than churches.

> The question then arises whether a Confessing Church movement ought to take a confessionally-based stance (that is, enrolling the faithful) or discern where in society the gospel of Jesus Christ demands our vigorous resistance and who the allies are in such resistance. Given the pluralistic character of our society, only the second of these is a live option.[218]

Hunsinger continually insisted that the crisis was in fact theological as well and that the theological challenge had to be met as such. He asserted the centrality of doctrine. Politics (and ethics?) he assigned to the periphery. Centrality and periphery form one whole; in fact the one without the other is meaningless, but substance and application must be distinguished.

This seems to be an unfortunate way of putting things. If the kingdom of God is the subject of the Gospel proclamation, how can the claim be made that politics is peripheral? Such a scheme does not really serve to clarify the nature of confession, the relation of doing theology to resistance.[219] Nor is such a scheme necessary for Hunsinger's insistence that the church be centered, that its sense of identity is essential to any reciprocity between church and world.[220] That insistence, in fact, indicates that ecclesiology as political theology is central to the substance of the gospel.

## 5.3. *Kairos: A challenge to the churches*

Hunsinger and several of his respondents pointed to the praxis of base communities and to the method of liberation theologies as hopeful signs and examples for a confessing movement. Various calls to prophetic resistance have been issued in terms of a discernment of *kairos*. The South African *Kairos Document* (Cf. II.2.6.) stimulated response from other quarters: *Kairos Central America: A Challenge to the Churches of the World* and *The Road to Damascus: Kairos and Conversion* (a joint document of Africans, Central Americans and Asians). More may be on the way in Europe, the Middle East, the United States or elsewhere, but the three documents mentioned above provide sufficient basis for reflection. I refer specifically to their joint publication with commentary by Robert McAfee Brown in *Kairos. Three Prophetic Challenges to the Church.*[221]

What is a *kairos*? The term is a transliteration of a Greek word for 'time' and can be contrasted with another Greek word *chronos*. *Chronos* is time passing by, the succession of moments, minutes, months and milleniums. *Kairos* is a time, a moment, that is not to be missed, a special or right time, a time of opportunity or decision, a time of fulfillment.[222] Jesus' coming out began with the announcement of such a time. "Fulfilled is the *kairos* and nearby is the kingdom of God: change your minds and trust in the good news." (Mark 1:15)

The documents speak of a moment of truth. Such a moment is a favourable time, a time of grace, for it offers a unique opportunity for repentance and conversion, change and decisive action. It is a dangerous time for if it is missed the consequences will be unforeseeable and the loss immeasurable. Judgement will come. It is therefore a time to be discerned and acted upon.[223]

The *kairos* thus indicates a critical conjuncture, a crisis in the time. There is thus a close relation to the application of the *status confessionis*, as Brown indicates. No longer can one agree to disagree. No longer can contrary positions be tolerated as complementary. 'Both/and' is no longer possible. It is 'either/or'. A decision must be made.

What is the situation which has evoked such a contemporary *kairos*? The documents seem to agree in scope. The crisis is that of devastating economic and political oppression. The cause is colonial and contemporary imperialism and the manipulated (so-called "free") market. The scandal is the complicity of Christians and churches and 'Christian' societies, not in the least the United States. Condemnation is directed at ideological caricatures of theology which are labeled hypocrisy, heresy, apostasy, blasphemy, and idolatry. The commitment is to the struggle of the poor as subjects of their own liberation. The calling is to Christians everywhere to let themselves be converted to God's option for the poor and to participate in ecumenical solidarity and resistance.

The documents are "hard-hitting" as Brown points out and rich readers of the West, especially of the United States, are warned to brace themselves.[224] But the point of the documents is that the facts are hard, terribly and fatally hard, that the truth must be confronted, that the struggle must be engaged for God's sake. Any question of details is thus utterly subservient to the severity of the crisis and the urgency of the task.

Will the *kairos* be met? For it calls, in the first place, for the conversion of all those who call themselves Christian and are not yet on the side of the poor. It calls for the conversion and transformation of churches everywhere. Are Christians and churches meeting the moment? Some are, as Berrigan has indicated. Will such declarations of *kairos* help others to conversion? It might turn out that the *kairos* will spread itself out over the *chronos*. That is to say that, if any widespread change is to come, it will be in a slow process. At best the *kairos* documents can serve to accelerate a process that will have to be spearheaded by confessional communities.

Brown asks whether it is time for a *Kairos USA* document. He provides an initial checklist and invites additions. The question arises: Does the scope become so broad that a *kairos* is hardly conceivable? The checklist turns into a project that assumes a process spread through time. The *kairos* becomes then a reflective rather than active enterprise. It becomes the task of ethics and ecclesiology itself.

## 5.4. *Conciliar process: justice, peace, integrity of creation*

*Dietrich Bonhoeffer: An ecumenical council for peace*

In 1934, in the same year that the Barmen declaration was issued and the Confessing Church became a fact in Germany, Dietrich Bonhoeffer issued in an international setting a call for an ecumenical council to speak a word of peace to the world.[225] For Bonhoeffer peace was not a question, but a commandment. And that commandment was in fact the reality of the church. It was the inseparable bond in Christ beyond all boundaries. Christians can thus not take up weapons against each other, for to do so would be to take up weapons against Christ.

How does peace come about? Not by means of security or guarantees. Peace is to be dared and ventured. The way to peace is the way of the cross. Who can then call us to peace so that the world will hear?

> Only the one great Ecumenical Council of the Holy Church of Christ over all the world can speak out so that the world, though it gnash its teeth, will have to hear, so that the peoples will rejoice because the Church of Christ in the name of Christ has taken the weapons from the hands of their sons, forbidden war, and proclaimed the peace of Christ against the raging world.

*Heino Falcke: The ecclesiology of peace*

The church did not speak and the world went to war, but the hope that the ecumenical church would speak a word of peace was not forgotten. The hope was reiterated in 1983 against the background of the *status confessionis* on nuclear weapons in Germany. Specifically it was the East German delegation to the general assembly of the World Council of Churches in Vancouver that proposed a peace council. The ecumenical movement, however, had changed since Bonhoeffer's days. Other issues, commands of the day, had placed themselves on the agenda. No peace without justice, was emphasized by Alan Boesak and others from the third world. Peace had to be more than an anti-nuclear East-West arrangement. By Eastern Orthodoxy, attention was asked for creation and the threat to natural environments as well. It became clear, furthermore, that the word 'council' created ecclesiological difficulties for both Orthodox and Roman Catholic partners. But the thing had to have a name. The Vancouver assembly issued a call for the churches "to engage in a conciliar process of mutual commitment (covenant)[226] for justice, peace and the integrity of creation."

The English abbreviation became JPIC, emphasizing the three central issues (justice, peace, and the integrity of creation) and the challenge to human and natural survival. Of particular interest for the present purposes is the meaning and significance of the phrase "a conciliar process of mutual commitment (covenant)." What might that entail for the churches? Is there something like an ecclesiology of JPIC? One notable example is provdided by the considerations of Heino Falcke, who as a member of the East German delegation in 1983, was one of the initiators of the whole undertaking.[227]

Falcke points to three modern events that have enlivened the concept of an ecumenical council. In the first place he points to the Second Vatican Council and the subsequent hopes for institutional reform and popular participation.[228] In the second place he points to the Council of Youth engendered by the community of Taizé as a charismatic complement to the Second Vatican Council. Taizé has become a sign of a springtime in the church, of a truth lived out in meditation and reconciliation, a praxis of community and sharing.[229]

In the third place Falcke reflects on the challenge presented by Bonhoeffer.[230] Falcke does not expect, as Bonhoeffer did, that the world will listen, gnashing its teeth. (Nor does it seem to me that Bonhoeffer, in the time that he wrote his letters and papers in prison, would still have expected that.) Important, however, is not to what extent Bonhoeffer's political expectations were realistic, but that he placed the concept of a church council in the context of political reasoning and responsibility. Bonhoeffer named only one concretization, refusal of military conscription, but he did so by emphasizing the universal character of the church as a decisive argument against ecclesial and political nationalism.

That universality (catholicity) was rooted in Bonhoeffer's christology, especially his understanding of "Christ existing as community." Just as Christ is Lord of the entire world, so is the church in essence one, and has the task of speaking Christ's word to the world. Falcke refers to this as an ecclesiological consequence of the first Barmen thesis. Jesus Christ, the one word of God, is ecclesiologically interpreted and concretized as the one ecumenical church.

Loyalty to the universal body of Christ precedes political loyalty to one's own people and state. Christians are thus not to take up arms against each other. This ecclesiology of peace thus embodies a truth and a reality that the church is as the body of Christ. If Christ is our peace, then the church as the body of Christ is to be the embodiment of peace.[231]

Does this ecclesiological argument discriminate between Christians and non-Christians? Is not Christ wounded whenever a weapon is directed at a fellow human? Falcke insists that the ecclesiological argument has a universal dimension. Bonhoeffer anticipated the understanding of both the Second Vatican Council and the the Uppsala assembly of the World Council of Churches that the unity of the church is a sacrament and sign of the unity of humanity.[232]

An ecumenical council would have the task of validating and effectualizing this understanding of the unity of church and humanity. The task must be undertaken comprehensively by combining ecological sensibility, economic solidarity, and irenic responsibility.[233] That in turn entails an appreciation of the varieties of contexts and challenges. The task of shalom is different where people are hungry or disappearing in the night from where they are overfed and overarmed. The conciliar challenge is to discern and relate those differences of experience[234] and so enable mutual participation. Common commitments are to be made in the form of covenants that reflect God's covenant with creation and humanity.

Falcke employs any number of understandings which have already been encountered: eucharistic community, *kairos* and conversion, communicative processes, the solidarity of the body of Christ. The interrelatedness is of great interest and importance, but the terminological density is undeniable. I therefore turn to the task of a closer interpretation of one term, that of 'conciliarity'.

## 5.5. *Conciliarity*

*Dietrich Bonhoeffer: Is the ecumenical movement church?*

Bonhoeffer was quite active in the budding ecumenical movement of the early 1930's. He sought to reflect on the theological, i.e., ecclesiological, basis of that movement.[235] That issue became for him a test case when the mutual relation of the Confessing Church and the ecumenical movement became acute.[236]

The crucial question for Bonhoeffer was whether the ecumenical movement, in its visible representation, was a church. Had the ecumenical reality of the church as attested in the New Testament found visible and appropriate expression in the ecumenical organization? Cooperation in the ecumenical movement assumed the reality of the one church, confessing one Lord. Should not the ecumenical movement thus assume the reality and authority of the church for itself?

The relation of both the German Christian church and the Confessing Church to the ecumenical movement made the decision unavoidable in Bonhoeffer's view. If the Confessing Church were correct in its absolute rejection of the German Christian movement, then contacts via ecumenical relations had to be rejected as well. The ecumenical movement had to decide with whom relations were to be maintained, with the German Christians or with the Confessing Church. To decide on that matter would be to decide on matters of confession. To decide on matters of confession would be to assume and appropriate the authority of the true church. Nothing less than witness to the truth and the unity of the church were at stake. The ecumenical movement did not decide, and with Bonhoeffer the Confessing Church effectively withdrew from explicit participation in the ecumenical movement. But the question had been raised.

*Ernst Lange: An ecumenical utopia*

Ernst Lange's penetrating look at the ecumenical movement reflects his role as an active and committed participant. His question is similar to Bonhoeffer's. What is meant by the description of the ecumenical movement as a movement of the churches?[237] His manner of answering the question is that of reviewing a conference of the Faith and Order section of the World Council of Churches at Louvain, Belgium, in 1971. Lange seeks to analyze the theme of the conference, "The Unity of the Church and the Unity of Mankind," and particularly to interpret the considerations on the concept of conciliarity.

Again the terminological density is ineludible, but it seems to serve the weight of the concerns. Lange is concerned with what might be called a multi-dimensional conflict on the unity of the church. I indicated at the beginning of this chapter Lange's recognition that the divisions of the world divide the church and that the church, particularly in the person of its theologians, adds to and aggravates the divisiveness.[238] Need the realities of racism, classism, sexism and so many other forms of discrimination be enumerated? Need the forms of economic interests, cultural chauvinism, social oppression and political violence be explicated? The marginalized are no longer a marginal problem.[239] The church finds these divisions in its own heart.

The unity of the church must not only confront the divisions of the world but also comprehend the diversity of human existence and expression.[240] There are differences of culture and color, of health and handicap, of sex and age, of natural and cultural varieties, that need to be appreciated and appropriated for the life of the church. Otherwise they too will be exploited into further divisions.

Complicating the two-fold challenge of human diversity and sinful division, is the fact that the church necessarily separates itself from the world by gathering the faithful and creating a distinct community. It is a mistake to equate that separation with the limits of belief and salvation, but the fact of a distinct religious community is itself a provocation susceptible to misunderstanding and misuse. The gathering of the 'elect' is itself in danger of misrepresenting its own cause by asserting its own identity at the cost of others, whether in the church or in the world, or by accommodating its identity to some particular group or interest.[241] The result is a proliferation of churches, with cultural, national, and denominational divisions. And it is this "parochialism" of the churches which is their most extreme perversion.[242]

As if these divisions and diversities were not themselves sufficient cause for conflict and confusion, the ecumenical movement must also confront a conflict on strategies: reconciliation or liberation; looking to that which divides or to that which binds; unity by common service or by common confession; unity anticipated in eucharistic community or patiently waited for in eucharistic abstinence? It is, however, this conflict on strategies which provides the strategy of the ecumenical movement, just as the diversities and divisions provide the agenda. The ecumenical movement is in fact a staging of those conflicts, the attempt to organize and appreciate them and make them fruitful for the life of the church.[243]

The ecumenical movement is thus a dynamic conflict that enlivens the unity of the church. Unity can only be understood as interaction of variety. Variety and diversity are appreciated as the spectral profusion of unity as they provide the sources and resources for unity. However, the attractive image of interaction and profusion holds within it the sources of real conflict and the struggle for truth. What holds it together is the common hope for truth and the common task of responsibility. Consensus and conflict are mutual aspects of the process of unity. That process of consensus and conflict, of interaction and profusion, is called conciliarity.[244]

Conciliarity is thus the name which the church gives to its common search for truth and to the task of discerning its responsibility. It is a constant structure of the life of the church - locally, regionally or worldwide - practiced in prayer, deliberation and decision. It is practiced in the faith that the Spirit will be working to provide reconciliation, renewal and transformation. It is a model of fundamental democracy. Unity is not organized hierarchically, but entrusted to the processes of discussion and interaction. Any church council must attain the consent of the grass roots. Decisive is the recognition that the question of truth must remain open towards the future. Conciliarity is concerned not only with truth but also with method.

A more concrete description of all this is for Lange "eucharistic community." Eucharistic community is the unity of the church and the very goal of the ecumenical movement. And eucharistic community implies a eucharistic ethic.[245] The Christ of the eucharist is the same as the Christ of the poor.[246] Sharing the bread of the eucharist is a symbol of the sharing of all bread.[247] If that be true then questions of social justice, church unity, and human community are not simply questions of the credibility of the church, but of the very identity and integrity of the church. It is the church as church that is at stake.

If the Christ of the eucharist is the Christ of the poor, then the poor and the marginalized are central to the unity and conciliarity of the church. They need to be heard first. Their cause must lend direction to the life of the church. The deliberations of Louvain on the handicapped in the church express this. They call to memory that Jesus Christ was rejected and broken and still a model of human wholeness.[248] The presence of the handicapped are a reminder of the limitations of human existence. They are a reminder that the strength of Christian community is to be found in weakness.[249] They are a reminder, one might also suggest, of the need of a new awareness of bodiliness.

What is to become of all of these considerations? The power of the ecumenical movement lies only in its arguments, but it has become common knowledge that arguments do not change structures. In fact the parochial identities of churches and the parochial consciences of Christians make them unable to engage themselves wholeheartedly in the ecumenical experience and the conciliar endeavor.[250] To cite the problem is not to solve it, but Lange's book is one great plea for a new understanding of our identities as Christians and churches. It is in effect a plea for ecumenical encounter.

The future of the church is the ecumenical movement. The ecumenical movement is the church seeking its own unity and seeking shalom in a terribly divided world. The church does not seek a different peace than the world, but it seeks it in a different way, from its own perspective. The only way for the church to seek unity and shalom is the conciliar project of the ecumenical movement. It is the common task of "all in each place" (the local church) and "all in all places" (the ecumenical church).[251] In fact the ecumenical enterprise is the only way of actuating the four fundamental criteria of the church: unity, sanctity, catholicity and apostolicity.[252] From that perspective the church is sign and promise of the *shalom* of God.

Lange asks whether relating essence and task of the church is a "functionalizing" of the church, in which the church is defined in terms of its contribution to the survival of humankind.[253] However, a reversal is also possible, in which the unity of the church is not conceived in terms of the unity of humanity, but in which the unity of humanity is conceived and confirmed from the perspective of the church in God's world. Lange's concern is with the identity and integrity of the church itself. Division and unity are matters of the *esse* of the church, not simply its *bene esse*.[254]

This can be further illustrated by noting how Lange derives the direction of the conciliar and ecumenical endeavor of the church from the life praxis of Jesus. Lange notes four "humanizing directions". The first is Jesus'inclusion of outcasts, his practice of love that transcended social limits and tended toward universality. Second is Jesus' movement from dominion to service, from strong to weak, from subjection to liberation. Priority is ascribed to that which is down under. Third is the way in which Jesus filled all reality with promise and thus sanctified the profane. Fourth is Jesus' anticipation of eschatological possibility in reality, rather than limiting possibility to reality.

With this orientation on the life praxis of Jesus Lange fills the terminological structure with critical direction. Conciliarity, ecumenicity, and unity take on a particular quality. The ecumenical utopia can be concretely anticipated in critical, conciliar, conflictful praxis.

*Ulrich Duchrow: Conflict over the ecumenical movement*

Lange pointed to the legitimacy and necessity of conflict in the ecumenical movement. Ulrich Duchrow, writing ten years later, would seem to agree. His concern is how the conflict is organized. The criticism he formulates in his book, *Conflict over the Ecumenical Movement. Confessing Christ Today in the Universal Church,*[255] is directed towards a concept of "reconciled diversity" which evades the conflict by letting differences be. The problem for Duchrow is not just parochialism, but also confessional particularism, especially of global confessional bodies like the Lutheran World Federation. Duchrow fears the demise of the ecumenical project, not as an institution, but in its radical orientation to unity, catholicity, and conciliarity in its relation to the unity of humankind in a divided world.

The criteria that Duchrow uses are the classic marks or attributes of the Nicene-Constantinopolitan creed: one, holy, catholic, apostolic church. He appeals to Jürgen Moltmann and Wolfgang Huber in his application of those attributes to the praxis of the church. He quotes Moltmann.

> What form is to be taken by Christ in the Church in a world of hostility? By the Church sanctified in the Spirit in a world of poverty? By the catholic Church as it testifies to the Kingdom in a world of violence? By the apostolic Church in the world of the cross? Is the situation in which the Church finds itself in this society not bound to stamp it with the signs of poverty, suffering, liberation, and partnership? ... The marks of the Church will then become *confessional signs in the conflicts* which today are really splitting and dividing humanity. Let us therefore extend the ecclesiology of tradition, which is oriented towards unity, into an ecclesiology oriented towards conflict in the world situation of today.[256]

How can a divided body of Christ confess Christ in a divided world? The most important specific challenge, according to Duchrow, would seem to be the recognition of the North-South situation as a confessional issue. In more general terms, Duchrow's concern is to contextualize the confessional problems. Traditional confessional differences can no longer be imposed on quite different third world contexts. Those same traditional confessional differences need to be overcome in common confession in the face of the questions dividing humanity.

How is this contextualization to take place? In other words, how is a conciliar process of "all in each place" and "all in all places" to be organized? The primary focal points of the church are the local and universal (ecumenical) forms, all in each place and all in all places.[257] In the local church the eucharist is celebrated and the word is actualized in the concrete situation. The practice of fellowship seeks to transcend all natural, cultural, economic, and political divisions. The local church shares in the catholic nature of the church by sharing the same apostolic faith and participating in the fellowship of a universal network of churches.

Two other forms of the church are noted: the regional church and initiative groups. Regional churches can support the local churches in assuming and performing their contextual responsibility. Initiative groups, orders, and discipleship groups can help the church face specific issues and break new ground. Both regional churches and initiative groups must, however, fulfill two conditions in order to participate in being the church: "(1) they must serve the eucharistic, confessing, ecumenical community of Christ in each place; and (2) they must serve the total fellowship of all local churches." By thus relating the forms of the church, Duchrow seeks to envision the organization of the church confessing ecumenically.

*Aram Keshishian: Conciliar fellowship*

Aram Keshishian, Archbishop of the Armenian Church in Lebanon, has provided an investigation of how the concept of "conciliar fellowship" has served as a model of unity in the World Council of Churches.[258] Keshishian closely relates conciliarity and catholicity and roots them in the local church as a eucharistic community. Just as the church is essentially catholic in the interrelatedness of unity and diversity, so also the church is essentially conciliar in the interaction of unity and diversity. The conciliar tradition from its beginnings in the early ecumenical councils is related to the task of preserving or restoring the unity of the catholic church. Conciliarity itself is a mark of the church (L. Vischer) or just another name for the church (Y. Congar). The church is a *concilium oecumenicum*.[259]

This is evident in the understanding of the local church. The local church is catholic by means of its 1) faithfulness to the particularities of its place; 2) its openness to other places; and 3) its communion with other local churches.[260] Thus the catholic nature of the church assumes the stuff of conciliarity: communication and common deliberation, convergence and consensus. (Keshishian's evaluation seems quite conciliatory. Fundamental differences between Roman Catholics, Orthodox and Protestants are indicated, but conflict receives little attention. At the same time his contribution would not be Orthodox if it did not emphasize the centrality of the bishop as administrator of the eucharist. But Keshishian is also aware that the regional function of the bishop which makes of the "local" church a regional reality is at odds with true locality.)

Keshishian exposes a critical point of tension. His conception of conciliar fellowship is not one of eucharistic community that would first require agreement (unity) on doctrine and the episcopacy. At the same time he states that the "unity of the church is not just a theological agreement, but a visible fellowship that a local church lives in communion with other local churches." And further: "Conciliar fellowship necessarily presupposes the unity of the church."[261] The question is thus raised whether conciliarity is a goal or means, feature, or pattern, form or vision, way or reality.[262] To simply state that it is all of the above, as Keshishian suggests, may be correct, but it would hardly serve to clarify matters, unless the intention is to radically relate (or integrate) means and ends.

Keshishian agrees that the ecumenical search for visible unity cannot remain open-ended. Conciliarity constitutes for him a threefold challenge: to institutionalized confessionalism of Protestantism, to universalism and centralistic uniformism of Roman Catholicism, and to radical parochialism of Orthodoxy.

*Bert Hoedemaker: Local community in a global society*

Bert Hoedemaker likewise emphasizes the local and global (ecumenical) poles of the form of the church and draws two central conclusions.[263] The first point concerns the confessing character of the church. Drawing real limits can only occur locally. The *status confessionis*, e.g., must be the commitment of a local community. It is there that word and sacrament, community and service touch the daily lives of people. It is there that decisions of faith are made and a life of discipline in the face of real risks is practiced. It is there that the consequences become visible and practicable.

The local community must secondly open itself to the breadth and depth of the global community. Local confession resounds in ecumenical communication (conciliarity). It is an appeal to common confession and solidarity and an openness to appeals from other communities. The conciliar practice of the church, or more specifically, of an ecumenical council can have a market function. Local confessions and appeals can be communicated and considered, even if they are not mutually compatible.[264]

Hoedemaker's question is whether concrete (local) obedience and authoritative, confessional stances by regional or ecumenical bodies can be combined in the way Bonhoeffer and Duchrow have advocated. Global awareness, a new reality of church history in this century, is at the same time an awareness of fragmentation and deep division, of seemingly insurmountable expansiveness. It is awareness of any number of conflicts in the world and contextual differences. No council can speak with unabashed authority. Thus Hoedemaker's analysis of the present situation of church and world serves to heighten the realization that the authority of any council lies in its reception by local communities at the grass roots level.

This does not mean that the market function of conciliar practice is non-committal. It is not a 'free market.' The unity and common commitment of local confession and ecumenical communication is the question that is central to both enterprises. It is the abiding question that Bonhoeffer emphasized: "Who is Jesus Christ for us today?"[265] And this question is to be asked and answered at the points of conflict in the world, in the context of experiences of suffering and struggle. It is there that the fundamental questions of humanity and faith are to be confronted.[266] The question of the presence of Jesus Christ in the midst of various conflicts and contexts is to be a guide in creating local community and seeking ecumenical communication.

The *status confessionis* and/or a conciliar process for justice, peace, and integrity of creation cannot, therefore, have as their primary aim declarations of the church, but can only be moments or movements, whether local, regional, or global, in the conciliar practice of local confession and ecumenical communication. All is dependent on the quality of that community and that communication.

One might question Hoedemaker on the nature of ecumenical commitment. If conciliarity is a mark of the local as well as ecumenical church, then ecumenical communication would seem to possess a confessional quality. Its very presupposition, as Bonhoeffer indicated, is the unity and catholicity of the church, the essential character of ecumenical communication. It will never and can never be non-partisan. Was Bonhoeffer not correct that the ecumenical movement should have decided between German Christians and Confessing Church? Were not ecumenical bodies correct in confirming the *status confessionis* in the context of apartheid as an expression of solidarity with the appeal coming from South African Christians?

Hoedemaker points to the difficulty of confessing at any but a local level, as if it is not difficult enough there. Nevertheless, it should be reckoned with that at times local confession may lead to regional or even global confession. Ecumenical confession needs local consent and confirmation, but it need not yet be universal in an absolute sense in order to be catholic. In other words, the sense in which the ecumenical movement is the church and assumes the authority of the church cannot be answered in general terms. Rather the question should be kept alive.

One other thing is noteworthy in Hoedemaker's understanding of the church. If the primary focuses of the church are local and global (ecumenical), then all cultural and especially national relations become secondary. Understanding the relation of the church to the world primarily in terms of its relation to the state and its government becomes inadequate. Traditional concepts of church and state need revision. The relation of church to world is much more plural and needs to be oriented to the points of conflict in the world.[267]

*Margot Kässmann: The eucharistic vision*

The juncture of ecclesiology and ethics is central in the eucharistic vision of Margot Kässmann.[268] The task she undertakes is to relate issues of poverty and justice to the ecumenical discussions on the unity of the church, especially in the context of the World Council of Churches. How can BEM (baptism, eucharist and ministry) and JPIC (justice, peace and integrity of creation) be tied together? How might an ecclesiological basis be provided for a "church of the poor" that can shape the unity of the church? Kässmann sees the possibility of a convergence of the concern for unity and the concern for witness and practice in a "eucharistic vision." In fact she even suggests that "the eucharist is the pivot on which ecclesiology and ethics can turn and in which the local and the global, contextuality and intercontextuality, eschatology and history, unity and diversity can meet" so that the tension between dogmatics and social ethics can be overcome.[269]

According to Kässmann the unity of the church is not a product of dogmatic, confessional agreement, but arises out of eucharistic practice. At the same time it seems necessary to explicate the ethical dimensions of the eucharist. "Those who celebrate the eucharist together are the church - a challenge to any hierarchical thinking. Those who celebrate the eucharist together are community - a challenge to any division according to race, class, sex, or possession. Those who locally celebrate the eucharist together are a community in solidarity with brothers and sisters in the whole world - a challenge to any thinking governed by particular interests. The celebration of the eucharist thus stabilizes Christianity in an existent unity that contradicts confessional borders. And it establishes a unity that contradicts the economic and political divisions of the world."[270]

Not only is the eucharistic vision which Kässmann unfolds appealing, one might also hope with her that it will in fact serve the ecumenical processes of convergence and consensus. Difficult to understand, however, is her apparent concern to demarcate the eucharistic vision over against other conceptions. She considers the *notae ecclesiae* and the *status confessionis* too intellectual, the classic attributes too ahistorical, and ecclesiological appeals to the kingdom of God too triumphant. The eucharist possesses for her more an experiential, praxis oriented, constitutive and creative character.[271]

It would seem too simple to point out that it remains to be seen whether the eucharistic vision can succeed where other notions have failed. More important might be to realize that the eucharistic concept, whatever its advantages, is itself in need of (proper) explication in the face of misuse and reductionist approaches. Nor is an understanding of the church as sacrament, which Kässmann holds, immune to triumphalism, privatism, exclusivism, and indifference to the world. The eucharist can probably only serve convergence and consensus when it is essentially understood in terms of and in relation to all the other attempts to intertwine ethics and ecclesiology. For all of them, including the eucharist, are explications and/or expressions of the fundamental reality of the church itself, the *ekklesia*, the body of Christ. The meaning and identity of the church is in turn to be rooted in the prior reality of the praxis of Jesus and the apostles.

## 5.6. *On catholicity and conciliarity*

*Bonhoeffer on church fellowship*

In an essay on "The Question of the Boundaries of the Church and Church Union" (1936)[272], Bonhoeffer stated that the Reformation detached the question of what the church is from the question of who belongs to the church. Furthermore, the definition of the church, i.e., a determination of the limits of the church as a confessional unity, is not something that can be decided for all times, but is rather a continual process of church decision in response to limits that confront the church from outside.

This is in keeping with the interpretation of the *status confessionis* derived from Bonhoeffer. The church recognizes a threat to its integrity, formulates and confirms the sense in which the church is at stake, and in so doing redefines itself, i.e., determines what is and is not tolerable in the church as the church of Jesus Christ, all in response to a particular challenge.

Less clear perhaps in the context of the present investigation is the relation of 'who' and 'what'. The suggestion derived from the *status confessionis* debate was that the church is not to be exclusively defined in terms of marks of the church (such as administration of word and sacraments), but also to be understood as the flesh and blood reality of the members of the body of Christ. In other words, the church is to be defined both in terms of 'what' and 'who'. The latter is necessary if the church is indeed made for humans and not humans for the church. Both aspects, 'what' and 'who', are of essential importance, whatever their possible tension and relative emphasis might be.

This, however, is not in substantial conflict with Bonhoeffer. Bonhoeffer was objecting to racial or cultural definitions of the church, reducing membership to an exclusive quantity. At the same time he could speak of church fellowship as a qualitative totality, a given total unity. To speak of the church as the reality of its members is to indicate an inclusive totality, a fundamental inclusiveness. Common is the application of attributes or marks of the church such as unity, sanctity, catholicity, and apostolicity to the human solidarity of the body of Christ.

*Defining conciliarity*

'Conciliarity' has referred historically to the workings and legitimization of those official church gatherings that were to decide matters of doctrine and authority.[273] In the ecumenical movement the term has taken on a broader meaning, as evidenced in the discussion above. The aspects of common deliberation and reception, the emphasis on ecumenical communication and local confession, would seem to tend towards a fundamental democratization of conciliarity. If the Christ of the eucharist is the Christ of the poor, then not only is the pursuit of justice essential to the life of the church, but also the voice of the poor to the processes of conciliarity. (Lange and Kässmann) Where Bonhoeffer placed conciliarity in the context of political responsibility (Cf. Falcke), Lange and Kässmann radicalized and Hoedemaker localized the practice of that responsibility. Keshisihian correlated conciliarity and catholicity (unity) and suggested the radical interrelation of means and ends in terms of conciliarity.

Conciliarity serves then to indicate the way in which the church interacts with itself, both locally and ecumenically. It is a manner of critically communicating and seeking consensus, of organizing conflicts and responsibility. Furthermore, ecumenical communication (conciliarity) has a particular context and content. Its context is the divisions of church and world that call for attention to the points of conflict, the experiences of suffering and struggle, the life of the poor and the weak. (Lange, Hoedemaker) The question who Jesus Christ is is asked in the context of the conflicts of the world. This contextualized content is joined in the processes of conciliarity to the challenge of organizing communication and community life.

*Defining catholicity*

Catholicity is an expression of the fullness and wholeness of the church that includes both unity and diversity. (See II.3.6.) For the rest it is a complex and contested concept.[274] 'Catholic', as a synonym to 'Roman' or 'orthodox' or 'one true' church, is a disputed, often polemic attribute. Nevertheless, common ground can be found. Catholicity indicates a universality of all persons and peoples, all times and places.[275] In that sense catholicity possesses an eschatological thrust. At the same time it is a quality of the church and a calling to Christian identity.

A joint theological commission of Roman Catholics and representatives of the World Council of Churches (1968) signalled four "aberrations" of catholicity:

> the restriction of communion to certains races, nations or social classes; the formation of sects or parties within the body of the church; denominational pride to the detriment of others; and the misuse of the concept of catholicity in order to legitimate doctrines and practices which are not congruent with Christian identity.[276]

Within the World Council of Churches it has been consequently suggested that the ecumenical process can serve to "achieve an even broader catholicity" in the attempt

> to bring people of all times, of all races, of all places, of all conditions, into an organic and living unity in Christ by the Holy Spirit under the universal

> fatherhood of God. This unity is not solely external; it has a deeper, internal dimension, which is also expressed by the term 'catholicity'.[277]

Closely related to this, but more critically formulated, would seem to be F.O. van Gennep's attempt to understand catholicity in terms of covenant. Not only does the word covenant provide a clear biblical reference, it also indicates a binding together (community) of the strong and the weak. This lends to the church an exemplary or pro-existential significance. It implies a church for the world.[278]

Catholicity is generally understood in close relation to the notions of unity, holiness and apostolicity, in keeping with the Nicene-Constantinopolitan Creed. Catholicity has been defined (again within the World Council of Churches) as "the quality by which the church expresses the fullness, the integrity, and the totality of life in Christ".[279] The use of the term within the *status confessionis* debate was similar. Within that same debate, however, the term also possessed the critical sense indicated by Van Gennep. Less explicit in the above definitions is the reference to the human (flesh and blood) reality of the body of Christ (e.g. Duchrow) and the community of (sisters and) brothers (Barmen). (Cf. II.3.6. and II.4.6.) These references are, however, in keeping with the above descriptions of catholicity and may be seen as critical vantage points on catholicity from the point of view of the *status confessionis* debate. Catholicity can thus be understood as the quality of fullness and integrity of the church, its community (unity) and diversity, its inclusive nature critically attuned to the weak and the threatened.

*Catholicity as method*

It has been seen that both the *status confessionis* and conciliarity (whether in general or in terms of the conciliar process for justice, peace and the integrity of creation in particular) presuppose the catholic nature of the church. Conciliarity is the interaction of the variety and diversity of the church in the struggle for convergence and consensus, solidarity, and unity. The *status confessionis* is a critical and crucial defense of the solidarity of the body of Christ as a catholic community. A conciliar process under the name of JPIC is not just another program for the church, but the essential organization of its social and political identity. The *status confessionis* is not just another theological slogan, but a critical defense of the church's unity, identity, and integrity.

The recognition that conciliarity presupposes unity and catholicity requires a clarification of method. (Cf. Keshishian.) An understanding of catholicity as both quality and calling (see above) suggests that the proper methodology of the church catholic is to practice the goal which is to be pursued. There is no way to peace; peace is the way. There is no way to an ecumenical movement; the ecumenical movement is, as movement, the way. The way to unity is the practice of unity (as the interrelatedness of variety). The way to conciliar relations is the praxis of conciliarity (as the committed and conflictful interaction of diversities and divisions). The way to eucharistic community is not that of exclusive conditions, but eucharistic hospitality. The way to inclusive community is inclusion.

Catholicity, just like unity, sanctity, apostolicity, conciliarity, and ecumenicity, is both an attribute and a criterion of the church. It is a believed reality, but as a reality it serves as a critically shaping force. In that sense it both qualifies and creates the identity and integrity of the church. Identity and integrity are neither simply givens nor norms to be fulfilled. They create their own reality in being attributed and ascribed, believed and practiced.

It might serve to further clarify the matter by pointing out that it is not the same as the question of credibility. Much is made presently of the credibility or incredibility of the church. But credibility, like happiness, can hardly be pursued for its own sake. Doing something simply for the sake of appearing credible borders on hypocrisy. Lack of credibility may serve a heuristic function in indicating points of friction. However, the issue at hand is not the credibility of the church in the sense of its reputation, but the integrity of the church in terms of its own identity.

Here the question might be raised whether this concern for the identity and integrity of the church is not self-serving. If the church is for the world, is not its credibility precisely the crucial issue? Should the church not be less concerned with its own catholicity and conciliarity, and so forth, and more with effective healing of the wounds of the world? Is the debate on the *status confessionis* not an egotistical identity crisis in a world waiting for a good neighbor? These questions on the church's credibility and effectiveness have to be heard and weighed. It remains the case, however, that such questions are of a heuristic rather than intrinsic nature. They point to severe self-serving interests that have continually compromised the church, but they cannot alter the fact that the only justification for the church's existence is precisely its particular perspective on the healing of the world, the unity of humankind and the way of peace. That perspective is rooted in its understanding of its own identity as a particular experiment and practice of human community.

That particular orientation may find itself quite at odds with notions of credibility in the surrounding world, but the church stands or falls on the basis of its inclusive, catholic practice in the name of Jesus of Nazareth. Its confession is its praxis and its praxis is its confession. Being an inclusive community, preaching and practicing good news to the poor and the unconditional love of God, the praxis of catholicity and conciliarity, constitute the very method of the church to heal the wounds of the world. The church does not seek a different peace than the world, according to Lange, but it seeks it in a different way.

### *Considerations*

*On the inclusive community of Christ*

1. The question "Who is Jesus Christ for us today?" is the formative and determinative question for local community and ecumenical communication.
2. "The Church, the local Church as a member of the ecumenical Church, includes Israel as its presupposition and the world as its promise. The love in which the Christian community has its reality is grounded in its faith in the God of Israel and in His Messiah Jesus, and is sustained and given its life by its hopeful participation in the universal community whose redemption is promised with the coming of Christ. In community with Israel, the Church has its faith; in community with the world it expresses its hope; sustained by this faith and hope it finds itself as a community of love." R. Osborn
3. The inclusive character of the community of Christ is a reflection of the praxis of Jesus in his inclusion of the outcast and the priority he attributed to the poor, the marginalized, and the weak.
4. The inclusive character of Christian community is tested not only at its margins and limits but also in the manner in which a central place is yielded to the marginalized.

*On confession and conciliarity*

5. The local community centered around an inclusive eucharistic practice is the focal point of Christian confession.
6. Confession needs concretization in specific commitments and covenants guided by ecological sensibility, economic solidarity, and irenic responsibility.
7. Priority in the confessing movement of the church is not to be attributed to declarations or confessions, but to strengthening and supporting already present confessional communities (as resistant, resilient, repentant, and remnant communities).
8. Essential to the development of those communities is the development of networks for ecumenical communication as a place of human encounter and confronting conflict.
9. Of importance for the quality of the life of the church is the linking of regional networks and initiative groups to the confession and eucharistic fellowship of local churches.
10. Confession understood in the context of conciliarity as praxis seeks clarity, but not exclusion. It seeks allies.
11. Conciliarity is the church's way of organizing the conflicts inherent to its common life. It understands unity in terms of interaction and encounter. It is the practice of a method on the basis of a claim to truth.

12. Placing conciliarity in the context of political reasoning and responsibility is a correlative of relating the unity of the church to the unity of humankind. Both are a recognition of the political substance of the church and the gospel.
13. *Status confessionis* and conciliar process (JPIC) both assume the catholic quality of the church as their precondition.
14. The proclamations of *kairos* place the church before the same urgency as the *status confessionis*. In both cases the response may turn out to be more of a process spread out in time.
15. The relation of the church to the world is shaped by its own centeredness and identity. The relation of the church to the world is more varied than traditional views of the relation of church and state would suggest.
16. The method of the church catholic is to practice what it pursues, to actualize its identity. The method is to live the reality of the solidarity of the body of Christ, to embody the praxis of Jesus.

## II.6.

## THE FUTURE OF THE *STATUS CONFESSIONIS*

### 6.1. *The history of the status confessionis*

The review of the *status confessionis* debate presented here began rather late, in the 1930's. The history of the term goes back to Reformation and counter-Reformation days, when the early Lutherans were hard pressed in the Schmalkaldic wars. According to the Interim of Leipzig the Protestants were allowed some doctrinal freedom if they would conform to the rites of the Catholic church and recognize episcopal authority.

Melanchton was agreeable. Cultus and church order were for him matters of indifference, *adiaphora*, that did not affect the central confession of the Reformation. Flacius opposed Melanchthon. In a state of persecution and confession nothing is indifferent. (*In statu persecutionis et confessionis nil est adiaphoron.*) Resistance was to be maintained at all levels. Flavius' position seems to have received support in the Formula Concordiae. (*In statu confessionis nihil est adiaphoron.*) Nevertheless, the terminology remained loose and unclear, and the issue was hardly resolved.

As such it could be applied to the protest of several church ministers of Hamburg against a new operahouse at the end of the seventeenth century. The moralization of the term was easily accomplished.

In 1817 King Friedrich Wilhelm III decided to force union upon the Lutheran and Reformed churches under his sovereignty. The result was that Lutherans and Reformed debated on their confessional identity. The term *Bekenntnisstand* (situation or stance of confession) was employed, but did not quite become a technical term of specific clarity.

This history does little to clarify the contemporary usage of the *status confessionis*. The term was at times wielded in the theological and ecclesial arena without ever truly clarifying or deciding matters. Bonhoeffer and others took it up as a useful and forceful instrument in the German church struggle, but it seems that Bonhoeffer infused the term with new meaning and relevance that it had not previously possessed. Of particular note is the shift from *adiaphora* debate to matters of *essentia*.[280] Bonhoeffer's concern was not with matters that might otherwise and under different circumstances be considered indifferent, but with matters that were to be regarded as indisputable in principle. Bonhoeffer employed the *status confessionis* in relation to the very being and essence of the church.

## 6.2. *The purpose of the status confessionis*

> The essential purpose [is] to deliver both internally and externally the firmest possible message of witness and confession in the clearest terms providing maximum support for those who in a critical situation are inspired by their faith to seek genuine church unity and fundamental changes leading to reconciliation in the society.[281]

Such was the intention of the Dar es Salaam assembly of the LWF in the interpretation of M. Schloemann. Such a cumbrous description betrays the problematic character of the *status confessionis* The result is a *status controversionis*.[282] The entire point, however, is not theological controversy or ecclesial conflict, but the confession and praxis of the one, holy, catholic and apostolic church. The issues need to be faced on their own merit and not circumvented by theological circumlocution. The point of the *status confessionis* or of a *kairos* for the church is the recognition of crisis and division in the life of the church and the urgent call to response and solidarity. The church divided is a *contradictio in terminis* that must be reconciled. The conflict must be organized. The truth which the church is must be embodied. Communication must take form in community. The question that is put to the church is how to understand and organize its common life so as to live the solidarity of the body of Christ. How is the church to live its own identity and maintain its integrity in the world?

The present review of the debate on the *status confessionis* would seem to indicate that the *status confessionis* is not so much an exceptional case as an intensification or concentration of the ethical enterprise of the church. Making the *status confessionis* an exception robs us of the possibility of explicating criteria to determine its use or meaningfulness. Viewing it as a condensation of ethical concerns and ecclesiological identity in a critical context allows it conversely to shed light on the entire project of ecclesial ethics.

## 6.3. *The usefulness of the term status confessionis*

Is the *status confessionis* as an ecclesial-theological term a useful instrument for putting the question to the church? Must it not be admitted that the *status confessionis* has failed to fulfill its intention? Indeed, the *status confessionis* has failed in that it has not generally helped to rally consensus and arouse solidarity. It has rallied debate and aroused animosity. One must, however, differentiate. Admittedly the term allows for misunderstanding, but a significant portion of the misunderstanding derives from fundamentally different understandings of the nature and mission of the church in the world, of what confessing Christ is all about, and of the political nature of the gospel. The affirmation of a *status confessionis* has often been more of an occasion for fighting out those differences than the direct cause of confusion.

Might it be better to substitute the term *kairos*, with its biblical roots, for *status confessionis*? There are some differences. The term *kairos* does not necessarily contain the connotation that the integrity of the church itself is at stake, but it does convey a sense of urgency and decisiveness. Or is such terminological juggling, like the consideration of *processus confessionis* or *casus confessionis*, trivial in the light of the challenges being issued? The fundamental debate on the understandings of confessing Christ and the nature of the church will continue whatever the terminology.

It can be admitted that the term *status confessionis* has no clear tradition, is not an ecumenical term, is materially imprecise, is subject to inflationary usage, and has been asserted without due reference to the processes of conciliarity.[283] Any number of other objections might easily be cited. For all such reasons there is no need to insist upon terminology. There is no use in insisting upon the *status confessionis*, even if it be right, if it does not work. But is there a substitute that might avoid the manifold misrepresentations and yet still provoke the incisiveness intended by the *status confessionis*? Can the terminological debate be resolved by another term?

It has been seen that the catholic quality of the church has far reaching ethical significance. It points to the indisputable solidarity of the body of Christ. If that be recognized, then the *status confessionis* as a term might be forgotten, as long as its incisiveness is not ignored. The possibility arises, consequently, to shift attention to the essential and ethical significance of the classic attributes of the church. It would seem feasible to reformulate the essential concern of the *status confessionis* in terms of the unity, sanctity, catholicity, and apostolicity of the church. Especially the term catholicity provides direction and substance for understanding the ethical identity of the church. Such a shift might not resolve the debate, but perhaps recast it in more fruitful terms.

### 6.4. *The praxis of the status confessionis*

Even if the term *status confessionis* be relinquished, much can and should be learned from the *processus confessionis*. First of all, it should be recalled that the *status confessionis* (or its equivalent) is not in the usage and intention of its advocates something declared or created, but a crisis recognized, confirmed, and answered. It is not something planned, but provoked. It is not a threat to unity, but a defense of unity. It seeks not excommunication, but is the test case of communication. It seeks not division, but renewed consensus on the confession. It does not degrade those of a different mind, but urges discernment of a particular crisis. It is not triumphant, but confesses guilt. It requires a singular concentration, local concretization, and theological clarity. It cannot be categorically limited by formal criteria such as duration, direct participation, or persecution, for it involves the solidarity of the body of Christ, the church in its catholic and ecumenical dimensions.

With or without the term the praxis of the *status confessionis* will continue. It will continue, according to Berrigan, in the discerning praxis of confessing communities. In the life of resistant, resilient, repentant, and remnant communities the identity of the church receives profile and preserves its integrity. The praxis of the *status confessionis* continues in the life of those communities that have discerned the questions and acted upon them and are thus putting the question to the ecumenical church.

The *processus confessionis* is consequently part and parcel of the practice of conciliarity. For it involves organizing the conflicts and consensus on the identity and confession of the church in a process of ecumenical communication. Such a process is shaped and informed by those theologians who reflect on the ethical identity of the church. It is the purpose of the following section of this study to explore several such contributions. The history of the *status confessionis* serves to remind the participants in conciliarity what the stakes of ecumenical communication are. In that way the *status confessionis* might serve to enlighten and enliven the entire project of understanding the ethical identity of the church. Conversely, a broader perspective on how ethics and ecclesiology are related can serve to shape a climate of conciliarity and a context of self understanding in which the crises and challenges for the church can be recognized and answered.

Shifting attention to the classic attributes of the church involves directing attention as well to their modern translations: solidarity, ecumenicity, and conciliarity. In particular a transition will be made from the *status confessionis* to an understanding of the ethical quality of catholicity and from the *processus confessionis* to the calling of conciliarity. Together, catholicity and conciliarity indicate the inclusive nature of Christian community and ecumenical communication. Their location is confessing, eucharistic community. Their (confessed) reality is the body of Christ. Their reference is the inclusive praxis of Jesus.

### *Considerations*

1. The *status confessionis* is not to be isolated as an exceptional case, but to be exploited for the light it can shed on the entire project of ecclesial ethics.
2. The history of the *status confessionis* debate leads to the conclusion of a terminological failure. The fundamental theological debate will, however, continue.
3. Attention can be shifted to the ethical significance of the classic attributes of the church, namely, unity, sanctity, catholicity, apostolicity. Their

modern translations are solidarity, ecumenicity and conciliarity. Their location is confessing, eucharistic community. Their reality is the body of Christ. Their reference is the inclusive praxis of Jesus.

4. The challenge of the *status confessionis* and of a *kairos* put the church to the question of its identity and integrity in a divided world. The question is clarified and communicated in the life of confessing communities.

# III. THEOLOGIANS INFORMING THE CHURCH

## *Envisioning Christian Community*

The review of the *status confessionis* debate pointed to fundamental questions and perspectives on the ethical nature and task of Christian community. It was asked whether the issues might be better apprehended by shifting attention from the *status confessionis* terminology to the classical attributes of the Christian church and their modern translations. Particularly the terms 'catholicity' and 'conciliarity' presented themselves as interpretive tools for restating the issues and intent of the *status confessionis*. Together, catholicity and conciliarity indicate the inclusive nature of Christian community and ecumenical communication.

At the same time it would seem that a broader investigation of the relation between ethics and ecclesiology could serve to provide further substance to the understanding of catholicity and conciliarity and perhaps rescue the issues from the isolation and distortion of the *status confessionis* debate. In that way a climate and context might be engendered for recognizing and answering the crises and challenges indicated by the *status confessionis* and by a *kairos* for the churches.

The strategy followed here is that of enlisting the contributions of several theologians who explicitly relate ethics and ecclesiology in their theological projects. I do not take those selected to be representative in a general sense. I take them to represent themselves and their particular communities and to fruitfully provoke further thought on the (ethical) vocation of Christian community. Nor are all the reviews provided in this section of the same nature and quality. In some instances only one or two major works are discussed. In other instances more extensive treatment was judged to be desirable. The intent is not to be exhaustive or definitive, but to relate (on a limited scale) the substance of the *status confessionis* in its ethical and ecclesiological dimensions to a more constructive and coherent understanding of the ethical formation of the church.

Dietrich Bonhoeffer, who provides the basic direction and inspiration for the entire study, has already been treated in various contexts. It is now time to attempt a more summary and systematic review, however brief. Bonhoeffer combines both confessional (christological) and extrovert emphases to characterize the nature of responsible Christian community. Similarly Paul Lehmann understands the *koinonia* as both subject and object of God's fellowship-creating activity in the world. It is attention to transcendence that transfigures both the church and the body politic.

The most extensive treatment is given to Stanley Hauerwas, who in a very different way contributes to a fundamental framework for a communitarian ethic. He is concerned with the distinctive identity of Christian community, its particular perspectives (narratives), and its practice of non-violence and hospitality.

The relation between ethics and ecclesiology is as much implicit as explicit in liberation theologies. Enrique Dussel is one of those who in a characteristic way has explicated his understandings on ethics and community. In fact, community for him is the essence of Christian life and of the reign of God. The treatment of Leonardo Boff is limited in its critical assessment of one particular book. In this way no justice is done to his significant theological work as a whole. Nevertheless he is included as a complement to Dussel for the sake of his perspective on the catholic nature of local community and for the sake of dialogue with him on a critical understanding of the concept of Christian community.

Elisabeth Schüssler Fiorenza directs our attention more strongly to matters of exegesis and biblical interpretation. She is included here also for the way in which she is quite explicit about the ecclesiological and ethical context from and toward which she works. The project of an *ekklesia* of women is to be noted for its appeal to an inclusive understanding of Christian community and its liberationist import. At the conclusion of the review of Schüssler Fiorenza, brief attention is given to the vision of Rosemary Radford Ruether on exodus-community and its dialectical relation to institutional (patriarchal) churches. Finally, Letty Russel receives a treatment similar to that of Boff. Her ecclesiology is of particular interest due to the way in which she combines various perspectives. She envisions a church in the round that is attentive to the central place of the marginal in the household of God.

# III.1.

## DIETRICH BONHOEFFER ENGENDERING RESPONSIBLE COMMUNITY

Two key expressions of Dietrich Bonhoeffer, one taken from the beginning of his theological work and one from the end, might serve to summarize his thought on church and ethics. In *Sanctorum Communio*, written as his doctoral dissertation, Bonhoeffer spoke repeatedly of "Christ existing as community."[284] In the letters and papers from his last years in prison is found the notion of a "church for others."[285] These two fundamental notions, which span a period of seventeen years, indicate a fundamental direction of his theology. Bonhoeffer's role in the *status confessionis* debate and in the call to conciliarity has already been encountered. At this point an attempt will be made to more generally examine his vision of the ethical task in the context of the community of Christ. The historical development of Bonhoeffer's thinking on church and ethics has been well traced by Thomas Day[286]. The task here is only to gather various insights of Bonhoeffer into the nature of Christian community as the subject of Christian ethics. The two central expressions cited above will serve as two poles on which to string the various findings.

### 1.1. *Christ existing as community*

Bonhoeffer began his doctoral thesis with an investigation of the concept of person. He asserted both the integrity and relatedness of the human person, with the emphasis falling upon the human person as a person-in-relation, a person intended for community, both an individual and a social being, and in both respects an ethical being. It would seem that sociality and community are understood to be both a context and a calling for the human person. Personhood is from and for others.[287]

Two comments might be made at the outset. One is that the emphasis on sociality is not a disregard for individuality. The integrity of the human person is respected.[288] The emphasis on sociality provides the context of individuality and of the development of human personality.

The second comment is that Bonhoeffer's description of personhood in terms of relatedness is immediately ethical. Because he engaged transcendental and idealistic philosophers, the question might be raised whether he did not confuse categories of being with ethical categories, 'is' and 'ought'. Is this one more example of the naturalistic fallacy?[289] However, Bonhoeffer's point was ultimately not philosophical but theological. Person and community were understood in relation to the Christian notion of God. He was concerned with the social intention of all Christian concepts.[290] Relatedness is both an essential and ethical dimension of human existence. This is inherent to the Christian understanding of the nature of creation. Ethics is at the heart of the God-given human interrelatedness. Shaping those relations from the heart of God is what the biblical story is about.

It is not primarily Bonhoeffer's philosophical inquiries, but his primary intention of explicating the nature of the church as a "revealed reality"[291] that is relevant here. By closely relating the concepts of person and community he arrived at a notion of a collective person, of which "Christ existing as community" is his primary example. Bonhoeffer understood the church to be the body of Christ in the sense that the church is the very presence of Christ.[292] Christian community is Christ present as a social reality, a reality with as reference the empirical church, "a locatable, human community"[293]. The believed reality is that which is believed of empirical community, even if the full identity is an eschatological one.[294] Bonhoeffer "asserted not that the church is nothing more than, but that it is nowhere else but in the concrete human community."[295]

The church is thus a given reality, a reality grounded in the revelation in Jesus Christ. It is not a matter of becoming the church (potentiality). The church with all its ambiguity *is* Christ existing as community. It is this reality which is then put into working (actualized) by the Holy Spirit.[296] "The body of Christ is both real presence in history and norm for its own history."[297] The calling of the church is thus to be itself, to conform itself to its identity as body of Christ.

The content of this calling is response to the love command. The community of Christ is the fellowship of love in obedience to God. It is selfless love that seeks only obedience to God and lays no claim on the other. It is precisely this selfless love that evokes reciprocity and forms community.[298] Love is the will to maintain fellowship, as Bonhoeffer would later say.[299] Community, it may be concluded, is both God's purpose for humanity and God's means towards that end.

'Being together' and 'being for one another' are the concrete social acts that constitute Christian community.[300] The former expresses itself, e.g., in bearing one another's burdens. Where one suffers, all suffer; where one rejoices, all rejoice. The latter takes form in service, intercession, and mutual forgiveness. Being for one another carries within it the seed of being for others. Again it becomes clear that Bonhoeffer's understanding of the social character of personality, of the social acts that constitute community, and even, one might say, of the social nature of God, imply a specific ethic. Relatedness is qualified relatedness.

To be sure Bonhoeffer stated that the structuring principle of Christian community, proxy (or substitution, deputyship, as a translation of 'Stellvertretung'), is not an ethical but a theological concept.[301] He later stated that "God has founded his church beyond religion and ethics"[302]. In the essays which are gathered in his *Ethics* he would also reject the ethical endeavor to know good and evil, to derive human conduct from ethical principles or to rely upon conscience as an ethical guide. This critical usage of the term 'ethics' should not prevent us from seeing that his concern was fundamentally ethical, i.e. a concern for shaping concrete human relations, a concern to engender human responsibility.

## 1.2. *The church as the subject of ethics*

In *Ethics* Bonhoeffer stated that "the point of departure for Christian ethics is the body of Christ, the form of Christ in the form of the church, the formation of the church according to the form of Christ."[303] This "point of departure" entails various aspects.

Bonhoeffer maintained that the knowledge of God resides primarily in the community as community. The community knows more than its individual members.[304] Revelation occurs in the community.[305] Thomas Day comments:

> Bonhoeffer saw the community whose linchpin is Christ's insistent Word as the unique social location of ethical insight. All knowledge and human sensitivity is social. Christian insight is communal.[306]
> Ethical thought, like all theological knowledge, is only possible as ecclesial, communal thought. Christian ethics is reflection at the service of a particular community.[307]

It is thus the community that is the primary subject of the knowledge of God's will, i.e., of ethics. The individual believer is in need of that context in order to discern what must be done. The individual question 'What must I do?' is embedded in the (biblical) question 'What must we do?'[308] It is in the community that the word of the Lord is heard and understood. The ethical enterprise is a joint venture of the community, a dialogical and interactive enterprise.

Bonhoeffer's task of training young theologians in the Finkenwalde seminary of the Confessing Church provided him the opportunity to put his ideas into practice. Again Day summarizes:

> Nothing less than living together, conviviality, sharing of resources and risk, common daily prayer and discipline, all this was necessary if the Word of God was to be heard, obeyed, and proclaimed in the land. Such was Bonhoeffer's conviction and experience in those years.[309]
> Where and how is the call of Christ to be heard now? Only in the prayerful common reading of the scriptures...In this community's explication of the scriptures the Word of God is heard.[310]

In another context Day comments on *Sanctorum Communio*:

> In the community Christians can speak to each other the Word which enables and commands being for others. And they can help each other towards making and executing responsible decisions by sharing information and possible models for action and by encouraging sympathy. Such counsel must not become command if it is to enable the other's freedom rather than rob him of responsibility. The community is the basis and strength of all individual life and insight.[311]

It is in this light that Bonhoeffer rejected conscience as a guide to ethical thinking and behavior. Ethics is not a matter of individual reflection, not a self-centered activity, but a matter of social perception and sensitivity.[312] It is in this light also that Bonhoeffer's rejection of ethics as knowledge of good and evil[313] or as a system of moral principles[314] is to be understood. "The church must not proclaim eternal principles but commands for today."[315] It is social sensitivity, and not moral abstractions, that must govern ethical thinking and behavior. The love of neighbor is love of the concrete human other. That is the orientation for Christian love.[316] Again I make use of Day's summary.

> What is to be done will be determined by our neighbor's concrete and changing needs...In each specific situation the neighbor's needs are the shape of God's command. To look at any set of principles or even to the revealed law of God, rather than to the neighbor is sin...in each instance we must be sensitive to the real needs of our brother and sister. Where is this sensitivity and insight to be had? Only in community, in being with and for others. Christian ethics is *common* sense. The church is the community of those who recognize the Word of God addressed to them in their concrete situation and demanding their response.[317]

Although he was at times hardly hesitant to offer ethical directives (concrete commands), Bonhoeffer can appear radical in his rejection of ethical principles and the like to the extent that one could fear ethical arbitrariness, a fully situational ethic. This fear is countered, however, not only by his steadfast orientation on the biblical revelation, but, more specifically, by his location of ethical activity in the community.

> For Bonhoeffer there is no Christian ethic in the sense of an ordered system of principles from which the moral value or property of this or that act can be deduced. But there is a community of persons gathered in response to God's word to be with and for each other. Christian ethics is ecclesiology taken seriously.[318]

> The continuity of Christian ethics consists in the living community and not in any conceptual system, whether, dialogical or whatever.[319]

### 1.3. *Church for others*

The church as the point of departure for Christian ethics is not just a matter of communal reflection. The church is itself an ethical reality. "The Christian community is not simply the receiver of the Christian revelation. Today it is the revelation, the form of Christ in the world for us, "Christ existing as community."[320] "The church is the place at which the taking form of Jesus Christ is proclaimed and occurs. Christian ethics is at the service of the proclamation and this occurence."[321]

It becomes clear in *Ethics* that what occurs in the church is intended for all humanity.[322] All the world is called by the church into the fellowship of the body of Christ which is a given reality in Jesus Christ.[323] Thomas Day points out that in *Ethics* a shift in emphasis occurred. The primary point of departure of Christian ethics became the reconciliation in Christ rather than the community of Christ. The church is still integral to the ethical scheme, but as that part of humanity in which Christ has already taken form in anticipation of the whole of humanity being actualized as the body of Christ.[324]

The sentence in *Sanctorum Communio*: "Not only is Christ both donum and exemplum for humanity, but one human is the same for another."[325], might now be carried further: Christ existing as the church is likewise both donum and exemplum for humanity. The church is to be a paradigmatic human community in the service of justice. "The church is only the church, when it is there for others."[326] It is Christ existing as the church for others.

> And so the three central ideas of his mature theology seem to be: Christ, church, world. And 'these three are one'. The church consists of those human beings in whom Christ stands in the place where the whole world is meant to stand and acts as deputy for the world. The church serves the world and summons it into the fellowship of Christ's body.[327]

Ethics is still rooted in the community but clearly in the context of the world and of the reconciliation of the world in Christ. "Bonhoeffer believed that Christ is forming community in this world, that the Christian revelation becomes tangible in the responsible being for others which it creates."[328]

Is the distinction between church and world collapsed? Does the church surrender its own vernacular to a "non-religious interpretation," to use another phrase from Bonhoeffer's latter days? The question has two sides. Indeed the church needs to be opened to the world in order to be inclusive of others. The church is called to identify with others. At the same time Bonhoeffer advocated the arcane discipline, the hidden life of the church, in which the church maintains its own identity. And never did Bonhoeffer surrender the reference to Christ in his understanding of the church. His ecclesiology is to a great extent christology. The church retains its identity in its confession and expression of Jesus Christ. But Jesus Christ is the "human for others" and identification with Jesus Christ is "being for others."

### 1.4. *The politics of the church*

"Church history is the hidden center of world history."[329] These words from *Sanctorum Communio* are echoed in the lectures on the church from 1932.

> Where God speaks with his church, she is the center of all human places, even though she appears to people to be the most dispensible...She is the critical center, from which all is judged. God hinself is the crisis, not the preacher, not the church. Nobody knows ahead of time where the center will be. According to historical measures it can lie at the periphery, like Galilea in the Roman empire and Wittenberg in the sixteenth century. But God will make the place visible and everyone must pass by. The church can only witness to the center of the world which only God makes to be the center. She must attempt te create space for God's work.[330]

Important is the qualification that the church is not something different than the world but itself part of the world. "The church is a piece of qualified world ... the presence of God in the world, not a consecrated sanctuary, but a world called by God to God."[331] It is a piece of the world with a calling.

> The church is the city set upon a hill, the *polis* which God has founded on earth. Consequently its 'political' character is part and parcel of her sanctification. World remains world and the community remains the community, but God's word goes out from the community over all the world as the message that the earth is the Lord's and all that is in it. There is no personal sanctification apart from this visible delineation of the community. Such is a disregard for the body of Christ.[332]

In these words which again reflect the community as the proper location of Christian faith and obedience, the political nature of the community is described as the strategic starting point for the proclamation of the Lordship of God. "Bonhoeffer saw the Christian churches as the foci of the new history of humankind, the places where people's being together for others has already begun, the centers from which this new humanity reaches out to all."[333]

It would seem that Dietrich Bonhoeffer continued to hold to the premise that Christian community is both God's purpose for humanity and his means to that end. The community of Christ, the church, remained in his view the central strategy of God's ethics. Nevertheless the ponderings on the church from prison reflect his severe disappointment in the established churches as he had known them, the German evangelical church, the Confessing church as well as the ecumenical movement. At the same time such ponderings pointed to a new vision of the church. The familiar passage on the "church for others" requires closer examination.

> The church is the church only when it exists for others. To make a start, it should give away all its property to those in need. The clergy must live solely on the freewill offerings of their congregations, or possibly engage in some secular calling. The church must share in the secular problems of ordinary human life, not dominating, but helping and serving. It must tell people of every calling what it means to live in Christ, to exist for others. In particular, our own church will have to take the field against the vices of hubris, power worship, envy, and humbug, as the roots of evil. It will have to speak of moderation, purity, trust, loyalty, constancy, patience, discipline, humility, contentment, and modesty. It must not underestimate the importance of human example (which has its origin in the humanity of Jesus and is so important in Paul's teaching); it is not abstract argument, but example, that gives its word emphasis and power.[334]

What significance might this revisioning of the church have for its centrality? Of course, the center described above is a theological and not a sociological location. It refers primarily to the church's task and calling and not its organization and status. But form and content are interrelated here. A new role for the church will entail a new positioning. The context of concern for the secular is increasingly a secular society and a marginalized church (at least in Bonhoeffer's Germany and those countries of similar culture).

Is it appropriate for a marginalized church (which is not the same as a church which seeks proximity to the marginalized) to claim for itself a theological center? Can this pretention of both the elliptical two kingdoms doctrine of Luther and Barth's concentric understanding of the political location of the Christian community still be maintained? Is the claim to a center not historically tied to the assertion of secular church authority and domination and thus to the Constantinian compromise? Is it thus responsible to speak of a center or epicenter? Does not the term center serve to confuse rather than clarify the precarious relation of the church to the world in both its theological and sociological dimensions? And finally: Is God's activity in the world centered?

Thomas Day suggests (in his maximum interpretation) that Bonhoeffer overcame his wrestling with the traditional Lutheran thinking in two realms by means of the musical image of polyphony.[335] Reality, life is multidimensional. That would mean that the relation of the church to the world likewise is multidimensional. The concept of a church for others or a church for the world exposes the need for a restatement of the relation between church and state, a relation which must be seen within the perspective of the relation between a multi-dimensional church and a multi-dimensional world. An ecclesial ethics will need to seek an understanding of political faithfulness and responsibility which is not dependent on a particular model of church-state relations but rooted in the nature of the church itself.[336] The church need be centered, i.e., maintain its own identity in the world, but may well find its own center off-center.

A related issue is the common juxtaposition of Romans 13 and Revelation 13, also made by Bonhoeffer[337], but in effect too formal. The suggestion is that Paul in his letter to the Romans commends obedience to a reasonable government, whereas John's understanding of a diabolical (Roman) government in his apocalyptic vision should lead to total disobedience. It should not be overlooked that both the apostle Paul and the prophet John had the same Roman empire in mind, and not only the government contemporary to their writing but the state in general. We must not forget that it was the same government that Paul called 'servant' which crucified the Messiah and persecuted the apostles, including Paul. On the other hand the persecution of the church was at the time that Revelation was written probably not all that severe. And the theme of Revelation is not just the persecution of the church but also and equally the seduction of the church. Both Paul and John seem to concur on the response of the believers: overcoming evil with good by means of non-violent discipleship and discriminating witness. Both agree with Peter: We must obey God more than men. As also with Jesus: Render to Caesar what is of Caesar and render to God what is of God. It is essentially the identity of the church that defines its response to the state, not the always dubious identity of the state.

## 1.5. *In search of responsible community*

At the heart of Bonhoeffer's theology was the church, the life of the community. Bethge points out how Bonhoeffer, alongside the Lutheran markings of the true church, namely, word and sacrament, emphasized the life of the earthly community, the church as the real body of Christ on earth.[338] Day summarizes that churches "are 'Jesus Christ existing as community' as long as the Word is there proclaimed and gathers around itself a community whose being together and for each other is concretely symbolized in the Christian sacraments."[339]

What has often been understood in more individualistic terms as discipline, Bonhoeffer understood as the discipleship of the community. He commented once on the church struggle: "I believe the whole thing comes down to a decision on the Sermon on the Mount."[340] In this light it is to be noted that his interpretation of the Sermon on the Mount in *The Cost of Discipleship* is essentially ecclesiology.[341]

Community remained the name of the game even in the time of conspiracy and imprisonment. Day suggests that the increasing "worldliness" of the community that Bonhoeffer proposed was accented by Bonhoeffer's participation in the "worldly" circle of the conspirators. Any inconclusiveness of his prison thoughts is attributable not just to the circumstances of confinement but also to the fact that the primary concern was not a new theology in and of itself, but the requisites of a new community that could take up the tasks at hand.

> His immediate concern was the structuring of a new Christian church as a paradigmatic human community which comes together in response to a call from beyond itself and whose conviviality is open to all of humankind.[342]
>
> The first priority was to shape in Christ a community in which further reflection on the ethical implications of the gospel would be possible and meaningful.[343]
>
> Interpretation was not the primary task at hand. The immediate need was the structuring of responsible communal life in secular society...Only in full engagement in social life does one learn to believe. One must live a while in a community in order to understand how 'Christ takes shape in it'. Thus Bonhoeffer's first priority remained the communal living of the Christian message, and his project climaxed in proposals for future church structures.[344]

Such was Bonhoeffer's project, a continual search for responsible community, a search often disappointed. There arose in the Evangelical Church no general protest to the Aryan measures. Nor did even the Confessing Church concur on Bonhoeffer's call to solidarity with the Jews. Despite his insistence on community as the location of Christian faith and obedience, his decision to participate in the conspiracy was not and could not have been supported by communal consensus. At best it might be said that the decision was taken in the context of the new, largely secular community of the conspirators.

The primary motivation for that decision was not to be found in a general consideration of the permissibility or necessity of violence or in an application of Revelation 13 in the direction of total resistance. Participation in the conspiracy was an act of responsibility. It assumed responsibility for the past, for the guilt of Germany. It took on responsibility for the future, that the coming generation might continue life. The act of responsibility was an act of historical freedom that could hardly be ethically validated or ecclesially supported. It was in its time and context a borderline case that was nevertheless dictated by historical necessity.

The diabolic stupidity dominating Germany could not be confronted by an act of edification but only by an act of liberation.[345]

The conclusion would seem to be that Bonhoeffer's biography did not enjoy the communal theology and shared responsibility he advocated. The challenge and urgency of the task he defined remain, for it was precisely the will to solidarity and community that motivated participation in the conspiracy. In accounting for that participation Bonhoeffer wrote:

> The Christian is called to sympathy and action, not in the first place by his own suffering, but by the sufferings of his brethren, for whose sake Christ suffered.[346]
>
> We need to learn to regard people not so much on the basis of what they do and leave undone, as on the basis of what they suffer. The only fruitful relation to people - particularly the weak - is love, i.e., the will to be in community with them.[347]

These lessons from the experience of resistance had also provided a new perspective on the world.

> There remains an experience of incomparable value. We have for once learnt to see the great events of world history from below, from the perspective of the outcast, the suspects, the maltreated, the powerless, the oppressed, the reviled - in short, from the perspective of those who suffer...This perspective from below must not become the partisan possession of those who are eternally dissatisfied; rather, we must do justice to life in all its dimensions from a higher satisfaction, whose foundation is beyond any talk of "from below" or "from above."[348]

From this perspective the "borderline case" proves exemplary, as Bethge has pointed out. Conspiracy and its attending violence are not in themselves exemplary. They were simply and specifically the command of the day and must not be abstracted. Exemplary is the assumption of responsibility, "being for others" as participation in the sufferings of Jesus, the "human for others." This original christological confession of Bonhoeffer contained within it an ethical commitment that informed his ecclesiology.[349] The question is whether it will yet inform and form the church.

### *Considerations*

1. For Christian theological ethics, relatedness is qualified relatedness.

2. An understanding of community as the primary subject of the knowledge of God's will lays primary emphasis not on concepts and principles of ethics but on social perception and sensitivity, being with and for others.
3. Being with and for others is part and parcel of the identity of the church. The scope is all humanity, the world. The focus is the church as proxy for the world.
4. The church is centered in its attention to Christ and its common life. That center may serve to put the church off-center in the world. The relation of church to world is multi-dimensional and not centered in the relation to the state.
5. The church is confronted with its own collective irresponsibility by the exemplary responsibility of Bonhoeffer and his fellow conspirators. For the church to engender responsible community, it will need to account for its own irresponsibility and heed the example given.

# III.2.

## PAUL LEHMANN
## MAKING HUMAN COMMUNITY HUMAN

Paul Lehmann was a friend of Dietrich Bonhoeffer. Like Bonhoeffer he finds his focal point for thinking about ethics in the fact and nature of Christian community.[350] Using the transliteration of the New Testament Greek word for community, he speaks of *koinonia* ethics. The context of Christian community provides the juncture between two other contexts that shape Lehmann's approach, namely, human circumstance and divine activity. That divine activity is itself focused upon human community.

### 2.1. *What God is doing in the world*

Focus on Christian community directs Lehmann's attention to "the concrete, personal and purposeful activity of God".[351] All questions as to the will of God, the application of commandments, the interpretation of scriptural texts, the search for guidelines for Christian behavior, and so on, are to be viewed within the context of the dynamic of divine activity. This contextual approach is understood by Lehmann to be a liberating contribution by the Reformation to ethics, providing as it does

> the possibility of ever fresh and experimental responses to the dynamics and the humanizing character of the divine activity in the world. This meant for ethics the displacement of the prescriptive and absolute formulation of its claims by the contextual understanding of what God is doing in the world to make and to keep human life human...Ethics could now be a descriptive discipline, not in contrast to a normative discipline (a distinction which presupposes another context), but in the sense of providing an account of the transformation of the concrete stuff of behavior, i.e., the circumstances, the motivations, and the structures of action, owing to the concrete, personal, and purposeful activity of God.[352]

The nature of this activity is political and ethical. "Let it be noted that the signs which point up what God is doing in the world are ethical signs."[353] "Now the formative biblical images which point to and describe the divine activity in the world are political images, both in the pneumatological and in the fundamental senses of the word."[354] This latter is further explicated:

When we say, then, that God is a 'politician', and that what God is doing in the world is 'making or doing politics', it is the Aristotelian definition and the biblical description of what is going on that we have in mind. According to the definition, we may say that politics is activity, and reflection upon activity, which aims at and analyzes what it takes to make and to keep human life human. According to the description, what it takes to make and to keep human life human in the world is "the unsearchable riches of Christ...the plan of the mystery hidden for ages in God who created all things; that through the church the manifold wisdom of God might now be made known to the principalities and powers in the heavenly places...until we all attain...to mature manhood, to the measure of the stature of the fullness of Christ."[355] (Quotations are taken from the letter to the Ephesians.)

It is to be noted that Lehmann speaks of signs and images, of biblical description and story, of parable and presence. While his purpose is essentially theological and christological, biblical and revelational, his method is thoroughly imaginative and associative, parabolic and often paradoxical. The gain in creativity is at times a strain to clarity, but presents at the same time an attempt to do justice to the challenge of contextuality. His point is that there is no simple logic or application of ethical norms, principles, and concepts to the human condition. Human predicament is complex and the divine activity is dynamic, but God acts where the interplay of biblical image and human situation serves to humanize human life.[356] The concern is to allow divine transcendence and presence (or in christological terms: the lordship of Christ) to concretely affect human life and shape community.

I will return to this matter, but want to point to the congeniality with Bonhoeffer. Bonhoeffer insisted that the church speak only concrete commands for the day. Ethics was to be seen as social sensibility. Lehmann contextualizes the ethical enterprise. Ethical principles, natural law, and casuistry short cut the ethical challenge and end up in abstractions. The approach of Bonhoeffer and Lehmann despite any generality of their formulations is an attempt to reckon concretely with the presence of God in human affairs.

### 2.2. *Koinonia ethics*

Similar to Bonhoeffer Lehmann proposes (with particular reference to the letter to the Ephesians) "that the *koinonia* character of Christian ethics is derived from the nature of the church as the 'body of Christ'...[The] church, the fellowship which is the body of Christ, the *koinonia*, is the fellowship-creating reality of Christ's presence in the world."[357] That is to say that 'Christian' ethics has its focus in the church as the fellowship in which the divine activity (of humanization) both comes into view and is structured.

> Just as there is no Messiah without his people, so there is no real presence of Jesus in history without or apart from the true people of God which as the work of the Holy Spirit is always at the same time a spiritual and visible reality. It is this reality of the *koinonia*, whatever the word for it may be, which denotes the concrete result of God's specifically purposed activity in the world in Jesus Christ. We might therefore say that Christian ethics is *koinonia* ethics.[358]
>
> The hidden (*koinonia*) character of the church and the empirical (*ekklesia*) character of the church are dynamically and dialectically related in and through God's action in Christ, whose headship of the church makes the church at once the context and the custodian of the secret of the maturity of humanity. Regarded in this way the reality of the church is an ethical reality because what God is doing in the world becomes concrete in the transformation of human motivation and of the structures of human relatedness which are the stuff of human fulfillment.[359]

It is important that the church, understood as "the context of ethical reflection", is not just a place where Christians can think about ethics, but is itself an ethical reality, a concrete expression of "the corporate structure of God's activity in the world."[360]

Bonhoeffer emphasized that the primary subject of the knowledge of God (and thus of God's will) is the collective person of the church. More explicitly Lehmann emphasizes the *koinonia* not only as the subject of ethical knowledge but also as both object and subject of ethical praxis. The church is object of the divine activity of humanization (and the creation of human fellowship) and at the same time subject of ethical activity by means of its participation in that work of humanization. This means that the ethical reflection of the church is reflection upon the divine praxis which the church is.

> The penultimate chapter of the biblical story is the story of the eucharistic community in the world. Here is the laboratory of maturity in which, by the operative (real) presence and power of the Messiah-Redeemer in the midst of his people, and through them of all people, the will to power is broken and displaced by the power to will what God wills. The power to will what God wills is the power to be what man has been created and purposed to be. It is the power to be and to stay human, that is, to attain wholeness or maturity. For maturity is the full development in a human being of the power to be truly and fully himself in being related to others who also have the power to be truly and fully themselves. The Christian *koinonia* is the foretaste and the sign in the world that God has always

> been and is contemporaneously doing what it takes to make and to keep human life human.[361]

Lehmann refers to the *koinonia*, ("the fellowship-creating reality of Christ's presence in the world") as a hidden character of the church, "dynamically and dialectically related" to the empirical church, "neither identical with nor separable from the visible church", a sort of "ecclesiola in ecclesia", "a leaven in the lump".[362] The ambiguity of the empirical church precludes any identification, but Lehmann's manner of speaking at this point should not detract from the emphasis which he also lays on the concrete human and political reality of the divine activity. The real interest in the fellowship-creating reality of Christ's presence and in the divine activity of humanization is not only its hiddenness but its concrete transformation of humanity and its concrete structuring of human fellowship.

> [The] empirical church points, despite its ambiguity, to the fact that there is in the world a laboratory of the living word, or to change the metaphor, a bridgehead of maturity, namely the Christian *koinonia*. In the *koinonia* a continuing experiment is going on in the concrete reality and possibility of man's interrelatedness and openness for man. In the *koinonia* ethical theory and practice acquire a framework of meaning and a pattern of action which undergird the diversity and the complexity of the concrete ethical situation with vitality and purpose.[363]

The dynamics of Lehmann's *koinonia* ethics lend further substance to Bonhoeffer's notion of a "church for others", or as formulated in *Ethics*, "for the world."[364] "Christian life is lived not only in the church but also in the world; and whatever God is doing in and through the *koinonia*, he is also doing in the world."[365] The fellowship-creating presence of Christ is structured in the church, but the scope of the divine, political activity is humanity. The *koinonia* possesses a sign character for all humanity, for the divine economy includes believer and non-believer alike.[366]

## 2.3. *"What am I to do ?"*

Lehmann defines the theological discipline of Christian ethics as "the reflection upon the question, and its answer: What am I, as a believer in Jesus Christ and as a member of his church, to do?"[367] In light of all the emphasis on the *koinonia*, it is to be noted that Lehmann formulates the question in the first person singular. It might seem that the plural form: "What are we to do?" (Luke 3:12; Acts 2:37) would better reflect the "corporate structure of God's activity in the world".[368] Lehmann, however, does not employ the plural, and the singular has its own right. Interrelatedness is essential, but it serves integrity and maturity.[369] Nancy Duff indicates that Lehmann's position is not characterized by egalitarianism (or hierarchy) but by heterogeneity, which celebrates difference and is oriented to reciprocal responsibility.[370] Concreteness and contextuality of Christian ethics as well as integrity and interrelatedness of the human person would seem to suggest both the singular and plural.

*Koinonia* ethics means "that it is from, and in, the *koinonia* that we get the answer to the question: What am I, as a believer, in Jesus Christ and as a member of his church, to do?"[371] The indicative form of the question is also related to the reality of the *koinonia*.

> [The] ethical question - in the *koinonia* - is not 'What ought I to do?' but 'What *am* I to do?' because in the *koinonia* one is always in an indicative rather than in an imperative situation. There is, of course, also an imperative pressure exerted by an indicative situation. The 'ought' factor cannot be ignored in ethical theory. But the ethical factor is not the primary ethical reality. The primary ethical reality is the human factor, the human indicative, in every situation involving the interrelationships and the decisions of men. In the *koinonia* something is already going on, namely, what God is doing in the situation out of which the ethical question and concern arise to fashion circumstance and behavior according to his will. This is why a contextual ethic does not lead to ethical anarchy or ethical expediency.[372]

It is to be noted that the indicative of ethics is not just salvation in a general or individual sense ("Individuals are 'saved' into the *koinonia*, not one by one."[373]), but the ethical reality of the church. It is this ethical reality (indicative) that shapes and forms the ethical activity of Christians. This ethical reality is essential to a contextual ethic which might otherwise fall prey to excessive subjectivism or individualism, anarchy, expediency, cultural bias, and so on.

The ethical question is, to be sure, complex and problematic. And it may be granted that "the real problem of Christian behavior is not knowing that one is to do the will of God but doing the will of God which one knows."[374] Nevertheless, humans

> are genuinely perplexed by the diversity and complexity of human motivation and of behavioral options which make up the stuff of the ethical situation. The truth is that the more ethically sensitive a person is, the more likely he is to know...that even if he is prepared to acknowledge that he is to do the will of God, he comes thereby only to a still more troublesome perplexity, namely, what is the will of God which he admits he is to do?...For Jesus, the will of God is always problematic enough to have to be unpretentiously asked for and trusted.[375]

> Asking for and trusting the will of God are recommended by Jesus not only because of the complexity of the ethical situation but also, and more basically, because of the complexity of the will of God itself...There is no formal principle of Christian behavior because Christian behavior cannot be generalized. And Christian behavior cannot be generalized because the will of God cannot be generalized. ...It cannot be too strongly stressed that the Decalogue presupposes the covenant and, in a world in which God is at work and man is destined to find fulfillment in the service of God, sharply focuses upon the concrete human occasions of obedience.[376]

This is the complexity and paradox of the Christian ethical situation.

> The fact is that outside the context of the divine activity it makes no sense to talk about the will of God; and within the context of the divine activity, the question about the will of God exposes the paradoxical character of the ethical situation of man. The paradox is that we do not know the will of God which we will and we do not will the will of God which we know.[377]

It should be clear that the complexity and paradox have also a positive value for Lehmann. He states that the "complexity, in the context of the *koinonia*, is an occasion for the fulfillment, not the frustration, of the rich diversity of Christ's giving."[378] He could probably similarly state that the paradox of the ethical situation of humankind is an occasion for maturity, full humanity.

At any rate the classic problem of discerning the will of God is placed in the context of the problem of discerning the activity of God, which is humanization. That does not serve to simplify the ethical question. It does, however, root the ethical question in the ethical reality of the (diversity of the) *koinonia* and the ethical challenge of maturity. Answering the ethical question means participating in the *koinonia* and seeking human maturity.

> All the interrelationships of men are drawn into the orbit of the way life looks from within the *koinonia*. The thrust of the *koinonia* into the world means that all ordinary conduct is socialized rather than universalized, because in the *koinonia*, and this means in the ethical reality of Christian faith, the maturity and the humanity of man stand or fall together. A mature humanity and the 'new humanity' are identical.[379]

All this follows from the basic orientation and goal of Christian ethics.

> Christian ethics is oriented toward revelation rather than toward morality. Christian ethics aims, not at morality, but at maturity. The mature life is the fruit of Christian faith. Morality is a by-product of maturity."[380]

Christian ethics stands or falls therefore with the quality of the Christian *koinonia* and the maturity (humanity) of the Christian person. This makes of Christian, contextual ethics a daring, delicate, and disputable enterprise. But such are the demands of human fellowship and maturity. Such are the dynamics of Christian faith and community. "The *koinonia* is always there in the community of faith where prophetic-apostolic witness to revelation and response to the fellowship in the Spirit coincide."[381] The result is that the primary focus of Christian ethics is not on the rules and regulations of ethical behavior, but on the ethical subjects: God, the church, and the believer.

## 2.4. *Socialized conscience*

Lehmann, like Bonhoeffer, discerns the ambiguity of conscience[382], but where Bonhoeffer rejected conscience because of its individualistic character, Lehmann seeks to redeem conscience for the ethical enterprise by socializing it within the context of a *koinonia* ethic.[383] The significance of conscience is found in human freedom and sensitivity to respond to the challenge of God's humanizing activity in the face of dehumanization. Conscience is not choosing between good and evil, whether in assent to an external good or as an internal act of will, i.e., conscience is not a moral capacity. Rather conscience is that "which forges the link between what God is doing in the world and man's free obedience to that activity."[384] Lehmann points out that the biblical location of human responsibility is not conscience but the heart.

> The conscience knows by a kind of internal sight, a cognitive seeing which condemns the knower out of the inexorable disparity between his own nature and the order against which he has offended. The heart knows by a kind of sensitivity at once central and total which marks the person as a whole; this relational knowledge involves man as a doer in a behavioral response to a God whose claim upon him is the foundation of his humanity.[385]

Conscience is not indispensable to a Christian ethic. If, however, it is to be appropriated for purposes of ethical analysis, it must be understood as "the conscience immediately sensitive to the freedom of God to do in the always changing human situation what his humanizing aims and purposes require."[386] The biblical example is to be found in the discussion by Paul of eating meat offered to idols (1 Corinthians 8 and 10). There Paul deals with considerations of conscience; however, it is not one's own conscience but the conscience of the other that is the occasion for ethical decision. This does not present a new criterion of action, but offers a relation of human consideration and response.

Conscience, "as the internal arbiter of human action, is transposed from the self to the neighbor."[387]

The function of conscience is no longer to accuse or excuse, but to express "the pre-eminent claim of my neighbor's conscience upon and over my own."[388] "The neighbor's conscience is the concrete bearer of whatever ethical significance and function may be claimed for conscience...This conscience-relation [between one's neighbor and oneself] is a relation of human claim and human response through which no human action is ethical in itself but all human action is instrumental to what God in Christ is doing in the world to make and to keep human life human."[389]

Lehmann calls this a 'theonomous conscience', governed and directed by the freedom of God alone. In terms of the Corinthian passage there is on the one hand a legitimate claim to liberty (autonomy): "All things are lawful." There is on the other hand a "relation of human claim" (heteronomy): "Not all things are helpful." The ethical response is, however, that of free obedience (theonomy).

The question arises whether 'theonomy' provides an adequate solution or synthesis to the polarity of autonomy and heteronomy. A 'free obedience' remains heteronomous. Even an understanding of ethical behaviour as a choice for one's own humanity or for one's true self (*autos*) cannot preclude the experience of heteronomy. Nor is the ethical question 'What am I to do?' ever void of heteronomy. The question always entails an external claim, even if the claim is contextualized in the community or believed to be coming from God.

That no human behavior is thoroughly autonomous must also be clear from Lehmann's description. All human behavior is conditioned not only by physical and structural determinants, but also by the ethical dilemmas and bottlenecks that characterize human existence, i.e., the real disturbances of human life or community (or even of non-human reality) that give occasion to ethical crises. Furthermore, if humanity does indeed find its origin and purpose in God, then there are also theological conditions to meaningful human existence and behavior. Lehmann concurs with Karl Barth that the condition or precondition of the human ethical predicament is a fundamental disturbance.[390]

It should be remembered that the disturbance and the complexity have a positive value for Lehmann. They provide the opportunity for human responsibility and maturity. A (Christian) theological ethic entails an informed disturbance and a sensitized accountability, tuned to the history of law and prophets and apostles, to the human history of God and the Messiah. This information, this history is not an absolute standard or rule of human behavior, but a shaping force and a critical guideline. It is not a solution to the ethical dilemma, but a disturbing promise in the concrete ethical situation or relation. It is the opportunity for ethical concretization and creativity.

With such terms as autonomy, heteronomy or even theonomy Lehmann does not clarify the ethical condition. The problem cannot be reduced to a question of which law or rule (*nomos*) we must look to, whether hetero- or auto-, nor transcended by an appeal to the divine. More helpful than the concept of theonomy would seem to be Lehmann's own category of maturity. For maturity involves the capacity to deal with (distinguish, evaluate and relate) the various claims and commitments that humans experience. It includes the capacity to responsibly describe the concrete context and environment of ethical decision in terms of divine and human activity.

### 2.5. *The transfiguration of politics*

There is one particular issue to which Lehmann has devoted attention, namely, that of revolution and revolutionary violence, in his book *The Transfiguration of Politics*.[391] The subtitle included only on the dust jacket[392] indicates the christological foundation: *The Presence and Power of Jesus of Nazareth in and over Human Affairs*. The goal is that which has been encountered all along: humanization. The hope is that the passion and action of revolution can be formed and informed by transcendence.

Lehmann positively evaluates the concern of revolutionary movements with "making time and space make room for freedom" as an authentic sign of the human.[393] The proximity to the divine activity in Jesus Christ of making and keeping life human is for him evident. Revolution needs to be qualified, lest it go the way of all revolt and devour its own children in programmatic violence. The question of power is central. It requires not just transformation (a change in the form of power) nor transvaluation (a shift in the kind and use of power), but transfiguration as a turning point in human events. The transfiguration of Christ serves as the parabolic model of the ingression of "things that are not" into "things that are."[394]

True to his descriptive approach Lehmann looks more to the meaning of revolution than to a moral evaluation of it. Revolutions are not made; they just happen. And they happen when people feel themselves severely wronged in their basic humanity and freedom. They are aroused by the sentiments of justice to revolt. Such an arousal is a sign of moral transfiguration, a turning point in the course of human events.[395] As an example Lehmann points to the conspiracy of which Bonhoeffer was a member, particularly the assassination attempt of July 20, 1944.[396]

The category for properly understanding revolution is not ethics, law, or sociology, in Lehmann's view, but apocalypse. Revolutions are *kairotic* actions seeking a revision of political priorities. The movements against imperialism, colonialism, and racism are divinely appointed judgements on the failures of the political to nurture human community.[397] Violence is not so much an endemic nemesis of revolution, but a sign that politics have arrived at a moment of truth. The risk of violence may in a given situation be seen as inevitable though it can never be justified. If, however, it becomes policy, then revolution forfeits its transfiguring power and devours its own children.[398]

The revisioning of political priorities involves the priority of freedom above order and of justice above law. Justice (righteousness) is not a specific norm, but "a relational term that refers to the social reciprocities in which man acts, which actually function in a directional way, and at the same time in very diverse ways." Righteousness is the focus of the practice of love and is to be understood in terms of covenant. Of the practice of justice in human society the poor are a test case.[399]

The point in attending to the concept of justice is the implicit priority which Lehmann attributes to it and to freedom above the issue of violence. In fact it is the intended subordination of power to purpose and violence to liberation that forms the point of the book. The crucial question becomes the sovereignty of God (the lordship of Christ) in its liberation of power and limiting of violence.

What is peculiarly absent in Lehmann's treatment of revolution and the transfiguration of politics is the *koinonia*. I find only two references. One is a singular sentence that the agenda for the transfiguration of humanity derived from the biblical story might also be arrived at by the language and life of the community of faith, which is the church.[400] The suggestion is not explicated. B. Harvey asserts that this absence of the *koinonia* robs the perspectives on power and revolution of historical concreteness.[401]

The other reference is not an understanding of the political task from the context of the *koinonia* as one might have expected, but a task assigned to the "people of God." It is derived from an understanding of revolution as supplication, a prophetic appeal "to a sovereign ideal of justice or humanity or to the judgement or grace of God."[402] Revolutionary and biblical politics coinhere, according to Lehmann, in the providential presence and pressure which is "making time and space make room for the freedom and fulfillment that being human takes." The transfiguration of politics and power "requires an identification of the people of God with the suppliants of history."[403] The transfiguration of human community requires transcendence.

### *Considerations*

1. The primary ethical task is not the prescription of norms for behavior, but the (evaluative, historical) description of context in terms of divine activity, Christian community, and human predicament. Such a three dimensional contextual approach is an attempt to do justice to the presence of God in human affairs, to the humanizing project of human community, and to the complexity of ethical responsibility.

2. Christian community as "the fellowship creating reality of Christ's presence in the world" is both object and subject of ethical praxis. Christian community may be an experiment in the practice of humanity and maturity.
3. A resolution of the problem of conscience as well as of the tensions between autonomy, heteronomy, and theonomy can be guided by the concept of human maturity as a discrimnating and evaluative capacity of ethical subjects.
4. Christian ethics stands or falls with the quality of Christian community and the maturity of the Christian person.
5. The primary task of the Christian community in the midst of social upheaval is to discern the meaning of events. The contribution of Christian witness is to insist upon the subordination of power to justice and humanity. The task of Christian supplication draws attention to transcendence as that which can transfigure politics by revising its priorities and by making room for human freedom and fulfillment.

## III.3.

## STANLEY HAUERWAS
## THE CHURCH AS A SOCIAL ETHIC

The church does not have a social ethic. The church is a social ethic. This conviction lies at the heart of the theological project of Stanley Hauerwas and immediately indicates the intimacy of the relation he draws between the church and Christian ethics.

An attempt, however, to display the theology of Hauerwas proves more complicated than his seemingly blunt and simple claim that the church is a social ethic might cause us to suspect. He seems able to combine a classical and medieval understanding of the virtues with a gospel ethic of the radical reformation. He appeals to a traditional and narrative approach to ethics and arrives at a defense of nonviolence. He lays claim to the universal thrust of Jewish and Christian ethics while insisting upon the particular and distinctive characteristics of the same. Such are the gathered insights of an evangelical Methodist who was greatly influenced by a Mennonite while teaching at a Roman Catholic institution, to mention only one phase of his intellectual development.[404]

Hauerwas' intent is to display the inherently practical nature of Christian convictions and theology. Although those convictions defy strong systematization;[405] nevertheless his "overriding concern has been systematic, namely, to understand how Christian convictions can claim to be true without distorting or giving a reductionistic account of what in fact Christians ought to believe."[406]

### 3.1. *The narrative mode of moral reflection*

What is meant when it is said that the church is a social ethic? What is the understanding of ethics underlying such a claim? It will be necessary to look into the themes and concepts that Hauerwas employs in his moral reflection, such as virtue and character, narrative and tradition.

The binding factor would seem to be the concept of narrative, not as the central focus of Hauerwas' theology, but as a fundamental concept and context which serves to clarify the interrelation of the various other themes.[407] "The nature of Christian ethics is determined by the fact that Christian convictions take the form of a story, or perhaps better, a set of stories that constitute a tradition, which in turn creates and forms a community."[408]

Essential to Hauerwas' understanding is the intertwining of story, tradition and community. The story of God's calling of Israel and of the life of Jesus requires the formation of a corresponding community. The church is the community where the story is remembered and rehearsed, where the tradition is preserved and provoked.[409] "From this perspective the church is the organized form of Jesus' story."[410]

This last formulation is reminiscent of Bonhoeffer's description "Christ existing as community", though one hardly finds any reference by Hauerwas to Bonhoeffer. In common is a normative understanding of the church in that the church is not merely a shared response to the biblical story, but, as Lehmann would also agree, a participation in the continuing story of God's purposes. "Church" functions as both a descriptive and normative category, a matter that will require further attention.

At this point the affinity of Hauerwas' position to the moral theory of Alisdair MacIntyre[411] with its fundamental claim on the narrative form of moral reasoning[412] is to be noted. At issue is a critique of the "standard account" of morality which would aspire to moral objectivity from a neutral (self-alienated) standpoint, by appealing to categorical principles of rationality or universal standards of a supposed human nature. It is argued that this modern aspiration, stemming from the Enlightenment, has proved inconclusive and is ultimately illusory. It does not and cannot do justice to the fact that all morality is dependent upon particular traditions and to the way in which narrative is essential to the intelligibility of moral reasoning and moral agency. We cannot make ourselves morally understood without appeal to the narrative form of our activity in the context of a particular moral tradition. It is not our neutrality that informs and forms our moral being and behavior but our vested moral interest.

The critique of the "standard account" does not entail a wholesale rejection of that account. On the contrary, the various ethical theories, principles, and perspectives that have been developed constitute a substantial contribution to the moral discourse if sufficient attention is paid to the narrative context from which they have been abstracted.[413] The consequence of this critique of various ethical theories (such as utilitarianism or formalism, teleology or deontology, as well as of apparently logical and objective conceptions like categorical imperative, universalizability, the ideal observer, etcetera) is to recognize the relative legitimacy of such moral perspectives and modes of argument, but not to mistake them for rational moral foundations or categorical principles in and of themselves. Intrinsic value (deontology) and the weighing of effects and results (teleology) are both significant moral considerations, but neither is sufficient in itself to constitute a moral theory. They both must be displayed, argued, and related within some (narrative) context.

Another way of putting the whole matter is the following: "Our argument, put in traditional terms, is that the moral life must be grounded in the 'nature' of man. However, that 'nature' is not 'rationality' itself, but the necessity of having a narrative to give our life coherence. The truthfulness of our moral life cannot be secured by claims of 'rationality' in itself but rather by the narrative that forms our need to recognize the many claims on our lives without trying to subject them to a false unity of coherence."[414]

Hauerwas' primer on Christian ethics, *The Peaceable Kingdom*, thus opens with the assertion that "the very nature and structure of ethics is determined by the particularities of a community's history and convictions."[415] In other words, ethics is a social and historical discipline that always requires an adjective or qualifier. Consequently the Christian's task is not the search for moral absolutes or universal principles (as exemplified by the Enlightenment), but the appropriation of the biblical story, which through the praxis of the Christian community forms and informs ethical substance and sensitivities.

A narrative approach emphasizes on the one hand that ethics always reflects the particular convictions of historic communities[416] and recognizes on the other hand that narrative is an essential mode of Christian understanding. Indeed, there is no more fundamental way of knowing God, the world, or the self than through a narrative display of their history. There is no more adequate way of expressing their identity and the contingent nature of their relations.[417] Narrative is the form that the biblical revelation takes in telling the story of God's dealings with Israel and in Jesus Christ. Narrative is the means that we have of explaining ourselves, who we are, and why we do what we do. Narrative is thus the primary source of an understanding of God and the (moral) world in which we live. Narrative is, consequently, the means of relating ourselves to each other, to the world, to our past and present and future, to God.

Narrative thus understood entails a claim to truthfulness, specific claims about the nature of reality. The story must ring true. If it does not, then it fails to warrant belief. Truthfulness is not just concerned with facts as such, but with our faculties of interpretation and imagination that help us to see ourselves as we are and envision the world as it is and is meant to be.[418]

## 3.2. *Transformation, truthfulness and tragedy*[419]

It is not enough for learning to see and envision, to interpret and to imagine, that we be informed by the Christian story. Christian ethics involves human formation and transformation as well. The gospel is a self-involving story, for "there is no way to speak of Jesus' story without its forming our own. The story it forms creates a community which corresponds to the form of his life."[420]

Envisioning the world as God's creation and ourselves as participants in his kingdom project does not come naturally. Although Hauerwas does not care to summarize or simplify this fundamental alienation of humankind commonly called sin, it would seem that he is most concerned with self-deception, the inability, perhaps the fear or refusal to be truthful, and the resulting proneness to violence in order to camouflage a lack of truthfulness.[421]

What ethics is about, what the Christian story is about, is how the self can be transformed to see the world truthfully.[422] It is Hauerwas' claim that the story characteristic of Christians and Jews provides

1. power to release ourselves from destructive alternatives;
2. ways of seeing through current distortions;
3. room to keep ourselves from having to resort to violence;
4. a sense for the tragic: how meaning transcends power.[423]

The gospel, the biblical story, provides a way of living truthfully and enables one to accept tragedy without resorting to violence. A tangency with Lehmann can be pointed to. Lehmann similarly saw the need for power to be governed by purpose in making room for human freedom. Hauerwas goes on to emphasize a sense of the tragic, the ability to accept powerlessness and insolubility in order to avoid resorting to violence.

Hauerwas presents the four features listed above as criteria for judging among stories. He wants to emphasize that a narrative account of ethics, while not providing an objective moral bedrock, nevertheless need not fall into a thoroughgoing moral relativity. It is possible to judge among stories, not so much by weighing arguments, as by displaying the effects of various stories, the sort of persons and communities they shape.[424] A tree is known by its fruits and the proof of the pudding is in the eating.

Strictly speaking, the four features listed above are not general criteria for distinguishing between rival stories, as Hauerwas initially suggests, but a presentation of and a claim about what the biblical story has to offer. In the friendly and not so friendly competition between coexistent ethical traditions and contingent moral narratives, Hauerwas defines his cause in terms of truthfulness, tragedy, and peaceableness as his own particular interpretation of the biblical, especially the gospel, narrative.

### 3.3. *The ethical journey*

The substance of Hauerwas' understanding of truthfulness and peaceableness needs further explication, as do the transformation of self and the formation of community which he advocates. First, however, it would seem helpful to understand how Hauerwas envisions the task of ethics and theology and the shape of Christian life. There again it appears how intertwined his conceptions are.

> Thus story is a way to remind us of the inherently practical character of theological convictions. For Christian convictions are not meant to picture the world. They do not give a primitive metaphysics about how the world is constituted. Rather the gospel is a story that gives you a way of being in the world. Stories, at least the kind of stories I am interested in, are not told to explain as a theory explains, but to involve the agent in a way of life. A theory is meant to help you know the world without changing the world yourself; a story is to help you deal with the world by changing it through changing yourself.
> This is the reason...that ethics cannot be separated from theology...Thus the truth of religious convictions at least involves how the self is formed to rightly know the world as it should be but is not, except as it is subject to divine and human agency.[425]
> Theology is a practical activity concerned to display how Christian convictions construe the self and the world. Therefore theological claims concerning the relation of creation and redemption are already ethical claims, since they situate how one works methodologically.[426]

These notions of story, of practical activity, of construing the self and changing the world, of a way of life imply a fundamental conviction that all of this is going somewhere. To illustrate this Hauerwas makes use of a distinction by Gilbert Meilaender, who

> suggests that two of the most basic metaphors determining how the Christian life is to be understood are those of journey and dialogue. The latter basically sees the Christian life as going nowhere...That is to say, the Christian is simply caught within the dialogue between two voices with which God speaks: the accusing voice of the law and the accepting voice of gospel. Hearing the law, he flees to the gospel. Hearing the gospel, he is freed to hear what the law requires. But hearing what the law requires, he must again flee to the gospel. Life is experienced as a dialogue between these two divine verdicts, and within human history one cannot escape that dialogue or progress beyond it.[427]

A similar "back and forth" movement occurs, according to Hauerwas, when the conception of the Christian moral life is dominated, as in a great deal of Protestant theological ethics, by the notion of command. Life is "seen as the response or failure of response to individual commands."[428] "The Christian obligation, in the light of this metaphor, is obedience to law and performance of the will of God. The object of the moral life is not to grow but to be repeatedly ready to obey each new command." The result of this is, according to Hauerwas, an "individualistic and occasionalistic understanding of the self."[429]

This critique of the dialogue metaphor and of the dominance of the notion of command in *Character and the Christian Life* is contrasted with the formation of the ethical self in terms of virtue and character. The appropriate metaphor is that of a 'journey'.

> [The] underlying contention...is that the moral life, and in particular the Christian moral life, requires a teleological conception of human existence that gets somewhere rather than forever being a movement between the "back and forth."...when the Christian life is conceived as a journey, a process is implied through which people are graciously transformed by the very pilgrimage to which they have been called.[430]

The Christian moral life is in need of substance and should be conceived of as having duration and direction. It consists of becoming the sort of person and the sort of community that God wills. It involves growth and continuation by means of formation and transformation. Hauerwas does not reject the metaphor of dialogue or the notion of command, but he wants to place them "in a larger framework of moral experience"[431] by arguing that "the metaphor of journey is and surely should be the primary one for articulating the shape of Christian existence and living."[432] For example,

> God's command comes not just as an action directive for specific decisions but also as the command to be perfect as he is perfect. God's command comes as judgement because the self has a duration that allows for growth and development. The command comes as forgiveness because we can do nothing to change our past, but we are not condemned to repeat it.[433]

Or put yet another way:

> The biblical commandments do not command us arbitrarily; rather they call us to be holy as God is holy, as we have learned of holiness through God's faithfulness to us. Therefore, like God we are called to be what we are and to do what we do because God is that kind of God. Such a morality requires no "foundation;" it is enough that we know it to reflect the very nature of God."[434]

If there is a "foundation," it is provided by "the narrative display of God's holiness in Scripture," more specifically by "the story of Christ."

> Such a foundation is not extra-rational; indeed, it is a claim about reality, namely, that our existence is God-given and -formed. Such a claim is properly interpreted, as are all claims, within a community that seeks to understand its world. At least the beginning of wisdom in human communities is the recognition that our lives are narrative dependent, that we are pilgrims on a journey, even if we are not sure what that journey

> entails. That we Christians witness to a man's life, a man called Jesus, who is the heartbeat of our life and the meaning and form of our existence becomes intelligigble (and therefore rational) in the light of such narrative dependency.[435]

It is the narrative context as well as the journey metaphor that provide the framework for Hauerwas' ethical enterprise.[436] It is the story (or stories) of Israel and Jesus (as well as the ongoing journey that is called the church) that provide the particular substance of his moral perspective.

### 3.4. *Jesus existing as the kingdom*

It is Hauerwas' conviction that "Christian ethics is specifically formed by a very definite story with determinative content."[437] The entire framework that Hauerwas erects is intended to "help us understand the moral significance of Jesus' life, death and resurrection,...the Jesus we find portrayed in the Gospels."[438] Hauerwas is particularly disturbed by "cosmic and ontological" Christologies that "tend to make Jesus' life incidental to what is assumed to be a more profound theological point. In particular the eschatological aspects of Jesus message are downplayed."[439]

It became clear above that narrative and journey constitute the framework for Hauerwas' attention to the biblical tradition and the church. Hauerwas claims conversely that the particular story and community that are his starting point imply precisely the historical, narratable understanding of ethics he has more broadly defended.

> Theologically and ethically the significance of Jesus for determining the meaning and content of the kingdom implies that history assumes an importance that cannot be ignored as it often is by other forms of ethical reflection. For the particularity of Israel, Jesus and the Church must be taken up constitutively into what those who proclaim Jesus as Lord and Christ regard as true and good and right. The kingdom does not start with nature, with the notion that the perfection implicit in creation be reformed by divine assistance; rather the kingdom starts as the hope of a people called by God, which for Christians is defined by the life and death of the crucified Christ. The universal scope of the kingdom is rooted in the universal scope of God's reign. What we can know of God and his kingdom is always given through the history of Israel filtered through the light of Jesus' cross.[440]

In this careful attention to form and content of the life of Jesus (as portrayed in the Gospels[441]) Hauerwas is in basic agreement with John Howard Yoder's description of the posture and politics of Jesus, including Yoder's ensuing ecclesiology and nonviolent ethic.[442] The pilgrimage, the journey, which constitutes the moral life of the Christian, is nothing else than the nitty-gritty of discipleship to Jesus within a community marked by truthfulness and nonviolence. And that discipleship is common participation in the reality of the kingdom of God, just as Jesus' own life was a manifestation of that kingdom. Hauerwas emphasizes that

> Jesus' teaching was not first of all focused on his own status but on the proclamation of the kingdom of God. Jesus, it seems, did not direct attention to himself, but through his teaching, healings, and miracles tried to indicate the nature and immediacy of God's kingdom.[443]

This implies no "low Christology" but the recognition that any christological claims must be made subsequent to the narrative portrayal of Jesus as God's anointed who proclaims and manifests the kingdom. For Hauerwas, in fact, Jesus is the story of the kingdom.[444] "Put starkly, Jesus himself is the meaning and content of the kingdom."[445] Hauerwas can quote Barth: "Jesus is Himself the established Kingdom of God," and agree with Origen that Jesus is the *autobasileia*, the kingdom in person. The force of this identification is to emphasize that the kingdom is not just an ethical ideal.[446] Close attention to the narrative relation between Jesus and the kingdom indicates that Jesus did not have a social ethic (i.e. a kingdom ideal), but that his story is a social ethic (i.e. an erupting reality).[447]

Borrowing from Bonhoeffer one might describe this position in terms of "Jesus existing as the kingdom." At any rate it is clear that Hauerwas lays emphasis on the concrete story of Jesus and the proclamation of the kingdom as that which provides the contours and context of an ecclesial ethic. Where Bonhoeffer emphasized discipleship,[448] and Lehmann the divine activity of humanizing human life,[449] the added force of Hauerwas' description is his emphatic appeal to the life of Jesus and the content of the kingdom.

According to Hauerwas Jesus defined the kingdom in that he "challenged both the militaristic and ritualistic notions of what God's kingdom required - the former by denying the right of violence even if attacked, and the latter by his steadfast refusal to be separated from those 'outside'."[450] The effect of both challenges would seem to be a fundamental inclusiveness of the kingdom, so that there is an essential relationship between the welcoming of the stranger and the ostracized, on the one hand, and the posture of nonviolence on the other.

This is reflected in another mark of the kingdom: the call to discipleship. That call is a radical break from security and possessions, including the possession of ourselves, as the things that are the source of our violence. This dispossession, which is the cross, is not a general self-sacrifice, but the confidence that forgiveness and love are alternatives to the coercion of the world.[451]

That confidence is the confidence that the kingdom has become a reality in and through Jesus.[452] He defines where this world is going. He enables his followers to view this world eschatologically, i.e. "in terms of a story, with a beginning, a continuing drama, and an end."[453] Hauerwas admits that the controversy on whether the kingdom is coming, present, or still to come, is hardly resolvable in the terms in which it is raised. His concern, however, seems not to be the resolution of that controversy, but the context of the continuing drama with its present and future possibilities. That drama entails claims about the nature of God's rule and about the real opportunities for a life of truthfulness and peaceableness.

Again, the Christian life is not one governed by morality or by obedience to commands or principles. Rather it emanates from a confidence in the truth of a particular story. It is a life shaped by that story by learning to be faithful to that story. It is not an easy story, for it challenges our illusions, and it reveals the violence that we have stored up within us. The blessed irony, according to Hauerwas, is that by forsaking our illusions and violence we do not lose our individuality, our self, or our autonomy, but become in fact substantial selves, truthful individuals, and free persons.[454] Or, to put it in terms that Hauerwas uses elsewhere: We appropriate character and we learn the skills and virtues that (the Christian) life requires.[455]

> True stories thus require extensive training in skills commensurate with that story. The Christian claim that life is a pilgrimage is a way of indicating the necessary and never-ending growth of the self in learning to live into the story of Christ. He is our master and from him we learn the skills to live faithful to the fact that this is God's world and we are God's creatures...We learn such a truth only by being initiated into it by others. That is why the question of the nature and form of the church is the center of any attempt to develop Christian ethics. And it is to that subject we must now turn.[456]

## 3.5. *The church, a gesture of the kingdom*

### *The church is a social ethic*

In following Hauerwas while he turns his attention to the church, one does not leave his concern for the kingdom. Once again the concerns are intertwined.

> Focus must be brought to bear not only on the eschatological fulfillment of the promise of the kingdom, but on the concrete ecclesial community established in its name. The kingdom of God is the hope of the people

> whom God has called out among all the nations. The question of ecclesiology, therefore, precedes strategy for social action. Without the kingdom ideal, the church loses its identity-forming hope; without the church, the kingdom loses its concrete character.[457]

It should be clear that Hauerwas does not identify the kingdom with the church. He is well aware that there is more to the kingdom than the church. Such is the hope to which the biblical stories give witness. His point, however, is that

> the church as that community formed by Jesus' story is not incidental for understanding God's kingdom. For...the virtues that form and are formed within the church are in fact a foretaste of the kingdom. To be sure, the church is not the kingdom, but neither is the life Christians share together something less than the kingdom's inbreaking. For the hope necessary to sustain the journey and pilgrim alike is in fact the first fruits of the kingdom, which we know to be God's will for the whole of creation.[458]

Repeatedly the church serves as the pivot on which everything turns in Hauerwas' writings. Indeed the church is for him a sort of "ontological necessity."[459] Hauerwas' position on "the practice of the church's story"[460] might best be expressed in a couple of extensive quotations.

> The emphasis on narrative, therefore, is not first a claim about the narrative quality of experience from some unspecified standpoint, but rather is an attempt to draw our attention to where the story is told, namely, in the church; how the story is told, namely, in faithfulness to Scripture; and who tells the story, namely, the whole church through the office of the preacher...The story is not self-referential but rather creates a people capable of being the continuation of the narrative by witnessing to the world that all creation is ordered to God's good end. The church is the necessary context of inquiry for the testing of that narrative...The church is crucial for the intelligibility of the story that Christians have to tell...The church is the community that is at once the storyteller as well as a character in the story that is required by Christian affirmation of God's redemption of the world through the people of Israel and the cross and resurrection of Jesus of Nazareth.[461]

When the church and its narrative are so interwoven, the meaning of the claim that the church does not *have* a social ethic but rather *is* a social ethic begins to emerge.

> The claim that the church is a social ethic is an attempt to remind us that the church is the place where the story of God is enacted, told and heard.

> Christian social ethics is not first of all principles or policies for social action but rather the story of God's calling of Israel and of the life of Jesus. That story requires the formation of a corresponding community which has learned to live in a way that makes it possible for them to hear that story. The church does not have a social ethic but is a social ethic then, insofar as it is a community that can clearly be distinguished from the world. The world is not a community and has no such story, since it is based on the assumption that human beings, not God, rule history.[462]

The background is set for Hauerwas' contention that "the authority of Scripture is a political claim characteristic of a very particular kind of polity."[463] Regarding scripture as authoritative means to appropriate the biblical narratives as a way of knowing and being faithful to the truth.[464] Attributing authority to the biblical narratives is an act of remembrance and witness, dependent upon and giving shape to the life and identity of a particular community. Such an approach to scripture is, furthermore, in keeping with the process of remembering and reinterpretation that gave birth to the texts of biblical literature.[465] The biblical narrative is not singular, but full of variety and tensions. "The canon marks off as Scripture those texts that are necessary for the life of the church without trying to resolve their obvious diversity and/or even disagreements." The canon thus provides not a simple summary, but "the classic model for the understanding of God."[466] Canon is thus not an accomplished fact, but a task, challenging us to be a distinct kind of people.[467]

Hauerwas' judgements on the world (as on liberalism and on the 'standard account' of ethics) are sweeping. More important at this point, however, is to note two matters that require further clarification. One is the formal distinction (and relation) between church and world. The other is the specific nature of the church's life that makes of it a social ethic and that distinguish it concretely from the world.

*A particular universalism*

What makes the church distinctive is the particularity of the narrative that makes the church "the storied society"[468] that it is. The church is not called to be morally good, but to learn to live faithfully to the stories of Israel and Jesus, to be a community where the truth of those stories is lived and spoken.[469] The first social task for the church is therefore not, e.g., to do this or that to make society more just, but to remember its own origins and history, to be the kind of community capable of nourishing its life by the memory of God's presence and of the history of God's people. Hauerwas emphasizes specifically that it is a great social challenge and a radical political act to learn to remember the history of the Jews (Israel past and present) as essential to the church's own history.

Such remembering is radical because it provides a prophetic understanding of the Christian community and its relationship to the world. It entails a radical change in the political form of the church, for it is a call for the church to be a new distinctive people amid the nations.[470] It is through an exclusive commitment to Israel and by means of the church that God wills to bring all people into his kingdom.[471]

Historically what has happened instead is that "Christianity took the universalism of the messianic hope and fused it with the ideological universalism of the ecumenical empire."[472] The result was a decisive shift in the logic of moral argument of which Constantine is the symbol.[473] At that point it becomes the concern of moral discourse not to give the Christian community its particular, distinctive color, but to direct the moral behavior of any- and everyone and to contribute to the workings of society and the state. The central concern becomes acceptability and effectiveness rather than faithfulness.

For Hauerwas such a 'universalism' results in cultural and social imperialism. He agrees with Brueggemann's description of the empire as essentially sectarian.[474] And he finds it

> odd that those who are so committed to the liberal values of the Enlightenment characterize the pacifist position as sectarian since they are usually the ones that develop justifications for Christians in one country killing Christians in another country on grounds of some value entailed by national loyalties. Surely if any position deserves the name 'sectarian' it is this, since it qualifies the unity of the church in the name of a loyalty other than that to the Kingdom of God.[475]

It would seem that some differentiation is advisable in discussing the various forms of 'universalism' so that one might also reckon with the possibilities and merits of an 'enlightened' pacifist universalism. At the same time one could agree with Hauerwas' critique that so many so-called universalist ideologies and liberal or Christian ethics that have accommodated themselves to the needs of the nation-state are in fact anything but universal. In contrast to that is Hauerwas' position that Christian convictions concerning the particularity of Israel's messianic hope, convictions concerning also the nature of the reign of God over creation and of the unity of the church, provide a significant hope and a relevant political posture of universalist dimensions in a terribly divided and violent world. They provide, e.g., a "trust that the other's life, as threatening as it may first appear, is necessary for our own."[476]

Van Gerwen points out that Hauerwas' location of the ethical enterprise in a particular community serves to avoid the extremes of both subjectivism and universalism. "Community has to provide an objectivity to the agent's moral character which is both contextual (particular, appropriate to the agent's perspective and sociocultural setting) and visionary (challenging, gift, discipline putting a demand and ideal before the agent)." Van Gerwen labels this a middle position that is typical for a "phenomenological understanding of ethics which concentrates on the objectivity of a shared cultural product."[477]

With regard to Hauerwas' qualification of the world, i.e., of contemporary society, as being essentially liberal, Van Gerwen suggests that such a view, while perhaps more appropriate to the United States than to European democracies, is a rather optimistic view of the world. Van Gerwen is of the opinion that a faceless bureaucracy has usurped liberalism, political vision, and moral purpose. Van Gerwen asks how the church is to live in a world dominated by a faceless bureaucratic monster which is already in our midst.[478]

One might then ask, without denying the general thrust of Hauerwas' critique of liberalism, whether liberalism could not in some practical respects also be seen as an ally of the church in the struggles for humanization. The Dutch theologian F.O. Van Gennep has made a plea for a renewed dialogue by the church with significant modern ideologies such as liberalism, socialism, anarchism and feminism, which he understands as products of the Enlightenment.[479] Van Gennep was more positive than Hauerwas about the contribution which those ideologies could make to the pursuit of freedom, justice, and equality. Van Gennep felt that such ideologies have served a corrective function in society as well as in and for the church (and its ethics). Van Gennep was himself convinced of the particularity of the church and its story, but emphasized for purposes of communication and the pursuit of truth a cultural openness and the practice of dialogue.

Noteworthy is Hauerwas' assessment that liberalism presents a primary challenge to the church in light of its predominance in western societies. It might also be the least catholic of the enlightenment ideologies. At the same time Van Gennep serves as a reminder that behind the ideologies essential questions lie, questions (e.g. regarding the nature of freedom and justice) which are more important than the ideology itself. Van Gennep is well aware of the totalitarian tendencies of all ideologies and therefore seeks dialogue with the dissidents in each tradition.

*Creating a contrast*

Hauerwas remains adamant about the necessity for the church to live its own life. In a footnote he is even willing to label that distinct common life a "normative form of sectarianism"[480]. For him the originality of the first Christians resided not in the peculiarity of their beliefs but in their social inventiveness in creating a new community. Their formation of a community distinct from the world was a reflection of how their belief in God had been transformed in the encounter with Jesus. The challenge is for the church to be a "contrast model",[481] a servant community which takes time to care and nurture friendships, a faithful manifestation of the peaceable kingdom in the world, a community of peace and truth in a world of mendacity and fear[482], a place of hospitality to the stranger, a place of unity in a divided world,[483] a living alternative.[484]

Hauerwas goes so far as to challenge the idea that the primary task or concern of Christian social ethics is to make the world better or more peaceful and just.[485] A church for others and for the world (Bonhoeffer) and the attention of the *koinonia* to what God is doing in the world (Lehmann) are not what he has in mind. Not that he is unconcerned with the world. He is simply convinced that God's strategy of transforming this world begins with the creation of a transformed people, an alternative society, a church that *is* a social ethic. Without such a contrast the world would have no way of recognizing its own worldliness, i.e., its self-made dividedness and violence.[486] Without attention to itself the church would lack the virtues to be such a people, would lack the skills of interpretation and discrimination for recognizing the possibilities and limits of society.[487] Thus any sense of the church being for the world seems to be qualified in terms of the church being for the kingdom.

In the light of this social task the existent disunity of the church is a scandal. Hauerwas' primary concern is not with the divisions of doctrine, history, and practice, whatever their significance, but those of class, race and nationality.[488] This "scandal", this discrepancy, not only reveals a failure of the church to be the church, i.e., faithful to its particular origins and history, but reveals also a tension in the theological project of Hauerwas between his theological claims about the church as being a social ethic and the factual disunity and disarray in the life of the church. (See III.8.1. below.)

*Integrity*

It is Hauerwas' concern to recover "the integrity of the church as an alternative political community."[489] The primary concern might be said to be simply the integrity of the church, but there is the recognition that such a concern implies a very particular political posture and a particular interpretation of the world. Yet the primary emphasis on the integrity of the church as such is not unimportant. The question is whether Hauerwas does not state the dualism between church and world too strongly.[490] Like Yoder he emphasizes that the way of Jesus implies its own distinctive posture. However, it should be recalled that the distinctiveness resides in the particularity of the narrative and in the integrity of the community and not in distinctiveness as such. To be sure, Hauerwas wants to make clear that his claims for the distinctiveness of the church and Christian ethics do not imply any assumption of superiority or Christian dominance (as if there were some neutral vantage point from which to pass such judgement), but are meant to remind us of the radical nature of the gospel.[491] It follows that the integrity and alternative character of Christian community need not imply a categorical distinctiveness, but rather a particular identity.

This is seen as well in Hauerwas' recognition that one may find persons who, while not themselves Christians, better manifest God's peace than Christians do. Hauerwas insists upon and hopes for cooperation with such people for securing justice in the world. The basis for such cooperation is not a general morality, but testimony to the wideness of God's kingdom.[492] It is not necessary that Christians always agree. More important is the nature of their agreements and disagreements. The political process (moral discourse) in which moral issues are adjudicated must be shaped by the concerns and convictions peculiar to the nature and tradition of the church and also be governed by love.[493] Such is necessary if the church is to be(come) a community that corresponds to its own story and truth and be(come) in that manner a social ethic.

It may be, according to Hauerwas, that such a social ethic is "but a gesture". And yet gestures are the very embodiment of our values and concerns, our means of communicating with one another and of shaping our world. "In this sense, the church is but God's gesture on behalf of the world to create a space and time in which we might have a foretaste of the Kingdom."[494] Through gestures, not in the least those of the sacraments and worship, the story is learned and acted out. However, it must be clear that the quality of those gestures and the validity of the church's common, social and ethical life are dependent on its integrity. Upright living is to be understood as a mark of the church.[495]

### 3.6. *The practice of imagination*

The ethical enterprise of Hauerwas is based not only on the expectation of a distinctive community, but also of a particular kind of people. The integrity of the community implies the integrity of its members as persons of virtue and character, of vision and imagination. Conversely, such persons must be formed and transformed, such virtues and vision must be learned and appropriated by participation in the life of the community. It is in community, through examples and teachers, through embodiment of language, gestures, and moral practices, that individual character is formed.[496]

The convictions and the practices that make up the substance of our moral life are not of our own making nor can they be obtained piecemeal. We inherit, learn, appropriate, and revise them by sharing in the ethical endeavor (tradition) of a particular community. In traditional theological terms, personal sanctification requires a sanctified people where the tradition and the examples of the saints are remembered, enacted, and carried on.[497]

Hauerwas would challenge members of the church to understand themselves to be involved in a "moral adventure", constantly seeking a better understanding of what it means to make God's story their own, enriching one another by displaying that story in their own lives, and opening themselves to the challenge of others and of new understandings of truthfulness.[498]

Although to my knowledge Hauerwas does not explicitly discuss the matter, the language of appropriation and sanctification, of character and growth and agency, can throw light upon the discussion of autonomy versus heteronomy versus theonomy. These three variants seem to reflect the notion of command (and the metaphor of dialogue) and within that context they form a problem, at least a tension. When, however, the metaphor of journey or of growth becomes predominant, then the three variants in question become various moments or aspects of ethical development.

Hauerwas realizes that integrity requires that one live faithful to personal history.[499] That understanding, it seems to me, is not unrelated to the concern for autonomy. Not that we are self-made persons, but that we can appropriate our selves and be the sufficient cause of our own actions (agency), i.e., we are creative moral subjects who can give directions to our lives.

At the same time, Hauerwas insists that a virtuous life and the appropriation of character depend upon the existence of communities which have been formed by narratives faithful to the character of reality.[500] This heteronomous aspect is not to preclude autonomy, but the recognition that a human self is fundamentally a social self. Sociality, human community, the relation to others (heteronomy) is necessary to form the self, to shape its character and identity, to provide the conditions for its becoming a responsible, mature moral being.

When Hauerwas speaks of making God's story one's own story, that might be considered a more or less theonomous experience. Yet as long as humans remain pilgrims, the tension between autonomy and heteronomy will be felt and experienced. It hardly seems helpful to understand autonomy and heteronomy to be mutually exclusive or prematurely resolvable. Rather they are polar aspects of the moral experience, just as individuality and sociality are polar aspects of human existence and personality.

Whatever the relative emphasis on the individual or the community, they are, in Hauerwas' understanding, essentially allies in the task of living out Christian convictions. Those convictions are themselves a morality, and embody a morality.[501] They create an alternative. Forgiven people can be a social ethic by exemplifying in their (common) life an alternative to Babel and Mammon, to mutual fear and violence.[502]

Living such an alternative is a test of the imagination. "Christians are a people whose imagination has been challenged by a God who has invited us into an otherwise unimaginable kingdom."[503] Christian ethics requires the creation of space, psychologically and physically, for the imaginative formation of a common life, for envisioning new possibilities and embodying alternatives to the necessities of this world. Imagination is not only a matter of the mind, but of our passions and bodies, of our total selves as well.[504]

Such an alternative is present in the celebration of the common meal, where habits and relations are enacted contrary to habits of disunity and distrust. In the meal the stranger is welcomed because he enhances rather than threatens our own being. In the meal peaceableness is practiced as people participate in a shared history, making others' histories a part of their own.[505]

### 3.7. *The politics of peace*

There are numerous paths that could now be pursued to further display the theological enterprise of Stanley Hauerwas. Of interest might be his claim that the proper practice of medicine as well as an appropriate form of sexual life are dependent on the particular practices and convictions of a (political) community.[506] Or one might consider the challenge presented to a community by the presence of the mentally handicapped.[507] Little attention is given to the poor and issues of poverty. Hauerwas would probably place relative priority on a common life with or among the poor and the powerless, rather than on the issue of poverty as such.[508] It is precisely at this point, however, that the radical nature of Hauerwas' non-violence becomes evident. It is, in conclusion, the matter of peaceableness that deserves further attention.

In stating that "the question of violence is the central issue for any Christian social ethic,"[509] Hauerwas is insisting that the pursuit of justice may not usurp the issue of power and violence. He has gone so far as to suggest that justice is a bad idea for Christians.[510] Modern conceptions of justice are variably abstract and self-contradictory, but nevertheless legitimize all sorts of claims. The concept of justice is appealing to the church, he suggests, because it promises social influence and relevance. It thus serves as an equivalent for natural law. At the same time it is essentially theocratic, revealing a will to power. The advocacy of justice by liberation theologies likewise owes too much, in his view, to Enlightenment ideals and lacks a proper account of justice. Related to this is Hauerwas' concern that the concept of liberation as a dominant metaphor will diffuse the distinctive witness of the church.[511]

Hauerwas assures his readers that he does not want to do away with the pursuit of justice, but he overstates the case. His criticism is suggestive and his contribution to a better concept of justice hardly substantial. How can any biblical ethic be developed without central attention to the concept of justice? If there is in fact no generally accepted Christian theory of justice, then Hauerwas (and other Christian ethicists) should be working hard to explicate one. Any approach will indeed need to be discriminating, but in the meantime there are sufficient examples of blatant injustice, whatever the theory, as raw material for reflection.

In that context one can then consider what seems to be a basic point for Hauerwas, namely, that nonviolence, in its rejection of the particular interests of power, is integral to the pursuit of justice. The question of justice is first of all a self-involving question, not one to be solved by appeals to revolution or the state.[512] A focus on the coercive aspect of politics is a failure to enliven the political imagination by seeking intellectual and institutional alternatives to violence and non-coercive forms of power.[513] Hauerwas rightly refuses to capitulate to the argument that nonviolence involves withdrawal from responsibility (the sectarian accusation). At issue is the very form of responsibility.[514]

Besides this political defense of non-violence, there are three other levels at which Hauerwas explicates his position of nonviolence. The heart of the issue is for him the question of discipleship as a matter of loyalty to Jesus Christ and conformity to the form of the kingdom. Insisting as always on the reality of the kingdom, Hauerwas does not see the essential tension as being that caused by unrealized ideals, but a tension between faithfulness and unfaithfulness.[515] A Christian pacifism, inasmuch as it incorporates the virtue of patience, is therefore not to be judged by its observable results, although results are indeed sought. For peaceableness is a quality of character and action, a reflection of Christian hope in the peacemaking of God.[516]

This trust in the peaceableness of God is reflected at another level in Hauerwas' assertion of the incompatability of truth and violence. Truth is precisely a challenge to all of the illusions, fears, lies and half-truths on which our disorder and violence are based, including the illusion of our own apparent peaceableness. Truth "gives us the confidence to rely on nothing else than its witness. A 'truth' that must use violence to secure its existence cannot be truth."[517]

Truth for Hauerwas is combined with truthfulness, peace with peaceableness. There is, finally, the level of the life of peace, which is not so much a matter of convictions and certainties as of character and community. Peacemaking is the very form of the church, the form of human relations and personal integrity which are governed by forgiveness and reconciliation. It is the form of unity that appreciates differences and welcomes the stranger, a unity that is not the assumption of some abstract universality, but that is given in actual contact of peoples.[518] These are the tests of real truthfulness and peaceableness: the challenge of the stranger, the intractableness of human differences, the recalcitrance of the manifold divisions in the world. Peace is an activity requiring patience and courage.[519] Truth and peace must be comprehensive and resilient enough to include the stranger. Hospitality and nonviolence are together constitutive of the identity of the church as both bear witness to the fundamental inclusiveness of the kingdom of God.

### *Considerations*

1. The power of the gospel story is its self-involving character and its ability to form and inform community.
2. The church is the community where the biblical story is remembered and rehearsed, where traditions are preserved and provoked. In that context the ethical enterprise is essentially historical and creative.

3. Christian ethics receives its specific color from the life and cross of Jesus and from the proclamation and reality of the kingdom.
4. The Christian life is to be understood as a journey. Ethics is about the task of enabling persons to be pilgrims and sojourners, a wandering people. (The image of pilgrims on a journey provides a context for appreciating autonomy, heteronomy, and theonomy as various moments in personal transformation.)
5. The more the church allows itself to be formed and informed by the gospel, the more it *is* rather than *has* a social ethic.
6. The integrity of the church lies in neither its distinctiveness nor its universality as such, but in its particularity, that is to say, in its attention to the particularities of the biblical stories of Israel and of the Jew Jesus.
7. The problem of power is a test of political imagination. Concepts of justice need to be examined with a view to their coercive elements.
8. The biblical story enables a practice of truthfulness as a capacity to confront tragedy, welcome the stranger and resist violence. Hospitality and non-violence are essential characteristics of the community of Jesus.

## III.4.

## ENRIQUE DUSSEL
## FACE-TO-FACE WITH THE POOR

> The essence of the Christian life is community: being together with others. This is also the essence of the reign of God: to be together with God, face-to-face with God in community.[520]

It is this affirmation that underlies the communitarian ethic of Enrique Dussel. But this reality of human relatedness and community is being interrupted and negated by the practice of domination, the sin of oppression, such as experienced by the poor of Latin America. The conflict between that affirmation and its interruption forms the driving force of the theological project of Dussel, a project which he undertakes as a participant in the endeavor of liberation theology: reflecting on the life (praxis) of Christian community in the struggle to liberate the poor.

### 4.1. *Sharing bread*

The theology of liberation (and in this context I refer to the Latin American phenomenon[521]) is an expression of protest, a protest against the structural impoverishment and dehumanization of the masses of Latin America. That protest, including the social analysis behind it as well as the prophetic pretentions of its expression, will require further attention. However, it would be incorrect, according to Dussel, to understand the project of liberation theology (or the movement of base communities to which that theology is secondary) as being simply reactionary. The method of liberation theology is not that of a negative dialectic, i.e. it is not just a negation (critique) of negation (oppression).[522] Liberation theology begins with an affirmation, a "radical principle", which is "the face-to-face of the person-to-person relationship in the concrete, real, satisfied, happy, community, in the gladness of being one with God and one with our brothers and sisters, the members of the community."[523]

Dussel sees this affirmation expressed in the picturing of the original apostolic community in the second chapter of Luke's "Praxis" of the Apostles[524] (Acts 2:42-47). Praxis, in Dussel's usage, is the active relatedness of persons to one another. It is proximity, being face-to-face, the real presence of one person to another. That relationship, if it is to be truly personal and authentic, is a relationship of infinite respect. It is love as *agape*, love for the other as other.[525] It is "charity" in the sense of the respectful gift of ourselves to each other.

This (Christian) love is lived in the plural, in mutuality, as a people established in the face-to-face of unity, i.e. community (Greek: *koinonia*).

> Rooted and established in mutual, respectful love, grounded in the charity of its free and unfettered participants as persons, as individuals fulfilled in a life in common, the Christian community is celebration, and a celebration that takes up or assumes the totality of life.[526]

That celebration of life finds expression in the satisfaction of each one's needs, again as exemplified in the original apostolic community. It is this understanding of need and its satisfaction that renders intelligibility to the eucharist, to community, to justice and the reign of God. It is the fulfillment or disregard of the other's need that is "a principle and an absolute criterion of the last judgement" as pictured in Matthew 25.[527] "Sharing bread, holding all things in common, and selling one's possessions and goods all indicate the radical nature of love that is respectful of the loved person(s)."[528]

Whatever else can be said of all these things, Dussel concentrates the understanding of the eucharist, of community and justice, of judgement and the reign of God, of life and love, all in the simple act (praxis) of sharing bread.

## 4.2. *The poor*

*Domination*

Contrary to this praxis of community is the praxis of domination, as an interruption of community and the negation of the other as other. This "original sin" (i.e. inherited social condition) of domination as an alienated social relationship makes of the dominated other a thing, a means. And the failure to respect the other as other is an offense to God as absolute Other. It is idolatry which has become embedded in our institutions and oppressive structures.

Quite concretely - and the reader must never forget the context out of which liberation theology is written - this all means poverty. The dominated other is not just marginalized and alienated and humiliated. He or she is denied life, denied bread, denied the fundamental means of life. That is what it means to be poor. And Dussel takes the time and effort to once more explain how the socio-politico-economic system that dominates Latin American life robs the people of the fruits of their own labor and production, robs the poor of their own bread and life.[529] The system is a totality ("the world") which would simultaneously feed upon and exclude the poor.

This social reality is understood biblically in the relation between rich and poor. These terms, besides referring to concrete persons, also function as "dialectical categories".

"Poor", in the biblical sense, denotes the dominated, oppressed, humiliated, instrumentalized term of the practical relationship called sin.. The constitutive act of the "poor" in the Bible is not lacking goods, but being dominated, and this by the sinner. The poor are the correlative of sin. As the fruit of sin, their formality as "poor" constitutes the poor or oppressed, and as such, the just and holy.
The "poor" are those who, in the relationship of domination, are the dominated, the instrumentalized, the alienated. Outside this relationship they can be "rich".
The poverty or want suffered by the poor is not the sheer absence of goods. No, the poverty of the poor consists in having been despoiled of the fruit of their labor by reason of the objective domination of sin.
Thus the life of the poor is accumulated by the rich. The latter live the life of the rich in virtue of the death of the poor. The life of the sinner feeds on the blood of the poor...[530]

It might be argued that the biblical understanding of sin is more varied than the dialectic of rich and poor that Dussel describes. However, one need not understand Dussel to be reducing the concept of sin to this juxtaposition of rich and poor, but rather to be highlighting a fundamental, if not the foremost, dynamic of the biblical judgement on the human (social) condition. In that sense his formulations are incisive. God's will, whether as community or kingdom, is the sharing of bread. Robbing the poor of their bread is the idolatry of the rich, the "original" sin of domination.

*Holiness, that is, exteriority*

By virtue of their alienation and victimization by the system of domination the poor are identified as "holy", i.e., exterior to the system. The term "exteriority" seems to possess an internal dialectic in Dussel's usage. On the one hand the poor are the 'exteriorized' (although Dussel does not use the term directly in this way[531]) in the sense of marginalized, those reduced to the status of non-persons. They are the product of alienation, a troublesome by-product of the system, but for which there is no place within the totality of the system.

On the other hand the "poor are the others stripped of their exteriority, of their dignity, of their rights, of their freedom, and transformed into instruments for the ends of the dominator..."[532] In that sense their alienation and dehumanization result from the failure to respect their exteriority, their otherness as otherness, their humanity and holiness.

Dussel appeals to Levinas' (phenomenological) understanding of the transcendental other, but wants to apply the same to political economy. The "other", the "poor person" confronting the system by demanding justice, is to be understood as "the metaphysical *reality* beyond the ontological *being* of the system as a totality."[533] In other words, it is the cry of the poor that must be the starting point, not the existing system as system. The demand is justice, not the justification of powers that be.

The poor are, furthermore, not only the manifestation of the sin of the system and as such the revelation of injustice. They are also the location (and occasion) of the epiphany of God.

> In the system the only possible locus of God's epiphany is those who are non-system, what is other than the system, the poor. Jesus' identification with the poor (Matthew 25) is not a metaphor; it is a logic. God, the other absolute [or: the Absolute Other], is revealed in the flesh (the system) by what is other than the system, the poor.[534]

In this view there is in the exteriority of the poor and the priority of God a coincidence of otherness which occasions an "internal transcendence".[535] The theological recognition of the otherness of God and the christological understanding of Jesus' identification with the poor are brought to bear both on the significance of the poor in the divine economy and on corresponding human strategies of liberation.

*To liberate the poor*

The presence of the poor is a constant in human history. "Never will there cease to be poor upon the earth; wherefore I command you: Open your hand to your brother [sister] the poor one, the needy of the land." (Deuteronium 15:11) Every system, every totality, produces its poor. Every freedom, every revolution, creates new poor. Every morality, i.e. every prevailing social order as a system of practices, as a totality, proves unable or unwilling, to allow for the other as other.[536] Every 'universality' turns out to be a particularity in disguise.

> But in every human situation there are the poor, the oppressed, who constitute the correlative of sin and the domination of sin. These here-and-now poor are concrete persons, objectively determinable in real worlds, that of Aztecs, Incas, Chinese, Bantus, capitalists, socialists. There can be no innocent "mistaken identity". Everyone knows, in each concrete situation, who are poor and oppressed, who have fewer opportunities, goods, values, rights, and so on. Hence the principle, "Liberate the poor" is absolute (not relative), and nevertheless concrete (not universal - with a "universality" that in reality is only particularity with false claims to universality).[537]

Thus the priority of the poor in their exteriority and the constant presence of the poor in human history result together in an ethical absolute: the liberation of the poor. Changing contexts and historical contingencies will ever require renewed analysis and contemporaneous responses. This lends prophetic realism and eschatological reserve to all projects and strategies of liberation.[538] Still the ethical critique will be constant in its rationale and structure, in its attention to the truly poor in a particular moral or practical system. It is from them that ethics will derive its criteria for the judgement of contemporary social situations and their institutions.[539]

It becomes evident that Dussel maintains a critical concept of the poor. Although he does not elaborate it in those terms, the effect seems to be not only to criticize and attack the prevailing (capitalist) ideology in Latin America, but also to warn against absolutizing any new ideologies of liberation or whatever. A simple Marxist scheme, for example, will not do. The poor must ever again be rediscovered.

Dussel devotes a good deal of attention to an analysis of work, production, value, accumulation, flow of capital, etcetera, as they affect the life and exploitation of the poor. Such is a necessary task in the project of liberation and not only in his context. Therefore, it need not be so much a criticism of Dussel as a further inquiry to ask about the poor who are not robbed of their products simply because they have no products, simply because they can produce no bread, either because they miss the means or because they miss the capacities. One might think of the landless, the "unemployed", the homeless, the expelled, the discriminated, and also the street children, the mentally and physically handicapped, the disabled, those with psychic and emotional limitations or disturbances or with troubled personal histories, etcetera. Dussel's understanding of the poor might allow for these categories as well. Important is the recognition that the disregard, disrespect, discrimination, and domination of the other, of the poor, is multifaceted.

Dussel's attention to the poor serves to radicalize an understanding of the inclusive nature of the kingdom, or, as he prefers to say, the reign of God. Hauerwas emphasized Jesus' rejection of particular, exclusive interpretations of the kingdom. Dussel emphasizes the priority of the poor as the cutting edge and principal criterion of a Christian ethic. This is not to be understood as an abstract ethical principle, but as a recovery of community, the reaffirmation of the other as other (as exterior), the praxis of mutual love, sharing bread face-to-face.

The identification of Jesus[540] with the "least" in the parable of the last judgement (Matthew 25:31-47) plays a significant role in the priority given to the poor. That leads to two quite different considerations.

First of all it is not clear that "the least of these my brethren" refers in a literal sense to the poor generally. Of course the interpretation of this passage is not uncontested. See, e.g., the very thorough examination of the whole history of interpretation of the passage by S.W. Gray.[541] It would seem that Jesus is referring more specifically to the lost sheep of Israel. His whole life can be seen as a mission to those who were lost, ostracized, impoverished, sinful, and sick, i.e., the "exterior" of Israël, those suffering exclusion from the community of the people. The parable expresses a similar but slightly shifted concern, not in terms of an inner Jewish debate on the inclusiveness or exclusiveness of the believing community, but rather with a view to the treatment of the poor of Israel by the Gentiles ("the nations").

In light of the history of the Jews since Jesus told the parable, the interpretation that the "least" stand for all of Israel might seem a very good one. On the other hand the intention may be that when the peoples, the gentiles, are gathered at the end of time and are to be judged, the incisive criterion will not be just whether one was 'friendly' to Israel, but whether one saw and responded to those of Israel in special need or danger, the poor of Israel, the least of Jesus' ("these my") brothers and sisters, such as he had gathered around himself.

Secondly, whatever the interpretation of Matthew 25, it should be seen that the claim of Jesus' identification with the poor is not dependent on this one passage. Rather, such an identification issues from a reading of the entire gospel accounts. It is reflected in Jesus' self-understanding of his mission, as I indicated above, and is concisely expressed in the reading from the prophet Isaiah in the synagogue in Nazareth. (Luke 4:16-30.) The passage is of importance because it not only establishes the mission to the poor, but also, in the harsh words of Jesus to his townspeople, gives an indication of a healing and deliverance in which the gentiles also might share. Of course, both concerns already belonged to the tradition of Israel. In that sense the parable of the last judgement, as parable, might also serve to enliven the imagination and enlighten ethical praxis regarding whichever poor wherever. Important in this respect is Dussel's insistence that Jesus' identification with the poor is not a metaphor but a logic.

The question that arises with regard to the interpretation of Matthew 25 is the relation of the "priority of the poor" to the "priority of Israel" in the interpretation of the biblical message. The calling of Israel and the concern for the poor are arguably both part of the strategy of the God of Israel. One might even note that both coincide in the poor of Israel. Jesus' mission, according to his own claim, was first to the lost and the least of Israel but, in that regard, to Israel and for the sake of Israel. At the same time the gospels narrate how the encounters, confrontations and conflicts resulting from his mission carried hem beyond the bounds of Israel.

The question becomes further what the "priorities" of Israel and the poor mean for the community of the followers of Jesus. The question becomes acute in light of the claim at times made by the church to supersede Israel. The question is further complicated by liberation theology's challenge to the church in terms of God's preferential option for the poor. An ecclesial ethic like that of Dussel needs to clarify these questions in an ecclesiological interpretation.

What Dussel does do is to carry the understanding of the poor even further by asserting that the poor are concrete persons and peoples and at the same time represent a transcendental, metaphysical category, a locus for the epiphany of God. This is ethics as fundamental theology. Dussel refers to Zubiri and Levinas in asserting that reality, in this case the impoverished other, transcends being, in this case the prevailing system.[542] This philosophical claim is tied into biblical understandings, into the otherness of God, into christology and also into a theology of creation. "The whole idea of creation indicates precisely that before the self there is an Other."[543]

*A utopian perspective*

The command to liberate the poor, as Dussel emphasizes, is absolute (valid everywhere and always) and nevertheless concrete (related to specific poor)[544]. At the same time it is ever again related to those who are exterior, to those outside in ever changing historical constellations. This lends to the entire project of liberating the poor a utopian character. For it is the attempt to continually "see everything 'from outside' - outside the obvious, the taken-for-granted, the traditional."[545]

Dussel is well aware of the eccentricity, both in a literal and figurative sense, of this position, but that is exactly his point. Using the Exodus motif he explains:

> The poor set out on their journey. They pass beyond Egypt's frontier, they transcend the horizon of the system, they cross the barrier of death. Now there is nothing to follow, no one to heed, but the Lord. They have now embarked on the nothing-of-the-system, the non-being of the prevailing morality. They are on the road to the "wilderness" (Heb., "bamidbar", "in the wildernis", is a theological category). The "wilderness" (Matthew 3:3; 4:1) is exteriority, the expanse over which domination no longer has sovereignty.
>
> Praxis as an action and a relationship of the members of the community, of a people that has transcended the morality of sin...is utopian, meaningless, absurd, mad, subversive, destructive, dangerous for the system left behind, left in the past.[546]

The reign of God, the gospel, represents a Christian utopia. Poverty and exteriority represent an openness to the future, to transcendence.[547] The command to liberate the poor as well as the journey of the poor themselves derive vitality and viability from that perspective. Dussel is confident that this ethical demand, despite its contingent and utopian character, can be met. His confidence is grounded in the possibility and potential of prophecy and community.

## 4.3. *The prophetic community*

According to Dussel the poor and the oppressed are "predisposed to a comradeship of solidarity with any member in pain," predisposed to community.[548] (I take this to be not so much an assertion as an observation, in keeping with the method of liberation theology as reflection on praxis.) As victims of domination they are, to be sure, subjects of poverty.

> But as the poor grow in awareness, they hear the voice of the other, the other poor among the people, and they are transformed into subjects, agents of the reign - its primary builders, its principal protagonists.
> The poor are evangelized or receive the "good news" in which they are "happy", "blessed" by God, and so on, because they are poor. Thus they come to awareness that they are the subject, the agent, of the reign of God, but only insofar as they are active participants in its construction...the passive objects of the domination of sin, the poor, have become the active subjects of the reign.[549]

In other words, the poor by receiving and responding to the good news become a people, a community. "People" is here a theological category, expressing "the presence in the world, in history, of holiness or goodness as communty, as institution."[550] It remains a "utopian community", having no place in the system. Yet:

> From outside the world, outside the flesh and the system, in virtue of its actual, concrete solidarity, it can exercise the concrete function of liberation and service to the poor, to the people, in the form of criticism of that system. It is this prophetic community that makes the "crowd" a people, and makes the "poor" a historical subject.[551]

The Christian community - and Dussel has in mind the base communities of Latin America - exercizes a "prophetico-pedagogical function of liberation".[552] There is a dialectical relation or correlation between prophet and people. This is expressed in the exodus image. "Moses became a prophet when he committed himself to the liberation of the oppressed people. The people became authentic when they left Egypt and moved into the promised land."[553] Although not directly so stated by Dussel, the community might be envisioned as the coincidence of prophet and people. The poor need to be called out of the land of domination into community. The prophet must be rooted in the concrete praxis of community. One can speak of coincidence because it becomes clear that, for Dussel, the prophet is not just a lone voice in the wilderness, and that prophecy becomes a community challenge and function. He challenges the church, as poor church and as church of the poor, to follow Jesus and to be prophetic, to serve the very poorest and to work for the liberation of the poor, specifically in Latin America.[554]

### 4.4. *Sensibility and celebration: the eucharist*

"In community the just share bread."[555] Dussel emphasizes that

> The feeding of the hungry, or for that matter the very activity of eating when performed by the hungry, is a "spiritual" activity and not merely a material one, because it is an act of service, of diakonia, of love, of risk (because it is against the system).[556]

In other words, things such as food, housing, clothing are not only objects of consumption. They become material, "sensible" signs of goodness when they are given and shared in true service, when they exemplify the praxis of liberation and justice.

Dussel emphasizes corporality, bodiliness, feeling in the flesh, sensibility.[557] He means that which touches the "skin", the sensations of pain or pleasure, of hunger or satisfaction. Sensibility refers both to one's own sensations and to one's sensitivity to the sensations of others. Poverty then denotes the negative side of that sensibility of the other: his or her need as hunger, thirst, homelessness, cold, and the like. As a result sensibility is placed in the context, not only of the physical, but of the ethical, communal, political, and economic as well.

This context is further highlighted by pointing to the alliance between domination and "ascetical morality". Where the body is demeaned for the sake of the "soul" and all things "spiritual", there is no sensibility for the (needs of) others, there is no justice for the poor, there is no restraint to torture.

> An ethics of liberation is corporeal: it is affirmation of the flesh, of sensibility; it is sensitivity to the pain of another (when that pain is the result of the sin of domination). ...Sensitivity (or com-miseration, compassion - the capacity to suffer with another) to the pain of another becomes the very criterion of praxis. The criterion is a "corporeal" one: "I was hungry..." The commitment it calls for, however, is "spiritual": it is the Spirit that moves me to the service of my neighbor.[558]

In a similar manner Dussel wants to understand the relation between bread as a product of common human labor and the bread of the eucharist. Before bread can be shared in the eucharist, the grain has to grow in the earth, the bread has to be produced, and the product must be shared freely or obtained in justice. The bread shared, as bread that can really be eaten and as shared in face-to-face community, implies a whole scale of technologies, of economic and political relations.[559] Sharing bread in the celebration of the eucharist is not just to be understood in its sacramental sense, but also in its economic significance.[560] There is not only the 'symbolic' communion of the participants, but also a literal-material solidarity. Or to put it more adequately, perhaps, the literal-material significance and the economic and sensible qualities of sharing bread are real dimensions of the symbol or sacrament of the eucharist.

Bread is life. Sharing bread is sharing life. Sharing bread is realizing justice. Dussel would also understand the bread as a sign of the life of the prophet and martyr in the struggle for justice. Making these links between the bread of labor and the bread of the eucharist, the life of the poor and the life of the martyr means for him the link between "economy and eucharist, the essence of Christianity."[561]

## 4.5. *The reign of God*

It has already been stated that the sharing of bread is the common praxis of the eucharist, of Christian community and of the reign of God. It then becomes clear how the eucharist can be understood as an eschatological sacrament of anticipation of the coming kingdom,[562] how the reign of God is realized "in a special way in the small Christian community (in the interpersonal, concrete, daily face-to-face, in need satisfied, in the justice of equals, in the liberty of persons respected in the present)."[563] In fact Dussel speaks at times of "the community of the reign" which is built by service and not by coercion and domination. "The martyria of the utopia of justice, the praxis of service, the love of justice, alive and operative in the face-to-face relationship, moves, converts, animates and vivifies."[564] In other words, the community is the praxis of seeking justice and the reign of God.

A critical question that has been directed towards liberation theology in a general sense pertains to the relation of divine initiative and human activity in the coming of the kingdom.[565] The concern would seem to be that the true kingdom might be preempted if liberation becomes a human project or accomplishment. Stated in such terms, however, the criticism appears somewhat abstract. Dussel, Boff, Míguez Bonino, and Gutiérrez, e.g., seem clear in understanding the kingdom as an initiative of God which will find in God its culmination as well. God defines and determines the kingdom. There is certainly no reduction of the kingdom to human activity or to the church (as in Christendom). That would undermine the historical responsibility and critico-liberating function of the church.[566] The reign belongs to God and at the same time God calls upon the chosen people and the followers of Jesus not to wait for the kingdom (although there are times of waiting and one must also be wary of over-activism), but to expect the reign of God, to particpate in it expectantly, to anticipate it, to live it. The emphasis in the New Testament proclamation falls on the present dynamics of the coming of God's reign. The expectation is self-involving in a praxis of love and justice.

Of course, there need always be reflection - and the theologians of liberation insist that it be committed reflection - on the concrete virtues, strategies, actions, and the like, that make up the praxis of the expectant community. It is at that concrete level that real questions can be asked. In what ways does the praxis of a particular community or a particular struggle for justice relate to the way of discipleship and the communitarian spirit?

For the rest one must probably remain somewhat agnostic about the relation between divine and human activity or between the historical and the eschatological. It is not clear how a general appeal to categories of the historical or of the eschatological can render specific criteria, as if the meaning and nature of history or of the eschatological or of the apocalyptic were in themselves fully clear. Instead close attention should be paid to the specifics of the narratives of Israel and the prophet from Nazareth. How did they form their history in the interpretation of the torah? How did their expectation inform their praxis? From there one can ask how a community of followers of Jesus can take up the expectation in a contemporary praxis.

That is the context for understanding the expectation of Dussel and others that the movement of base communities and liberation theology is something new and revolutionary, an "outstanding moment in history", a movement of a new people toward liberation, a movement "toward a new historical type of humanity".[567] It is noteworthy that one of the forescripts in Dussel's history of the church in Latin America is taken from Revelation 21:1. "Then I saw a new heaven and a new earth..." All such convictions are an expression of historical judgement. Such judgements are risky, audacious, but precisely for that reason they should be taken with seriousness. How prophetic those judgements will prove to be will remain to be seen, but they are an attempt at interfacing history and eschatology. (See II.5.3. below.) At any rate they emphasize once again that history does require judgement.

### 4.6. *Church and world*

*The exterior community*

If the import and impact of the reign of God on the life of the community is to be understood in terms of its specific praxis, how does Dussel envision the task of liberating the poor? How does the church realize its prophetic function? It could be similarly asked how Dussel describes the church in its relation to the world. The answer reveals that the relation of the church to the world is not a part of ecclesiology but that "ecclesiology is theology that deals with the political aspect of theology."[568] The church is defined specifically in terms of this task. The community is to be understood and organized around apostolate: prophecy, mission, and service to exteriority.[569] Her identity is exterior because divinity and the poor are exterior. Solidarity becomes the contemporary name of catholicity and mission.[570]

This means that Christianity is not to be understood as a private matter, neither that of a private individual nor of a private club. It is life in community understood from outside that community.[571] The complement of this position is that the church, properly understood, will never become or identify itself with a political state.[572] In fact Dussel maintains that Christianity invented the secular state. "The church needed not-to-be-the-state", i.e., needed to be distinct from the state in order to fulfill its prophetic function.[573] Although one might question the historical quality of this assertion, one can take Dussel to be suggesting that if the secular state should not exist, then the church would have to insist upon its invention by distancing itself from the injustice and idolatry of the state.

This distinction from the political state defines precisely the political function of the church as a community in the diaspora, an eschatological religious community. To be sure Dussel can suggest that Christian community is religious and pedagogical and not political in that it, like the synagogue, refrains from the assumption or exercise of power.[574] At another level, however, this is precisely its political significance, the position from which the community can exercise its prophetic, political function. That function is to invade the world from outside, to destructuralize the totality of sin and domination, to provoke in the name of exteriority a crisis in the midst of totality. In order to do so it must preserve its own exteriority and non-conformity, which is its holiness. And exteriority means poverty. "Only when the church identifies itself with the poor and the oppressed can it accomplish its prophetic function."[575]

To be sure the church in the concrete is also in the world and assumes the errors of the world. Dussel insists that no ecclesiology can overlook the fact that both subjugators and subjugated are to be found in the institutional church, but he maintains that "to accept the church as it is is to betray the church in its very essence."[576]

*Subversion*

Dussel is convinced that the effect of the church's mission is subversion. He prefers the word "subversion" to "revolution", because what is involved is not a turning back (*revolvere*) but a putting on top that which was hidden below (*subvertere*).[577] By way of contrast one should note his criticism of postwar moral theologies of the West (beginning with Tillich, Niebuhr and Barth) as being merely "reformist", failing to criticize the system as a totality. A single sentence is devoted to Hauerwas.

> Hence neither does the theological attempt of a Stanley Hauerwas manage to so much as surmise the remote legitimacy of criticizing the capitalistic system, being enveloped by it and presupposing it as a totality.[578]

This indictment is made despite Hauerwas' fundamental critique of liberalism, that modern ally of capitalism. But as Dussel does not further specify his understanding of Hauerwas one need not speculate on the matter. The point is clear and that is the rejection of a reformist ethical critique.

In opposition to the reformist mold Dussel advocates a fundamental critique. "Liberation ethics arises as a theory preceded by and demanded by a praxis opposed to the system as a totality." In the context of the world-wide, structural crisis of capitalism "the first task is to penetrate and overthrow the basis of the system and replace it with another basis, one beyond, transcending the present system."[579] This is the consequence of appropriating the point of view of the poor.[580] From the vantage point of absolute poverty and oppression the changes that are needed are not reformist but fundamental, for the system must be challenged as a whole. Again it should be emphasized that this entails not merely a negation of the system, i.e. it is not simply a negative dialectic. Rather it is a prior affirmation of the other, the exterior, which is the origin of any negation.

*Violence*

The necessity of revolutionary changes or, in Dussel's terminology, fundamental subversion confronts us with the question of the means of subversion.

> The cultural and theological awakening of Latin America as oppressed and dependent, forces us to rethink our situation in the light of faith as a means of escaping the apparent dead-end with its perpetual underdevelopment. But it brings the Christian face to face with the possibility of having to choose the way of revolution as an expedient for liberation and as a means of transforming the oppressed into free persons and at the same time liberating the oppressor who alienated himself by regarding the oppressed as nothing more than "things".[581]

The question of revolution is often understood in terms of the question of violence in the form of armed insurrection. It is an incisive contribution of Dussel that he differentiates between forms of violence (and non-violence), that he recognizes how the ways of the political hero and the prophetic community might diverge, and that he still insists that revolution should not lead to new domination but to the liberation of the oppressor as well as the oppressed.

In his history of the church in Latin America Dussel responds to those who defend non-violence.[582] He states that he "personally" does "not believe that nonviolence is a viable option for Latin Americans who want to effect change." Nor does he consider violence as such to be condemned by either Old or New Testament. Unjust violence is condemned, but violence as passion he considers to be a meditative attitude that is justified by its purpose. "The New Testament does not condemn violence, but rather proposes 'prophetic violence' as the supreme way of being a person." This is the violence of the kingdom of heaven (Matthew 11:12), the subversion of the beatitudes. The prophet pledges his life for the sake of unmasking injustice, but without the use of arms, without killing, although risking being killed. "Jesus had no desire to enter into the dialectic of mutual annihilation."

Dussel distinguishes between the violence of the oppressors and the violence that challenges the oppression at the risk of own well being. Dussel notes that "Some are desperate or ideologically convinced that there is no other way but to take up arms (subversive armed violence)." There is also a contextual consideration in the recognition that there are instances of tyranny and injustice that leave no choice. Nevertheless such violence is equivocal, and there exists an unequivocal sign.

> In response to the oppressive violence of the bourgeois-militarists, neocolonial state - the worst kind of violence - there exists the prophetic subversive violence, which utilizes neither offensive nor defensive arms. It is the violence of the "Word of God" that is directed to those who hurl insults at the Cross, and that raises oppressed people to an awareness of their value and initiates the process of liberation.

The method is that of the "pedagogy of the oppressed" (Freire). It does not prepare one for new domination following the elimination of the oppressor as in the use of subversive armed violence, but it prepares one for liberation wherein the dominator will be humanized in the liberation of the dominated.

Dussel distinguishes this prophetic violence not only from armed violence but also from the conditions of non-violence. Subversive prophetic violence is violent in that it confronts, shocks, and harasses those who live as part of the oppressive structures. The intent is to humanize the oppressor by denouncing his "good conscience". The evil of the structures must be revealed and the structures destroyed.

> Moreover, this violence is subversive because it puts down the universally held values such as money, prestige, and "having more," and exalts the basic values of equality among people, justice, and liberty for all. But the means advocated are not guns, grenades, and bombs, but rather the pen and the committed life.

This prophetic violence shares with armed subversion the risk of death. But there is a difference.

> The death of the prophet is martyrdom -unequivocal "testimony" that liberates the oppressor, the police, or the army that assasinates him. The

> death of the hero for a cause, even a just cause, is not the death of a saint. Between the hero and the saint lies the distance of the equivocal sign of the struggle that attempts to annihilate the dominator and the unequivocal sign of the struggle to liberate the dominator and the dominated in a historical process which in the last analysis is eschatological because no stage of history is absolute, ultimate or the Kingdom of God on earth.

The issue of violence proves again to be crucial to the understanding of the identity and task of the community. Two emphases of Dussel are to be noted. First of all, the question of violence is radicalized by the insistence on the necessity of fundamental political, social, and economic changes. The primary issue is subversion of totality. The nature of that struggle, and it is a struggle of life and death, cannot be other than compounded by force, passion, violence. Secondly, Dussel carefully seeks to define a form of subversive violence that is characterized by inclusiveness. The oppressor must be humanized, not eliminated. Dussel is correct in understanding this as being a forceful endeavor, destructive of the values and structures that the oppressor has created. At the same time Dussel is himself unequivocal in his respect for otherness, i.e. the assertion of the humanity of the dominator, however great his sinfulness.

*After the revolution*

It is not necessary in this context to dwell long on the matter, but it can be noted how the struggle for liberation and subversion leads to the question of the just society. The bread of the eucharist implies the matter of technologies and structures for the just production and distribution of bread. Dussel calls this a theology of the state. One might label it a theology of the political in a more general sense.[583] At any rate there is the role of the hero who not only organizes the oppressed for the struggle against domination, but who also "turns his or her life toward the construction of a new homeland, a new historico-political order."[584]

It is not surprising that Dussel has in mind a form of socialism. That he approaches the topic critically will hardly need mentioning. The issue is worth mentioning because the choice for a democratic form of socialism bears affinity to the understanding of the nature of Christian community. A single quote will suffice.

> In the society of real socialism, then, the individual will require the organization of the community-as-subjectivity, the utopian horizon of a community constituted in the exercise of democratic freedom, full participation in or conscious personal management of the productive process, control in planning - in the total responsibility of fulfilled members of a human organic community, and a human community that means to move toward the future, not to return to the past.[585]

What these practical considerations of Dussel make clear is that a praxis and theology of liberation is not simply a theology of hope, but is concerned with concrete strategies and movements of struggle and liberation. One might ask Dussel to display those strategies more specifically and argue his choice for socialism more explicitly. That would add force to his theological project.

### 4.7. *Ethics and the theology of liberation*

"Liberation theology's fundamental theology is community ethics." The complement to this is the recognition "that theology is ecclesial, by its origin and by its finality - if by church we understand the people of God in its totality..."[586] This is a consequence of the fundamental method of liberation theology which is reflection on praxis. The antecedent of this theology is the real praxis of a community, of a people, specifically of the poor.

"Praxis" seems to have primarily three references. It can refer to the 'praxis' of the poor in the sense of their oppression and destitution.[587] This praxis cannot provide the focus of liberation, but it constitutes the crisis which forms the actual starting point of liberation theology: the real life vantage point of the poor.

> To situate the poor - to describe their origin and the concrete modes of their appearance in our age - is the radical sine qua non for the initiation of a theological (theoretical), critical, prophetic discourse on liberation. This then is fundamental theology, for it is the premise, the a priori, the prime conditio sine qua non, of all the rest of theology.[588]

An ethics of liberation starts from the affirmation of the real, existing, historical other, and not only from a phenomenological approach, as must be remembered, but from the standpoint of political economics.[589]

There is a complement to this that Dussel describes in contrast to what he understands to be the dominant question of European and North American theologies: "Is it possible to believe?" The prior inquiry of liberation theology on the other hand relates to the situation and subjectivity of the theologian or believer: What is the praxis behind the question? Whence, i.e., out of which historical social situation, do I engage in theology? That is "the first chapter of all theology."[590]

In the second place, praxis can refer to the struggle for liberation.[591] Liberation theology is committed theology, convinced that the encounter with the poor, with the other in his or her exteriority, is a transforming and self-involving experience. The reflection on the struggle is a contribution to the ongoing struggle.

Thirdly and finally, praxis refers to the life of the base communities.

> Ethics is the affirmation of life emerging from the experience of community, the experience of the relationship of respectful love among sisters and brothers.[592]
>
> Ethics requires, as antecedent condition of its possibility, the concrete, real life of the community, such as the one Jesus was in the process of founding with his apostles. It was the praxis of that community which generated the norm, "Happy are the poor!" In that community, factually and really, in actual community relationships, the poor were happy, satisfied, treated as persons. And from out of this concrete experience, ethical norms and requirements were derived.
>
> Community relationships of justice, real ethical relationships (...bodily relationships) are the essence and foundation of ethics, the real starting point of the ethico-prophetic critique. The critique as such may emerge on an ideological level. But it originates on an infrastructural, practical level: that of community relationships themselves.[593]

In a way this description is reminiscent of assertions by Hauerwas that ethics is a function of living communities and the narratives and traditions which form and inform them. Dussel is likewise critical of a reduction of morality to imperatives, principles, natural law conceptions, and the like as being at the least abstractions and at the worst so many attempts to elevate particular conceptions to universal status.[594] He is concerned with the virtues and practices which actually give shape to the community, although he more than Hauerwas emphasizes the material modes of the relationships in community. He is convinced, similar to Hauerwas, that: "The Bible can be interpreted only in the living tradition of the particular Christian community", but, Dussel continues: "only when it is read and contemplated from the 'place of the poor', from the 'perspective of the poor'."[595]

It is precisely this attention to the poor which is for Dussel the ethical key. Amidst the contingencies of moral communities and ethical traditions the philosophical category of exteriority and the economic destitution of the poor coincide to establish an ethical absolute. Of course, Dussel understands this ethical absolute in terms of the narrative of Israel and the prophet from Nazareth. That is the common ground on which he can confront Hauerwas. However, it seems that, whereas by Hauerwas the weight of argument falls primarily upon tradition (narrative) and the community which it forms, Dussel emphasizes the coincidence of the narrative with the philosophical-economic understanding of exteriority.

The same might be expressed in recognizing, as above, that for Dussel praxis is not simply the praxis of the community of Christ. For that reason, although Dussel emphasizes the intentional, practical character of community life just as Hauerwas does, his understanding of the Christian community rings more inclusive, that is, more 'worldly' and less 'sectarian' than that of Hauerwas.

That leads to a further comment. The term *orthopraxis* (or *orthopraxy*) is a prior and more comprehensive term than *orthodoxy*. Orthopraxy includes and is the very context of any orthodoxy. It renders orthodoxy any meaning that it might have. Yet even when orthopraxy is understood to reflect the abiding responsibility for the poor,[596] it would seem to share with orthodoxy a normative, conformative approach. Somewhat contrary to this is the entire method of praxis, reflection on praxis, and renewal of praxis as a radically critical approach. The emphasis would then not fall on orthopraxis, but on a (dynamic) liberative praxis on the basis of a critical, narrative approach.

This is similarly the implication of the image of journey which one also finds in Dussel's writings. The exodus motif provides the image of the poor setting out on their journey.[597] Dussel sees the image as being fundamental to the very concept and reality of liberation. There is a departure from somewhere (Egypt, i.e. domination), to somewhere (the promised land, i.e. just relations, or, eschatologically, the reign of God) and the journey itself (the searches and struggles of the wilderness).[598] This description lends a degree of concreteness to the journey metaphor. Dussel can state that "The whole of community ethics is a 'road under construction'".[599] Yet he is convinced that "there are sufficient pilgrims that the way is being charted."[600]

> "Traveler, there is no road, therefore make a road and walk," (Antonio Machado) and little by little you will be able to follow the road that has been made.[601]

## *Considerations*

1. The basic affirmation of Christian life is the celebration of being together in the praxis of community. The central expression of Christian community and of the reign of God is the praxis of sharing bread. The bread of the eucharist must be the bread of (the struggle for) justice.
2. The inclusiveness of the kingdom finds its cutting edge in the strategic priority that God assigns to Israel and the poor. Or put another way, it is the biblical attention to the covenant and the poor that guides the ethical praxis of the Christian community amidst the contingencies of moral traditions and perspectives.
3. There is a coincidence of otherness in the priority of God and the exteriority of the poor which points to an "internal transcendence."
4. The presence of the poor as a constant of history evokes the continual task of discerning their presence and struggling for their liberation. Christian community authenticates itself where the voice of the prophet and the struggle of the people coincide.

5. "Ecclesiology is theology that deals with the political aspects of theology." The identity of the church is exterior because divinity and the poor are exterior. Solidarity becomes the contemporary name of catholicity and mission.
6. Christian community is called neither to coopt or coerce the coming of the reign of God, but to expect and anticipate it, to participate in its dynamics. The distinction between the historical and eschatological dimensions of the coming of God's reign can serve to draw attention to their interfacing in the narratives of Israel and the prophet from Nazareth.
7. More central to the political task of the church than either reform or revolution is subversion as a fundamental challenge to the totality of the existing order from the perspective of the poor (the exterior).
8. The variety of violence requires discriminate evaluation. A critical category of evaluation is inclusiveness. The concept of "prophetic violence" points to the necessity of struggle that might be veiled by appeals to non-violence. The prophetic community while seeking to practice inclusive, unarmed subversion, needs at the same time to be attentive to the role of the political hero.

## III.5.

## LEONARDO BOFF
## *ECCLESIOGENESIS*

### 5.1. *Church and community*

One of the strengths of Latin American liberation theology, of its ecclesiology and communitarian ethics, is its concrete ecclesial reference to base Christian communities. In fact, the theological method of liberation theology as a reflection on praxis presupposes the prior existence of those concrete communities. Not only is there a reference to real existing communities, there is also a (critical) reflection on their common life and their position within the larger body of the church(es). In order to examine that ecclesial reference more closely the contribution of Leonardo Boff on "ecclesiogenesis"[602] is enlisted. Although his frame of reference is primarily Roman Catholic, his considerations transcend those limits.

Boff is concerned with the ecclesial quality of the base communities, whether they are "church" in the full sense of the word. The suggestion he is refuting is that the base communities are somehow ecclesialy deficient, lacking universality, lacking perhaps a priest and/or a proper expression of the sacraments, lacking a regular relation with the church hierarchy, etcetera. His argument might be understood as an apologetic for the base communities, but such a label hardly does justice to the moving description he provides of the dynamics and significance of those communities.[603]

According to Boff the base communities do not confront us with simply a movement within the church (or a sort of para-church organization).

> These are church itself, among the people, in the church's foundations. The base communities are a response to the question: How may the community experience of the apostolic faith be embodied and structured in the conditions of a people who, in Brazil as throughout Latin America, are both religious and oppressed? The church communities...are genuinely church assimilating the characteristics of the people, church in which the people can express their faith in a key that belongs to their own culture, to their own values, to their yearning for a liberation that will bring participation and communion in justice.

What are the characteristics of these communities? Boff emphasizes initially the role of the laity. It is the laity of the church who most clearly represent two concerns of Boff. As laity (from the Greek *laos*, people) they are members of the people (the poor masses, the *ochlos* of the Gospels). As members of the church they participate in the sacramental character of the church, the church universal. In other words they combine both human community and faith. Indeed, these are, for Boff, the two primary elements that constitute the church: authentic community and explicit Christian consciousness.[604]

The result of this is to turn the church upside down. The emphasis falls not upon the hierarchy or the institution, but upon the life of the community. The significance of the organizational aspect is secondary as a ministry of unity, integration and coordination, of assistance and direction, similarly on all levels, from pope to (lay) monitor of a base community. In mutual apprenticeship and openness all must serve the good of the community,[605] for the communitarian spirit is taken to be the essential orientation of Christianity.

In fact, Boff's description of the base communities, which is similar to the representation of them by Dussel, is intertwined with a specific interpretation of the gospel.

> The communities are built on a more vital, lively, intimate participation in a more or less homogeneous entity, as their members seek to live the essence of the Christian message: the universal parenthood of God, communion with all human beings, the following of Jesus Christ who died and rose again, the celebration of the resurrection and the Eucharist, and the upbuilding of the kingdom of God, already under way in history as the liberation of the whole human being and all human beings.
> Christian life in the basic communities is characterized by the absence of alienating structures, by direct relationships, by reciprocity, by a deep communion, by mutual assistance, by communality of gospel ideals, by equality among members.[606]
> Christianity with its values rooted in love, forgiveness, solidarity, the renunciation of oppressive power, the acceptance of others, and so on, is essentially oriented to the creation, within societal structures, of the communitarian spirit. (...) Jesus' whole preaching may be seen as an effort to awaken the strength of those community aspects.

The project of engendering community and the project of liberation coincide here. "Church community means church presence - the living community experience of the gospel, the organism and 'organization' of salvation-liberation in the world."[607] The same can be expressed in two findings of an inter-church meeting of base communities in Brazil in 1978, commenting on the economic, political, and cultural despoiling of the poor: "(1) the main root of this oppression is the elitist, exclusive, capitalist system; and (2) people resist and are liberated to the extent that they unite and create a network of popular movements."[608]

Community forms in this project a counterpoint to both the institution of the church and to society in general. Neither the institution nor society can ever become fully communitarian. Both remain in a polar relation to community, but the communitarian has an ethical priority ("supremacy") above either the institutional or the societal. And that supremacy finds its most adequate expression in a strategy of small groups, face-to-face communities. As a leaven within the church[609] and as society's utopia[610] the base communities constitute a reinvention or rebirthing of the church (ecclesiogenesis). This phenomenon of small groups, of small communities within church society, is in itself not new. Decisive is the perspective. Boff presents not just an argument for face-to-face relations from a perspective of group dynamics. He is reflecting on a movement of intentional community among the poor themselves as a primary mode and political strategy of their liberation.

Boff argues that the local base communities are full manifestations and representations of the church catholic (universal). Catholicity is not a geographical, statistical, sociological, or even historical concept, but is a question of true identity. That identity does not consist in being a part or piece of a whole, but in an orientation towards the whole. The universality of the church as an openness to all sides is a sign of the universal element in God's salvific will. The particular church is not the whole church but represents this universality wholly in her openness and koinonia.[611] Consequently, Boff can assert that "The church sprung from the people is the same as the church sprung from the apostles."[612] For the church sprung from the people, however different in form and expression, is a full embodiment of community and faith in God's inclusive kingdom.

## 5.2. *Latency or birth*

It is clear that Boff is concerned to establish the legitimacy and catholicity of the base communities in themselves. He must do so, in light of his Roman Catholic context, as a counterpoint to the hierarchical domination. He insists that the church can "spring" from the people and is not dependent on a supposed priority of the (hierarchical) institution. Consequently this concern issues in a specific conception regarding a "latent church". In this view the church is not transplanted deductively by the institution, but implanted inductively. That is to say that the implanted church is not so much something new, but an explication, purification and prolongation of "the already existing, latent church." Before the arrival of the institutional church, the Spirit has already been moving to activate people and shape an anonymous church by grace and forgiveness. The arrival of the institution to implant the church requires that the church enter into dialogue with the culture and religions of the country in order to render explicit and conscious the presence of God's Spirit.

The basis of this conception, if it be faithful to the method of reflection on praxis, would be the observation that the people, i.e. the poor, come together of themselves, with or without the church. The essential qualities of community such as a praxis of solidarity, face-to-face relations, mutuality, respect of otherness, etcetera, are not dependent upon the explicit presence of the Christian church. More theoretically, it might be said that the concept of community is not only a theological category, but essentially an anthropological category as well. Community is a human phenomenon. The institutional church, in Boff's view, only adds explicit consciousness and direction to the implicit (immanent) work of Christ and the Spirit.

The problem with this conception is that it seems to assume a peculiar combination (or opposition) of various and distinct categories. Immanence and latency are juxtaposed to institution and hierarchy. It assumes that that which comes from outside (extra nos) comes from above, not from transcendence, but from a dominant class (e.g. of priests and bishops). Why, however, does Boff limit himself to a contrast of only two conceptualizations, having previously stated that there are as many ecclesiologies as basic ecclesial structures, each limited in itself and therefore in need of other forms of expressing the whole mystery of the church.[613]

Another conceptualization is possible that would envision an institution, not as a hierarchy, but simply as organized continuity ("network") in service of the gospel. The one who brings the gospel as Gods message of liberating community is not a representative of the hierarchy or of the institution as such, but simply an evangel of the communitarian spirit of God. He or she is not sent by superiors, but goes out from the community into the world, to the people, to the (other) poor. Whether the evangel will encounter "already existing" community and of what quality remains to be seen. Of course, he or she should be respectful of the otherness of the encountered culture or practices (whether religious or otherwise), for that is an essential quality of the communitarian spirit that he/she wishes to engender. But what therein can be affirmed and what would need be transformed (or liberated) for the sake of the gospel remains to be seen.

As an anthropological concept "community" is plural, general, multi-interpretable. As a theological concept "community" is a critical concept and cannot be presupposed or assumed. Or is "community" in the sense of Boff not to be taken as an anthropological category, but as a category of poverty? Is his intention not to speak of community in general terms, but of the community of the poor. The assumption - or is it again an observation? - might then be that since the poor are the locus of Gods epiphany, their community will be an expression of how God wills to create liberating community. In other words, are the poor the locus of God's epiphany not only in their poverty, but also in their community?

Such an approach would preserve, perhaps, a critical sense of "community". And let it be emphasized how much can be learned from the poor in terms of community spirit, concretely. However, Boff's theory seems unsatisfactory. The ultimate criteria are in the end not derived from the community as such, but from the gospel. The community of the poor is, to be sure, the locus for hearing, reading, and understanding the gospel, is itself part of the hermeneutical process, but Boff's own statement that the "latent church" need be explicated, purified and prolonged, makes of that latency such a vague concept that its critical and substantial value becomes questionable.

One may rejoice in whatever parallels, affinities, shared values, and alliances which the church might discover among the poor and popular movements. Often the church finds others who are ahead of it. All too often the church has failed to respect the reality of other communities and the values of their cultures. It would seem more proper to respect those persons and movements in their otherness and therefore also in their worldliness, rather than to annex them in terms of latency or immanence. If it is recognized that the work of the Spirit, the dimensions of the kingdom, as well as the realm of the human and the good, transcend the bound of the church, then there is no need to interpret all such dynamics ecclesiologically. It is enough to discern and ascertain the occasions for cooperation and celebration.

A people, a (secular) community of the poor legitimizes itself or not and can be understood with respect to its own self-understanding. Christian community, on the other hand, involves not just an additive (i.e. an explication of the implicitly present, the latent), but a critical, prophetic origin. Dussel does well to emphasize the prophetic aspect in the genesis of the people of God and of Christian community. The prophetic community understands itself in terms of its calling to participate in the liberation of the people, that the poor might become a people, that the utopia of community might leaven society. Evangelization is then not simply explication, but the occasion for a real birth, for new creation.[614] In other words, Boff's concepts of rebirth and ecclesiogenesis might be better expressed without the use of the categories of latency or immanence.

### 5.3. *The people of Israel*

A related matter is Boff's appeal to E. Peterson in making of the historically contingent "fact that the Jews, God's chosen people, did not believe in the Lord" a constitutive element of the church. "It is of the very concept of the church that it is essentially a church of Gentiles."[615] Boff sees the result of this as a "passage from Israel to the Gentiles", opening the way for acculturating and concretizing the message of Jesus without having to "pass by way of the pedagogy of the Old Testament."

Tied to this is a second thesis of Peterson: "The church exists only contingently upon the fact that the second coming of Christ was not imminent: in other words, that concrete eschatology was suspended and in its place the doctrine of the last end of the human being had entered the picture." In other words, a supposed turn from the eschatological to the historical perspective accompanied or even motivated the turn to the Gentiles. The expectation of the

Kingdom of God by the Jews is replaced by the historical mission of the church as a substitute for the unrealized kingdom.

It seems strange that Boff, who otherwise is insistent upon the historical (as in the question of whether Jesus willed the church) can treat the question of the Jews so schematically. There is first of all the fact that the original, apostolic Christian community was Jewish. And the normative "Christian" community in the apostolic writings consisted of the reconciliation of Jews and Gentiles. The Christian church is Jewish in origin. It consisted initially of those Jews who recognized in the life and teaching of Jesus the incisive expectation of the kingdom. It was joined by those Gentiles who recognized in the teaching of the apostolic (Jewish) community on Jesus as the annointed of the true God an unheard-of promise. It was decided that no Gentile need first become a Jew to share in the expectation of the coming kingdom. It was not decided that the community of the followers of Jesus preempted the place of Israel as the people of the promise. The disbelief of the majority of the Jews in the messianic quality of Jesus does not wrest them of their chosenness. The otherness of Israel as the people of the abiding covenant cannot be superseded by the church.

Secondly, the eschatological quality of Jesus' message and ethic was not a contingent perspective that can be replaced by a historical perspective. Jesus' message was fundamentally eschatology, the immanent expectation of the kingdom as an interpretation of the consequence of the history of Israel and of the character of God. That the expectation was and is both eschatological and historical is a problem for the modern mind-set and for our theological categories. In the gospel accounts, however, it is the very dynamic of the coming of the kingdom. There the issue is not "already" or "not yet", but the very coming, inbreaking of God's reign into the human realm. It is questionable whether an interpretation of the nearness of the kingdom solely in terms of temporality is adequate. The primary intention of the proclamation of the nearness of the kingdom was to emphasize the dynamics of God's reign as evidenced in the proclamation of good news to the poor and the restoration of the lost and the least to the community of the holy. The proclamation of the kingdom was both promise and calling, an interfacing of eschatology and history.

Do these critical comments on Boff's interpretation of the calling and eschatology of Israel as well as on his conceptions of latency detract from his contribution to an understanding of the catholic quality of local communities? That need not be the case. For the catholic quality resided not in latency or historical conceptions as such but in Boff's explication of the communitarian spirit in its relation to the liberation of the poor. That is the thrust of his plea for a rebirth of the church in a project that is both ethical and ecclesial.

*Considerations*

1. Stressing the role of the laity draws attention to the identity of the church in terms of authentic community and explicit Christian consciouness. Community, as the expression of the catholic nature of the church, has priority above the demands of institution and society.
2. Ecclesiogenesis is a way of drawing attention to the coincidence of engendering Christian community and the praxis of liberation. A common mode of both projects is the creation of networks of solidarity.
3. Christian community is qualified community, qualified by the biblical narrative and by the presence of the poor. While claiming and witnessing to its own identity and catholicity, Christian community needs to respect the otherness and integrity of other communities.
4. The problem of the immanence of the kingdom is not adequately stated solely in terms of temporality. The primary intention of the proclamation of the nearness of the kingdom was to emphasize the dynamics of God's reign as evidenced in the proclamation of good news to the poor and the restoration of the lost and the least to the community of the holy. This points to an intimate relation between the persistence of the people of the promise and the promise of the kingdom.

## III.6.

## ELISABETH SCHÜSSLER FIORENZA RECONSTRUCTING THE *EKKLESIA* OF WOMEN

> My point is not only that the "discipleship of equals" preceded the "patriarchalization" of the church but also that it was repressed rather than replaced. Although the discipleship community of equals or women-church was submerged and often oppressed by ecclesiastical patriarchy, it has never ceased to exist. Rather than conceptualizing church history as a history of decline (or progress, depending on the point of view), I conceptualize it as a history of struggle. Insofar as the Bible is the model for both women-church *and* patriarchal church, it is also the paradigm of this struggle.[616]

What is to be done with the fact that the Bible has served both to inspire women in their struggles for liberation and to suppress women in the interests of patriarchy? What is to be made of the fact that the Bible not only includes admonitions that women be silenced but that women have indeed been effectively silenced and forgotten in any number of ways in both the biblical writings and church tradition? The task that Elisabeth Schüssler Fiorenza undertakes is one of creative imagination in the reconstruction of Christian beginnings, in the remembrance of forgotten foresisters and in the reappropriation of the heritage of women-church.

As with Dussel here again a fundamental affirmation appears. It is the affirmation of the reality of women and women-church despite their disregard and repression by patriarchy. What does Schüssler Fiorenza mean by the term patriarchy?

> I do not use the concept in a loose sense of 'all men dominating all women equally,' but in the classical Aristotelean sense. Patriarchy as a male pyramid of graded subordinations and exploitations specifies women's oppression in terms of the class, race, country, or religion of the men to whom we "belong." This definition of patriarchy enables us to use it as a basic heuristic concept for feminist analysis, one that allows us to conceptualize not only sexism but also racism, property-class relationships, and all other forms of exploitation or dehumanization as basic structures of women's oppression.[617]

The focus is on the oppression of women, but the range of the definition suggests that it might prove illuminating for the position of any who are poor and powerless under patriarchy. Conversely the expression women-church is not used in an exclusive sense "but as a political-oppositional term to patriarchy."[618] Women-church proves to be a strategic, provocative term, yet essentially affirmative and inclusive by virtue of its rejection of the exclusiveness and repression of patriarchy. The strategy, however, requires that first the silence surrounding women be broken, that the sufferings and power of women be illuminated.

## 6.1. *Advocacy reading*

*The task of reconstruction*

Reconstructing the reality of women in the early church must deal with the fact that the biblical texts are androcentric, that is, written by males or at least from a male perspective. The real information on women is sparse, often prescriptive rather than descriptive, often distorted by biased translations or traditions of interpretations. And yet despite themselves the androcentric texts provide useful hints on the reality of women in the early church.

Schüssler Fiorenza employs all the tools of historical-critical scholarship on the Bible in an imaginative reconstruction of the historical reality of early Christian communities.[619] The task of reconstruction involves not only correcting misleading translations and misguided interpretations, but also reading the silences, gleaning the texts of incidental information. It is concerned not only with proof texts on women, but with the texts in their entirety. It seeks to comprehend not only the intention and meaning of a text in itself, but also the context in which and to which a text is a response. Schüssler Fiorenza's reading of the texts is from the outset a community oriented project in its recognition that the texts do not present doctrine or orthodoxy so much as represent the life and faith of living communities. It is the life and practice of early Christian communities (plural!) that Fiorenza seeks to rediscover historically.[620]

Indeed most of the texts are prescriptive, if not in form then by intent. Nevertheless they provide information for an imaginative description. For example, the injunction that women should not prophesy with uncovered heads reveals that there existed a lively praxis of prophesying by women. Paul seems not only to have been concerned to regulate the behavior of women in the churches; he also was careful to send greetings to women who were his coworkers, fellow leaders, and servants. The position of women in the gospel accounts and a comparison of their roles in relation to men, especially the male disciples, reveals their prominence as followers and as leaders in the community of disciples and in the early church.

Although it is not feasible here to reproduce Schüssler Fiorenza's careful exegetical work in detail, it should be pointed out that she ascribes priority to the descriptive task. Her first concern is with historical reconstruction, not with theological justification.[621] She is, for example in the gospel accounts, more interested in the narrative that includes women than with the stress on word or proclamation typical of form criticism. The emphasis falls on story and praxis, rather than text and ideology.[622] The priority ascribed to description above prescription is a matter of method, but at the same time the means serves a specific end, namely, that of making women visible. By the force of its cumulative argument the descriptive approach lends, despite any disagreement on detail which there might be, substantial support to the project of reconstruction and the resulting conclusion.

> Women had the power and authority of the gospel. They were central and leading individuals in the early Christian movement. Women as church have a continuous history and tradition that can claim Jesus and the praxis of the earliest church as its biblical root model or prototype, one that is open to feminist transformation.[623]

The basic historical thesis is that the equality and leadership of women in the early church precedes the canonical texts.[624] The ideological (androcentric, patriarchal) prescription in the texts does not always correspond with what was the actual social reality.[625] Needed, therefore, is not only an understanding of the historical-theological meaning of the texts, but also a critical theological evaluation of their functions in the history of the church as well as in the life of the contemporary church.[626]

*A critical evaluative feminist hermeneutic*

The task of feminist reconstruction requires a specific feminist hermeneutic. As noted above such a feminist hermeneutic makes use of the critical analytical methods of historical biblical scholarship, but it combines their use with the theological goals of liberation theologies.[627] It shares with liberation theologies an advocacy stance, contrary to supposedly value-neutral scientific investigation.

> Similarly liberation theologies insist that revelation and biblical authority are found in the lives of the poor and oppressed whose cause God, as their advocate and liberator, has adopted. A feminist critical hermeneutics of liberation shares the "advocacy stance" of liberation theologies but, at the same time, it elaborates not only women's oppression but also women's power as the locus of revelation. As the root model of Christian life and community the Bible reflects women's strength as well as their victimization.[628]

The recognition that the Bible is for women both a source of power and a source of oppression requires defining a feminist hermeneutic critically over against a number of fronts. There can be no simple appeal to the Bible, nor to the ecclesial or academic traditions of interpretation, and not even to prophetic canons of liberation hermeneutics. But contrary to post-biblical feminist rejection of the Bible as thoroughly and hopelessly androcentric, Schüssler Fiorenza takes up the task of critical feminist evaluation. She insists on the one hand that the forgotten past of women's sufferings and struggles deserves to be remembered and reclaimed. She is convinced on the other hand that the use of the Bible in past, present, and foreseeable future to suppress women does not allow women of biblical religion to abandon that book, but rather requires their critical appropriation of it. These ethical and political considerations are joined to ecclesiological and religious concerns.

> In the last analysis, such a project is not just geared toward the liberation of women but also toward the emancipation of the Christian community from patriarchal structures and androcentric mind-sets so that the gospel can become again a "power for the salvation" of women as well as men.

How then is a feminist hermeneutic to be defined? While it shares critical tools of biblical scholarship, it does not share the value-neutral ideals of a great deal of the academic establishment. Rather than asserting how feminist criticism might contribute to more value-neutrality, Schüssler Fiorenza argues that "Intellectual neutrality is not possible in a historical world of exploitation and oppression."[629] By thus emphasizing the contextualization of any scholarship, she calls all biblical interpretation, whether academic or ecclesial, conservative or liberative, to specify its political options and intellectual presuppositions. In fact a feminist evaluation must direct its hermeneutics of suspicion towards what it perceives as the androcentric presuppositions and models of a great deal of scholarship. The intention is to transform androcentric scholarship and knowledge into truly human and inclusive scholarship and knowledge.[630]

Schüssler Fiorenza is likewise critical of doctrinal and canonical approaches to scripture. Her fundamental point, in some ways similar to that of Hauerwas, is that the Bible has no authority independent of the community to which it belongs. This would seem to be the hermeneutic complement to the recognition that the Bible was not written to present doctrine but to represent the life and faith of Christian communities. On the one hand it is mistaken to reduce the Bible to a canonical prooftext for orthodoxy or historical factuality. On the other hand it is mistaken to try to distinguish between essence and accident of the texts or to select a canon in the canon to support neo-orthodoxy or prophetic liberation.

Schüssler Fiorenza includes in her criticism feminist colleagues such as R. Radford Ruether, who has proposed a method of correlation to prophetic critique, and L. Russel, who has sought to distinguish between constant and changing traditions with reference to the eschatological future of God's liberation.

Such feminist reductionist approaches, as Schüssler Fiorenza understands them, fail to critically evaluate the androcentric character of the biblical traditions, including that of the prophets, as a source not only of power but also of oppression of women. That is the point which apologetics for biblical authority, however liberative in intention, likewise overlook. Furthermore all of these doctrinal and canonical, subcanonical and correlative approaches adhere, according to Schüssler Fiorenza, to an "archetypal biblical paradigm that establishes universal principles and normative patterns."[631] Instead she proposes an understanding of the Bible as prototype.

> Both archetype and prototype denote original models. However, an archetype is an ideal form that establishes an unchanging timeless pattern... A prototype is critically open to the possibility of its own transformation. ... A hermeneutical understanding of Scripture as prototype not only has room for but requires the transformation of its own models of Christian faith and community.
>
> Such an understanding of Scripture not as mythic archetype but as historical prototype provides the Christian community with a sense of its ongoing history as well as of its theological identity. ...it is able to acknowledge positively the dynamic process of biblical adaptation, challenge, or renewal of social-ecclesial and conceptual structures under the changing conditions of the church's social-historical situations.
>
> Such a theological understanding of the Bible as prototype cannot identify biblical revelation with the androcentric text, but maintains that such revelation is found in the life and ministry of Jesus as well as in the discipleship community of equals called forth by him. ... Insofar as the model proposed here locates revelation not in texts but in Christian experience and community, it can point to the actual practice of the churches which define explicitly or implicitly biblical authority and the canon of revelation with reference to their own acknowledged or unacknowledged centers of ecclesial power. While the Roman Catholic Church has made explicit such a hermeneutical procedure, other Christian churches implicitly and practically follow it.

This last statement suggests that Schüssler Fiorenza - if she is correct - may not so much be *proposing* a specific hermeneutical theory as *exposing* the way hermeneutics generally works. She proposes a paradigm shift, but the shift may be more in the way of looking at things than in the way of doing things, that is, more in the way of looking at what is in fact being done. Does not every interpretating community factually and effectively canonize its own perspectives and praxis? An understanding of the Bible as prototype and root model does provide a different paradigm for describing hermeneutics. Nevertheless, it can be asked if the actual functioning of Schüssler Fiorenza's critical evaluation of biblical writings significantly differs in a formal sense from that of other uses and/or appeals to scripture. Does she not by sifting and sorting the texts also arrive at a sort of canon within the canon, if not in a primary, then in a secondary sense?[632]

Answering these issues would require a concrete and detailed account of the ways in which biblical texts actually do function in the life and praxis of specific communities. In the meantime any evaluation of Schüssler Fiorenza's evaluative hermeneutic must explicate its own evaluative context. She clearly displays her own shift in paradigm by asserting that the canon or norm for evaluating (androcentric) biblical traditions and their subsequent interpretations, is not to be derived from the Bible itself, but to be formulated within the struggle for the liberation of women and all oppressed peoples.[633] The hermeneutical center for her own feminist biblical interpretation is the *ekklesia gynaikon* or women-church, the movement of self-identified women and women-identified men in biblical religion.[634] She further argues that liberation theologies should develop

> more adequate heuristic interpretive models appropriate to specific forms of oppression. In short, the biblical interpretation of liberation theologians must become more concrete, or more "provincial", before an "interstructuring" of different interpretive models and a more universal formulation of the task of a critical theology of liberation can be attempted.[635]

Thus for Schüssler Fiorenza there may be any number of hermeneutical and canonical issues that still must be dealt with. But before they can be adequately treated and tied together, any number of unabashedly particular modes and models must be explored. Any hermeneutic model with comprehensive or catholic pretentions must begin by appreciating and incorporating those particular endeavors and their contributions to a critical and inclusive understanding of scriptures. At the same time those particular interpretive schemes retain their priority. No universal revelatory canon can be abstracted. Any revelatory canon must remain "specific since it is extrapolated from a particular experience of oppression and liberation."[636]

One might also say that it is extrapolated from the life and praxis of a particular community. It is at this point, however, that Schüssler Fiorenza is critical of Hauerwas. The appeal to a community of remembrance and forgiveness is not enough. The community must be one of repentance and reform as well, will it be liberated from its own oppressive past and present practices and sustain not just a memory, but a dangerous, subversive memory and a critical liberative praxis and hermeneutic. Provocatively Schüssler Fiorenza states:

> Instead of asking whether an approach is appropriate to the Scriptures and adequate to the human condition, one needs to test whether a theological model of bibilical interpretation is *adequate* to the historical-literary methods of contemporary interpretation and *appropriate* to the struggle of the oppressed for liberation.[637]

While this statement follows from Schüssler Fiorenza's basic position and while its critical content is significant, does it not in fact overstate the case? The problematic character of preconceived notions of biblical authority and of reductionist views of a canon within a canon is clear. Yet any approach to the biblical texts, any method of interpretation, must be appropriate to the texts that it investigates. One could even argue that Schüssler Fiorenza does try to meet that criterium. For example, she points out that "the canon includes various, often contradictory theological responses to historical situations of the early church."[638] Subsequently she attempts to do justice to that recognition by means of a critical evaluation appropriate to the variety.

The assertion is that the Bible is no longer to be seen as simply an authoritative source, but as a resource for women's struggle for liberation.[639] Related to this is the difficulty in postulating a male Jesus as model or canonical norm for women.[640] The question arises what it then means to reclaim the narrative of Jesus and the history of the early church for women? What is entailed in attributing revelatory value to certain texts that transcend their patriarchal frameworks? Or to put it more directly: In what sense do the texts carry their own weight and is revelation allowed to speak up for itself?

If the question is put in that way, then the insistence of Schüssler Fiorenza upon the adequacy of method and the appropriateness to liberation would seem to be precisely her means of opening the texts so that the reality of revelation might speak for itself. The intention of her interpretation process in employing a particular method and perspective is not to curtail the biblical writings, but to reveal their dynamics and power. Her interpretive scheme begins where it does in the struggles of women in order to move to the story of God which turns out to have included women. It is that story, which does not possess abstract authority, but which does in the hermeneutics of Schüssler Fiorenza carry its own weight and comes to speak for itself.

The point is that revelation and authority do not exist abstractly in the texts of themselves but that revelation can be uncovered in a struggle with the texts. Hermeneutics cannot be reduced to one-sidedness. It is a process involving both the perspective of the interpreter and the attempt to let the story speak for itself. But if the story is to speak for itself, the texts must be ever again reread and the story (reconstructed and) retold.

More could be said on the hermeneutical method of Schüssler Fiorenza, on suspicion and remembrance, on proclamation and actualization, but hopefully enough has been said here to clarify her basic position. She points out that any communitarian ethic must be conscious of its hermeneutic context. And she raises fundamental questions about how a community in fact reads the scriptures. But a presentation and evaluation of Schüssler Fiorenza's contribution should not dwell solely on questions of method and theory, but also examine the fruits of her textual analysis and historical reconstruction. What is it that needs to be reconstructed in order to be reappropriated as a remembered past, a dangerous and subversive memory?[641]

## 6.2. *The praxis of Jesus*

*The inclusive wholeness of the basileia of Sophia-God*

The first thing that might be noted in Schüssler Fiorenza's picturing of Jesus is not so much what he said and did, but the context in which he understood himself and his ministry. Two features are of central importance: the God of graciousness and goodness perceived as divine *Sophia* (wisdom)[642] and the inclusive wholeness of the *basileia* (reign) of God.[643]

Schüssler Fiorenza suggests that Jesus probably understood himself as a prophet and child of *Sophia*. Primarily in the wisdom literature of Israel one can find a conception of Israel's God and of divine wisdom as *Sophia*, sister, wife, mother, beloved and teacher. Contrary to classical prophecy, wisdom theology reflects no fear of goddess language, but uses that language to speak of the gracious goodness of Israel's God. In the justification of wisdom (*Sophia*) by her children (Luke 7:35) and in the invitation to all who labor hard and are heavy laden to come, to rest, and take up the yoke of learning (Matthew 11:28mm), Jesus manifested himself as a child and messenger of divine *Sophia*. In a lament over Jerusalem *Sophia*-Jesus expressed the desire to gather the children of the city as a mother hen her young (Luke 13:34).

It is such a gathering that likewise characterized Jesus' vision of the *basileia*. The central image and actualization of the *basileia* in the parables and praxis of Jesus was table fellowship as a festive meal. Jesus' central concern was not for ritual purity or moral holiness which, according to Schüssler Fiorenza, were typical of other groups in Greco-Roman Palestine. The thrust of the ministry and movement of Jesus was not the holiness of temple and torah, but the wholeness of the *basileia*.

> The Jesus movement in Palestine does not totally reject the validity of Temple and Torah as symbols of Israel's election but offers an alternative interpretation of them by focusing on the people itself as the locus of God's power and presence. By stressing the present possibility for Israel's wholeness, the Jesus movement integrates prophetic-apocalyptic and wisdom theology insofar as it fuses eschatological hope with the belief that the God of Israel is the creator of all human beings, even the maimed, the

> unclean, and the sinners. Human holiness must express human wholeness, cultic practice must not be set over against humanization. Wholeness spells holiness and holiness manifests itself precisely in human wholeness.[644]

Not the holiness of the elect, but the wholeness and inclusiveness of all, of every child of Israel became the measure and mark of the *basileia*. Such was the praxis and vision of Jesus that mediated God's future into the structures and experiences of his own time and people. The power of God's *basileia* was experienced and realized in healings and parables, in table community with both the righteous and sinners, in sharing bread with the poor and celebrating the sabbath with both men and women. All of this reflected the graciousness and goodness of *Sophia*-God, a God of all-inclusive love,

> who accepts everyone and brings about justice and well-being for everyone without exception. The creator God accepts all members of Israel, and especially the impoverished, the crippled, the outcast, the sinners and prostitutes, as long as they are prepared to engage in the perspective and power of the *basileia*.[645]

*Discipleship of equals*

The reality of God-*Sophia*, reflected in the inclusiveness and wholeness of the *basileia* vision, gave rise to a gathering of followers in a "discipleship of equals." It was a movement of impoverished and disinherited, of outcast and marginal people, of despised and downtrodden, in the same praxis of inclusiveness and equality lived by Jesus-*Sophia*. The majority of Jesus' followers was drawn from the scum of Palestinian society. They shared their meager bread and practiced an equality and solidarity from below. They possessed not so much an alternative lifestyle as an alternative ethos of reborn hope and refound dignity.[646] They actually experienced the eschatological reversal of the last becoming first, of happiness for the poor.

Schüssler Fiorenza points to numerous examples of the inclusion of women. In fact women were a significant part of the movement, experiencing healing and acceptance, following and anointing Jesus, serving as examples and serving the movement. The memory of a woman who anointed Jesus is exemplary. She is remembered for her act of prophetic love. Jesus defended her against the protest of male disciples who used the poor as an argument against her. But her name has been forgotten and the poor are still with us.[647]

There is another story of a likewise nameless woman who occupies a unique place in the gospel accounts of Jesus ministry. It is the story of a gentile woman, a Syrophoenecian. (Mark 7:24-30) As Schüssler Fiorenza points out, the narrative is distinct from all other controversy dialogues in the gospels in that Jesus did not have the last word. It is, one might suggest, as though it is the woman herself who in her witted response represented divine *Sophia* as she moved Jesus to broaden his vision.

> The gracious goodness of the God of Jesus is abundant enough to satisfy not only the Jews but also the gentiles. ... The Syrophoenician respects the primacy of the "children of Israel," she nevertheless makes a theological argument against limiting the inclusive messianic table community of Jesus to Israel alone. That such a theological argument is placed in the mouth of a woman is a sign of the historical leadership women had in opening up Jesus' movement and community to "gentile sinners."[648]

This "apostolic 'foremother' of all gentile Christians" thus extended the inclusiveness of the *basileia*. Schüssler Fiorenza initially points to three distinct groups of people for whom Jesus claimed the *basileia*: (1) the destitute poor; (2) the sick and crippled; and (3) tax collectors, sinners, and prostitutes.[649] Such an unfolding of the Jesus movement illuminates how that claim included women. In light of such manifold inclusiveness Schüssler Fiorenza does not consider the social category of the poor to be sufficient to describe the inclusive character of the Jesus movement. Not all of the outcasts who got involved in the movement came from the poor. It is necessary to add the category of the marginal.[650]

Dussel is one of those who focuses on the category of the poor and gives primary attention to the means of production and impoverishment. At the same time he employs the categories of rich and poor to express the systematic of domination and oppression. His use of the category of domination, like Schüssler Fiorenza's use of the category of patriarchy, provides a tool for the illumination of multiple and intertwined forms of oppression.

Schüssler Fiorenza emphasizes how patriarchal oppression and economic exploitation are interrelated in the same social-economic systems. The majority of the poor and starving are women. Of this Mary, the mother of the messiah, is a symbol, in her representation of the hope of the poor. Mary not only proclaimed the promised eschatological reversal; she did so as a woman.

The reference to the mother of Jesus leads to a final peculiarity of the community of followers of Jesus. As inclusive as it was, it encompassed no "fathers." Not only did Jesus' call to discipleship disrespect patriarchal family bonds and disrupt the peace of patriarchal households, it also subverted relations of domination by taking the child and the slave as the primary paradigms of discipleship. When Jesus heard that his family was looking for him, he responded by pointing to his followers and stating, "Whoever does the will of God is my brother and sister and mother." (Mark 3:35) Schüssler Fiorenza notes: "Those who live the gracious goodness of God are Jesus' true family, which includes brothers, sisters, and mothers, but, significantly enough, no fathers."[651]

In addition there is the injunction that the disciples call no one father, there being only one father, namely in heaven. (Matthew 23:8) Schüssler Fiorenza concludes that the monotheistic fatherhood of God, elaborated as the gracious goodness usually associated with a mother, does not serve to legitimize but to reject patriarchal structures of domination. Liberation from patriarchal structures is thus at the heart of the *basileia* vision of Jesus.

### 6.3. *The praxis of the early church*

*Galatians 3:28*

Schüssler Fiorenza understands the early Christian missionary movement to have exemplified the same inclusiveness and egalitarian character as the Jesus movement. A key expression of the theological self-understanding of the emerging church is to be found in Gal 3:28.

> There is neither Jew nor Greek;
> there is neither slave nor free;
> there is no male and female;
> for you are all one in Christ Jesus.

Schüssler Fiorenza, with many others, takes this text to be an adaptation and/or application by Paul of a pre-Pauline baptismal confession. The three paralleled pairs seem to reflect the inclusive categories of the Jesus movement. The parallelism suggests that in each pair the same sort of claim to equality is being made. If the text can be understood as a baptismal confession, then it proclaims that all the baptized are equal.

There is evidence that slaves, male or female, expected freedom from their initiation into the Christian community.[652] At any rate gentiles, slaves and women could expect equal status and responsibilities within the social relationships and structures of the community.[653] In other words, Galatians 3:28 is not only to be understood as a statement about the baptized individual, but first of all as a communal Christian self-definition. In the Christian community no religious-cultural divisions and no structures of dominance may be allowed to determine the nature of community. Of course, differences remain. Galatians 3:28 does not mean there are no longer men and women in Christ, but that gender roles and sexual relationships determined by patriarchal marriage and society are no longer constitutive of the new community in Christ. The unity and equality advocated are not anthropological but ecclesiological.

It may be debated to what extent there was a socio-political component to this ecclesial egalitarianism, e.g., what influence the early Christian communities could have had or did have on the institution of slavery. Schüssler Fiorenza recognizes that Paul focused on the moral and ecclesial behavior of the believers with only limited emphasis on the social-political reality of the death of Christ and the existence of Christians in terms of new creation.[654] She is, furthermore, critical of the understanding of the cross of Christ in terms of universal atonement, the suggestion being that such an emphasis tempers the socio-political and thus the egalitarian-liberative force of the gospel of the cross. (Short of looking into the literary-historic aspects, one might consider that the conception of universal atonement can likewise be understood in terms of a radical egalitarianism.)

The outcome of such considerations should not detract from what Schüssler Fiorenza describes as the actual alternative possibility and praxis of equal ecclesial-social status within the Christian communities. Full membership was afforded to all regardless of social, marital, or sexual status. Functions and leadership were distributed according to ability and charisma. Such emancipatory practices made the movement attractive to slaves and women,[655] and the evidence that both were prominent in the early movement is substantial. Schüssler Fiorenza examines two aspects of the influence and importance of women in the beginning churches: their position as matrons ("patrons") of house churches and their active role in missionary activity.

*Matrons and missionaries*

It was the house church, as a space for worship and preaching, for social and eucharistic table sharing, that was often the starting point for the missionary movement in a new city or district. It presupposed some well-to-do member of the movement who could provide the necessary space and economic resources for the community.[656] It was the sphere of the house, in which women often had primary if not sole responsibility, that provided women the opportunity to also assume primary responsibility for the community and its gatherings in the house church. The structure of the house church is to be best understood in terms of the patronage relations of contemporary religious associations of Greco-Roman society. The patron (or matron) provided not only hospitality and financial support, but also leadership and influence.[657] Primary example is Phoebe, who in Romans 16:1,2 is referred to as a sister, deacon and benefactor/patron.

Besides indicating the prominence of women among the prophets in the early Christian communities, Schüssler Fiorenza also points to the role women played as missionaries, particularly in the practice of missionary partners. There are several women to whom Paul refers as co-workers, deacons, sisters, and/or apostles, who worked with him on an equal basis.[658] It is significant that many such missionaries administered both the word and the eucharist.[659] Also important to note is that the Jesus they proclaimed and commemorated was understood in terms of the Spirit and *Sophia* of God.[660]

The result of Schüssler Fiorenza's reconstruction of the emerging Christian movement is to indicate organizational structures and a social framework that make women's leadership both plausible and intelligible.[661] The egalitarian ethos of the Jesus movement was carried over into the early Christian missionary movement.

*Pastoral patriarchy and suffering service*

Whatever its social impact, the alternative practice of equality exemplified by the early churches existed in tension with contemporary patriarchal society and households. It is not surprising that the new sense of kinship and freedom that the missionary movement engendered was considered to be politically subversive, undermining as it did the prevailing social order. It is Schüssler Fiorenza's contention that this tension became the occasion for introducing the Greco-Roman patriarchal order into the house church movement.[662]

She points on the one hand to the development of a monarchical episcopacy, with its beginnings in the pastoral letters of Christian scriptures, and to the patriarchal ethos of the household codes on the other. Gradually the practice of charismatic and communal authority expressed in alternating leadership accesible to all the baptized was replaced by authoritative male officers.[663] The household codes, with their emphasis on submission for slaves, women and children, served to support that development. The original intent of the application of the household codes to Christian morals may have been apologetic for purposes of lessening the tension with the prevalent social order. With the introduction of Aristotelian notions of hierarchical domination and patriarchal submission, the genuine Christian vision of equality was lost.[664] As a result women's leadership became a marginal matter[665] and slavery could be tolerated.

While the patriarchalization of the church became historically the dominant institutional mode, it was not the only thing being proposed.

> However, since the Gospels were written at a time when other New Testament authors clearly were attempting to adapt the role of women within the Christian community to that of patriarchal society and religion, it is all the more remarkable that not one story or statement is transmitted in which Jesus demands the cultural patriarchal adaptation and submission of women.

The primary witnesses are Mark and John. Far from being apologetic or adaptive, the Marcan gospel states that giving offense and experiencing suffering must not be shunned. "Domination-free leadership in the community and being prepared to undergo sufferings and persecutions are interconnected."[666] Instead of slaves, women, and children being admonished to obedience, they are pictured as the paradigms of discipleship. Anyone in a position of leadership is to to become like them, indeed to become their servant.

The marks of the Johannine community are altruistic love and alternating service in which women are included. "At crucial points of the narrative women emerge as exemplary disciples and apostolic witnesses."[667] It seems that the gospel writer was aware that such preeminence of women is controversial, but the egalitarian praxis of Jesus is unquestioned.

John and Mark thus concur in their emphasis on service and love as the core of Jesus' ministry and as the central demand of discipleship. It should be noted that the "call to service is addressed to those who are in power, to those who are first in community, not to those who are least."[668] Its function is thus not that of maintaining submission to patriarchal interests, but of "fostering the praxis of the early Christian ethos of coequality in discipleship."

## 6.4. *The ekklesia of women*

The reconstruction of early Christian beginnings as a discipleship of equals enables women to reclaim their own biblical roots and heritage and reclaim their own selves in the church. By reappropriating the past and by reclaiming the sufferings and struggles of their foresisters, women experience the subversive power of the "remembered past" as a "dangerous memory." This reality of women, past and present, in both their oppression and power, allows women

> to build a feminist movement not on the fringes of the church but as the central embodiment and incarnation of the vision of the church that lives in solidarity with the oppressed and the impoverished, the majority of whom are women and children dependent on women.[669]

Solidarity together with commitment and accountability form the life praxis of what Schüssler Fiorenza calls the *ekklesia* of women. The image of an *ekklesia* of women serves two purposes. On the one hand it serves to bond women together in a communal experience of God's presence. It emphasizes that the movement and gathering of women in biblical religion is church. Schüssler Fiorenza joins in with those who emphasize that "to embrace the gospel means to enter into a community."[670] At the same time she insists that the community which the gospel calls into being is a discipleship of equals. The gathering of God's people around the table for eating, drinking, talking, sharing, giving and receiving must not exclude women from breaking the bread and deciding their own spiritual and political affairs.

It must not be forgotten, and that is the second point, that the term for church in the New Testament, *ekklesia*, is not so much a religious as a civil-political term. (Similar to Lehmann, Schüssler Fiorenza emphasizes the political character of formative biblical images.) "It means the actual assembly of free citizens gathering for deciding their own spiritual-political affairs."[671] The *ekklesia* of women is therefore a movement of women, as people of God, to claim their own religious powers, to participate fully in decision making processes and to nurture each other as women Christians.

Schüssler Fiorenza seeks to avoid a number of possible misunderstandings. While rejecting the location of women at "home in Eden," as the so-called Christian right would have, she is also critical of the Exodus image. The Exodus image, while compelling women to leave so much behind which they might treasure (loving community with children and men, shelter and happiness), overlooks the fact that there exists no reservoir free of patriarchal influence.[672] An *ekklesia* of women cannot escape patriarchy, but must learn to creatively and constructively challenge it.[673]

The criticism of the Exodus image is directed at Radford Ruether. Radford Ruether has articulated a dialectical relationship of Women-Church to the institutional patriarchal churches in terms of an Exodus-community.[674] She emphasizes that social analysis is not enough. Women need intentional feminine communities of faith, worship and nurture to sustain their own spirituality and struggle. Women-Church is a necessary separatist strategy in the face of the continued refusal of institutional churches to respond to the needs and identities of women.[675] It seeks to create a space for women to articulate their own experiences and communicate them in dialogue with alternative Christian and religious options.[676] At the same time dialogue can be maintained with and within the historical cultures of the parent institutions.[677] The choice between conformity or disconnection should be rejected for the sake of dialectical relations and networks of community relationships.[678]

Radford Ruether would seem to agree with Schüssler Fiorenza in the claim that women can make to being church. Whereas women have traditionally existed in marginal spaces, they are increasingly becoming subjects of their own spirituality and Christian praxis.[679] Radford Ruether asserts that women are not in exile from the church, but that the church is in exile and exodus with women, awaiting a new wholeness of cohuman community liberated from patriarchy.[680] Thus for Radford Ruether, as for Schüssler Fiorenza, women-church is not an exercise in ideological separatism, but a strategy to empower women and transform the church.[681]

Schüssler Fiorenza's criticism of the Exodus image seems to focus on the accompanying suggestion that there might be a space or place free of patriarchal influence. While the formulations of Radford Ruether might suggest that at some points, her primary concern is for strategic spaces and structures in which women can create their own cultures, nurture their own spiritualities and develop their own critiques. A spearpoint of the strategy is directed against clericalism as a primary foundation and means of patriarchal power.[682] With these concerns Schüssler Fiorenza would seem to concur when she employs the metaphor of an open space in which women can formulate their critique and struggle in the face of patriarchy.[683] Not unimportant is the suggestion of the Exodus image that the church needs to be going somewhere, namely towards liberation from the bonds of patriarchy.

Both Radford Ruether and Schüssler Fiorenza likewise realize that the *ekklesia* of women is a plural movement. Radford Ruether emphasizes the varieties of commitments and communities belonging to the network of women-church.[684] This reflects again her understanding and support of dialectical relations with the institutional churches.

Schüssler Fiorenza has likewise reflected upon the significance of various strategies and analyses within the (Christian) feminist movement. She understands them not in a positivistic contradictory sense, but in terms of a democratic pluralism of rhetorical strategies.[685] That understanding would seem to reflect the complex character of patriarchy that combines and intertwines various forms of oppression according to race, class, sexuality, etcetera. The praxis and theory of the *ekklesia* of women must therefore appreciate and appropriate the differences of experience and perspective of women of different color, sexual orientation, social situation, and whatever.

At the same time, it need be realized that pluralism generally functions in a stratified sense. Differences are made into differences of status. Those descriptions of status need to be "denaturalized", just as descriptions of women (or 'woman') should not appeal to a feminine nature.[686] It becomes clear that the socio-political emphasis of Schüssler Fiorenza is not to be understood in contrast to a theological approach but in opposition to anthropological-essentialist understandings of human natures and status. Radford Ruether has suggested that the original lie is the naming of differences among humans of race, gender and ethnicity as "good and bad, being and non-being."[687]

This critical appreciation of difference and plurality requires at the same time an ethic of solidarity if it is not to cripple the movement or tolerate reactionary tendencies.[688] That makes of the *ekklesia* of women an oxymoron, a combination of contradictory terms, in a critical space of openness and bonding. The *ekklesia* is an open forum but not a free market, for the context is the solidarity of women with their own selves and with the most oppressed of women.

This is significant for the understanding of identity. Schüssler Fiorenza adheres to an intersubjective theory which she takes from J. Benjamin. The intersubjective theory places identity in the relation between the self and the other, in the tension between equality and difference. The relation is one of mutuality between unity and division. This intersubjective understanding is expressed in the metaphor of a bounded open space.[689] It provides a political ethic of mutual recognition and respect in solidarity. The *ekklesia* of women constitutes a critical, political concept for the mutual relations of openness and solidarity, of self and other, of identity and difference, of unity and variety. The *ekklesia* of women provides a committed open space in which the divine presence can be experienced in the midst of that mutual identity and experience.

*Considerations*

1. The Bible, in so far as it provides a model for both women-church and patriarchal church, is a paradigm of struggle on the identity and nature of the church. This recognition raises the need for an evaluative hermeneutic.
2. The conflict between prescription and description that Schüssler Fiorenza exposes presents a double challenge. On the one hand it points to the need to confront the entirety of scripture. On the other hand it challenges traditional paradigms of biblical interpretation and use. Both challenges serve to enliven the hermeneutical imagination and to open the way to a more catholic approach to scripture by attention to the readings of particular communities. While the shift from archetype to prototype provides a model for the transformation of tradition and community, it does not yet formulate catholic criteria for the reading of scripture in the recognition that revelation must be allowed to speak for itself.
3. The holiness of the Jesus movement took the form of wholeness and inclusiveness. That found expression in a discipleship of equals in which women were exemplary followers and prominent leaders. The extension of the good news to the Gentiles seems to have been specifically prompted by women.
4. The nature of inclusiveness of the Jesus movement suggests adding the category of the marginal to that of the poor.
5. It is noteworthy that references to the discipleship family include mothers, brothers, and sisters, but no father, except the non-patriarchal, motherly Father in heaven.
6. The form of the house church allowed women to play prominent roles in community leadership. Parallel to that were women prominent as missionaries.
7. Hierarchical domination and patriarchal submission, which marginalize women and tolerate inequality (cf. slavery) are to be confronted with the call to service, suffering, and mutual love and with attention to the role models of slaves and children.
8. The assertion of an *ekklesia* of women is a critical political act of remembrance and appropriation of the heritage and equality of women in the church. It is a dangerous, subversive memory of both the oppression and power of women. Its life praxis is solidarity, accountability, and commitment.
9. The term *ekklesia* is to be understood in its civil-political meaning of the decision making process of free citizens. Women reject their marginalization and claim their own participation and gathering as central to the life of the church.

10. Women church is a provisionary strategy of creating an open and free space for women to claim themselves and nurture their own spirituality and struggle.
11. The relation (whether dialectical, strategic or otherwise) of the provisionary particularism of women church to the catholic quality of the church needs further clarification.
12. An appreciation of difference and plurality requires not just openness but also solidarity if it is to maintain its commitment to liberation and to discern the divine presence.

## III.7.

## LETTY RUSSEL
## *CHURCH IN THE ROUND*

### 7.1. *The table principle*

> The critical principle of feminist ecclesiology is a table principle. It looks for ways that God reaches out to include all those whom society and religion have declared outside and invites them to gather together. It measures the adequacy of the life of a church by how well it responds to the needs of marginalized persons for justice, hospitality, and hope.[690]

With the metaphor of the table Letty Russel entwines and envisions an inclusive ecclesiology from a feminist perspective. Her scope encompasses base communities and the World Council of Churches, Korean women and American homosexuals, ecumenical traditions and the contemporary *kairos*. She unfolds her vision of a *Church in the Round* through provocative examples and personal experiences, providing a concreteness and warmth to her ecclesiology. As with Leonardo Boff no justice is done here to her theological work by selectively reviewing one publication. However, some of the various perspectives she brings together are to be included here.

There may be any number of tables around which the life of Christian community can take place. Along with the table of the eucharist Russel envisions three more: the round table, the kitchen table and the welcome table. The round table connection indicates a form of leadership in the church, circular not hierarchical, sharing power and multiplying responsibility in order to inspire and empower those on the margins of church and society. The paradigm is not one of (patriarchal) position and competition, but of (matriarchal) partnership, mutuality, community, friendship, connectedness, teamwork and networks.

The kitchen table is the place of sharing solidarity, service, and the struggle for justice. It involves the recognition of a *kairos* for the churches. "The [*kairos*] documents represent a collective confession of the inadequacy of most ecclesiology and church practice for the crisis of suffering that people face in our groaning world."[691] At the same time, contemporary confessing communities are living a praxis that is engendering a new paradigm of the church committed to justice and liberation. The church does not have a mission, but participates in the mission of God by connecting with the marginal and the suffering.

The welcome table is a part of the American black church tradition, symbolizing the communion table and every other gathering at table.[692] It thus symbolizes the practice of hospitality and the affirmation of diversity. Jesus made clear that the "household of God is open to all persons, especially those who have been excluded or marginalized." Thus the welcome table, like Jesus' parables of the reign of God, indicate "God's choice to call those at the periphery...to the center of community."[693]

## 7.2. *The marginal focus of the household of God*

The metaphor "household of God" is derived from the domestic images in the parables and sayings of the gospel that point to the proclamation of God's reign and hospitality.[694] The term "household" serves to express the reality of the new creation "without using the patriarchal language of kingship, domination, and subordination." In an

> eschatological sense of God's householding activity in and beyond this world, "household of God" does not refer to the church, as it does in later Greek Testament books such as 1 Peter, but rather to God's New Creation. The church as a household of faith is called to be a sign of God's power at work among all the nations of the *oikoumene*, but there are other signs that point toward God's mended world house. Those who "fall in faith with Christ," and desire to share the faith and struggle of Christ's community, witness to Christ as the way to the New Creation.[695]

The understanding of the household of God, rooted as it is in the praxis of Jesus and the gospel narratives, is thus shaped by justice. And the primary relation of justice is to the marginalized. "Jesus' message is that he is found with the outsiders, not because they are any more righteous than the others, but because, as a group, they are the ones who help us know when justice is done and all are included."[696] (The emphasis on justice is necessary if the term household is to carry political connotations like the terms it replaces.)

The focus on the marginalized, which Russel emphasizes, suggests a dialectical reordering. This becomes evident in her reception of bell hooks (*Feminist Theory: From Margins to Center*). "From the point of view of those who are marginalized, it is an important form of empowerment to choose the margin as a place to stand and work or to move to the center in order to gain the ability to talk back."[697] Whereas women of color are recognizing the special vantage point of their marginality and claiming the center for their own contributions, Russel envisions white mainline churches moving from center to margins in order to share in the struggles for justice.[698] Russel labels this "situation-variability in dealing both with groups that have been powerless and those that have been powerful." The significance of the margin for the life and organization of the church needs to be further explored.

### 7.3. *Hospitality in the household of faith*

The justice connection is essential in Russel's view to the life and being of the church. The household of faith is a community of faith and struggle. In fact, she asks whether justice should not be considered a fifth sign of the church, alongside unity, holiness, catholicity and apostolicity.[699] She has herself emphasized diversity with unity, justice with holiness, connectedness and orthopraxy with catholicity, and mission with apostolicity. She suggests that the signs should be understood in a descriptive rather than prescriptive, dogmatic fashion. The point is that

> The church finds its own identity as a sign of Christ's work in the bringing of God's household by being a community of faith and witness, a community of struggle for the poor and oppressed, and a community of hope in the fulfillment of God's New Creation.[700]

The point is clear, but the question is whether adding justice to the classical signs serves that point. On the one hand the biblical notion of justice is prior to and arguably at the roots of classical ecclesiology. On the other hand, if one were to add justice in the present day ecumenical setting, then peaceableness and stewardship of creation would need to be added as well. In that sense the pursuit of justice and peace and respect for the integrity of creation could be viewed as essential expressions or contemporary translations of the classical signs. Also, one might then add another quality that is so central to Russel's own ecclesiology (like that of Hauerwas): the practice of hospitality. Hospitality in Russel's description would seem to be both the primary means of the pursuit of justice and the celebration of the graciousness of God.

> From a Christian perspective, community, or *koinonia*, is a new focus of relationship in Jesus Christ that sets us free for others. The community of faith and struggle is formed by its central commitment to Christ, but it is nurtured by its common struggle to live out the ministry of Jesus and his message of good news for the oppressed. The purpose of the community is to extend this welcome of God's household to all people, especially those who have been excluded by society.[701]

From this perspective Russel seeks to interpret the biblical concept of election, not in terms of a bestowed privilege leading to practices of domination, but as an expression of the compassion and hospitality of God.[702] There lies the basis for a unity that appreciates diversity. The righteousness and justice of God inform community life in such a way that "the question of sharing at Christ's table becomes a question of hospitality rather than of ecclesiastical unity."[703] Thus hospitality becomes one of the primary means of meeting the challenges presented by a contemporary *kairos* and by a feminist/womanist critique of the church.

> We need to subvert the church into becoming a church in the round, a church where spirituality of connection becomes a living reality because people are engaged with faith that connects them to the struggles for justice in a discipleship of freely chosen service in the name of Jesus Christ.[704]

***Considerations***

1. Russel's use of the term table provides a practical image of solidarity, shared responsiblity, and hospitality.
2. The metaphor "household of God" provides an expression of God's reign and hospitality in non-patriarchal terms. That the household of God is a household of justice needs to be emphasized in order to retain the political sense of the images of God's reign.
3. Focus on the marginalized suggests a dialectical reordering of the church (and society). The significance of the margin for the life and organization of the church needs further exploration.
4. Hospitality is a means of the pursuit of justice and of the celebration of the graciousness of God.

# III.8.

# CONSIDERING THE CLAIMS ON THE CHURCH

## 8.1. *An ascriptive method*

At a couple of points in his writings Hauerwas reflects on the objection that such a church as he advocates simply does not exist.[705] A variation on that theme is the criticism that the church that Hauerwas advocates is essentially sectarian, due to his concern for a distinct and separate life of the church.[706] (Added to that is traditional critique of the pacifist position that it fails to accept worldly responsibility.)

A somewhat similar critique is expressed by the Dutch sociologist M. Thung on very dissimilar Dutch theologians, G.H. ter Schegget and H.M. Kuitert, that whatever the political positions implied by their ecclesiologies, they both insist upon the sole right of theology to pass judgement on the church and hardly allow the social sciences to have a say in the matter. Her point is that many theological statements on the church are simply not applicable to daily church practice. For Hauerwas the word 'church' is not so much a descriptive term as a theological "claim" regarding God's creation of a new community. Dussel maintains that "to accept the church as it is is to betray the church in its very essence." For Ter Schegget it is in theology that the essence of the church must be determined. Thung replies that sociologists do not wish to argue that point. Their concern is not the essence of things but their practical, empirical forms.

It was Bonhoeffer's attempt in his dissertation, *Sanctorum Communio*, to put sociology (and social philosophy) to the service of dogmatics. However, it was not an empirical, descriptive sociology, but a phenomonological sociology that Bonhoeffer had in mind.[707] He was more concerned with the fundamental sociality of humankind than with empirical knowledge of the structure and functioning of the German provincial churches (*Volkskirche*). From that point of view he could, e.g., assert that the essence of the church was primarily expressed in the anonymous celebration of communion in a city parish, where people were gathered not out of human interest but solely around word and sacrament.[708] The same Bonhoeffer found himself several years later entwined in a struggle between the true and the false church. In disrespect of any empiricism a theological judgement was passed.

To be sure, not all these discussions are about the same thing. The dispute between sociologists and theologians is not the same as the "sectarian" debate among theologians. And the "sectarian" debate has a different context than the struggle between a "true" and a "false" church. However, there do seem to exist some common aspects, such as the concern for the relation between substance and form of the church as well as some concern for realism, whether that be a biblical or a human realism. (This latter concern has a parallel in the contrast of the kingdom as both a reality and an ideal.) It is not the intention to elaborate on all these criticisms or tensions here. It would seem more fruitful to examine how Hauerwas relates his theological ethics to real life churches and consequently to indicate a manner of envisioning the same relationship, and so deal indirectly (however inadequately) with the critique indicated above.

Hauerwas' reply to the "sectarian" accusation is direct. Such biased and muddled labels, he asserts, shortcut the discussion.[709] Instead, a rejection of his position must address his specific claims on the church, the biblical story, christology, nonviolence, the limits of liberalism, etcetera, and not just pass sweeping judgement on the outcome of his position. If for Hauerwas the word "church" is a theological claim, it is a claim about a church in the making. "In so far as we are the church" is a phrase that can be encountered more than once,[710] and there is explicit reference to God "making us his church."[711] Just as the kingdom is viewed as a reality which is breaking in, so the church is seen as a reality in the making, there "where people faithfully carry out the task of being a witness to the reality of God's Kingdom."[712]

For Hauerwas there are both descriptive and normative aspects of the Christian life that can be understood as a "pattern of expectation" regarding both who we are and what we can be expected to do. "The very idea of expectations combines the descriptive and the normative in the sense that what we ought to do is in fact what we are."[713] This is reminiscent of the position of Lehmann, for whom ethics is primarily descriptive "in the sense of providing an account of the transformation of the concrete stuff of behavior, i.e., the circumstances, the motivations, and the structures of action, owing to the concrete, personal and purposeful activity of God."[714] What Hauerwas adds to the position of Lehmann is a more concrete description of the divine activity in the contours of the kingdom and a more substantive view of human behavior in the context of community.

Hauerwas' concern is to help communities (congregations) appreciate the significance of their common acts, those activities that constitute their common life (not the least of which is worship) and in so doing, help the churches share their stories truthfully.[715] Hauerwas' manner of making that concrete is to provide a real life example, an example of a local congregation, which despite its limits and shortcomings, was moving in the direction that Hauerwas envisions.[716] The means of moving on were not primarily those of making decisions (although decisions were made), but of acknowledgement and appreciation of where and who that body of people as a Christian church were and wanted to be. Examples are how the celebration of the eucharist found further expression in a common meal with and for the neighborhood and how the intention to remain present in a depressed, racially mixed part of town implied the decision to repair the roof.

Similar to Hauerwas' approach, but in a very different setting, is the attempt by a Dutch Catholic, A.J. Baart, to *describe* a *proposed* form of moral discourse in/for the Dutch churches.[717] Baart seeks to provide an ideal-typical description of the manner in which moral deliberation can take place in the church. His description includes fundamental assumptions on the identity of the church and of the participants in moral discourse, as well as on rationality, along with simple rules (regarding, e.g., the use of power) for the carrying on of moral conversation. Of importance at this point is not the details of Baart's description, but his insistence that his model combines various and sundry elements of ethical reflection and moral discourse that really do exist, however scattered, and that are attainable, whatever the shortcomings. The "ideal" indicated is not a distant, unrealistic goal (with, at best, some ambiguous motivating power), but the condensation in a model that may not exist in pure form but that nevertheless provides a reasonable and coherent expression of existent examples.

In this manner the relation of a theological description to an empirical church is a selective, normative, exemplary one. And this seems to be not dissimilar to the critical function that a sociological approach can offer when it goes beyond empirical description to making concrete proposals for the organization of the life of the church. It shares then with Hauerwas a concern for the proper functioning of the church in order to reflect its proper purposes, i.e., pursue its proper journey.

At this point the question arises how far general or systematic observations on the issue at hand can be pursued. Which empirical church is being talked about? Is the concern with churches at large or local communities? And in which social or global context? Simply the description and interpretation of the context confronts us with innumerable empirical and normative dilemmas.

A critical ecclesiology offers its theological description of the church as a critical reflection on the praxis of the church. That critical reflection and theological description must reflect the contours of the empirical description of that same praxis. At the same time it seeks to provide a (normative, prescriptive) challenge to contextual and ecclesial empiricism, because it wants to contribute to a renewed self-understanding, a new definition, of the church in its context.

Consequently, whereas it is necessary to distinguish between descriptive and prescriptive approaches, it does not seem fruitful to oppose them. Instead, just as the description is wrought with prescription, one might seek to understand their methodological interrelatedness in terms of an 'ascriptive' approach. An ascriptive approach is to be understood in close relation to what has been indicated above on the theological method of reflection on praxis, for it involves a theological evaluation of the life of the church. It is reflection on praxis for the sake of enhancing that praxis and engendering new praxis. It is inconceivable without a descriptive reference. At the same time it makes theological claims about the church. It does so by appealing to theological criteria, particularly the biblical story and the traditions, lived and confessed, of the church.

To be sure both references of an ascriptive approach are plural: the lives and histories of churches on the one hand and biblical theologies and confessional traditions on the other hand. Can one then speak of "the church" in singular terms? There is a factual plurality of churches in both descriptive and prescriptive senses, a plurality of at times irreconciliable differences and not just diversity. At the same time there does exist a community of theological discourse on the "church". There is an ecumenical life of the churches in a Christian tradition going back to the life of Jesus of Nazareth and the praxis of the apostolic community. Making claims on the "church" is problematic to the extent that it involves a degree of abstraction. Speaking ascriptively of "the church" is, however, a legitimate theological enterprise in the attempt to further the theological conversation on the church, clarify its conflicting conceptualizations, and contribute to consensus on a form of common life suitable to the gospel of Jesus Christ.

Amidst the abundance and ambiguity of biblical interpretation and ecclesial description, of church history and theological reflection, an ascriptive attempt is made to sift and sort out a coherent and convincing claim on the nature of the church. The claim is a multi-dimensional appeal. It appeals to traditions, both descriptive and prescriptive, both practical and confessional, both historical and theological. At the same time it entails an appeal forward, an attempt at transformation and transfiguration of tradition and praxis.

The ascriptive approach advocated and applied here is thus an attempt to understand and reunderstand the church. It involves unfolding the inherent identity of the church, explicating the implicit, actualizing theological and practical resources in new contexts and configurations, and, by so doing, critically validating and transfiguring the perceptions and praxis of the church. It seeks to display, elaborate, elucidate, and evaluate particular perspectives of the self-understanding of the church (such as catholicity) and effectuate them in new ways for the common, ethical life of the church. It results in theological claims to be understood as reordered and reasoned expectations.

Such claims are necessarily made in dialogue with and by contrast to competitive claims, whether descriptive, prescriptive or ascriptive. The value of the tension between descriptive and prescriptive approaches (whether fruitful or incommensurable), the "truth" of any ascription, can only be determined in relation to concrete examples and claims. Similarly, the degree of "realism" of the present project can hardly be judged in general terms. It will have to prove convincing or not. It will be convincing to the extent that it can make a reasoned case rooted in tradition, both descriptive and prescriptive, and at the same time serving transformation and transfiguration.

## 8.2. *The church as a starting point for ethics*

The theologians reviewed share not only the method of staking theological claims on the church, they also share the presupposition that the church serves as a starting point for Christian ethics. The church as presupposition is not taken in an exclusive sense, for other perspectives, such as reconciliation, narrative, prophetic traditions, and transcendence, are enjoined along with biblical criticism and philosophical standpoints. Nevertheless, the church, the community of Christ, provides fundamental orientation. This is most explicitly and perhaps exclusively the case in the theology of Hauerwas. In the theology of Schüssler Fiorenza it is more implicit but no less radical.

*The church as subject and object*

In the various ecclesiologies the church emerges as both subject and object, an ethical experiment. The church as community is integral to the strategy of God in the world, as object of divine activity. The church is "Christ existing as community" (Bonhoeffer); "the fellowship-creating reality of Christ's presence in the world" (Lehmann); the focus of God's strategy for creating a new people (Hauerwas); the essence of Christian life and of the reign of God as the "face-to-face with God in community" (Dussel); expression of the essential communitarian spirit of Christianity (Boff); the experience of the inclusive wholeness of the *basileia* of *Sophia*-God (Schüssler Fiorenza); and the household of faith as "a sign of God's power at work among all the nations of the *oikoumene*" (Russel).

Whatever the various emphases, it appears generally that the focal point of the authors under review is the local community. The context of the church at large is present, but it is in the face-to-face experience of relatedness that God's work takes shape. Boff particularly emphasized the catholicity, the fullness of the local, base communities. It might be noted that Schüssler Fiorenza and Russel are the least explicit about the church as an object of divine activity. Schüssler Fiorenza, in particular, places more emphasis on the historical development and vision of the church.

The church as subject of ethical and political activity emerges in a "church for others" assuming responsibility for the world (Bonhoeffer). The church is the *koinonia* as the context of ethical reflection and participation in the work of humanization (Lehmann); itself a social ethic in the performance of scripture and the nurture of a distinctive life (Hauerwas); a prophetic community committed to the liberation of the poor (Dussel); a project of engendering community and liberation (Boff); an *ekklesia* for deciding spiritual-political affairs; and participation in the mission of God by connecting with the marginal and the suffering (Russel).

Common to the understandings of the church as a subject of ethical activity is the conviction that Christian ethics is a function of living communities, narratives and traditions, and not simply a literalist deduction from biblical texts nor a general appeal to ethical principles or theories. Ethics is a political, communitarian activity shaped, variously, by concrete commands, divine activity, narrative, and/or the commitment to liberation. Those various shaping factors reveal, on the other hand, the controversies among the theologians reviewed.

*Church and world*

Hauerwas specifically provokes controversy with his insistence upon the radical distinctiveness of the church. He would seem wary, though he does not discuss it, of Bonhoeffer's description of a "church for others". Whereas Bonhoeffer advocates responsibility for the world and Lehmann the humanizing activity of God in the world, Hauerwas suggests that the church is most helpful to the world by being faithful to itself. Not that Bonhoeffer and Lehmann would disagree, but their focus is more extrovert and distinctiveness is interpreted in a more temporary, anticipatory manner.

The controversy can be stated in a different way by comparing the positions of Hauerwas and Dussel on violence. The concern of Hauerwas with the integrity of the community of Christ, leads him to emphasize the peaceableness of the church (and vice versa). The concern of Dussel with the liberation of the poor, causes him to lend more emphasis to the pursuit of justice. Both advocate non-violence. Hauerwas does so, however, in a more principled manner and distances himself from ideological struggles. Dussel, on the other hand, advocates an unarmed "prophetic violence" and seeks proximity to the at times violent struggle for the liberation of the poor.

Schüssler Fiorenza and Russel do not directly treat the question of violence. They share with Dussel the emphasis on liberation and with Boff the conviction that the engendering of community can coincide with the task of liberation. Much more than is the case with Lehmann and Hauerwas Christian community is focused towards the marginalized, the exterior, the poor and the suffering. Peculiarly, in comparison with Hauerwas, the relation to the world among the liberation protagonists is more one of struggle in the world and yet less one of distinction from the world. This may be explained by the partisanship for the underdogs in the world. Solidarity with the world of the poor entails struggle against the world of the powerful.

*Inclusive and exclusive*

The relation of church and world raises the question of the inclusive and exclusive character of Christian community. The term inclusiveness has been used in several instances as an interpretive tool. It was encountered explicitly in the viewpoints of Schüssler Fiorenza and Russel. The question of the nature of inclusiveness has several dimensions. There is the question of the relation of an inclusive ethos to the exclusive character of a distinct belief (revelation) and community. Secondly it should be asked how partisanship for the exterior and the poor, the suffering and the marginalzed, is to be understood in relation to inclusiveness. A further tension can be framed in terms of Lange's rejection of parochialism (II.5.5.) and Schüssler Fiorenza's advocacy of a more "provincial" theology. (III.6.1.)

It must be admitted that inclusiveness is never absolute. There will always be those who find or feel themselves outside for whatever reasons. Any conviction, whether religious, moral, ideological or whatever, any way of looking at the world unavoidably will to a greater or lesser extent exclude other viewpoints. And to the extent that viewpoints and convictions make us who we are, competing viewpoints exclude not just each other on a theoretical and practical level, but also to various degrees the persons who hold those viewpoints. The exclusiveness is not simply a matter of contingency, incommensurability, cultural limitations and the like, but at times, perhaps often, the result of a clash of fundamental convictions on the nature of truth(fulness) and the manner of the good life.

Christian convictions are based upon a narrative of divine presence and passion in the history of Israel and the person of Jesus Christ. The biblical narrative is understood as revelation, an act of God, a moving of the Spirit. On the one hand it is claimed that Christian faith is a response to revelation, a product of the moving of God's spirit. On the other hand Christian faith is a product of human experience in a broad sense. It is a result of socialization, tradition, and reasoned reflection as well as personal experience and conviction. One could claim that human experience is the mode or landing area of divine presence. One might also, however, suggest that Christians and Christian community - in their own experience - are both object and subject of their own faith.

Any exclusiveness of Christian faith resides therefore not only in the claim on divine revelation but also in the human response to that revelation. It resides not only in the reasons of the hart as an unarguable appeal to a revealed truth, but also in the reasoned explication of Christian convictions and the religious experience of Christian community. The exclusiveness is a result both of a specific recognition of revelation in the particularities of Israel and of a particular stance, i.e., a specific direction in the commitment to follow Jesus.

It should be noted that the intention is informative and normative rather than exclusive,[718] but that such a particular orientation and specific commitment are for reason and praxis exclusive of (some) other claims to truth and practices of life. The claim is not that no practical truth or life direction are to be found outside of biblical revelation, nor that all other sources are to be rejected, but that biblical revelation provides a particular orientation and a specific (normative) perspective. No normative claim can be made for biblical revelation in a simple or literal manner, but the biblical narrative does provide a pattern of description and expectation with normative significance. Berkhof concludes that the relation of Christian faith to other truth claims is dialectical.[719] The claims to truth have to be sorted out. (In that respect the word catholicity has also been applied to the question of the "true church" and to matters of orthodoxy.) And the process of sorting reveals what criteria are maintained, and to what extent the specifics of revelation are compatible with and/or exclusive of other claims.

Hauerwas understands that process in terms of the embodiment of tradition and the practice of (political) community. It is to be noted that whereas he on the one hand emphasizes the particularities of the biblical narrative and the distinctiveness of Christian community, he simultaneously lays claim to an inclusive ethic of non-violence and hospitality. The enemy is to be loved and the stranger welcomed. Criticism is directed at the sectarian character of ideologies and imperialism. The particularity of Israel's messianic hope provides a hope and a political posture of universalist dimensions in a violent and divided world.

Similarly Van Gennep has put forward that the exclusiveness of divine activity is the precondition of the inclusiveness of divine activity.[720] Salvation is from the Jews, for the world. The catholic fatherhood of God is contrary to the tendency of groups to claim God for themselves. The revelation in Jesus Christ entails the recognition of the equal humanity and worth of every person as a child of God. This "catholic truth" motivates communication and community. Its concern is not simply unity, but the whole in its diversity.[721]

The significance of this way of relating exclusiveness and inclusiveness for the present study is the implicit suggestion that a catholicity of human beings has priority above a plurality of convictions. The insistence on baptism alone as criterium for membership in the church struggle of Nazi Germany was an exclusive position for the sake of an inclusive community of Jews and non-Jews. The rejection of the complementary thesis on nuclear armament (and thus of a plurality of opinions on the peace issue) was an exclusive position on the basis of an inclusive understanding of the reconciliation in Jesus Christ. That is the church's way of seeking the peace and unity of the world, not so much a different peace, as Lange emphasized, but a different way of seeking peace.

The inclusiveness bears a contingent rather than an absolute character. It is contingent to the claim to truth. And it is contingent to the embodiment of that truth in a catholic praxis, contingent therefore as well to particular ecclesial and political strategies for the sake of realizing full embodiment. The contingency of the claim does not, however, make it less critical, fundamental or radical. The ethos of Jesus, as Hauerwas and Schüssler Fiorenza in particular have indicated, is marked by a fundamental human inclusiveness, i.e., the attempt to restore (or realize) the fullness of human community.

*Parochialism, provincialism and particularity*

Lange criticized the "parochial" character of so many churches, the accomodation of their identity to some particular group or interest. The effect is the assertion of identity at the cost of others. The result is a proliferation of churches along ethnic, cultural, national and denominational divisions. Such churches no longer open themselves to diversity as the spectral profusion of unity. In misrepresenting the cause of a distinct Christian community such churches are an extreme perversion.

Schüssler Fiorenza advocated more "provincial" biblical interpretations, more concrete theologies, in order to appreciate the particularities of communities and their (liberating) struggles. In fact, she asserts the relative priority of those particular endeavors. The question might then be asked if she does not in effect propogate a new form of parochialism. Is provincial not just another word for parochial, even if placed within a liberation context?

The intentions, however, are different. The various intentions can be clarified by recalling the criteria for the catholicity of local churches put forth by Keshishian. (II.5.5.) The local church is catholic by means of its 1) faithfulness to the particularities of its place; 2) its openness to other places; and 3) its communion with other local churches. Schüssler Firorenza uses the term 'provincial' to emphasize faithfulness to the particularities of a locality (1). Lange uses the term 'parochial' to criticize the lack of openness to other places (2) and the lack of communion with other local churches (3). This does not mean that the attempt to be faithful to particularities, especially in the manner that Schüssler Fiorenza advocates, will not strain the openness to other places and local communities. It does mean that the particularities of any place have to be critically evaluated from the perspective of openness to others and that the whole must allow space and appreciation for the particularities. In that sense the term 'provincial' can be misleading in that it can carry the same connotations as 'parochial'. The term 'particularity' is preferable to the extent that it allows both for concreteness and openness.

*Marginality and priority*

Bonhoeffer spoke of the "incomparable" experience of viewing events from below, from the perspective of the outcast, the powerless, the oppressed, the suffering. Lehmann indicated that the poor are a test case of justice. Hauerwas insisted on openness to the stranger. Much more radically Dussel emphasized the term 'exteriority' to define the position of the poor outside the system. He consequently enfused the term with theological significance by understanding it in proximity to transcendence. The liberation of the poor became an ethical absolute. Schüssler Fiorenza explicated the advocacy stance of a liberation theology in general and the struggle of women as a hermeneutical center in particular. The question can be asked whether and how these claims with respect to a particular (partisan?) perspective express inclusiveness within the catholicity of the church.

It should be clear that for all of the authors the emphasis on the perspective of the poor and the marginal has a strategic significance. That does not make it less fundamental, as the very radical description of Dussel in terms of 'exteriority' makes clear. The strategic significance of the perspective of the poor and marginal is precisely in order to include the poor and the marginal in the whole, to restore and/or realize the wholeness of human community. It is particularly the conviction of the theologians of liberation that such community cannot be realized on the terms of the dominant, the rich, and the powerful. Women, the poor, and the marginal must become subjects of their own histories and communities.

On the one hand a term like marginality, used in a summary sense, indicates injustice, whether perpetrated or perpetuated. It points to the factual exclusion or near exclusion of others. On the other hand it is employed by Bonhoeffer and in liberation theology to indicate a liberating perspective. From the perspective of the marginal it can be better seen what is wrong with human society and community. From the point of view of suffering and struggle strategies can emerge for healing and realizing human community and society. Marginality points to a disruption of human community and to a reality of conflict, but at the same time to a perspective of "incomparable" value.

To be sure Bonhoeffer was quick to point out (III.1.5.) that the

> perspective from below must not become the partisan possession of those who are eternally dissatisfied; rather, we must do justice to life in all its dimensions from a higher satisfaction, whose foundation is beyond any talk of "from below" or "from above".

Similarly, the representatives of liberation theology began with a fundamental affirmation, a "radical principle" (Dussel) of community. Dussel's strategy of liberation is a choice for the oppressed and yet ultimately inclusive of the oppressor. An *ekklesia* of women is envisioned on the way to a community of men and women free of patriarchy. More extensively and more radically than Bonhoeffer, however, the theologians of liberation seek to explore and exploit the perspective of the poor and the marginal for particular ecclesial and political strategies.

A parallel appeared in the discussion of the *status confessionis*. The *status confessionis* was understood not to be a threat to unity but a critical defense of unity in its attentiveness to the excluded and the expendable. The intention of the *status confessionis* is not excommunication, but radical communication for the sake of the renewal of community. There was a degree of partiality in the *status confessionis* in its specific concern for (and solidarity with) Jew and black and those threatened by nuclear annihilation or hunger, but it was a necessary partiality for the sake of the whole and of humanity.

This strategic understanding of marginality is at the same time rooted in the biblical narrative and theological interpretation. Dussel pointed to Jesus' identification with the poor and asserted the coincidence of transcendence and exteriority. Schüssler Fiorenza emphasized the special invitation of Jesus to the impoverished, the outcasts, the sinners and prostitutes, as well as the extension of the invitation to the gentiles. The overriding concern remained wholeness.

Ter Schegget (in commenting on Van Gennep's conception of catholicity) has sought to comprehend the critical nature of Christian unity, grounded as it is in the calling of Christ.

> Christ, as one who passes borders, breaks through the borders in one direction, for that is the only way possible: He does not stop at the border that is set by the rich, the powerful and the dominant, because He is a stranger with the estranged and poor with the poor. Christ does not stand between the parties, nor above the parties, but as the mediator of God He stands on the one side for the sake of reconciliation of both sides. In that way he is the martyr as well. This must lend content to catholicity. The given orientation has no metaphysical or religious status, but it is an answer to the quest for that which transcends the system. The transcendent element, in light of the Messiah and his way, lies in estrangement, suppression, and the fate of the outcast.[722]

Faithfulness to particularity is thus qualified in terms of the priority of the particularities of the poor and the marginal. The church does not seek a different inclusiveness; rather, it seeks inclusiveness in a different way, by attributing priority to the margin. It does so by seeking solidarity and community among and with the poor and the marginalized.

*Christian ethics as ecclesial ethics*

It was stated above that the various authors under review concurred in taking the church as a starting point for ethics. It is in the *koinonia* that the activity and will of God is discerned. (Lehmann) The essence of Christian life and the reign of God is community. (Dussel) The church does not have a social ethic, but *is*, that is, embodies a social ethic as a particular community and political alternative. (Hauerwas) Christian ethics is ecclesial ethics, not in an exclusive or exhaustive sense, but in a fundamental sense. It has been seen that understanding the nature of the Christian community can provide direction and substance to Christian ethics, particularly Christian social ethics. The formation of community is a political act. (Hauerwas) Ecclesiology is political theology. (Dussel) In ecclesiology fundamental ethical decisions are made. In Christian ethics fundamental ecclesiological presuppositions are present.

Christian ethics is, according to the witnesses gathered here, no abstract ethical enterprise. The shape and continuity of Christian ethics is provided by biblical narrative and Christian tradition and by the embodiment of that narrative and tradition in Christian community. In that sense Christian ethics is not a formal or deductionist activity - although it engages in formal reasoning - but a practical enterprise. It seeks to be concrete and transformative.

This general description is, of course, in need of more specific explication. Several basic directions (criteria) have emerged. They have been summarized in terms of catholicity and conciliarity, inclusiveness and marginality, community and diversity. Several matters require further clarification: the organization of the church and its ethical discourse, the vocation of non-violence, as well as the description of the essential identity and integrity of the church. Such a constructive undertaking is necessarily hypothetical. The motivation for attempting it is the question how things might take shape in churches and Christian communities responsive to the *status confessionis* and to the theological interpretations presented above. The following section is an attempt to take up some of the issues needing further clarification in order to indicate some basic possibilities and perspectives.

### *Considerations*

1. An ascriptive ecclesiology combines descriptive and prescriptive elements in a pattern of expectation. It consists of a critical appeal to the self-understanding and praxis of the church for the sake of a coherent claim on the church.
2. Understanding the church as subject and object of ethical reflection and praxis is to understand the ethical enterprise as a function of tradition, narrative, and community life.
3. The inclusiveness of the church is contingent to the Christian claim to truth and to the embodiment of that truth in a catholic praxis. The intent of that truth claim and its embodiment is at the same time fundamental human inclusiveness.
4. Attention to marginality expresses the priority of the poor and the exterior within the search for unity.

# IV. THE ETHICAL FORMATION OF THE CHURCH

## *Defining ethics in defining community*

The church is some body.[723] And the body is on the move. In an issue of *Sojourners* magazine Jim Wallis traces what he understands to be "a prophetic convergence of the people of God."[724] Wallis sees a new vital ecumenism emerging which in the absence of fixed creeds and dogmas is delineating new theological ground. Wallis seeks to name that ground in terms of its biblical orientation, its transformative spirituality, its centeredness on Jesus and the reign of God, its rootedness in the sufferings and hopes of the poor and the marginalized, and its catholic quality (diversity and integrity). It is the common ground of a movement, an extended community, seeking to embody a life that is envisioned for society.

The significance of Wallis' description is that it is a reflection on a real existing movement of (confessing) communities and networks, of which he himself is an active and leading participant. It is a descriptive vision. He writes in the future tense in order to further the vision of the common ground that is already being shared. He ascribes to the movement a theology that is both existent and still in the process of emerging. It is thus Wallis' method as well as his terminology that are of interest. Although Wallis' article will not be further discussed here, it provides an interesting example. The nature of his reflections underlines the way in which theological vision can be rooted in concrete community. It is interesting to note that Wallis, in tracing a theological convergence, arrives at a communitarian ethos and ethic. It becomes evident that ecclesiology and ethics are his way of doing theology.

In the present study no direct look has been taken at the praxis and confession of exemplary communities, as informative as that might be. Rather the approach has been to review and analyze ecclesio-political debates and theological positions. A following step is to attempt to order those materials into a more or less coherent and constructive view on ecclesiology and ethics. Let it again be emphasized that the intent cannot be a full fledged ecclesiology or ethical project, but a proposal on how things might take shape in a church responsive to the challenge of the *status confessionis* as explicated above. Admittedly, therefore, all sorts of topics and issues will be touched upon that demand more thorough exploration and study. Nevertheless, their treatment has been generally (and necessarily) limited to the context and considerations provided up to this point. Only in a few instances has other literature been introduced. The intent is not thoroughness, but to indicate directions derived from the evaluation of the *status confessionis* and supplemented by the projects of several theologians.

Under the headings of the key terms conciliarity and catholicity a framework is developed for a constructive church ethics that is informed by the challenge of the *status confessionis* and the processes inherent to its recognition. The term conciliarity serves to indicate the processes and perspectives explicit in the *status confessionis*. Conciliarity is the climate necessary for the task of confession and solidarity in the church. The term catholicity serves to indicate the substance of the *status confessionis*, the inclusive praxis of relatedness, of community and diversity. Catholicity is an expression of the confession and solidarity of the church.

The question of *the process of conciliarity* (IV.A.) leads first of all to the proposed terminological shift from the *status confessionis* to the classic attributes of the church and their modern translations. (IV.A.1.) In the second place, perspectives on the reading of scripture are commented upon, especially in relation to the way in which Schüssler Fiorenza has brought certain issues to the forefront. (IV.A.2.) The stage is then set to explicate an understanding of the church as a community of ethical conciliarity. (IV.A.3.) How is the church to do ethics? Amidst all the emphases on community and conciliarity, it seemed necessary to clarify an understanding of individuality in the context of community. (IV.A.4.) The consideration of the processes of conciliarity concludes with a brief typology of the church in terms of a pilgrim community engaged in an ethical enterprise. (IV.A.5.)

The consideration of *the praxis of catholicity* (IV.B.) seeks to establish certain aspects of the identity and vocation of the church. Priority is attributed to the relation of the church to Israel. (IV.B.6.) In that context the formative question of the church, "Who is Jesus Christ for us today?" is considered. (IV.B.7.) Given the relation to Israel and the person and praxis of Jesus, it can then be asked what shape and quality inclusive Christian community might embody, how it might be organized and where it might be localized? (IV.B.8.) One particular vocation requires attention, namely the struggle to resist violence, as several of the theologians under consideration emphasized. (IV.B.9.) The exploration of the praxis of catholicity concludes with a brief description of the ethical reality of the church as both object and subject of ethical activity, as both *koinonia* and *ekklesia*, as the body of Christ in a praxis of mutuality and marginality. (IV.B.10.)

## *IV.A. THE PROCESS OF CONCILIARITY*

## IV.A.1.

## ATTRIBUTES OF THE CHURCH IDENTITY AND ASCRIPTION

### 1.1. *The ecumenical expectation*

At the conclusion of the review of the *status confessionis* debate (II.6.*Considerations*) the findings were summarized in the following proposal.

> Attention should be shifted to the ethical significance of the classic attributes of the church, namely, unity, sanctity, catholicity, and apostolicity. Their modern translations are solidarity, ecumenicity, and conciliarity. Their location is the eucharistic community. Their reality is the body of Christ. Their reference is the inclusive praxis of Jesus.

Directing attention to the attributes of the church is to relate the fundamental concerns expressed in the *status confessionis* to the historic confessions of the church in terms of its self-understanding and assumed identity. It is an attempt to actualize those historic descriptive terms for the life of the church. Such an approach is neither descriptive (on the assumption that the church is as it should be) nor simply prescriptive (in the presumption that it is enough to say what the church should be) but ascriptive. It has reference to things said and implied in the church's confessions and to the life of exemplary communities in which the praxis of Jesus can be recognized. It implies a critical ecclesiology in which descriptive and prescriptive elements are interrelated for the sake of enabling the church to be what it claims to be. (III.3.5.3.) In this respect Hauerwas has spoken of a "pattern of expectation." Not only is the church a community of expectant people, but something is to be expected of the church as well. A theological evaluation of the church, as reflection on praxis, raises expectations on the direction things are to take in the church.

It is to be expected, for example, that the ecumenical movement will make progress toward church unity. It is to be expected that the spirit of polarity, not in the least in ethical questions, will be overcome by the spirit of conciliarity. It is to be expected that the status quo of plurality will make way for catholicity. It is to be expected that patriarchy in the church will make way for the participation of women, the marginal, the dominated, and the poor. It is to be expected that divisions of race, class, culture, and sex will make way for networks of solidarity and the eucharistic celebration of reconciliation. It is to be expected that complicity in injustice and violence will be confessed and that the struggle for justice and the vocation of non-violence will be pursued. All of these things are occurring, here and there, tentatively and radically, slowly and rapidly, in specific communities and church movements. Whether and to what extent they will affect the church at large will, however, be a reflection of the qualities of conciliarity and catholicity. Such things can occur there where the church proves true to its own identity in being attentive to the biblical narrative and expectant of the reign of God in the world.

Ecumenicity is a vision of the whole gospel for the whole human, the whole church, and the whole world. Ecumenicity entails a recovery of both the doctrine of the church and the doctrine of the unity of humanity. (II.4.2.) It includes as well a recognition of the catholicity of creation. Ecclesiology is not just political theology, but has creational and cosmological dimensions as well.[725]

## 1.2. *Apostolic wholeness*

Schüssler Fiorenza has indicated that in the Jesus movement holiness took the form of wholeness in the "belief that the God of Israel is the creator of all human beings, even the maimed, the unclean, and the sinners...Wholeness spells holiness and holiness manifests itself precisely in human wholeness." (III.6.2.) The *status confessionis* has been understood primarily in terms of unity and catholicity, but the findings of Schüssler Fiorenza suggest that the same things can be said in terms of sanctity (holiness) and apostolicity.

This can be illustrated by pointing to the call to holiness in the context of commandments on social order in Leviticus 19. Holiness is no inherent characteristic, but identification with the ways of God in order to provide for the poor and the alien and to love one's neighbor as oneself. This understanding is echoed in the gospel accounts in the call to be perfect and merciful just as God is gracious and kind. (Mt 5:48; Lk 6:36) The gospel context is one of love even of enemies, kindness to the ungrateful and wicked, abstinence from judgement and the practice of forgiveness, in order to identify with and reflect the inclusive love of God. If, as Dussel has pointed out, holiness is exteriority, then the practice of holiness is attentiveness to exteriority.

It is the apostolic witness that points to holiness as wholeness and inclusiveness in the praxis of Jesus. Ter Schegget has pointed out that apostolicity is the primary and essential characteristic of the church. (II.3.6.) The substance of apostolicity is expressed in the gospel portrayals and in the original discipleship of equals. Unity, sanctity, and catholicity along with ecumenicity, solidarity, and conciliarity are attempts to explicate and translate the apostolic ethos for the continuing life of the church.

### 1.3. *The praxis of confession*

In the context of apartheid it became necessary to insist that the unity of the church is to be visible and manifest. Particularly the practice of the sacraments was seen to be a test case for church community. Where black and white could not share the common meal at one table, the fellowship of Jesus Christ was being denied and defiled. Furthermore, it was asked what the value of church or sacramental fellowship might be where black and white could not share a cup of coffee together. The unity of the church is expressed sacramentally in one baptism and one table of the reconciled, but it is the life of the church that lends intelligibility and meaning to the sacraments. The bread of the eucharist, Dussel insisted, must be the bread of justice. The community of the church must be a community of struggle and sensibility, of truthfulness and trustworthiness. More than being marks of the church, the life and praxis of Christian community are that which lend substance and integrity to the sacraments and to the word. The life of the church is the praxis of confession, just as the sacraments are the celebration of confession and the word is the explication of confession. The praxis of the church is the real life reference of confession. It is the embodiment of the reality of the body of Christ. The sacraments, the word, and the attributes of the church are all explications and expressions of that body. It is the community and diversity of that body that lend identity and integrity to a Christian (ecclesiological) ethic.

### *Considerations*

1. Directing attention to the classic attributes of the church is an ascriptive attempt to actualize the self-understanding and assumed identity of the church expressed in its historic confession and exemplified in the life of particular communities.
2. A critical ecclesiology can be understood as an exercise in ecumenical expectation.
3. More than being marks of the church the life and praxis of Christian community are what lend substance and integrity to the sacraments and the word.
4. Apostolicity, as the primary characteristic of the church, witnesses to holiness as wholeness and inclusiveness in the praxis of Jesus and in the discipleship of equals.
5. The reality of the body of Christ defines Christian ethics in terms of identity and integrity, community and diversity.

## IV.A.2.

## READING TOGETHER
## HEURISTIC ANNOTATIONS

### 2.1. *Reading in community*

Hauerwas' claim that the church is a storied community (III.3.5.) is a way of pointing to the fact that the church does not live from reading alone. Rather the church is the community where the biblical story is remembered and rehearsed, where traditions are preserved and provoked. (III.3.5.) The gospel is a self-involving story that forms and informs community and character. (III.3.2.) Or as Nicholas Lash has formulated: "The performance of Scripture *is* the life of the Church."[726] Reading the scriptures is thus a political enterprise for it assumes a particular community and context.

The hermeneutical approach of Schüssler Fiorenza would seem to both radicalize and relativize Hauerwas' position. (See III.6.1.) It radicalizes it by taking its starting point and criterion in a particular emancipatory community, an *ekklesia* of women. Remembrance is informed by a dangerous, subversive memory. Taking that particular community to be not just a context but a criterion would seem to relativize the formative power of scripture. Scripture itself is put to evaluation and formed by the community, even as it may still serve to form the community.

Schüssler Fiorenza's investigations provide not so much a hermeneutical model as a heuristic approach. The movement of women-church has demonstrated that its reading of scripture can be critical, creative, corrective, and constructive. An *ekklesia* of women provides a new space and new perspectives for a liberating (re)reading of scripture. Those readings may be critically evaluated from the vantage point of more traditional or academic readings, but the reverse is true as well. The fruits of those readings need also to be appreciated and appropriated for the sake of a critical hermeneutic.

It is not clear, however, how a canon of scripture taken outside of the canon is an improvement upon a canon within the canon. Nor does it seem to function in an essentially different way. To what extent does such a diverse community as an *ekklesia* of women provide identifiable criteria for the reading or interpretation of scripture? More important is that such a community provides vital questions and perspectives. Similarly a historical-literary approach provides critical tools and methods for exploring the texts. Certain conditions for interpretation are delineated, but that provides only the beginnings of a hermeneutic.

The intention here is certainly not to provide a hermeneutical model or methodology. The point is simply to emphasize the interactive and dialogical (catholic) nature of reading in community. Reading in dialogue means on the one hand that there is no simple center or criterion from which the texts can be read. Instead there is the interaction between texts and readers and contexts. Reading the texts as scripture, that is, with a view to their formative and informative power, implies attributing to them an essential heuristic role in the discovery of what God wants to reveal to and do.[727] Thus the texts are allowed to carry their own weight and have their own say. At the same time the readers can recognize the significance of the texts only by coming to them with their own contexts and questions and particular interests. The perspectives and contexts of the readers thus also play a heuristic role in the confrontation with the texts. Reading in community becomes reading in conciliarity as the various perspectives and contexts confront the various readings. Those readings may prove competitive with or exclusive of each other, but initially they provide clues for further reading and practice. For the real proof of any reading is to be found in its embodiment by a particular community.[728] In that way there arises a dialogue (interaction or interrelation) between reading and praxis.

In that dialogical process any number of particular readings by particular communities in particular contexts can be heard. They are also to be evaluated, but they are first to be heard if reading and interpreting is to do justice to the catholicity of the church. A conciliar church will furthermore appropriate a catholicty of methods and perspectives, not as criteria but as heuristic approaches. There is no single interpretive interest that can guide all reading.[729] Historical-critical methods can be joined to liberative perspectives. Prescription can be confronted with description. Straightforward and parabolic readings will variously be needed. All these can serve to revitalize and transform the reading of the biblical texts.

In that light Schüssler Fiorenza's proposal for understanding the Bible as prototype rather than archetype is significant. An archetype, as she defines her terms, "establishes an unchanging timeless pattern...A prototype is critically open to its own transformation" and "requires the transformation of its own models of Christian faith and community" even as it remains an original model. (III.6.1.) This need not, however, imply the location of revelation in Christian community and experience rather than in the texts, because the texts can only play their heuristic and formative role by having their own say. But then the evaluative and heuristic role of Christian community and its embodiment of tradition, human reasoning, and experience can likewise be heard.

Readings of the Bible on the question of slavery provide a prime example. If the Bible is understood archetypically, the church may resolve itself to slavery. After all, slavery is well rooted in the biblical narrative. Understood prototypically the church can discern a liberating and transforming direction of the biblical narrative that points toward the abolition of slavery. Other examples are conceivable. Archetypically war is a biblical pattern, and a theocratic Constantinianism might justify itself. Prototypically it might be seen that war must be overcome and church and state separated. Archetypically women have been excluded from ministry. Prototypically their leadership and power are seen to be essential to the life of the church. Archetypically poverty is tolerable, for the poor will always be with us. Prototypically the liberation of the poor becomes an absolute command. Archetypically homosexuals have been condemned and excluded. Prototypically their presence could yet be affirmed.

A prototypical approach allows scripture to shape discernment in areas where the Bible in a literalist or archetypical understanding may seem silent. Scripture as prototype opens the way for drawing analogies and descriptions that will inform moral perceptions and sensitivities, for example in medical ethics or environmental issues.[730] Prototype as an original model provides orientation and continuity as well as the means for renewal and creativity. It provides the resources for both identity and transformation. It provides a sense of history and direction. Of importance is not to insist on a particular terminology or advocate a comprehensive hermeneutic, but to explicate a process and a perspective. The point is that in reading, remembering, and rehearsing the biblical narrative the church is not just repeating, imitating, or copying, but is in fact going somewhere and becoming transfigured.

Knowing where things should be going in order to shape the transfiguration of community requires discernment. That discernment can be informed by any number of hermeneutic perspectives and heuristic approaches. It will involve not just reading scripture but also allowing ourselves to be read by scripture. It requires reading scripture for our own sakes, but also allowing scripture to speak against us. It requires putting difficult questions to the texts, but also wrestling with the difficult texts. There are no sure or simple criteria, only the exercise of common responsibility and the development of practical wisdom.[731] Good reading thus requires communal integrity and human maturity.

## 2.2. *Reading the gospels*

Reading in community does have a particular focus and that is the formative question: "Who is Jesus Christ for us today?" To know who Jesus Christ is one must read the gospels (the assumption being that the texts as we have them provide reliable witnesses). The gospel accounts are to be read with the variety of methods indicated above, with special attention to their Jewish context and to their Jewish interpreters. That reading will thus be critical and evaluative, but the purpose is to illuminate the person, praxis, and passion of Jesus and so to let Jesus speak.

Of course, the gospels are to be read in the context of the entire Jewish and Christian canons (along with other ancient Jewish and early Christian writings). Here also reciprocity and dialogue are to be observed. Jesus is not to be read into Tenach, but read from it. The prophets did not in a simplistic manner anticipate Jesus as the Christ, but Jesus chose and formulated his position within the traditions and expectations of his people. From that perspective he may illumine a reading of Tenach, but he does not eclipse it. The integrity of Tenach as Jewish scripture is to be respected, just as the integrity of the gospel accounts and other writings of the Christian canon is assumed.

To state that Christ is the center of scripture is a problematic description in its tendency to simplify the dynamics and contrasts of scripture. It would seem more appropriate to state that the focus of a Christian reading of the biblical texts is to discern who Jesus was and what his significance for the life of the church is. (Cf. Bonhoeffer: "the form of Christ in the form of the church, the formation of the church according to the form of Christ." III.1.2.) The figure of Jesus serves to illumine the biblical writings, just as they can serve to illumine an understanding of Jesus. They may do so in a variety of ways, by contrast as well as by consensus.

The readers are confronted, furthermore, with diversity among the original Christian witnesses to Jesus. The Christian canon displays a variety of christologies reflecting the life, practice, and witness of various communities. That variety needs to be neither harmonized nor exaggerated but appreciated. That diversity is a reflection of the emerging catholicity of the early church and can serve as a prototype for contemporary Christian witness. (Such diversity is not the same as there being no way of reconstructing the historical Jesus. The concern here is not with the historical problem, but with the catholic dimension of witness to Jesus.)

To state that the focus of reading in Christian community is Jesus Christ serves not so much to solve anything but to direct the searchings. It ends up revealing the "polyphonic character of Christ."[732] Reading in community entails openness to that diversity of witnesses. It means engagement in the process of discovery and discernment and rediscovery of who Jesus is and where he is going. It may then be said that reading in community becomes an exercise in conciliarity. It involves the critical ability of listening to the voices of others, often outsiders and strangers.[733] Of particular interest are the interpretations of Jewish readers and scholars.

This implies that common reading can serve a critical function with regard to the appropriation of scripture. The dynamics of any hermeneutic like the perspectives of any community are that they not only illuminate but also cast shadows on scripture. Reading needs to be practiced in and from the shadows and margins of scripture and not just from particular canons. Jesus himself cannot be simply summarized or appropriated, but must ever again be discovered and discerned in his otherness, his outsideness, and his marginality.[734] It is the person, praxis, passion, and presence of Jesus Christ that makes reading a communal and conciliar enterprise that draws attention to the margins and thus illumines the entirety of existence.

### *Considerations*

1. It is the heuristic interaction between (particular) readings and praxis that reveals the power and persuasion of scripture.
2. Reading in community entails openness to the diversity of witnesses to Jesus Christ.
3. Readings of scripture require not only hermeneutic models but also heuristic methods for reading the shadows and margins of scripture.
4. Understanding the biblical text as prototype serves to keep the reading of scripture open to transformation.

## IV.A.3.

## A COMMUNITY OF ETHICAL CONCILIARITY ORGANIZING DISCERNMENT

### 3.1. *The church put to the question*

What are the ethical resources of the church? It has been indicated in this study that orientation and direction for a Christian (communitarian) ethic is provided by the identity and integrity of the church. The recognition of the church's identity as an ethical resource was prompted and informed by the recognition of a crisis or crises in the church. Various names have been given to the crises and the challenges confronting the life of the church: *status confessionis*, *kairos*, and conciliar process for justice, peace and the integrity of creation. These crises represent not just ethical challenges or dilemmas for the church, but cut to the root of its integrity and common life. The fellowship of the reconciled finds itself divided by race, culture, class, and sex. The peace of Christ is disrupted by the weapons of Christians pointed at each other. The discipleship of equals is devastated by misuse of power and economic injustice. The integrity and catholicity of creation which forms the basis of our common life is violated.

The time is now, so we are told. There is a *kairos*, a time of decision and discernment for the church. The church is called to responsiblity. The church is called to its own confession and transformation. Is it called to its own reform or to its own subversion? How is the challenge to be met? How are the conflicts to be organized? Will the challenge be recognized and will the conflicts be confronted? Or will a peace of the church that is no peace prevail above the church's vocation of faithful living in non-violence and the pursuit of justice? The challenges to the church can be understood, not as threats to peace, harmony, and unity in the church, but as occassions for rediscovery and renewal of the church's catholicity, its community and diversity, its unity in Christ who is our peace. The conflicts inherent to the church can be discerned not as threats to the life of the church, but as occasions for discerning its identity in being for others and in appropriating maturity and humanity.

A crucial task for the church will be to learn to confess guilt and accept forgiveness. The church has seldom practiced what it preached in this respect. The capacity for confession, for straightforward acceptance of guilt, for admission of complicity, and for being embarassed and perplexed, such things are needed if the church is to learn forgiveness, learn what it means to become a forgiven people, liberated from its own violence and fears, from its own pride and resentment. (Although it is generally held, especially in political circles, that admitting uncertainty or wrongness is a sign of weakness, such a capacity would seem to require maturity and character.) The church might not only inform political sensitivities, but also open the way to its own renewal if it should take responsibility for its past of violence and patriarchal oppression.

Schüssler Fiorenza suggests another aspect of remembering the past. The histories of the poor, of women, of blacks, of native peoples, of heretics, of pacifists, of homosexuals, of dissidents, and of so many who have found themselves at the margins or pushed beyond them, all those stories of struggle and suffering need to be reconstructed and remembered. Such stories serve to dissettle the church and to change it. And yet such change is needed if the church is to come to reflect inclusiveness and wholeness.

The exemplary responsibility exhibited by Bonhoeffer confronted the church, and not only the church in Germany, with its own failings and shortcomings. It also indicated the direction for a renewal of the church. So also the *status confessionis* was intended simply as a call to repentance and renewal. The affirmation of a *kairos* has been put forth as a discernment of a grace still available. Communities of the poor and an *ekklesia* of women issue calls to the fullness of the *koinonia* of Christ. Such challenges are not created or declared. They arise. They can be recognized, confirmed, and answered. They shape confession. Confession can then take the shape of commitments and covenants guided by ecological sensibility, economic solidarity, and irenic responsibility. Those are ways of being faithful to the vocation of the church.

### 3.2. *Shaping the ethical enterprise*

The church is no answer machine. It does not know how things should be done, but it is committed to seeking a way, to allowing itself to be informed ever again by the biblical narrative, and to opening the way for inclusive participation. In many ways Christian community is eclectic in its ethical searchings. It is confronted with the lessons and questions provided by the struggles of ideologies and the histories of communities and societies. By virtue of its inclusiveness it is also confronted with all the sorts of ethical arguments, principles, and imperatives that people of the world bring with them. By virtue of the same inclusiveness it should withstand exclusive principles, totalitarian organization, and absolutist claims.[735] At the same time it will seek to shape ethical perspectives in response to the biblical narratives and in relation to its own life.

The contrast between a narrative approach to ethics and approaches advocating ethical principles or reasoned absolutes should be emphasized but not exaggerated. (III.3.1.) The relative legitimacy of ethical categories and moral rationality is not only to be recognized but also appropriated. The church is in need of clear and crisp moral thinking. At the same time it is a narrative display that can serve the task of relating and relativizing, selecting and rejecting, such considerations. In that respect the rational competence of narrative can be joined to the political competence of faith.

One need not exaggerate the differences between Lehmann's decriptive approach and Hauerwas' narrative emphasis. Hauerwas may understand the biblical narrative in a more prescriptive way than Lehmann. Lehmann may lend more formative attention to the human predicament and human events. On the other hand narrative by Hauerwas and description by Lehmann (who also emphasizes narrative) function in similar ways. Hauerwas and Lehmann concur in their rejection of more formal, principled approaches to ethics. They are both concerned with the shaping power of our contexts and perspectives. They both effectively understand the church as both a subject and object of ethical activity. They both realize that the project of Christian ethics stands or falls with the quality of Christian community and the maturity or character of Christian persons. Narrative may be understood as our way of providing a description of our context, of understanding ourselves and relating ourselves to each other, and of relating our story to the biblical story. (Thus both narrative and description could be related to the method of liberation theology as reflection on praxis.) The common starting point is the context of the community of God's people. The primary difference may be Hauerwas' more radical insistence on rooting ethics in the life of biblical community and Lehmann's greater attention to transcendence and to the continuing drama of divine activity.

Pointing to narrative is another way of pointing to the practical and cooperative nature of the ethical enterprise. The story is to be lived out in community. It is the community that provides substance to ethics. In the absence of objective standards a way must be found to lend shape and conviction to ethical formation. Under the threat of arbitrary subjectivism or emotionalism a way must be found to provide coherence and continuity. Living in community is a way of attempting that. The community can seek to preserve and transform its traditions, to develop habits and form character, to engender responsibility, accountability, maturity, and practical wisdom. That is the reason that Hauerwas emphasizes not only the content of ethical considerations, but also the character of ethical subjects, whether individual or communal.

The church does not find itself without resources in dealing with all sorts of subjects or situations on which the Bible may seem silent. For the church has a variety of perspectives and values and a tradition of practical wisdom on which to draw. The church cannot pretend to solve issues of the environment or medical ethics, but it can shape thinking on the values of life, the limits of responsible human power, and the kinds of communities and societies that are desirable. It cannot resolve the question of euthanasia, but it can ask what is needed to make life worth living, to endure pain, and to surround persons with support in the hour of crisis, as well as what are the limits of human possibilities. Ethics understood as the narration of a common life is not just concerned with the decisions to be made or with the disturbances in human existence, but with shaping lives and transforming existence by giving it direction.

Is there anything peculiar to Christian ethics? Does it possess a proprium? Its peculiarity hardly exists in any particular position or principle. In fact its own self-centered concern for its uniqueness, propriety, or credibility is ethically dubious. If there is anything peculiar to the ethical enterprise of the church, then it is the way in which Christian communities allow themselves to be formed, informed, and transformed by the biblical narratives and by the margins of human existence and divine presence. The more the church allows itself to be thus formed, the more it provides ethics with specific shape and color and the more it *is* rather than *has* a social ethic. The identity of the church lies in its attention to the particularities of the biblical story of Israel and the Jew Jesus. The integrity of the church lies not in its distinctiveness or universality or credibility as such, but in its life as an inclusive community attentive to the poor and the marginal. The peculiarity of Christian ethics is to be found in the perspectives that order and color its ethical enterprise.

### 3.3. *The organization of ethical conciliarity*

Hauerwas has drawn attention to James Gustafson's description of the church as a community of moral discourse.[736] Hauerwas has himself spoken of a community of character. Relating the ethical task to the quality of conciliarity suggests speaking of a community of ethical conciliarity. Discourse and dialogue are essential to conciliarity and their quality is dependent on the character and content provided by its participants. Nevertheless, conciliarity (cf. II.5.6.) more than discourse suggests the directional and participatory nature of ethical consultation in the community of Christ. A discourse may take satisfaction in plurality and complementarity. Conciliarity seeks to respect and reconcile diversity in order to work towards consensus. Discourse may be governed by arguments and rationality. Conciliarity seeks as well to guarantee inclusive participation, explore intuitions, exploit the imagination, arouse the tempestuous,[737] and discern new directions. Discourse might be easily dominated by experts, whether theological or otherwise. Conciliarity seeks to relate expertise to the experiences and perspectives of lay persons. Conciliarity is particularly aware of the distortions of power and status and therefore attentive to the voices of the poor and marginal, the interests of the unheard and the absent. Discourse may seek to reflect from a distance. Conciliarity acknowledges the value of critical distance and is aware that the question of truth must remain fluid and open, but seeks to engender commitment and covenanting. Discourse provides analysis. Conciliarity seeks to join analysis to action.

Such a contrast of discourse and conciliarity may be a caricature. It is not meant to disparage discourse (or treat Gustafson unfairly), but to make use of the suggestive force of terms and to indicate the direction of ethical conciliarity as an inclusive enterprise. Ethical conciliarity both assumes and seeks to engender a community of character. It realizes how often the final word in ethical discourse must be given to practical wisdom and discernment. It is aware that ethics must be lived out by people with sustenance and resilience, people with a capacity for perplexity and repentance, people with patience and daring.

This direction of conciliarity requires organization of ethical dialogue and praxis. It requires recognition of group dynamics, of sociological processes and the need for institutionalization.[738] It requires the organization of the conflicts inherent to the church. It requires not just hearing but listening. It requires a "round table" style of leadership that shares power and multiplies responsibility. (III.7.1.) It requires respect for cultural patterns and differences, but can also run counter to cultural restrictions. It will seek to actualize the catholic nature of the church in an open but committed space. It can take as a model the ("kitchen table") experiences of women-church with the dialectic of sistership and alienation.[739] It can learn from the pedagogy and organization of the poor in base communities. It can build networks for mutual information and solidarity in an ecumenical practice.

Ethical conciliarity might be understood as the application of the golden rule to the ethical enterprise. That entails granting the other what one desires for oneself: the enjoyment of bread and the enjoyment of dialogue. It includes "hearing the other to speech."[740] It is mutual participation in the project of giving shape to human lives, communities, and societies. It is the realization of a common humanity and of a common vocation. It is the praxis of the round table.

The method of the church catholic is to practice what it pursues, to actualize its own identity, and to live the reality of the solidarity of the body of Christ. That is a way of embodying the praxis of Jesus. Means are radicalized as concrete ways of participation in the desired ends. The church does not so much seek a different peace than the world as it seeks the same peace in a different way. The way to peace is the practice of peace. The way to ecumenical unity is the practice of ecumenical unity. The way to eucharistic community is the practice of eucharistic hospitality. The way to inclusive community is inclusion. (II.5.6.) Means, more than ends, are specific tests of Christian faith, for they are the means of participating in the present peace and the coming reign of God. A practice of ethical conciliarity will pay specific attention to the means of common life. That is another way of relating the unity of the church to the unity of humanity, a concrete manner of practicing inclusive community.

This inclusive practice of embodiment, of the radicalization of the means as participation in the ends, is the ethical equivalent of ecclesiological ascription. It parallels the ascriptive appeal to the inherent identity and the peculiar perspectives of the church of Jesus Christ as an inclusive community. The ascriptive approach is not simply descriptive or prescriptive, but includes an attempt to trace the prescription in the description.[741] It ascribes to the church what is implied in its confession and what is being practiced in proxy by exemplary communities. Perhaps more important than new confessions, is the strengthening and support of confessional communities and networks of solidarity that are already seeking to live as the body of Christ.

Conciliarity is an attempt to organize the conflicts inherent to community life, but it provides no guarantee that consensus will be attained or that communication will be maintained. The very assertion of catholicity as method, of radicalizing means, of practicing what is to be pursued, and of living the reality of the body of Christ serves to radicalize the conflicts in the church and to divide the spirits. The concealed exclusiveness of institutionalized unity, ideological plurality and indifferent complementarity are thus revealed. At the same time the recognition is engendered that certain matters are essential and in that sense indisputable in the confession and praxis of Christian community: the priority of Israel, the poor, and the marginal, and the integrity of inclusive table communion open to all. Certain tasks are recognized as being of utmost urgency, a *kairos* for the churches: the struggle for economic justice, the reconstruction of participation by women, and the vocation of non-violence. Certain provisional strategies can be affirmed: the movement of an *ekklesia* of women and the development of particular, indigenous theologies.

Conciliarity is organized cooperation in the pursuit of practical truth. (II.5.5.) It is *ekklesia* as a civil-political organization of decision-making and direction. It is unity understood as the interaction of variety between the poles of conflict and consensus. It is motivated by the pursuit of truth and the common task of responsibility. It is neither simply orthodoxy nor orthopraxis, with their normative and archetypical connotations, but the critical renewal and transformation of tradition, confession, and praxis. It calls for ethical configurations open to transcendence and transfiguration, the ordering and reordering of priorities. (For that reason worship is an essential context of ethics and the observance of the sabbath or of the Lord's day informs ethical sensitivities.[742]) The direction of ethical conciliarity is the transformation of community and the transfiguration of ethics.

The transformation of community implies the reorganization of community. That might include critical reconstruction of the constellations of power, ways of sharing responsibility and authority. That may involve reorienting the life of communities to specific tasks. That may entail relocating community towards the margins. That may imply regroupings: the expression of the ethos of catholicity by small minorities, breakthroughs in ecumenical unity and solidarity, sectarian concentration, or worldly orientation. Ethical conciliarity implies a process of the organization and reorganization of the church. And the history of the *status confessionis* shows that in that process the church will find its own identity and integrity at stake.

### 3.4. *The art and praxis of discernment*

Attention has been shifted (relatively) from principles and categories of moral rationality to the subjects of ethical reflection and action. Their mode of ethical reasoning is narrative. Emphasis has been placed on conciliarity and character, common life and maturity, practical wisdom and praxis, responsibility and accountability, commitment and consensus. Not concepts and principles are the primary guides, but social perceptions and sensitivities, being with and for others. The role of conscience may be recognized as well, at least as understood by Lehmann in terms of a socialized conscience. (III.2.4.) Or one might speak of a storied conscience. Conscience provides a location for dealing with the various claims of autonomy, heteronomy, and theonomy upon human lives. Maturity and character are the capacity to deal with them. Community and journey are the context in which they can be appropriated.

There is another term, familiar in Christian thought, that can be used to describe the discriminating capacities that have been indicated: discernment. Discernment is the capacity to penetrate the confusion and to distinquish the essential, to observe the unobtrusive and unheard, to perceive what is crucial and critical, to recognize the crisis and the *kairos*, to envision the direction things should be going. It requires alertness, sensitivity, and sensibility. In common usage discernment may indicate a heuristic capacity, an intuition or suspicion. Or, it may refer to a well informed judgement, the exercise of practical wisdom to decide a matter or determine direction. It may be an assertion of prophetic spirit or it may result from training in practical wisdom. It may be an individual charisma or it may be the result of common searchings. It can also be seen as an interplay of all those aspects, intuition confirmed by a good look at things, piercing insight supported by weighted reflection, individual perception consented to in common consideration. It is as interplay that discernment can be recognized for the artful praxis that it is. It is as interplay that the charisma of discernment can be understood as the guiding agency of ethical conciliarity.

### *Considerations*

1. The capacity for perplexity and for confession of guilt is crucial to the task of ethical discernment and church renewal.
2. The perspectives of the marginal, their struggles and sufferings, are essential to the inclusiveness and wholeness of the church.
3. The rational competence of narrative and the political competence of faith together shape the otherwise eclectic ethical enterprise of the church.
4. Community provides ethics with shape and conviction in the absence of (rationally) objective standards. It provides ethics with coherence and continuity in the face of arbitrary subjectivism.

5. The enterprise of ethical conciliarity stands or falls with the quality of Christian community and the maturity and character of its participants.
6. The ascriptive method of the catholic church looks to what is implied in confession and is being practiced in exemplary communities. The praxis corresponding to that method is the radicalization of means as participation in and practice of ends. It is to live the reality of the body of Christ, to embody the praxis of Jesus, and to participate in the coming of the reign of God.
7. The conciliar struggle for truth will entail the ordering and reordering of priorities. It will result in the transfiguration of ethics and in the transformation and reorganization of community.
8. The art and praxis of discernment, as the interplay of prophetic spirit and practical wisdom, is the guiding agency of ethical conciliarity.

# IV.A.4.

# INDIVIDUALITY IN COMMUNITY
# CHARACTER AND CREATIVITY

## 4.1. *The individual as a permanent margin of community*

Bonhoeffer asserted both the integrity and sociality of the human person. The focus of this study is on sociality in the form of community. That raises by implication the question of the integrity of the individual. No individual is identical with his or her significant communities. No community is viable without respect for the integrity of the individuals who make up the community. In that sense individuality is itself otherness, exteriority, subjectivity. It forms an essential element of the diversity of humanity and of the life of community. For that reason the individual is a permanent margin of community, a positive challenge to a praxis of inclusion and a permanent limit to the power of community. Attention to individuality strengthens the anti-totalitarian and anti-absolutist ethos of inclusive Christian ethics. It resists the tendency of normative community to coopt and normalize its participants.

Individuals may create problems for community. They may disturb community by their creativity or eccentricity. They may smother community by emphatic presence or leadership. They may burden community with their particular problems or perspectives. They may undermine community by their non-conformity. In many such ways individuals present a challenge to the life of the community. Whether such challenges will be understood to be positive or negative will depend to a great extent on the spirituality and inclusive capacity (hospitality) of community.

Relating individuals to community is not quite the same as relating them to each other, although community is obviously made up of individuals. Community is more than simply a gathering of individuals. It is their interrelatedness according to certain habits, intentions, agreements, forms of organization, and the like. It is a particular context for interrelatedness. Of course, every encounter between individuals has some context, but reference to a particular community shapes the form and experience of interaction and interrelation. Thus the spirituality and organization of community are formative for the way in which individuals can be included and appreciated, encountered, and themselves formed.

Christians share a common identity not just in their humanity but also in their relatedness to Christ and the community in his name. In fact, that common identity may exist more in a common relatedness than in any set of specific or inherent characteristics. That common identity may be shared in quite different ways. Participation in the common project of the church includes respect for individual eccentricities and identities, for cultural, sexual, and physical characteristics, as well as for the particular constellations of human personality. True inclusiveness includes diversity.

The social dynamics of individuality are similar to those of minorities. Just as the individual confronts the community with otherness, so also does the minority challenge the perceptions of the majority or dominant. Blacks confront whites, women confront men, homosexuals confront heterosexuals, and individuals confront community with difference and the possibilities of peculiarity. It is here that complementarity can be appreciated and allowed a legitimate place. It should be recognized that all such peculiarities and particularities of human existence may conversely constitute the parochialism of consciousness and conscience.[743] The danger of this for the majority and the dominant is generally greater, though not in an exclusive sense. Participation in the context of interrelatedness and inclusive community is an attempt to transcend the provinciality and subjectivity of one's own perceptions of being human and being a Christian. It may be undertaken on the basis of one's own individuality and characteristic perceptions.

It seems hardly possible to adequately describe the relation between the individual and community. Integrity and sociality, individuality and community, form two focal points for human existence. They may find a bedding in other aspects such as creatureliness. At the least, individuality and community are each other's presupposition.

### 4.2. *Character and responsibility*

Frits de Lange has pointed out that individualism is not in good repute among Christian theologians.[744] The term is often used in a suggestive sense identifying it with egoism. The sweeping derogatory uses of the term are in fact manifold and also misleading to the extent that they are not directed against the phenomenon of well developed individuals or individual responsibility, but against a far reaching privatization of our lives and our ethics. Not individual responsibility, but the lack of solidarity would then be the object of criticism. Of concern is an individualization process that undermines the assumption of responsibility, whether personal or communal.

De Lange has sought to ground the responsibility of the individual in his or her radical subjectivity induced by the confrontation with the other in the sense of Levinas. It is the original experience of accountability as disturbance that occasions subjectivity, disturbs identity, and radicalizes individuality. The constitutive power of this "original" experience is compelling. It is not to detract from it by asking about its relation to the formative power of ethical community. Hauerwas, quite differently, has indicated that we need community to learn the habits and wisdom that shape our lives ethically and that enable us to deal with the ethical challenges which confront us. It is that formation which should enable us to confront and welcome the stranger. Common is the perception that the other (or Other) may not be appropriated for ethics, for that would be a way of neutralizing his/her disturbing presence. At the same time, Hauerwas emphasizes that it is the upbringing with ethical habits and wisdom which enables and informs one's response to the other. The very capacity to submit to disturbance rather than (violently) reject it, the facility for "living out of control" (Hauerwas), is nurtured by the formation of ethical sensibility. Both disturbance and formation constitute the ethical situation. In that respect the encounter with the other can be experienced as both a disturbance and a gift.

Human individuality is a being from, with, and for others. The individual receives his/her life from others. The individual responds to others. The individual lives with others. In all this there is an inviolable integrity of the individual relating and interrelating with others and with community. The life of the individual is constituted by, though not reducible to, community. The life of the community is dependent upon, but more than the sum total of, the individuals who participate in it. A communitarian ethic is not an abrogation of individualism, but its contextualization. Community is not the center of Christian ethics, but its context. (Christian ethics is not centered any more than its perception of God is.) The community as the subject of inclusive ethics is the conciliarity of responsible and accountable individuals. Community in turn is a primary form of Christian responsibility, for community is the very form of being a Christian. Christian ethics depends on the quality of community and the maturity (responsibility) of its participating individuals.

The appeal of an individual to conscience will consequently demand respect. To say that is not to attribute inherent value to the concept of conscience. The matter of conscience is quite problematic as has already been indicated. Conscience is not a criterion of ethics, but a mode or location of ethical reflection and decision. Respect for the appeal to conscience is necessary because such an appeal is a way for an individual to assert his/her integrity and responsibility as an individual. The appeal to conscience (or to responsibility) is a reminder to community of its own limits, of the open character of ethical conciliarity, and of the borderline predicaments of human existence. Affirming the critical margin of conscience is a way of indicating that community must appreciate the charisma of individual discernment. It is another way of indicating that any orthopraxy or ethical configuration needs to remain open to its own transfiguration from the margins.

### 4.3. *Charisma and creativity*

The individual, whatever the challenge he or she presents to community, represents therefore a creative element in the life of community. Important is not just a general postulate of individuality for the sake of character and responsibility, but the concrete individuality of real persons in all their peculiarity and eccentricity, with all their diversity and disturbances, with all their colorfulness and enrichment. They provide the dynamics of conciliarity. The intent of a conciliar ethic is not social conformity or normative orthopraxis, but a critical, cooperative and lively ethical adventure. Again, conciliar community is more than the sum total of its participating individuals, but it thrives from their charismata and creativity. Attention to individual charisma and creativity contributes to Christian community as an experiment in wholeness, an exercise in embodiment, a discipleship of equals, an open committed space. (III.6.2./4.) It confirms catholicity as both diversity and community. It is in effect an assertion of freedom in community.

### *Considerations*

1. Individuals form a permanent margin of community.
2. Common identity is a common relatedness inclusive of individuality.
3. It is in the interplay of disturbance and formation that ethical responsibility is constituted.
4. The appeal to conscience is a critical reminder to community of its own limits and of the essential value of individual discernment.
5. Individuals in their creative and charismatic individuality represent freedom in community.

## IV.A.5.

## THE CHURCH AS AN ETHICAL ENTERPRISE THE COMMON JOURNEY

Christian community is a continuing story. Hauerwas has emphasized that a proper understanding of the Christian (moral) life understands it as going somewhere, a movement with direction. The metaphor for Christian life and existence becomes that of journey. "When the Christian life is conceived as a journey, a process is implied through which people are graciously transformed by the very pilgrimage to which they have been called." (III.3.3.) Other ethical notions like those of command or dialogue are given a context within the narration of the journey. Christian life is not simply one of occasionalistic obedience (or disobedience), but one of duration and direction, of formation and transformation, development and continuation.

The metaphor of journey and the notion of narration allow for ethical formation, the learning of habits and character, the practice of wisdom and discernment, as well as for growth in maturity and humanity. They provide as well a way of envisioning the continuation and transformation of tradition. Ethics becomes an undertaking, an enterprise, an endeavor, an exodus, in which new understandings can be attained and new configurations arrived at. Christian ethics has no set design of the future, no program or ideology. Rather it involves following a promise and a person. It is discipleship. It involves ordering and reordering priorities in order to order and reorder our common life.

The community of followers of Jesus can consequently be viewed as a company of pilgrims, seeking to develop the artistry and abilities needed to continue the journey. It may be a journey through time in remembrance and expectation. It may be a journey through space, rerouting and relocating the community. It may be an endeavor to consolidate and configure in the present. It is to be community with purpose and direction, and at the same time open to its own transformation and redirection. It is a hospitable company, welcoming the wayfarers and strangers whom it encounters, sharing its provisions and resources with them, lending everyone a say, enlivening itself with its own variety. It is on the move, as sojouners in strange lands, as travelers seeking their destination and as prodigals coming home. It seeks to confront dangers with patience and passion. It sustains itself with the stories and visions of its own tradition and life.

As a pilgrim company it holds within it a practice of catholicity, the solidarity of all the times and places that make up its life. In remembering, it enlivens the ties to the past, the original stories and the continuing traditions, the struggles and the sufferings, the empowerment and the guilt. In pausing, in celebrating, and in telling stories, it realizes the connectedness in the present, opens its life and learns solidarity. In expecting and hoping for the future, it discerns its direction and purpose, learns trust and responsibility.

The focus of Christian ethics is Christian community, not as a fixed configuration, but as a movement, *koinonia* and *ekklesia* in development, a process of conciliarity and inclusive participation. When journey and narrative are taken as modes of (ethical) conciliarity, they serve to root the processes of conciliarity in the origins and traditions of Christian community and relate those processes to human experiences. It is in being attentive to the stories of Israel and of the Jew Jesus that the community learns to be attentive to transcendence and exteriority, to open itself to its own transfiguration. In that way it learns to reckon with the coming of the reign of God. The focus is community. The scope is the reign of God, the future of God in the world.

***Considerations***

1. The focus of Christian ethics is pilgrim community. The scope of Christian ethics is the reign of God, the future of God in the world.
2. Journey and narration provide modes of relating the processes of ethical conciliarity to the origins and traditions of Christian community.

# IV.B.6.

# ISRAEL AND THE COMMUNITY OF CHRIST PRIORITIES

## 6.1. *Confronting the schism from Israel*

For at least six reasons any Christian ethic must begin with Israel. It is, first of all, from and through the history of the people of Israel that Christians know of the one eternal God, the sovereign of history and the creator of humankind and all that is. It is from and through Israel that they know who that God is, a God of justice and mercy, a God of the poor and the afflicted, a God who hears and acts, a God whose being is being for all humankind and for all creation.

Secondly, the God of Israel is a God of faithfulness and promise, and the promise to the people of Israel is irrevocable. (Rom 11:29) The fact of that promise alone means that Israel is the first thing to be said. Moreover, the prophetic vision of universal peace is that the peoples and nations will become pilgrims to Jerusalem and learn there the ways of God. (Is 2:2-4, etc.) Salvation is from the Jews. (Jn 4:22) The promise of peace for the nations is thus tied to the peace of Jerusalem.

And so, thirdly, that promise takes on a specific form in the covenants, commandments, and concrete history of God with Israel. The teachings, the narratives, and the practical wisdom of the *Torah*, the prophets, and the writings of Israel (together *Tenach*) provide substance to the task of ethics. They display an understanding of justice, arguably a better justice, in terms of covenant relations and historical experience. They inform political expectations with respect to loyalties, the purposes of power, and the fate of the poor. They indicate the condition of humankind and the ethos of inclusive humanity (Miskotte).

Fourthly, Israel provides the context for understanding the meaning of the life and death of Jesus and his proclamation of the reign (household) of God. The first task is not to understand Israel and its scriptures in terms of Jesus, but Jesus in terms of Israel and its scriptures. Without Israel there is no expectation of the kingdom or its messiah. Without Israel there would have been no prophet from Nazareth, no one who might be fitting to be the messiah. Bonhoeffer recognized that Jews keep the question of Christ open. (II.1.3.) And even when Jesus is confessed to be the messiah, Israel continues to enliven the question of who Jesus is and how he might be the messiah. What is the reality of the reign of

God? What is the relation between this our history and God's eschatological promise? How can it be claimed in this virulent and violent world that the messiah has come and the *basileia* of God begun? This claim and provocation of Christian confession is enlivened by the very presence and history of Israel.

Fifthly then, the context of Israel for Christian faith is not just a formal matter, but draws attention to the real passions and actions suitable to the expectation of the kingdom and to the teachings and practices of Jesus as one come to fulfill the law and the prophets and initiate the inbreaking of the messianic household of God. In what ways was Jesus a teacher and prophet of Israel? What is good news to the poor? How shall the first be last and the last first? How shall the least and the lost be gathered in wholesome community?

Sixthly, the original Christian community was essentially Jewish. The emerging Christian church was envisioned as the reconciliation of Jew and gentile. (Eph 2:11-22) Gentiles were afforded hospitality in the community of the people of God, as ingrafted branches. (Rom 11:17-24) The covenant of Jesus Christ is thus the way that gentiles might come to the God of Israel and learn the peace of Jerusalem. Communion with the God of Abraham, Isaac, and Jacob is inconceivable apart from community with Israel.

Thus the crisis of the catholicity of the church is as old as its schism from Israel.[745] The church circumvented the nature of that crisis by seeking a sectarian solution and proclaiming itself the "new Israel." One could suggest that it is not the Constantinian accommodation but the "disinheritance" of Israel that constituted the original sin of Christianity and made it susceptible to the imperialist temptation. The further history of ecclesial attitudes and actions towards Jews has made of the schism an almost insurmountable chasm, but the church would continue to deny its own origin and identity would it not wage the attempt to bridge the chasm. The words of Klappert (II.1.5.) can be recalled, that

> the decisive task of the ecumenical church is to theologically advocate the native right of Jewish Christians in the gentile church, to realize the admission of Judaism, the community of God as a people, into the ecumenical movement (abstenance from mission to Jews) and to guarantee and secure the socio-political right to existence of Judaism among the peoples (the struggle against all forms of Christian anti-Judaism and anti-Semitism).

Of course, dialogue with Jews will confront the questions of the identity of the messiah and of the related Jewish and Christian identities, but the Christian concern must be conciliarity rather than conversion. How else can the church learn? Israel has enough for itself with the divine promise. The Christian church, to the extent that it is gentile, needs Israel for its own salvation and for that of the world. The overwhelming gentile character of the church can hardly reflect the vision of the reconciliation of Jew and Gentile in Jesus Christ. It has been noted that the community of Jews and Christians cannot be limited and defined in terms of baptized Jews, but it is a question to what extent and in what manner baptized Jews can feel at home (reconciled) in Christian churches. An ecumenical extension inclusive of Jews and Christians will have to confront the Gentile domination of the church.

### 6.2. *Solidarity with justice*

Of equal priority is the struggle against anti-Semitism. The recognition that anti-Semitism is resistance to God makes of the struggle against anti-Semitism a witness to the one God whom Jews and Christians alike worship. Indisputable solidarity with Israel means solidarity with the socio-political right of Jews to exist among the peoples. If solidarity with Israel is first of all solidarity with the least of its children (Mt 25:40,45; cf. III.4.3.), then there may be situations and times when utmost attention need be given to Jews in the diaspora, but solidarity must also confront the fact of the Jewish state. What might be the response to the state of Israel?

It can hardly be seen as a necessity of faith in a general sense that Israel live in a modern nation-state, despite any theocratic interpretations of Jewish scriptures. However, what should the Christian position be when confronted with a particular state of Israel with a particular, historical origin and situation? Solidarity with Israel will clearly entail the right of Israel to its own state sovereignty. It will entail real attention to the security of its citizens and to the peace of the land.

But what is to be done when there is internal strife? How can the church pray and work for the peace of a divided Jerusalem?[746] The church finds itself in a somewhat impossible situation of needing to appropriate and repent of its past of complicity with injustice in general and anti-Judaism and anti-Semitism in particular. It needs, therefore, to seek not just dialogue but also solidarity with Jews and with their precarious political existence in the state of Israel. It needs at the same time to assess all states, including the state of Israel and its treatment of the Palestinians, critically.

There is no way out of the dilemma, no simple solution like solidarity with the one as Israel or the other as oppressed or supposedly with both. However, a direction can be sought by letting solidarity be informed by justice, an inclusive justice in terms of the biblical narrative. There is no political solidarity without solidarity with justice, for there is no viable politics without justice.

It has been argued that double standards of justice are maintained when Israel is judged by the standards of the *Torah*. The truth of that argument is that no double standards are acceptable. The ambiguity of that argument is the suggestion that there may be a standard of justice for Christians that is not informed by the *Torah* (or *Tenach*). Israel is not to be selected for harsh or unfair judgement. Christians must in all cases let their understanding of political justice be formed and informed by scripture. In staking their lives to the God of Israel Christians stake their lives to the biblical understanding of inclusive, covenantal justice, which they consider to be an arguably better justice for the sake of an arguably better politics.

Still much remains unresolved, and surely differences will be encountered. It is questionable whether *Tenach* is non-violent in the sense that the gospel advocates, despite the fact that Jesus' non-violence is, of course, thoroughly Jewish. Non-violence is not to be expected from the state of Israel. But the question is one of a responsible and viable politics, power in the pursuit of justice and freedom, purpose and peace, humanization and inclusive participation. Perhaps the agreements between the state of Israel and the Palestinian Liberation Organization will serve those purposes.

### *Considerations*

1. The schism of the church from Israel and the gentile domination of the church must be confronted with the priority of Israel and the Jewishness of Jesus in order to open the way to ecumenicity with Israel.
2. Solidarity with Israel is informed by the struggle against anti-Semitism and by solidarity with justice.

# IV.B.7.

# COLORING THE COMMUNITY FOLLOWING JESUS

## 7.1. *The confessional question*

"Who is Jesus Christ for us today?" This remains the formative and determinative question for Christian community and conciliarity. The question qualifies the ethical enterprise of the church as essentially christological, in both a confessional and contextual sense. There is for the church no ethics or meta-ethics without reference to Jesus Christ.[747] There is no reference to Jesus Christ without reference to his Jewishness and life praxis. And there is no reference to his life praxis without reference to the expectation and proclamation of the reign (household) of God.

Crucial and critical aspects of the life praxis of Jesus of Nazareth have been indicated. The reign of God was proclaimed as good news for the poor. The least and the lost were restored to fellowship. (III.4.2.) The first were put last and the last put first. Holiness took the form of wholeness, healing, and inclusiveness. In a discipleship of equals, women, slaves, and children found themselves in prominence. The outcast and the marginalized found themselves in a new household of brothers, sisters, and mothers under the gracious parentage of God. (III.6.2.) The praxis of Jesus and his disciples was thus one of service and suffering and subversion. (III.6.3.) It was characterized by truthfulness, inclusiveness, and non-violence. (III.3.4.) It was an historical community infused with eschatological joy and hope, celebrating in table fellowship the presence of God in the presence of Jesus. That person, rejected and broken, remains for the church the figure of human wholeness. (II.5.5.)

The person, presence, praxis, and passion of Jesus were thus intimately related to the coming reign of God. The claim that the power ("finger") of God was at work in him is understood in the gospels as the claim that in that work the reign of God was coming upon humankind, not here or there, but in their midst. (Luke 11:20; 17:21) The discernment of the power and presence of God is henceforth understood not just as anticipation or analogy, but as the very dynamic of the reign of God in its coming. There is no way to attain or bring about the *basileia* of God, for there is only present expectation and participation. The means are radically related to ends in a discipleship of faithfulness and following Jesus. In light of this reality of the reign of God, the world is viewed eschatologically in terms of the meaning of events and of a story that is going somewhere. The world is qualified in terms of the messianic household of God. An interfacing of history and eschatology takes place.

To relate the praxis of Jesus to the reign of God is at the same time to relate the praxis of inclusive community in his name and spirit to the reign of God. Christ existing as community (III.1.1.) and Christ existing as the kingdom (messianic household, cf. III.3.4/III.7.2.) can consequently be apprehended as two poles of one divine activity. Christ existing as community concretizes the inclusive graciousness of God in real human *koinonia* and *ekklesia*, in a discipleship of equals formed and informed by the praxis of Jesus. Christ existing as the kingdom draws attention to God's gracious inclusion of all humanity and all creation, to the catholicity and worldliness of God's purposes.

How much more could and should be said of Jesus of Nazareth, the prophet of the Sermon on the Mount, and Christ crucified and resurrected? The purpose, as Hauerwas has indicated, is not to imply a low christology, but to root all christology in the nitty-gritty of the life of Jesus. (III.3.4.) It is the recognition that no singular christology or typology does justice. That means that it is the question, who Jesus is, more than any particular answer, that is formative for the church. Insisting upon the continuing priority of the question is another way of stating that it is relatedness to Jesus, more than any specific conception of him, that is at the heart of Christian community and ethics. Living lives with him and thinking thoughts of him cannot be separated, but that life is the context of thinking and retains priority. Following preceeds confessing in the gospel narratives. That is not an absolute sequence, but it indicates that relation preceeds definition. Theology is a secondary act that reflects on the prior act of praxis. The confession required is not a description of him, but a stance with and for him. (Matthew 10:32f,40; cf. Luke 9:50;11:23)

### 7.2. *The embodiment of otherness*

F.W. Marquardt has pointed to the fact that a certain elusiveness characterized the life praxis of Jesus.[748] He often retreated, not only from the crowds and the conflict, but also from pre-set conceptions and definitions. Such retreating may be attributed partially to Jesus' own searchings and partially to his strategy, his sense of *kairos*, his patience until the appropriate moment. The fact that he retreated need not, therefore, in any way detract from his authority and personality. It remains, however, a characteristic trait of his relating to his followers as well as to the crowds, to his friends as well as to his enemies. Nor does the resurrection essentially alter that trait. The resurrection appearances were selective and limited. In the biblical narrative of those appearances who he is has yet to appear even as he is appearing.

Miskotte has pictured Judaism as a questioning existence.[749] And Bonhoeffer indicated that Jews keep the question of Christ open. (II.1.3.2.) The very structure of the gospel narratives enlivens the question of who Jesus was and is today. The diversity of witnesses to Jesus is as old as the presence and praxis of Jesus himself. Again, one need not exaggerate the differences, but neither need the church harmonize the diversity. The canon itself provides a variety of christologies. There is a diversity of witnesses to the one Jesus reflecting the life and practice of various Christian communities. Those witnesses encompass both community and diversity.

Jesus can be pictured in his context as a child of Israel sharing the expectation of the reign of God in the face of Roman repression and popular confusion. His teaching can be illuminated in terms of the central love commandments. Paradigm shifts are conceivable, for example, an understanding of Jesus in terms of feminine wisdom. It can be theologically affirmed that the Christ of the eucharist is the same as the Christ of the poor. And yet for Christian confession (and not only for historical reasons) Jesus himself remains elusive. For the "human for others" (Bonhoeffer) bears himself a characteristic otherness in his representation of transcendence and the coming of the reign of God on the one hand and in his solidarity with the least and the lost (the marginalized and the exterior) on the other hand. In that sense his being for the Other, his otherness, is his way of being for others. That in turns suggest that one needs others (e.g. in ecumenical communication) in order to approach who Jesus is.

### *Considerations*

1. There is for the church no ethics or meta-ethics without reference to Jesus Christ. There is no reference to Jesus Christ without reference to his Jewishness and inclusive life praxis. And there is no reference to his life praxis without reference to the expectation and proclamation of the reign of God.
2. It is the confessional question, "Who is Jesus Christ for us today?" more than any specific conceptions, that serves relatedness to Jesus.
3. In Christian confession Jesus represents otherness. His otherness is his way of being for others.

## IV.B.8.

## THE SOCIAL FORMATION OF THE CHURCH
## MARGINAL COMMUNITIES

Where is Christian community to be found? The first things to be said have been said: in proximity to Israel and in relatedness to Jesus Christ. But what of the church itself? In eucharistic community and solidarity? In confession and conciliarity? In a church for others? In *koinonia*? In a storied community of character? In a community for/of the poor? In a discipleship of equals, or more specifically, in an *ekklesia* of women? In all of the above? What do these descriptions imply for the organization and social formation of the church? What is the identity of the church and what is its relation to the world? An attempt to deal with these questions can pursue the conclusion drawn from Bonhoeffer: being with and for others is part and parcel of the identity of the church. The scope is all humanity, the world. The focus is the church as proxy for the world. (II.1.6.)

### 8.1. *The exterior identity of the church*

Significant is the claim that the church is characterized by an exterior identity, being for others. That claim is rooted in the identity of the church as the church of Jesus Christ. The church shares the double orientation to the other that Jesus embodied. The church is the church in its being for God, in its attention to transcendence and its discernment of the otherness of Jesus Christ. And the church is the church in its being for others, in its attention to the exterior of the earth and its participation in Jesus' praxis of being for others. Not that divine priority and human exteriority are the same, but that they coincide in an "inner transcendence." It is in and through otherness that God is revealed and known. (Cf. Dussel.)

Two possible misunderstandings are to be addressed. One is that a being for others, as Bonhoeffer envisioned, might be mistaken for social paternalism or misrepresented as superiority. That is to misunderstand the identity of the church as if the church were peculiarly in possession of something that could be handed out to the other. But no such thing is to be had. The church is *for* others in that it is *from* others. It can only be *for* others in being *with* others. Being for others is attentiveness to exteriority and transcendence.

There is often talk of the poor and marginalized as something exterior to the church, just as there is often a peculiar blindness for those of the margins who actually participate in the life of the church. The marginalized thus find themselves marginalized in the church as well. However, the thrust of claiming that the church is only the church when it is a church for others is to indicate that the poor and the marginalized are not marginal or coincidental, but central to the life of the church. Just as the divine strategy and activity is oriented towards Israel and towards the poor and the marginalized, so is the life of the church to be oriented towards the same. The concern is neither formal membership nor participation in church activities. The point is that attentiveness to the voice of the poor, whether in the church's midst or beyond its boundaries, is essential to the life of the church. The church respects the fact that the poor are the subjects of their own struggle even as it retains its own identity, but it relates its life to the life of the poor.

A second misunderstanding of the exterior identity of the church might be the evaporation of the life of the church in external activity, as if *being* for others could be reduced to *doing* for others. Being for others, however, is first of all an encounter with the other, whether as gift or disturbance. It involves attentiveness. Being for others takes the form in the church of being with and from others, of mutual encounter and the struggle for interaction. The identity of the church is allowing identities to be transformed and radicalized by others. Being for others is fundamentally a spirituality.

The church is qualified community, qualified by the biblical narrative in its attentiveness to the transcendent God and its orientation to the poor, the marginalized (the exterior), the weak and the suffering. The critical test of Christian community and unity is thus the presence and position of the marginalized. That is to say that the inclusive character of Christian community is tested not only at its margins and limits, but also by the manner in which the weak and the marginalized are central to the life of the church. (II.5.5.) Church unity is not an equilibrium, but is shaped by the priority of the vulnerable and the exterior. (II.2.7.)

Attentiveness to the margins and the marginal is, in fact, the church's way of seeking community and unity. Conciliarity is the organization of the conflicts inherent to the life of the church. It reflects an understanding of unity in terms of interaction and encounter, a unity that seeks both to reconcile and respect diversity. (II.5.5./II.2.7.) Christian community is inclusive community and humanity is inclusive humanity. (II.1.7.) Drawing special attention to the marginalized and the threatened is to recognize that the diversity to be reconciled is also one of differences in power, status, wealth, and opportunity. The conflicts are not to be reconciled by compromises, but by fundamental changes in the way things are. It is the failure of "church theology" (II.2.6.) to discern that differences hardly ever function in a neutral manner. There can be no uncritical appeal to peace and reconciliation. True inclusiveness must attribute not just equality but also priority to the weak and the suffering, the poor and the outcast. Catholicity must appreciate the particularities of those outside the "main stream" and appropriate their peculiarities for the life of the church.

The catholicity of the church is not simply inclusive of the last and the first, but takes form where the last become first. Community arises where there is room for the unwelcome. Conciliarity entails listening to the voiceless and the unheard. Justice means life space for those without the means of worthy existence.[750] Not neutrality but a critical priority is the strategy of inclusiveness. "Christ does not stand between the parties, nor even above the parties - but as the mediator of God he stands on the one side for the sake of the reconciliation of both sides."[751]

Catholicity should therefore not be confused with the greatest common denominator or with an abstract universalism. In Christian confession the unity of humanity is known only by way of a detour, that is, by way of the unity in God's calling of Israel and the church. Humanity in itself is not one but divided. There is no common story, no binding (moral) tradition that provides unity. Humanity is simply plurality and diversity and conflict. The biblical narrative is understood to display the solidarity of humanity (cf. Eve as mother of all the living, Adam in whom all die, Abraham in whom all are blessed, and Jesus in whom all are reconciled) as well as the possibility of human community (in terms of covenant, people and church).

## 8.2. *The location and organization of identity*

What form is the church to take in order to reflect the priority of the marginalized.? The difficulty, but also the dynamic, would seem to be that the movement to the marginalized and the intrusion of the stranger necessitate a shift in the location of the church. In that respect the church is not self-centered but finds its center moving to its own margins and the margins of society. (III.7.3.) However, in that very act of shifting, the church remains centered in its relatedness to Jesus Christ. If in fact there is something like a coincidence of otherness in the presence of Christ and the marginalized, then one and the same movement may move the church to the margins and center it in Christ.

This perspective presents a challenge to all sorts of centerings of churches in institutions, clerisy, hierarchy, denominationalism, confessionalism, class, culture, ethnicism, national boundaries and the like. It is a consequence of the claim that membership in the church is to be decided only by baptism in the Spirit of Jesus Christ and by no other criteria. (II.1.2.) It is the combination of the two primary constitutive elements of the church, inclusive community and Christian confession. (Cf. Boff: "authentic community and explicit Christian consciousness." III.5.1.) It is not contrary to the institutionalism of tradition or to recognized leadership, but it involves a reordering of priorities, a transfiguration of the church. It is contrary to exclusive standards of difference and discrimination as criteria for the formation of church community. It is, furthermore, a recognition that there are essentially only two forms of the church, the local eucharistic community and the global ecumenical church. (II.5.5.) All other forms of the church are to be evaluated with respect to their participation in and contribution to those two basic forms.

In this light how is the project of an *ekklesia* of women to be evaluated? How are separate gatherings of women to be understood in relation to the life of the church? In the first place it should be realized that women-church entails a significant element of protest. It entails the conviction that women have been systematically discriminated against and marginalized in the church as well as in society. It entails also the recognition that patriarchy is all-pervasive, in the structures of church and society and in the souls of humans, both male and female. The claim is that patriarchy has established itself as an epicenter in the life of the church and thus violated the inclusive nature of the church. Patriarchy has prevented women from being the subjects of their own faith and spirituality, of their own Christian life and participation in the church.

What strategy can women then follow? The proposal is that women need their own gatherings, their own places of spirituality and decision making. Might it be objected that such separation is sectarian or exclusive? Such an objection is a failure to see the very point that women are making, namely, that they have continually been formally marginalized and/or factually excluded. That leads to the claim that not women-church, but churches that marginalize women are sectarian. As long as churches do not respond to the needs and identities of women, women have no choice but to create their own spaces and strategies for the sake of remembering and appropriating their own sufferings and struggles.

Of course, some women are leaving the church, but the concept of a women-church need not carry that connotation. Rather, women-church is an attempt at ecclesiogenesis, a strategy for rebirthing the church to be inclusive of both women and men by rediscovering the power of women. It is not exclusive of men, but is directed against patriarchy. Therefore, it can focus, provisionally and temporarily, on gathering women to practice spirituality and solidarity, to become subjects of their own participation in Christian community. It is then a provisional and temporary particularism aimed at engendering a truly inclusive and catholic church. By seeking both to delineate their own spaces and to remain in dialogue with established churches, women can participate in the double task of appreciating diversity and seeking community. How long an *ekklesia* of women will be needed is consequently dependent on how long the churches need to free themselves of patriarchy.

An *ekklesia* of women provides a model of provisional particularism as a step towards catholicity, just as the poor have often needed to organize themselves without the patronizing of the rich and the hierarchy, just as blacks (and other minorities) in white societies have experienced their own churches as a haven for their own dignity and identities and culture. Such provisional particularism, if it remains open to other places and communities (cf. II.5.6.), can serve the interrelation between particular identities (social, cultural, sexual, ethnic) and common identity.

The need and form of such provisional and particular embodiments will depend on the specific context. A general strategy of evangelism or church planting along ethnic or cultural lines is, however, something quite different, and it must be asked if such a strategy will not eventually and unwittingly serve the interests of dominant society to divide and rule. The catholic calling of the church is to transcend and transgress the dividing lines of the world. The factual apartheid among, between, and in the churches must be radically addressed. And the strategy should be one of the priority of the marginalized and the exterior.

Nor is an ideology of pluralism acceptable. Plurality exists, of course, and is a fact that must be reckoned with. The question is whether much of the plurality tolerated in the church is the same as the diversity to be appreciated in catholicity. An appreciation of diversity is grounded in the unconditional love of God as known in Jesus Christ. The name of Jesus qualifies the unity and diversity. A "theology of the church" (II.2.6.) that in the name of reconciliation (or plurality) is tolerant of both parties, both the oppressors and the victims, perpetrates injustice. An ecumenical plurality that tolerates both admission and exclusion of women from ministry and that generally excludes homosexuals from ministry and table fellowship tolerates discrimination as well. Just as tolerance meets its limit in intolerance, so also the inclusiveness of the church confronts the practice of exclusion. Catholicity is a different manner of defining the inclusiveness and spaciousness of the church than pluralism.[752] When the fruit of pluralism is factual oppression or discrimination, then the catholicity of peoples and persons requires priority above a plurality of opinions and standpoints.

Are there then no limits, no occasions for exclusion? There are limits, but the limits are initially defined by inclusion. The interpretation of the *status confessionis* indicated that it does not represent an exclusive standpoint or excommunication, but that on the contrary it has been put forth as an essential defense of the catholic inclusiveness of the church. Limits are drawn against those who have already violated the inclusiveness by their exclusive practices, thus dividing the table fellowship of the church. The primary intention of confession is clarity, communication, and invitation, not exclusion. For that reason, any exclusion bears an awesome burden of proof. The task of inclusion remains that of transgressing limits and transcending tolerance in a practice of encounter and acceptance. An appreciation of difference and diversity, if it is not to turn reactionary or indifferent, must be informed by solidarity.

The unity of the church (as was especially indicated in the statements and confessions in the context of apartheid; cf. II.2.7.) is to be visibly manifested and practiced in worship and works. Unity is mutual exchange. It is community that seeks both to reconcile and respect diversity. In doing so it attributes priority to the poor and the marginalized, sharing the solidarity of Jesus with the least and the lost. It is thus a unity not for its own sake, but extrovert community seeking to exemplify the praxis of Jesus for the sake of God's reign in the world.

Such unity finds practical translation in the face-to-face of local community (Dussel), in the development of networks, in the practice of hospitality, in solidarity with the victims, in all those things that enable churches and Christians to transgress and transcend the dividing lines of this world. The church cannot fulfill this task in personal, religious encounter apart from the world, nor by simply proclaiming political solutions, however prophetic. Instead, the church will need to respond to the challenge by embodying ways of living together, by shaping community, and by seeking a position and a vocation amidst the political and social realities. Between the micro-scale of the privatized individual and the macro-scale of the impersonal powers and principalities, Christian community can provide a meso-niveau of personal encounter and responsible empowerment.[753] In that manner the church can provide organizational and institutional forms for a spirituality of being for others.

What then of discipleship groups, regional or national churches, and strategic organizations? (See II.5.5.) Discipleship groups in their practice of a specific lifestyle or ministry can inform the life of the church. The hope is that they will seek to relate their practice to the life of other local communities. The fear must be that established churches will let them be and ignore their voices. National churches and regional churches along ethnic or cultural lines are in particular danger of solidifying the national and cultural loyalties which hinder the catholic calling of the church. The accommodation by the church to national interests, especially in times of war, has been historically one of the most severe and fatal injuries to the life of the church. Strategic organizations for mission, diaconal work, economic sharing, and political activity may often be needed to spearpoint the movement of the church. Their temptation lies in their creation of self-sufficient organizations and cells. Christian cooperation needs to be rooted in communion.

The point of paying attention to all of these particular and/or strategic endeavors is the recognition that they may be expressing something that other churches are missing. All such traditions may be evaluated in terms of their participation in the catholic calling of the church, if at the same time their particular truth and significance are discerned. They should not, as has so often occurred in church history, be relegated to the heretical or quaintly historical. They quite often represent the deficits of the church in its dominant forms. Traditions have something to say to each other, and the traditions of the marginalized bear their particular truths.

The implication is an orientation toward the margins, whereas women-church has been understood as a movement from the margins to the center. Women lay claim to the center of the church. What should be moving, women or the churches? Russel speaks of "situation-variability", a dialectical reordering of margin to center and center to margin. (III.7.2.) To some extent it may be a question of perspective or starting point, but the challenge of the margin indicates that the center itself is problematic. It is not the vision of women-church that women move into the center of churches as they are. The movement of women in the church is intended as a renewal and liberation of the church from the centers of power, culture and confessionalism. That suggests churches themselves being re-centered. A regrouping and reorientation takes place around a new center. The center remains Jesus Christ, but the center is found in a new place, at what was previously a margin. Attention to the marginalized tends to decenter and relocate the church in order to recenter it. For that reason the ecclesiological task of the church can be envisioned as one of being attentive to the margins and of allowing itself to be reshaped (perhaps in the round, but perhaps in some irregular shape).

Churches and church communities will always be resistant to such recentering. They maintain their own inertia and weight in order to institutionalize their own particular traditions and experiences. Yet they will need to realize that such recentering is a part of their traditions and origins, as far back as Jesus' orientation to the least and the lost, as fundamental as the fellowship of Jew and Gentile. From that perspective the *status confessionis* can be seen not as a threat to unity, but as a call to a renewed unity of confession and obedience. (II.3.2.) The way of radical discipleship, rather than being sectarian, can be understood as a practice of hospitality and non-violent inclusiveness. (III.3.5.) An *ekklesia* of women need not be considered separatist, but as an invitation to catholicity beyond patriarchy. (III.6.4.) The "borderline case" of assuming radical responsibility can prove illuminating and exemplary for the ethics of the church. (III.1.5.) The marginal become "witnesses to the sanctity of the unity of the church."[754]

## 8.3. *Marginalizing the church*

The unity of the church has been related to the unity of humankind. That recognition serves to root the church in the world. It is not that the church could be any where else, but that the church has often submitted to the temptation to define its distinctive flavor at the cost of the world rather than for the sake of the world. The distinctive feature of the church that is being emphasized here is its inclusive praxis of confession and community. The strategy of that inclusiveness is attention to the margins. Attributing priority to the margins is the manner in which the church seeks its own unity and the unity of humanity. The location and vocation of the church in the world is thus similarly defined in terms of its attention to the margins.

This is to reiterate the conclusion that the primary political relation of the church is not to the state, but to the poor, the marginalized, and the suffering. (II.2.5.) This is also to suggest that the decentering of the church also serves to decenter it in the world. Bonhoeffer spoke of the church as a critical center from which all is judged. The church witnesses to the center which God makes known. That center may, according to historical measures, lie in the periphery, but the church seeks to create space for God's work. (See III.1.4.) And yet that theological center is located in the periphery, in the margins, in proximity to the least and the lost, in attentiveness to exteriority. Theologically speaking, that is not to say that God is never in the middle of things, never at the perceived center of the world and its business, but that even when God might be at the center, it is in order to transfigure that center in terms of transcendence and exteriority. The use of the term 'marginality' is an attempt to provide a social translation for (or relation to) transcendence and exteriority. (Cf. III.4.2.)

Reservations on centering the church in the world have been expressed above. (Cf. the discussion of Bonhoeffer's position in III.1.4.) The problem is the pretention, intended or not, in assigning the church a central position whether in the eliptical Lutheran doctrine of two kingdoms or the concentric Barthian conception of the Lordship of Christ. Such a political conception seems to reflect the Constantinian context and the particularities of western history. Even if the intention of the concept is to deny secular church authority and/or superiority, the church is nevertheless related essentially to the state and established in the center.

The church's position (and possible centrality) in society seems to be a fluctuating affair, on decline presently in the West due to the marginalizing effect of secularization, on the rise in some other places where it may serve social protest or spiritualizing escapism, and in a seemingly permanent diaspora in yet other places. Whatever the fluctuations, the moments in which churches stood at the center of society, not to mention at the centers of power, were hardly ever their most glorious and faithful moments. It was, to cite a contrary example, the critical distance of the Evangelical Church in East Germany prior to 1989 that enabled it to play a central role in the turn of events of that year. If, in addition, the present plea for an orientation of the church towards the margins is appropriate, then the term center would seem to confuse rather than clarify the precarious relation of the church to the world (and to the state), not just sociologically, but also theologically. Christian confession is that God's activity is centered in Jesus Christ and not in the world.

Confessing Christ and creating marginal community puts the church off-center in the world, and that may be another way of recognizing that the world has no unifying center. The world is its (sectarian) dividedness and plurality, and has no unity or center in itself. (III.5.3./IV.8.1.) The world is multi-dimensional in its pluriform existence: politics, economics, society, communities, organizations, individuals, ideologies, militaries, cultures, subcultures, religions, and so on (not to mention nature and the environment). A multi-dimensional world without a demonstrable center implies and requires a multi-dimensional relation of the church to the world, "polyphonous" in Day's interpretation of Bonhoeffer. (III.1.4.) The relation of the church to the world is not governed by its relation to state or society in a general sense, but by its understanding of the mission of Jesus to the marginal as a dynamic of the coming reign of God.

Of course, the political relation will continue to play a significant role, but the terms of political discipleship are not to be dictated by a particular model of the relation of church and state.[755] The observations on Romans 13 and Revelation 13 were that, despite the very different picturings of the state, they roughly concurred on the nature of political discipleship: overcoming evil with good by means of non-violent discipleship and discriminating witness. (III.1.4.) The words of Jürgen Moltmann are helpful:

> The theme of the New Testament is not a Christian metaphysics of the state, but the position of Christians on politics. Not a theological doctrine of the state, but a theological foundation for Christian political discipleship is taught.[756]

The terms of Christian political discipleship should not be simplistically summarized, but they are governed by the formation of marginal community, by the struggle to resist violence and practice justice, by solidarity and hospitality, by the very things that make up the life of the church.

Decentering the church in relation to the state and the world and centering it in its marginal task can serve to liberate the church from its fascination with the state. It might also serve to liberate the church from its obsession with its own freedom, whether in terms of a general freedom of religion or more specifically in terms of freedom of proclamation of the gospel. Freedom and integrity of the church are defined in its relatedness to and its centeredness in Jesus Christ. To that extent the church is not dependent on the state for its freedom, but can claim and create its own freedom in its self-marginalization. Political freedom (and religious freedom is a form of political freedom) is, of course, to be welcomed and worked for, not just for the sake of the church, but for the sake of humanity, and particularly for the sake of the politically endangered. The church, however, is not free if the marginalized are not free, for then the church finds itself obligated to the cause of the politically coerced.

To state that the formation of community is a fundamental political act is actually a redundancy, but it can be emphasized in order to point out the radical nature of inclusive community. Inclusive community is radical because it confronts the private and particular interests of the state, of ideologies, of social movements and of all sorts of other communities. It is always a question to what extent the state serves the unity of humanity (even the unity of its own society) rather than any number of private and particular interests. In that respect catholicity provides the church criteria for evaluating social movements and ideologies. They are to be evaluated not just on the basis of their partial truths, but also on the basis of their inclusiveness and methodology. They may, like alternative and heretical Christian movements, expose specific deficits that need to be taken into account. Here again catholicity points not just to inclusiveness in a general sense, but to marginality. The situation of the poor in society remains a primary criterion of justice and of evaluation of the political order and struggle.

In this manner a basis and specific criteria are also to be found for cooperation of Christians with non-Christians. In fact, relating the unity of the church to the unity of humanity assumes such an inclusive praxis. Of course, cooperation must be discriminating and discerning, but that is valid for non-cooperation as well. There are no grounds for annexing the humanizing and inclusive praxis of others as essentially Christian. Inclusiveness and humanization are not in themselves Christian. Christian living is oriented to the praxis of Jesus of Nazareth. It is confessional. Therefore a spirituality of being for others can recognize and respect the otherness of others. It seeks cooperation with others and affirms the peculiar contributions of others. It also respects the integrity and dignity of those others, whether individual or communal, just as it seeks to maintain its own integrity. Others may have more to say to us precisely as we respect their otherness.

Cooperation is thus not an assumption of an implicit or latent Christianity of others, but a testimony to the wideness of God's messianic reign. (III.3.5.4.) Christian political discipleship is governed by witness to the inclusive household of God. It is the reign of God rather than the state that is the primary political relation of the church, and, because the proclamation of the kingdom is good news to the poor, that relation takes the form of marginal community.

### *Considerations*

1. Being for others is being with, from, and for others as a fundamental spirituality.
2. Attentiveness to the margins and to the marginal is the church's way of organizing community and seeking unity.
3. An *ekklesia* of women can provide a strategy of provisional particularism on the way towards a catholicity of women and men.
4. Attention to the margins serves to re-center and relocate the church.
5. Confessing Christ and creating marginal community put the church off-center in the world.
6. The reign (household) of God and the people of the poor, not the state, constitute the primary political relation of the church.
7. A catholicity of peoples and persons has priority above a plurality of opinions and standpoints.

## IV.B.9.

## THE STRUGGLE TO RESIST VIOLENCE PERCEPTIONS AND PASSIONS

### 9.1. *The perception of violence*

Hauerwas has asserted "that the question of violence is the central issue for any Christian social ethic." (III.3.7.) Similarly, Bonhoeffer, Lehmann, and Dussel afford particular attention to the matter of violence. Their findings on political responsibility and violence should perhaps be complemented and contrasted with an analysis of patriarchal violence and the sufferings and strategies of women. That such an analysis is not included here is a recognition of certain limitations, but nevertheless a deficit.

Liberation theologians like Dussel have pointed to the difference between the institutionalized violence of oppression and revolutionary violence that challenges oppression. (III.4.6.) Revolutionary violence may in turn be met by repressive violence.[757] It should be clear that no judgement on revolutionary violence can be made without taking into account its nature and context, that is, without passing judgement on oppressive and repressive violence. Often the burden of justification is laid upon revolutionary violence rather than on the violence of the existing order and oppression. That is not only a double moral standard, but overlooks the fact that oppressive violence by its nature seeks perpetuation of the order of violence, whereas revolutionary violence often seeks a transition to an order of (relative) non-violence.

The extent to which violence has become institutionalized can be seen in the manner in which conscientious objection to military conscription has been tolerated in modern western societies. Not the person who is willing to kill another human being is required to give an account of his motives and reasons, but the person who rejects such killing. That is ethics turned upside down. If violence is to be admitted at all, it is the use of violence and the engagement in war that must be motivated and justified and not their rejection. War cannot be accepted as a normal mode of human relations in the face of which pacifism has to justify itself. From an ethical point of view military candidates should be screened to test their motives and reasons for commiting themselves to armed service. Instead, a standing army has become part and parcel of the accepted immoral fabric of our societies.

The pervasive presence of violence in human lives and societies need not be accepted as being just the way things are. Not violence, but non-violence should form the point of orientation for thinking and acting. This is the force of Hauerwas' argument that it is not pacifism (or non-violence) that is sectarian and elitist, but violence. (III.3.5./III.3.7.) For it is violence that serves particular national and/or economic interests. It is violence that more often than not serves the position of the privileged and the possessive. It is violence that serves to divide rather than reconcile.

In the midst of the divisions of apartheid and under the threat of mutual nuclear annihilation the confession was sounded that "Christ is our peace". (II.2.5./II.3.3./II.3.4.) Reconciliation was understood to be a formative reality for the life and practice of the church. Such assertions of the reality of reconciliation were not carried to the ultimate consequence of pacifism. Might it be argued that the conviction that something needs to be reconciled is also a recognition of the reality of hostility and injustice as something to be reckoned with? Indeed, hostility and injustice must be reckoned with in the sense that there is no reconciliation without their repudiation, no peace without justice. That is not the same, however, as attributing to them formative significance. For that would be to take the pervasive presence of hostility and injustice as being just the way things are.

The conclusion must seem to be that violence should be generally and categorically rejected. Yet even a repudiation of all violence must be discerning lest it serve to mask the violence of the existing order. Lehmann states that revolutionary movements and their accompanying violence need first to be understood. The primary task is to discern the meaning of events. (II.2.5.) It is only from there that an adequate response can be formulated and acted out. If that be true, then the first act of political responsibility is to discern and analyze violence in its various occurrences and configurations. In that process the political competence of faith can express itself in the art of discernment and in the analysis of the human condition provided by Christian convictions. (The narratives of violence in scripture, rather than being misused to legitimize further violence, could be explored for the sake of understanding the nature of violence.)

It has been argued that pacifism fails to reckon with the fact that the use of force is integral to politics. Hauerwas, on the contrary, argues that the use of force is more often a failure to engage in political imagination. (III.3.7.) It makes of politics a coercive exercise of might rather than a powerful art of formative imagination. It relieves politics of the task of seeking non-coercive forms of power and viable alternatives to the exercise of force. The interesting question is not in general terms whether we can organize our social lives without force and coercion, but how far we may succeed in organizing them by means of specific alternatives to coercion. Democracy is one such attempt, but there are other alternatives as well. Not just misuses of power need exposure. Positive practices of power ought to be explored as well.

In a very different way, Dussel points beyond the obsession with coercive violence by distinguishing between armed violence and prophetic violence. (III.4.6.) Prophetic violence is subversive but not coercive in that it seeks the liberation and not the annihilation of the dominator. That makes it an "unequivocal testimony." Nevertheless, Dussel is understandably respectful of the sacrifice of the political hero in his or her (armed) attempt to subvert the existing oppressive order of violence. Dussel recognizes as well that the vocation of resistance and subversion is hardly practicable without at least provoking violence. This is the dilemma of the "unequivocal testimony" of the prophet and the martyr. For Dussel it is not the vocation of the prophetic people to take up arms, but he does recognize the passion and force of resistance and the violence of its context. Prophetic resistance is both vocation and provocation. Resistance and non-violence together are essential characteristics of the prophetic vocation and identity of the church.

### 9.2. *The economy of violence*

One of the things that an analytical or descriptive (rather than a moralistic) view of violence might indicate is its inadequacy and costliness (rather than simply its wrongness).[758] What are the material and social costs of suppression? What are the moral costs of getting accustomed to institutionalized violence and the practice of war? Why do so many revolutions fail and end up devouring their own children? (III.2.5.) Or in what respect do they fail even when they succeed? Do modern political organization and military technology allow for violence within acceptable and calculable limits? (II.3.1.)

The nuclear debate has subsided, but the weapons, despite any reductions among the major powers, still exist volumnously. Evidently, the problems of nuclear proliferation have themselves become proliferated. Wars in Iraq and Yugoslavia have demonstrated the sheer unwillingness and/or impossibility of limiting the weapons trade. More and more civilians are the victims of warfare and violent strife. An idealistic revolution is hard to come by these days. Instead countries are torn apart by rival factions. Attention is thus diverted from the issue of internal revolution to that of international intervention. The criteria of just war, having found temporary application to concepts of just revolution, are being rehauled for legitimizing "just" intervention. The scale of warfare and the proliferation of violence seem to be again on the rise, confronting Christian community and confession with more difficult and diffuse dilemmas than the challenge of East-West nuclear hostility.

The renunciation of the spirit, logic, and praxis of modern warfare, whether nuclear or not, has become no less crucial. The catholic nature of the church remains victim to the crossfires of national and international interests with every victim who falls. So also the justification of revolution and intervention must be exposed. Even when, in a singular case, some understanding can be afforded to the desperate resort to violence and respect can be given to those who thus give their lives to combat injustice, the entire project of justification of violence ought to be abandoned. The rhetoric of justification has proven too prone to ideological misuse and the criteria for intervention too arbitrary. Violence (internal or external) is not a solution, as is suggested by its justification, but a restaging of the conflict.

Dussel further illumines that conflict by relating violence to the question of revolution and subversion, for that is a way of relating the question of violence to the question of bread, the question of justice and injustice, of hunger and the market economy. This serves to an extent to contextualize perspectives on violence. At the same time, relating violence to the context of an encompassing world economy serves to generalize those perspectives. World economy and international interests are so pervasive that local contexts are being violated and engulfed in international relations. In that respect also the stakes of the game are being raised.

The assertion of the *status confessionis* with respect to world economy at least raised the question of the violence being done to the body of Christ by institutionally perpetrated injustice and poverty. (II.4.) Dussel exposed the domination and oppression by the system as the death of the poor. (III.4.2.) The problem is not just one of excesses or incidental injustices, but of structural poverty and exploitation. If, in fact, the answer cannot be found in corrective measures or reform, then there is needed a renunciation of the spirit, logic, and praxis of the free market system with respect to its autonomous character and deathly consequences, with respect to the mechanisms of exploitation of both humanity and nature, with respect to the unbridled trading in instruments of war and death.

It can be questioned whether an understanding of the workings of world economy in terms of violence will stimulate economic relief. Many who do not (and perhaps can not) experience the violence of their daily economic affairs may thus be alienated from a closer look at the way things work. And the complexity of the system serves to conceal complicity. The term 'complicity' may even be subject to misunderstanding in terms of personal accusation and guilt. The question of guilt is also to be confronted, but it is to be imbedded within the recognition of a common humanity and the assumption of responsibility. (II.4.2.) The first responsibility must be to hear the witness of the poor on the economic system. Common participation in the world economic order leads to a common vocation to subvert the system, to resist and to seek alternatives. Common participation in the world economic violence and the structures of political organization leads to the recognition that we are not non-violent.

## 9.3. *The passion of responsibility*

The question of violence and non-violence is the question of the form of (political) responsibility. Hauerwas rejects the argument that pacifism evades political responsibility. Non-violence as a condition of justice is precisely an attempt to enliven political imagination. (III.3.7.) Conceptions of justice are to be critically examined with a view to their coercive elements. (III.3.8.7.) Dussel insists that struggle and resistance, passion and subversion, are conditions of the renunciation of violence. (III.4.6.3.) The ethical project of Hauerwas seems lacking with regard to the question of sharing bread as a question of justice and with regard to struggle and subversion as the context of non-violent praxis. Boff indicates, similar to Dussel, that the project of engendering community, ecclesiogenesis, coincides with the praxis of liberation. (III.5.1.) It is a discipleship of equals that overcomes violence and repression in its midst, and it is the passion for liberation that shapes the equality of the disciples. The discipleship of equals is a community of justice, sharing bread and passion and empowerment.

Christian community is not non-violent. It bears within it the conflicts and the scars of violence in this world. For that reason non-violence cannot be understood as a standpoint or principle but rather as a vocation. As a vocation non-violence reflects the early Christian conviction that it is better to suffer injustice than to inflict injustice. Similarly, Bonhoeffer stated that Christians cannot take up arms against each other without violating the presence of Christ in their midst. To be sure, the insistence upon peaceableness creates conflict within the church. That conflict is generally resolved in terms of some form of complementarity thesis. Instead the conflict needs to be continually reorganized in a praxis of conciliarity and ecumenical solidarity.

At the same time Dussel makes clear that Christian community cannot limit its concern to its own praxis of non-violence. It needs equally to be concerned with a praxis of justice that confronts the causes of violence in the world. Lehmann advocates attention to a transcendence that can transfigure politics and revolution. Hauerwas emphasizes a praxis of truthfulness that will unmask the manifold excuses for violence and enliven political wisdom and imagination. Dussel is more radically concerned with a fundamental critique of the economy of violence in order to subvert the existing totality.

There are thus alternatives to violence and their neglect is a contribution to violence. There are (relative) non-violent forms of power such as democracy and sociocracy. There are ways of organizing cooperation and communication that enable consensus. There are methods of non-violent resistance. There are examples of the exercise of the art of politics. There is a spirituality of non-violence as well as an ethos of the Sermon on the Mount. There are trainings to enlarge capacities for non-violence, and there are communities to teach character and resilience.

Christian communities can, therefore, turn to investing their energies and resources in learning and practicing non-violence. A general preference for non-violence is of no avail if it does not take the form of a commitment to shaping the strategies and spirituality of non-violence into a vivid and viable alternative. Violence is the context, but non-violence is the vocation and point of orientation. Dussel retains the word violence for the sake of its passion and purifying force. An option for non-violence should exemplify the same passion, not as an escape from violence, but as a transcendence of violence in the manner of Ghandi and Martin Luther King.

It is a passionate commitment to non-violence that lends integrity to the discernment of violence and the analysis of the economy of violence. It is the vocation of non-violence that provides Christian communities with identity and direction. At the same time it is their identity as inclusive Christian communities that leads them to resist the violation of the body of Christ in the violation of the bodies of their fellow humans and to renounce the economy of violence. Here, too, means are radicalized for the sake of participation in the ends of peace. "There is no way to peace. Peace is the way."

This position certainly tends toward a categorical rejection of any and all violence. It does not reach that point because it understands non-violence as a vocation rather than a category. It may be asked if there are any criteria for stopping short of a total rejection, any possibility of the justification of revolutionary or interventionist violence, any legitimizing motives or interests. One might understand that some resort to violence out of desperation. One may appreciate the fact that the courage to risk violence is more fitting than cowardice. And yet that entails no real acceptability of violence.

What hinders a categorical rejection is Bethge's judgement that Bonhoeffer's participation in the conspiracy was a borderline case and yet one of exemplary significance. (III.1.5.) It sprang from the recognition that the diabolic stupidity dominating Germany could be confronted neither by an act of edification nor by aquiescence in the fateful course of events, but only in an act of forceful liberation. Responsibility had to be assumed and it was assumed passionately. When all attempts failed, the passion of martyrdom had to be accepted.

A contrary viewpoint is the treatment afforded Bonhoeffer's participation in conspiracy by Stephen Fowl and Gregory Jones in their review of Bonhoeffer's performance of scripture.[759] The suggestion is that Bonhoeffer's lack of a formative community led him not only to strained readings of scripture but also to a regretful participation in resistance and conspiracy. Fowl and Jones do see (with McClendon) that the fundamental tragedy was the eclipse (or lack) of responsible Christian community in Germany. What they fail to appreciate is the responsible and exemplary character of Bonhoeffer's actions in the community of conspiracy. Thus they suggest that Bonhoeffer's affirmative reflections on the conspiracy from his prison cell can be attributed to extreme conditions and prison cell isolation, far from the "shared friendships and practices of Christian community" that might have formed his judgements differently.

Indeed, community can help us to read and perform scripture better, but there is no basis for the suggestion that Bonhoeffer read poorly due to his isolation in the prison cell. (Such a judgement is not only abstract, but also a failure to remember how Jeremiah and Paul contributed to scripture from prison and to recognize how Bonhoeffer and Martin Luther King contributed to an understanding of Christian and community life from prison.) The non-violent Bonhoeffer and his "cohorts in the resistance" were for the sake of the world and for the sake of the church living out responsibility passionately. They were standing in the place where the church had failed to stand by not even assuming responsibility. They failed as conspirators but they excelled in the passion of resistance and in exemplary existence for others.

Bonhoeffer sought no justification or legitimization. In fact he recognized the severe risk of such an act of responsibility. Appeal to responsibility did not solve the issues or resolve the complexities. Bonhoeffer was himself aware that it was an act that could hardly be ethically validated or ecclesially supported. He could hardly imagine a church or a community rallying around such an effort or intervention. At the same time one can hardly imagine how the church can afford not to allow Bonhoeffer's participation in the conspiracy to inform its perceptions of violence and to form its passions of non-violence. Furthermore, the example of Bonhoeffer, understood within the totality of his commitments and life, can only serve to deepen a commitment to and understanding of the vocation of prophetic resistance and radical non-violence.

### *Considerations*

1. The church is not non-violent. Non-violence is a vocation.
2. The primary task in confronting violence is to discern the meaning of events.
3. The institutionalization of violence which requires a justification of non-violence is ethics turned upside down.
4. Non-violence should be understood in terms of a strategy of political imagination and responsibility seeking non-coercive forms of power.
5. The question of violence is not just one of weapons and warfare, but also of the (economic) institutions that govern our lives. In that respect the renunciation of the spirit, logic, and praxis of modern warfare can be complemented by the renunciation of the spirit, logic, and praxis of the free market.
6. Prophetic resistance is to be practiced as a passionate vocation of provocation.
7. The vocation of non-violence is not the vocalization of positions on violence but the practical commitment to engendering alternatives.
8. The borderline (marginal) case of violence cannot be justified. It can only be critically risked in an act of responsibility informed by passionate commitment to non-violence.

## IV.B.10.

## THE CHURCH AS AN ETHICAL REALITY COMMUNITY

According to Dussel (liberation) theology begins with an affirmation, a "radical principle" of "the face-to-face of the person-to-person relationship in the concrete, real, satisfied, happy, community, in the gladness of being one with God and one with our brothers and sisters, the members of the community." In fact the "essence of the Christian life is community: being together with others. This is also the essence of the reign of God: to be together with God, face-to-face with God in community." (III.4./4.1.) For Lehmann "the church, the fellowship which is the body of Christ, the *koinonia,* is the fellowship-creating reality of Christ's presence in the world." (III.2.2.) Boff emphasizes that Christianity is essentially oriented to the communitarian spirit, that the project of engendering community coincides with the project of liberation. (III.5.1.) In several manners Hauerwas draws attention to Christian community as the focus of God's strategy for creating a new people, for making us who we can become. (III.3.) The most daring description is that of Bonhoeffer, of "Christ existing as community."

Community and covenant relationships are what God is about in the world in order to humanize the world and empower community to participate in the reign (household) of God. Community is a way of organizing human conflict and engendering reconciliation. That makes of community both an object and subject of ethical praxis, an experiment in humanity and maturity, an embodiment of social ethic. It makes of Christian community the focal point of Christian life and confession. The local eucharistic community is the place where Jesus is remembered, where his presence in communion is celebrated, and where ways are sought and found to participate in the coming of the reign of God. In sharing bread around the table of Jesus Christ and in sharing the bread of justice with the poor the community embodies the truth of the church as the body of Christ.

Christian community is, in the first place, not so much something done, but something in which Christians find themselves. It is fundamentally an affirmation of human existence and creatureliness, of individuality and sociality, of unity and diversity, of struggles and sufferings. It is both spiritual and corporeal, spirituality and embodiment. It is the dynamics of the body of Christ as a spiritual and corporeal reality. It is living with God by living together. Christian community is, in Russel's vivid images, round table partnership, kitchen table solidarity, and welcome table hospitality. (III.7.1.)

Lehmann and Dussel lay emphasis on *koinonia*, fellowship, communion, community. Boff's attribution of priority to community above institutional church or society would seem to suggest that the word community more than the word church indicates what the church is about. Schüssler Fiorenza on the other hand has emphasized the word *ekklesia*, church, specifically in its civil-political meaning of a body gathered for deliberation and decision making. (III.6.4.) Effectually the word 'community' has been used to indicate both *koinonia* and *ekklesia*. Christian community is *koinonia*: the experience of interrelatedness, mutual affirmation and respect, sharing bread, the practice of catholicity. And Christian community is *ekklesia*: the practice of conciliarity, of organizing conflicts and common life, of sharing responsibility.

While Christian community (the church) can be understood as both *koinonia* and *ekklesia*, Schüssler Fiorenza's lead suggests putting more *ekklesia* into (practical) ecclesiology, not at the cost of *koinonia*, but in order to validate the inclusive, political nature of Christian *koinonia*. It is the *ekklesia* that organizes the processes of (ethical) conciliarity and thus gives shape and profile to Christian confession and *koinonia*. It is the *ekklesia* that sustains the (ethical) identity and integrity of the church. It is the *ekklesia* that responds in decision and action when the catholic quality of the church is violated. It is the *ekklesia* that reorients and reorganizes the life of the church in the form of marginal communities.

### *Considerations*

1. The proper location of the church is the local eucharistic community where the bread of justice is shared in inclusive community around the table of Jesus Christ.
2. Christian community is both *koinonia* and *ekklesia*, both object and subject of ethical praxis, both a spiritual and corporeal embodiment of the life of Christ in human lives.
3. More *ekklesia* in practical ecclesiology can serve to validate the catholic nature of *koinonia*, to sustain the identity and integrity of the church as inclusive community and to reorganize the church in the form of marginal communities.

# V. EPILOGUE

## *The praxis of mutuality and marginality*

## 1. THE *STATUS CONFESSIONIS* AND ECCLESIOLOGY

Following Bonhoeffer's lead a clarification of the *status confessionis* has been pursued from the perspective of ecclesiology. In that way attention was focused on the nature of Christian community and solidarity. Whereas the German church struggle was dominated by questions of theological and ecclesial authority, Bonhoeffer pointed to (ecclesial) solidarity with Israel as the crucial issue. In the context of apartheid the unity of the church and the reconciliation of diversity were affirmed. Unity was understood not in a neutral sense but in terms of the priority of the poor and the marginalized. In the debate on nuclear weapons reconciliation in Christ was confessed as a fundamental theological orientation. In the context of (mass) impoverishment it was asserted that the integrity of the church and (the doctrine of) the unity of humankind were violated in the waste of human lives and the failure to take responsibility. In all of the above contexts the church came to be understood in terms of the body of Christ, as an ethical reality and praxis of human solidarity. Church unity was seen to entail concretely manifested community as a political reality. It came to be seen that the intent of the *status confessionis* is not exclusion or excommunication, but communication of the fundamental inclusiveness of the Christian ethos. The *status confessionis* is in essence a defense of the inclusive unity of the church.

It became apparent at the same time that the term *status confessionis* was problematic. As a term it served controversy rather than clarification. Its suggestive impact caused confusion in matters of confession and moralism in matters of ethics. Its communicative intention was overwhelmed by the excommunicative interpretations. It seemed necessary to seek alternatives for formulating the challenge intended in the use of the *status confessionis* terminology. A certain kinship was discovered in the conciliar process for justice, peace, and the integrity of creation and in the call for a *kairos* for the churches. The terminological explorations provided the suggestion that the *status confessionis* in its modern usage could be reinterpreted in terms of conciliarity and catholicity.

At the same time it became apparent that a terminological substitute was not enough. The challenge and questions raised by the *status confessionis* debate necessitated more systematic reflection on the relation between ecclesiology and ethics. That reflection could at the same time lend substance to a new terminology. To that end the theological projects of several theologians who explicitly related ethics and ecclesiology were explored. In those reviews Christian community emerged as an ethical reality, as both subject and object of ethical praxis. Questions arose as to the non-violent nature of the church, the manner in which justice was to be pursued, the priority of the poor and the marginalized, and the praxis of inclusive solidarity. Theological claims on the church were understood as the outcome of an ascriptive appeal to tradition, both descriptive and prescriptive, for the sake of a transformed understanding of the church.

In other words, if the *status confessionis* could be restated, then only in the context of a concept of the church. In fact, the concept of the church was the very context in which Bonhoeffer had originally understood the *status confessionis*. Restating the *status confessionis* would then entail doing ecclesiology, not in a comprehensive sense, but for the sake of delineating certain criteria and perspectives. An attempt to do that was framed in terms of conciliarity and catholicity.

The term conciliarity served to indicate the basic processes and perspectives underlying the challenge of the *status confessionis*. To begin with, the classic attributes of the church were seen to provide ethical substance and definition for an understanding of the church. Their implication was an inclusive community capable of a common reading of scripture and of a conciliar approach to ethics. The need was seen to appropriate the perspectives of the marginalized and the poor, to appreciate the value of the individual and the particular. Ethics could thus be understood as an enterprise, a continual challenge to confession and an ongoing transfiguration of the church.

The term catholicity served to express the identity and integrity of the church. It proved capable of relating unity and diversity and of establishing the inclusive ethical perspective of the *status confessionis*. The priority of Israel was seen as the first fundament of the church. In that context the confessional question, "Who is Jesus Christ for us today?", could be affirmed. To confess Jezus Christ meant in turn to participate in the praxis of inclusive human community, transformed by the reconciliation in Christ and transfigured with respect to the marginalized, the exterior and the poor. Consequently it was seen how attentiveness to transcendence and exteriority placed the church off center in human society. From that position and perspective the vocation of non-violence as prophetic resistance to armed and economic violence proved integral to the life of the church. It became evident how the church bears a political identity shaped not primarily by the state but by the reign of God and by its relation to the poor and marginalized.

The *status confessionis* on Israel can thus be understood as the abiding confession of the priority of Israel for the church. The *status confessionis* in the context of apartheid can be understood as the fundamental praxis of the gift of reconciliation in the church in recognition of the priority of the poor and marginalized. The *status confessionis* as protest against nuclear weapons can be understood as the confession of Christ as peace, of the body of Christ as a community of peace, and of its essential vocation to resist the sectarian spirit of violence. The *status confessionis* as a call of despair in the face of mass poverty is understood as the affirmation of the doctrine of the unity of humankind and of the solidarity of the body of Christ as well as the assumption of inescapable human and Christian responsibility for justice. The *status confessionis* is thus reunderstood in terms of a fundamental affirmation and defense of the identity and integrity of the church, of the inclusive wholeness of the reign of God, of the political and ecclesial praxis of Christian community, of conciliarity and catholicity, of the spirit of *koinonia* and *ekklesia*, of the life of marginal communities.

## 2. THE *STATUS CONFESSIONIS* AND THE PRAXIS OF LOVE

Enrique Dussel's understanding of Christian community in terms of the praxis of love (III.4.1.) suggests yet another way of reformulating the substance (if not the sharpness) of the *status confessionis*. By that I mean an explication of the meaning of love in the gospel accounts in close relation to what has been said on the inclusive love of God and the praxis of Jesus. It is the very praxis of Jesus that informs the Christian understanding of the love and graciousness of God. In the context of that praxis the various love commands are not so much demands as ways of participating in the love of God. The call to love God with all one's heart, soul, mind, and strength involves the total person in a response to God's unconditional and encompassing love. It makes of love, among other things, a praxis of responsibility.

The various love commands indicate a threefold praxis of Christian love, 1) for the sisters and brothers of the *koinonia*, 2) for the neighbor and 3) for the enemy, all under the sign of the love from and for God. All three have as a common core the inclusvie love of humanity in response to God's love of the world: 1) the mutual love of fulfilled humanity in the *koinonia*; 2) the material love of common humanity in the love of another human being; and 3) the mature ("perfected" Mt 5:48) love of reconciled humanity despite human hostility. It is the last of these three which Jesus calls *perisson* (Mt 5:47), that which is uncommon, remarkable, extraordinary, the something more he asks of his followers. Thus, that which is perhaps most characteristic of the community of Jesus lies in the relation of his follwers to the (hostile) world.[760]

This threefold praxis can hardly be understood in terms of concentric circles. The cutting edge of love in the gospel accounts is at the margins, where dividing lines are crossed, truth is critically pursued and hostilities are confronted. The question "Who is my neighbor?" serves to disturb and reorient love relations. Who is the other who comes into my life and into our common life? At the same time the enemy can at times be found too close for comfort in the *koinonia* or too personal in ourselves. Thus the three are one, overlapping, complementing, and contradicting each other. They might further be supplemented with a measured love of oneself (Rom 12:1f), a material love of creation, and the mystical love for God, again under the immeasurable mystery of God's love for mankind and all creation.

The golden rule of doing unto others as one would have them do unto oneself is another way of explicating love as the fulfillment of Tenach. How should we deny another what we desire or claim for ourselves? To love our neighbor *as ourselves* is not to make self-love a precondition for loving others, but serves as an orientation and a guide in the recognition that the other shares the same basic needs and humanity that I discover in myself. Love understood from Tenach is thus the subjective praxis of justice. Love is participation in the reign of God. It is the subjectivity of love that can serve to join identity and praxis, ecclesiology (dogmatics) and ethics, mysticism and justice.[761]

Love may, to be sure, involve an adventure into the darkness of existence. Daring love, whether in the form of interracial marriage, sharing at the table of the reconciled, or simply sharing bread and a cup of coffee, may run contrary to the forms and powers of apartheid in this world, racial, economic, or political. The non-violent vocation of loving's one enemy may lead one into suffering violence rather than inflicting it. The praxis of mutual and inclusive love in the *koinonia* may lead to a parting of spirits in the church. Love may be a harsh and dreadful thing.[762]

Love may as well be a thing of beauty. The practice of love is the fundamental affirmation of relatedness and the celebration of community. The face-to-face encounter is a daring enterprise, for who knows what the faces and what the mouths and eyes on those faces have to say to each other? But underlying the encounter is our being from, with, and for each other. It is a beautiful thing if people can enjoy life, have enough to eat, can be liberated from fear and oppression, can learn reading and writing and righteousness. It is a wondrous thing when someone finds comfort and companionship in his or her suffering. It is an awesome thing if one knows oneself included in the graciousness of God. The practice of love is a practice of the beauty of life, a practice of passion and perception.

Jesus critically illustrated the commandment to love one's neighbor with the parable of a merciful Samaritan. Jesus radicalized the love commandment with the conjunction to love enemies and bless one's persecutors. Jesus intensified the love commandment with the instruction to his followers to love each other as he had loved them. Thus the praxis of love takes shape in forms of marginality and mutuality. It becomes the experience and expression of inclusiveness under the sign of the graciousness of God.

**NOTES**

1 Along the edge,
outside the circle,
is where I feel
secure.

Invisible
am I,
unmentioned.
Silent,
still and
unmoved.

Different is what
I want to be.
Look into
my eyes.

In: *Wie geen doel heeft kan niet verdwalen. Gedichten*, a collection of poems on the occasion of the hundredth anniversary of Psychiatric Hospital Brinkgreven, Deventer 1992, p. 141. Printed here with permission. (Translation: M. Walton.)

2 Cf. M. Schloemann, "The Special Case for Confessing: Reflections on the *Casus Confessionis* (Dar es Salaam, 1977) in the Light of History and Systematic Theology", in E. Lorenz, ed., *The Debate on the Status Confessionis: Studies in Christian Political Theory*, p. 75.

3 *In Christ - One Community in the Spirit*, pp. 90-99.

4 E. Bethge, "Dietrich Bonhoeffer und die Juden", pp. 182-3. In German the four catchwords are: *Gleichschaltung, Reichskirche, Führerprinzip,* and *rassische Reinheit (Arierparagraph).*

5 M. Niemöller, "Sätze zur Arierfrage in der Kirche", in: W. Niemöller, *Kampf und Zeugnis der Bekennenden Kirche*, p. 71.

6 Cf. K. Meier, *Der evangelische Kirchenkampf*, p. 120.

7 W. Niemöller, *Der Pfarrernotbund. Geschichte einer kämpfenden Bruderschaft*, p. 37. The four points of the pledge read (in German):

1. *Ich verpflichte mich, mein Amt als Diener des Wortes auszurichten allein in der Bindung an die Heilige Schrift und an die Bekenntnisse der Reformation als die rechte Auslegung der Heiligen Schrift.*
2. *Ich verpflichte mich, gegen alle Verletzungen solchen Bekenntnisstandes mit rückhaltlosem Einsatz zu protestieren.*
3. *Ich weiss mich nach bestem Vermögen mitverantwortlich für die, die um solchen Bekenntnisstandes willen verfolgt werden.*
4. *In solcher Verpflichtung bezeuge ich, dass eine Verletzung des Bekenntnisstandes mit der Anwendung des Arierparagraphen im Raum der Kirche geschaffen ist.*

8 E. Bethge, *Bekennen und Widerstehen*, p. 66.

9 Ibid., p. 73.

10 Ibid., p. 66.

11 K. Barth, *Theologische Existenz heute!*.

12 Ibid., pp. 26-27. The phrase is: "Theologie und nur die Theologie zu treiben."

13 Ibid., pp. 59-60.
14 E. Bethge, "Dietrich Bonhoeffer und die Juden", p. 183.
15 D. Bonhoeffer, *Gesammelte Schriften II*, pp. 126-130.
16 Ibid., pp. 128-129.
17 E. Bethge, *Bekennen und Widerstehen*, p. 62.
18 D. Bonhoeffer, *Gesammelte Schriften II*, p. 128.
19 P. Lapide, *Jeder kommt zum Vater*, p. 42. "Aus jüdischer Sicht war Barmen ohne Erbarmen..."
20 E. Bethge, *Bekennen und Widerstehen*, p. 117.
21 Ibid., p. 115.
22 Ibid., p. 122. Bethge quotes from K. Barth, *Eine Schweizer Stimme 1938-1945*, p. 90. See also Bethge, "Dietrich Bonhoeffer und die Juden", p. 192, where Bethge points to the Church Dogmatics, vol. II.2., published (in German) in 1942.
23 E. Bethge, *Bekennen und Widerstehen*, p. 113. Bethge refers to *Evangelische Theologie*, 28/10, 1968, p. 555.
24 Cf. P. Lapide, "Bonhoeffer und das Judentum", p. 118.
25 D. Bonhoeffer, "Die Kirche vor die Judenfrage", *Gesammelte Schriften II*, pp. 44-53. Cf. E. Bethge, "Dietrich Bonhoeffer und die Juden", p. 185.
26 E. Bethge, "Dietrich Bonhoeffer und die Juden", p. 174. Cf. G.B. Kelley/F.B. Nelson, *A Testament of Freedom*, p. 137-8.
27 P. Lapide, "Bonhoeffer und das Judentum", p. 118. "Wer heute Bonhoeffers Stellungname zu Juden und zum Judentum analysieren will, muss vor allem die Hybris der Rückschau vermeiden."
28 D. Bonhoeffer, *Gesammelte Schriften II*, p. 50.
29 Ibid., p. 51-53.
30 Ibid., p. 53.
31 Ibid., pp. 62-69.
32 Ibid., pp. 62-63.
33 Ibid., pp. 65.
34 Ibid., p. 68.
35 Ibid., pp. 90-119. "Erstform des Betheler Bekenntnisses."
36 Ibid., "Vorbemerkung des Herausgebers", p. 88.
37 Ibid., p. 115.
38 Ibid., p. 117. Cf. p. 88. Translation taken from G.G. Kelley/F.B. Nelson, *A Testament of Freedom*, p. 144.
39 E. Bethge, "Dietrich Bonhoeffer und die Juden", p. 192f. Cf. C.R. Müller, *Dietrich Bonhoeffer's Kampf gegen die nationalsozialistische Verfolgung und Vernichtung der Juden*, pp. 203-230, 295-303, 317-329.
40 Ibid., p. 208. Cf. P. Lapide, "Bonhoeffer und das Judentum", pp. 122f.
41 Ibid., pp. 197-198.
42 Ibid., pp. 199f.
43 Ibid., p. 198.
44 D. Bonhoeffer, *Gesammelte Schriften III*, p. 324.
45 E. Bethge, "Dietrich Bonhoeffer und die Juden", p. 198.
46 D. Bonhoeffer, *Ethik*, p. 122.
47 E. Bethge, "Dietrich Bonhoeffer und die Juden", pp. 186, 192.
48 Ibid., p. 193.
49 Ibid., 198.
50 Ibid., p. 200. Cf. D. Bonhoeffer, *Ethik*, p. 95.

51 *Kirchliches Jahrbuch der Evangelischen Kirche in Deutschland 1945-1948*, pp. 19-29.

52 E. Bethge, *Bekennen und Widerstehen*, p. 76.

53 W. Krusche, "Schuld und Vergebung - Der Grund christlichen Friedenshandelns", p. 5f.

54 Ibid., p. 9f. The *Darmstädter Wort* can be found in the *Kirchliches Jahrbuch der Evangelischen Kirche in Deutschland 1945-1948*, pp. 220-222.

55 *Kirchliches Jahrbuch 1945-1948*, pp. 224-227.

56 *Kirchliches Jahrbuch 1950*, pp. 4-6.

57 W. Krusche, "Schuld und Vergebung", pp. 11f.

58 Ibid., p. 64.

59 D. Bonhoeffer, *Ethik*, pp. 118f.

60 W. Krusche, "Schuld und Vergebung", p. 5.

61 D. Bonhoeffer, *Ethik*, p. 123.

62 W. Krusche, "Schuld und Vergebung", p. 1.

63 See J. Moltmann, ed., *Bekennende Kirche wagen. Barmen 1934-1984*. The conference was organized by the Society for Evangelical Theology and the Reformed Federation in Wuppertal-Barmen, February 27 to March 1, 1984.

64 Ibid., pp. 267-269.

65 Ibid., p. 121.

66 Ibid., pp. 91f.

67 Ibid., p. 77.

68 Ibid., p. 91. Klappert refers to K. Barth's sermon on Romans 15:5-13 in *Theologische Existenz heute 5*, Munich 1933, p. 11f and Fr.-W. Marquardt, *Die Entdeckung des Judentums für die christliche Theologie. Israel im Denken Karl Barths*, 1967.

69 Ibid., p. 99. Cf. K. Barth, *Eine Schweizer Stimme 1938-1945*, pp. 87-89.

70 Ibid., p. 123.

71 Ibid., p. 75.

72 "Wat wij wel en wat wij niet gelooven", in H.C. Touw, *Het verzet der hervormde kerk*, pp. 227-232.

73 P.F.Th. Aalders, et al, "Geen Neutraliteit", pp. 22-23.

74 A.A. Spijkerboer, "De 'status confessionis' en de politiek", pp. 134-142.

75 See J.W. de Gruchy/Ch. Villa-Vicencio, eds., *Apartheid is a Heresy*, pp. 148-153.

76 See J.W. de Gruchy, "Towards a Confessing Church: The Implications of a Heresy", in: J.W. de Gruchy/Ch. Villa-Vincencio, eds., *Apartheid Is a Heresy*, pp. 75ff. The article was titled "Die Tijd Vir'n 'Belydende Kerk' is Daar" and appeared in the periodical *Pro Veritate*.

77 Ibid., pp. 154-159.

78 E. Bethge, *Am gegebenen Ort*, p. 135.

79 Ibid., p. 137.

80 Ibid., p. 138.

81 E. Bethge, *Bekennen und Widerstehen*, p. 80.

82 E. Bethge, *Am gegebenen Ort*, p. 138.

83 "Das Problem der 'weissen' lutherischen Kleinkirchen im Bereich der Apartheid. Von der Mahnung in Evian zur Suspendierung in Budapest", *epd-Dokumentation* 12/85, 11 March 1985, p. 3.

84 "Kampf um das Recht und Streit um die Wahrheit. Ausgewählte Stellungnahmen zur LWB. Erklärung über Status confessionis in Südlichen Afrika", *epd-Dokumentation* 26-27/83, June 6, 1983, pp. 8-11.

85 *In Christ - One Community in the Spirit*, pp. 179-180.

86 See E. Lorenz, ed., *The Debate on Status Confessionis: Studies in Christian Political Theology*, as well as the documentation indicated in the preceding notes.

87 See *epd-Dokumentation* 12/85, pp. 11-14.

88 Silousio M. Bengu and Ishmael Noko, in "Status Confessionis and Church Unity", p. 38, resp. p. 56.

89 E.g., in the various contributions to J.W. de Gruchy/Ch. Villa-Vicencio, eds., *Apartheid is a Heresy*.

90 Ibid., pp. 161-165.

91 Ibid., p. 10.

92 Ibid., pp. 175-182.

93 J.W. de Gruchy, *Liberating Reformed Theology*, p. 215.

94 E. Bethge, "Een korte meditatie over de belijdenis van Belhar 1982", in H. Berkhof, et al, *Met de moed der hoop*, pp. 104-105.

95 Bethge, *Bekennen und Widerstehen*, p. 195.

96 *The Kairos Document. Challenge to the Church. A Theological Comment on the Political Crisis in South Africa.* I use for the present purposes its inclusion in R. McAfee Brown, *Kairos. Three Prophetic Challenges to the Church.*

97 Ibid., p. 26.

98 "Statement on the WARC decision", September 17 1982, in J.W. de Gruchy/Ch. Villa-Vicencio, *Apartheid Is a Heresy*, pp. 173-175.

99 J.W. de Gruchy, *Liberating Reformed Theology*, p. 213.

100 Ibid., p. 216.

101 See Chr. Loff, "The History of a Heresy", in J.W. de Gruchy/Ch. Villa-Vicencio, eds., *Apartheid Is a Heresy*, pp. 10f.

102 *Epd-Dokumentation* 26-27/86, p. 58.

103 Ibid., p. 74.

104 I have taken these descriptions from G.H. ter Schegget.

105 *Epd-Dokumentation* 12/85, pp. 30-32.

106 G. Krusche, *Bekenntnis und Weltverantwortung*, p. 126.

107 G. Stalsett in "Status Confessionis and Church Unity", pp. 16-17.

108 De Gruchy, *Liberating Reformed Theology*, p. 217-218, in a quote from the *Occasional Bulletin* of the *Belydende Kring*.

109 J.W. de Gruchy, *Apartheid Is a Heresy*, p. 80. See also Sh. Govender, "Een belijdende kerk in Zuid Afrika", in H. Berkhof, *Met de moed der hoop*, pp. 95, 99.

110 Sh. Govender, "Een belijdende kerk in Zuid Afrika", in H. Berkhof, *Met de moed der hoop*, pp. 100-101.

111 U. Duchrow, in E. Bethge, *Bekennen und Widerstehen*, p. 198.

112 Quoted by G. Krusche, *Bekenntnis und Weltverantwortung*, p. 147, from a speech in Baden, Germany, 1981.

113 U. Duchrow, *Conflict over the Ecumenical Movement*, p. 342.

114 It is hardly feasible here, as was done with the considerations at the conclusion of the previous chapter, to refer to a specific document or person for each consideration. Rather the considerations represent positions common to several or reflect more general perspectives gleaned from the debates.

115 H. Thielicke, *Die atomwaffe als Frage an die christliche Ethik*, p. 30.

116 "Anfrage an die Synode der Evangelischen Kirche in Deutschland," in *Kirchliches Jahrbuch der Evangelischen Kirche in Deutschland 1958*, pp. 30-32.

117 It would go too far to treat the immense discussion of the application and applicability of just war principles to nuclear warfare, although it has some affinity to the *status confessionis* discussion. A recent review of just war theory in the United States with a view to its future is to be found in J.B. Hehir, "Just War Theory in a Post-Cold War World", *Journal of Religious Ethics* 20/2 (Fall 1992), pp. 237-257. An advocate of the deterrent use of atomic weapons, H. Thielicke, (*Die Atomwaffe als Frage an die christliche Ethik*, p. 20.) stated in 1958:

> The only possible conclusion that can be made must apparently be, that first of all there may be no nuclear war, and that secondly the old issue of Christian theology whether a *justum bellum* is permissible has become outdated and is no longer applicable to an atomic war.

Why the criteria of just war are outdated remains unclear, unless the intent is to admit nuclear weapons. That the just war theory has hardly been effective and has been misused more than used is a matter of historical record. One could, however, actualize the principles of just war in order to reject nuclear weapons.

118 *Kirchliches Jahrbuch der Evangelischen Kirche in Deutschland 1958*, pp. 36f., 45.

119 E. Wolf, ed., *Christusbekenntnis im Atomzeitalter?*. See especially E. Wolf, "Die Einheit der Kirche im Glauben und Gehorsam," pp. 30-77.

120 Ibid., pp. 35, 39, 57, 62, 70, etc.

121 Ibid., pp. 43-44.

122 See the interesting rejection of both atomic weapons and political arguments by W. Busch, "Sünde? Sünde!", in B. Klappert/ U. Weidner, eds., *Schritte zum Frieden*, pp. 42-44. Busch asserts that atomic weapons are not weapons but means of mass annihilation.

123 H. Vogel in *Kirchliches Jahrbuch 1958*, p. 24.

124 H. Asmussen, ibid., p. 36.

125 W. Künneth, quoted in B. Klappert/U. Weidner, eds., *Schritte zum Frieden*, p. 107.

126 E. Wolf, ed., *Christusbekenntnis im Atomzeitalter*, p. 108.

127 "Heidelberger Thesen 1959", in: *Frieden wahren, fördern und erneuren*, pp. 76-87.

128 B. Klappert/U. Weidner, eds., *Schritte zum Frieden*, pp. 109-111.

129 E. Wolf, ed., *Christusbekenntnis im Atomzeitalter*, p. 43.

130 B. Klappert/U. Weidner, eds., *Schritte zum Frieden*, p. 126.

131 Ibid., pp. 133, 138.

132 E. Wolf, ed., *Christusbekenntnis im Atomzeitalter*, pp. 16, 54, 90.

133 *Het vraagstuk van de kernwapenen*.

134 See the summary in *Pastorale brief over de kernbewapening*, p. 6.

135 Ibid., pp. 5-8.

136 In the English translation which appeared in the *Ecumenical Review* of July 1981, pp. 249f., the word "belijdend" that I have literally translated as "confessing" was paraphrased "as believers." That may be more fluent English, but I hold for the present purposes to literalism.

137 H. Berkhof, "Das politische Zeugnis der Kirche zwischen Prophetie und Weisheit" in R. Wischnath, ed., *Frieden als Bekenntnisfrage*, p. 24.

138 *Pastorale brief over de kernbewapening*, p. 7.

139 H. Thielicke, *Die Atomwaffe als Frage an die christliche Ethik*, pp. 28, 32, 33.

140 E. Anscombe, quoted by G. Hunsinger in *Katallagete* 10/1-3 (Fall 1987), p. 102.

141 Das Moderamen des Reformierten Bundes, "Das Bekenntnis zu Jesus Christus und die Friedensverantwortung der Kirche," eine Erklärung, 12 Juni. 1982, *epd-Dokumentation* 38a/82, Frankfurt 1982. The declaration was also included in R. Wischnath, ed., *Frieden als Bekenntnisfrage*.

142 See the study document of the Evangelical Church in Germany, *Frieden wahren, fördern und erneuern*, p. 58.

143 "Gesellschaft für Evangelische Theologie" which issued its findings in a position paper "Den Frieden Ausbreiten", edited by J. Moltmann, in B. Klappert/ U. Weidner, eds., *Schritte zum Frieden*, pp. 260-263.

144 See the foreword to the declaration by H.J. Kraus.

145 Quoted by K. Stoll, *Status confessionis. Das Bekenntnis des Glaubens zu Jesus Christus im Zeitalter der atomaren Gefahr*, p. 64. Lohse also expressed regret that there had been no internal discussion on the matter within the EKD, to which the MRB was affiliated, prior to publication of the document.

146 Kirchenleitung der Vereinigten Evangelisch-Lutherischen Kirche Deutschlands (VELKD), "Kommuniqué", Hannover, 10. September 1982, in *epd-Dokumentation* 45/82, p. 16.

147 Rat der Evangelischen Kirche in Deutschland (EKD), "Kommuniqué der 36. Sitzung am 16./17. September 1982, *epd-Dokumentation* 45/82, p. 17.

148 See, e.g., A. Haarbeck, *epd-Dokumentation* 50/82, p. 20, and K. Stoll, *Status confessionis*, pp. 11, 21-25.

149 Quoted by R. Wischnath, *Frieden als Bekenntnisfrage*, p. 104.

150 J. Garstecki, "Vertrauen wagen - Phantasie für den Frieden in der bedrohten Welt," *epd-Dokumentation* 43/83, p. 71.

151 K. Stoll, *Status confessionis*, p. 206.

152 Both are quoted by G. Hunsinger, *Katallagete* 10/1-3 (Fall 1987), p. 102.

153 T. Rendtorff, "Der Friedensstreit bedeutet Gefahr für die Kirche," *epd-Dokumentation* 50/82, p. 43, in a reprint from the Frankfurter Allgemeine Zeitung.

154 *epd-Dokumentation* 38a/82, p. 3.

155 *epd-Dokumentation*, p. 2.

156 See H.J. Kraus, "We gaan naar een principieel pacifisme," *HN-Magazin*, June 28, 1986, pp. 24-25.

157 Cf. K. Stoll, *Status confessionis*, pp. 107, 109.

158 U. Möller, "Zum Problem des status confessionis", in R. Wischnath, ed., *Frieden als Bekenntnisfrage*, p. 259-260.

159 U. Duchrow, *Weltwirtschaft heute - Ein Feld für Bekennende Kirche?*, p. 136.

160 W. Huber, "Bekenntnis in der Gefährdung des Friedens," in R. Wischnath, ed., *Frieden als Bekenntnisfrage*, pp. 297-298. See in the same book: U. Möller, pp. 267-269, and H. Falcke, p. 302.

161 G. Krusche, "Confidence Rather than Deterrence," in P. Abrecht/N. Koshy, eds., *Before it's too late. The Challenge of Nuclear Armament*, p. 95.

162 Ibid., p. 32.

163 Ibid., pp. 30, 97-99.

164 *epd-Dokumentation* 47/82, p. 35.

165 D. Bonhoeffer, "Kirche und Völkerwelt", *Gesammelte Schriften III*, p. 217. The official English version on page 448 reads:
They cannot take arms against Christ himself - yet that is what they do if they take up arms against one another.
The German seems to me more poignant, and I have given a more literal translation in the text.

166 The "Absage an Geist und Logik der Abschreckung" was spoken at a synod of the Federation of Evangelical Churches in the GDR at Halle 1982. The renunciation of "Praxis" was added at the synod meeting in Potsdam in 1983. See *epd-Dokumentation* 43/83, p. 63-65.

167 *epd-Dokumentation* 43/83, pp. 46-48.

168 See "Resources for Study of 'Christian Obedience in a Nuclear Age'", p. 87.

169 One page leaflet of the Lutheran Peace Fellowship, St. Paul, Minnesota.

170 These following two points are summarized in the "Resources for Study" of the Presbyterian Church (U.S.A.), pp. 89-90.

171 E. Bethge, "2. Thesenreihe zum Problem 'status confessionis'," in R. Wischnath, *ed., Frieden als Bekenntnisfrage*, pp. 234-235.

172 Kerk en Vrede, "Uitnodiging tot belijden".

173 U. Duchrow, in J. Moltmann, ed., *Bekennende Kirche Wagen*, pp. 140-141.

174 J. Moltmann, *Bekennende Kirche Wagen*, pp. 19-20.

175 E. Bethge, "2. Thesenreihe zum Problem 'status confessionis'", in R. Wischnath, ed., *Frieden als Bekenntnisfrage*, p. 232.

176 G.H. ter Schegget, *Volmacht in onmacht. Over de roeping van de christelijke gemeente in de politiek*, pp. 244-331. My first treatment of the *status confessionis* ("*Status confessionis* and the status of the church", unpublished paper) dated from the same time that my mentor Ter Schegget wrote on the subject.

177 P. Staples, "Catholicity", *Dictionary of the Ecumenical Movement*, p. 134f.

178 See F.O. van Gennep, *Katholiciteit en pluraliteit*, p. 3ff. Van Gennep appeals to the Russian term *sobornost*, unity in diversity, that has also been related to conciliarity. See, e.g., E. Lanne, "Conciliarity", *Dictionary of the Ecumenical Movement*, p. 212.

179 W.A. Visser 't Hooft, in: N. Goodall, ed., *The Uppsala Report*, p. 320.

180 H. de Lange, mimeographed copy. Cf. *epd-Dokumentation* 26-27/83, p. 100-101.

181 Theological conference of "Die Gesellschaft für Evangelische Theologie" and "Der Reformierte Bund" under the title "Barmen 1934-1984" in Wuppertal-Barmen in 1984. Papers and a concluding declaration were published in J. Moltmann, ed., *Bekennende Kirche wagen. Barmen 1934-1984*.

182 Ibid., p. 269.

183 U. Duchrow, *Weltwirtschaft heute - Ein Feld für Bekennende Kirche?*.

184 Duchrow refers to Luther's "Ein Sermon vom dem hochwürdigen Sakrament des heiligen wahren Leichnams Christi und von den Bruderschaften" 1519. See pp. 62ff.

185 Ibid., pp. 67-68, where Duchrow examines "Von Konziliis und Kirchen."

186 Ibid., pp. 68ff.

187 Ibid., p. 73.

188 Ibid., p. 73-73. Cf. E. Lange, *Die ökumenische Utopie*, p. 144.

189 Ibid., p. 253. See also pp. 20, 118f., 207f., 282.

190 Ibid., p. 140.

191 Ibid., p. 292.

192 Ibid., pp. 171, 181, 189, 198, 203-206, etc.

193 Ibid., p. 203-204, where Duchrow points to a North American Catholic theological and biblical defense of the free market system in response to the bishops letter on the economy.

194 Ibid., p. 171.

195 L.A. Hoedemaker, "Het schema van de wereld and het belijden van de kerk", p. 346.

196 R. Dickinson, "Vragen bij Duchrow's oproep tot 'status confessionis' van het economisch system," in *Verzuim en verwachting*, pp. 342-345.

197 K. van der Poort and J.B. Sybrandi, in *Verzuim en Verwachting*, p. 364.

198 U. Duchrow, *Weltwirtschaft heute*, pp. 172, 189.

199 Ibid., pp. 168, 189, 191ff., 201.

200 Ibid., pp. 160, 278f.

201 L.A. Hoedemaker, "Het schema van de wereld en het belijden van de kerk", p. 350.

202 U. Duchrow, *Weltwirtschaft heute*, pp. 231-241.

203 See A. van den Berg, *Churches Speak Out on Economic Issues*, that surveys twenty documents and includes a bibliography of many more.

204 *Economy as a Matter of Faith*, p. 41.

205 *Christian Faith and the World Economy Today*, pp. 39f., 44.

206 *Christian Faith and the World Economy Today*, p. 22ff. This aspect was also prominent in the conciliar process component "integrity of creation".

207 E. Lange, *Die Ökumenische Utopie, oder was bewegt die ökumenische Bewegung?*, pp. 196, 224, 226.

208 Ibid., p. 193.

209 G. Hunsinger, "Barth, Barmen and the Confessing Church Today", *Katallagete* 9/2 (Summer 1985), pp. 14-27. Responses were published in vol. 10/1-3 (Fall 1987). See also G. Hunsinger, "Where the Battle Rages: Confessing Christ in America Today", *Dialog* 26/4, pp. 264-274.

210 R. Osborn, "Is the Church Political?", *Katallagete* 10, p. 61f.

211 *Katallagete* 10/1-3, p. 99.

212 Ibid., p. 76.

213 Ibid., p. 43. Hauerwas felt that the analogical approach of Barth would not do.

214 Ibid., p. 53.

215 Ibid., p. 65.

216 Ibid., p. 12.

217 Ibid., p. 14.

218 Ibid., p. 47.

219 *Katallagete* 9/2, p. 25.

220 *Katallagete* 10/1-3, p. 93.

221 R.M. Brown, *Kairos: Three Prophetic Challenges to the Church*.

222 Ibid., pp. 3f. Of course, any (theological) dictionary of Greek can also be consulted, but my primary concern is with the understanding conveyed in the documents and in the commentary on them.

223 Ibid., pp. 5-7.

224 Ibid., pp. 12f.

225 D. Bonhoeffer, *Gesammelte Schriften I*, pp. 212-215. The English version is to be found on pp. 447-449.

226 It is interesting to note that F.O. van Gennep seeks to understand 'catholicity' in terms of a covenant theology. See *Katholiciteit en pluraliteit*, p. 15ff.

227 Heino Falcke, *Vom Gebot Christi, dass die Kirche uns die Waffe aus der Hand nimmt und den Krieg verbietet. Zum konziliaren Weg des Friedens. Ein Beitrag aus der DDR.*

228 Ibid., p. 18f.

229 Ibid., pp. 21ff.

230 Ibid., pp. 26-35.

231 Ibid., p. 84.
232 Ibid., pp. 30f.
233 Ibid., p. 25.
234 Ibid., p. 34.
235 See, e.g., D. Bonhoeffer, "Zur theologischen Begründung der Weltbundarbeit," (1932), *Gesammelte Schriften I*, pp. 140-161.
236 D. Bonhoeffer, "Die Bekennende Kirche und die Ökumene" (1935), *Gesammelte Schriften I*, pp. 240-261.
237 E. Lange, *Die Ökumenische Utopie*, p. 33.
238 Ibid., pp. 197f., 224f.
239 Ibid., p. 170.
240 Ibid., p. 248.
241 Ibid., p. 226.
242 Ibid., p. 229.
243 Ibid., pp. 51f.
244 Ibid., pp. 246ff.
245 Ibid., pp. 70-73.
246 Ibid., pp. 182 and 199.
247 Ibid., p. 116.
248 Ibid., p. 185.
249 Ibid., pp. 217f.
250 Ibid., pp. 259.
251 Ibid., pp. 12, 22, 95.
252 Ibid., pp. 291, 299.
253 Ibid., p. 149.
254 Ibid., p. 198.
255 U. Duchrow, *Conflict over the Ecumenical Movement.*
256 Ibid., p. 31. Duchrow refers to J. Moltmann, *The Church in the Power of the Spirit*, New York 1977, p. 56.
257 Ibid., pp. 350-352.
258 Aram Keshishian, *Conciliar Fellowship. A Common Goal*, Geneva 1992.
259 Ibid., p. 23.
260 Ibid., pp. 33f.
261 Ibid., pp. 65, 71.
262 Ibid., pp. 3-5.
263 I refer primarily to two publications of Bert Hoedemaker. The first is an article "Het schema van de wereld en het belijden van de kerk", pp. 346-352, in *Verzuim en Verwachting. Gelovig Belijden in de Wereldeconomie*, a special issue of *Wereld en Zending* (1988/4) devoted to Duchrow's appeal for a *status confessionis* on world economy. The second is a pastoral memorandum of the general synod of the Netherlands Reformed Church entitled *Gemeente-zijn in de mondiale samenleving* (1988). Although the latter does not bear his name, Hoedemaker is its principal author. I hope I correctly portray his own position when referring to it.
264 L.A. Hoedemaker, "Het schema van de wereld en het belijden van de kerk", pp. 349-350.
265 *Gemeente-zijn in de mondiale samenleving*, pp. 10-11.
266 Ibid., p. 38.
267 Ibid., pp. 99-101.

268 M. Kässmann, *Die Eucharistische Vision. Armut und Reichtum als Anfrage an die Einheit der Kirche in der Diskussion des Ökumenischen Rates*, Munich/Mainz 1992.

269 Ibid., p. 22. See also pp. 257, 286, 289.

270 Ibid., p. 344.

271 Ibid., pp. 23, 324f.,329, 331.

272 D. Bonhoeffer, "Zur Frage nach der Kirchengemeinschaft", *Gesammelte Schriften II*, pp. 217ff.

273 E. Lanne, "Conciliarity", *Dictionary of the Ecumenical Movement*, p. 212.

274 P. Staples, "Catholicity", *Dictionary of the Ecumenical Movement*, p. 134ff.

275 Ibid., p. 135. Staples refers to Thomas Aquinas.

276 Ibid., p. 137.

277 Ibid., p. 137. The extended quotation is taken from a report to the fourth assembly of the World Council of Churches in Uppsala 1968, "The Holy Spirit and the Catholicity of the Church".

278 F.O. van Gennep, *Katholiciteit en pluraliteit*, p. 15ff.

279 P. Staples, "Catholicity", *Dictionary of the Ecumenical Movement*, p. 137.

280 Cf. C.R. Müller, *Dietrich Bonhoeffer's Kampf gegen die nationalsozialistische Verfolgung und Vernichtung der Juden*, pp. 29, 36.

281 M. Schloemann, "The Special Case for Confessing: Reflections on the Casus Confessionis (Dar es Dalaam 1977) in the Light of History and Systematic Theology", in E. Lorenz, ed., *The Debate on Status Confessionis. Studies in Christian Political Theology*, p. 48.

282 Chr. Rave in *Verzuim en Verwachting*, p. 355.

283 Ibid., pp. 83, 85, 112, 129, as well as comments by W. Huber, "Die Friedensfrage als Bekenntnisfrage. Status confessionis und Konziliarität", *Die status confessionis und die Einheit der Kirche*, Loccumer Protokolle, p. 160.

284 D. Bonhoeffer, *Sanctorum Communio*, p. 76, etc.

285 Idem, *Widerstand und Ergebung*, p. 415. Literally: "The church is only the church when it is there for others." The notion of being for others is, however, already present in *Sanctorum Communio*, pp. 121ff.

286 Th. Day, *Dietrich Bonhoeffer on Christian Community and Common Sense*. See also the article by Day, "Conviviality and Common Sense: The Meaning of Christian Community for Dietrich Bonhoeffer", in A. Klassen, ed., *A Bonhoeffer Legacy*, pp. 213-236.) Day attempts to understand changing emphases in Bonhoeffer's theology from the context of his changing communities: family, academia, 'Volkskirche', Confessing Church, seminary community at Finkenwalde, and the collective conspirators. "Our focus on the relationship between the communal context and the socio-ethical content of Bonhoeffer's theology has highlighted his move from concern for a wholistic concept of Christian community to commitment in [a sequence of] more or less churchy communities which he recognized as Christian more by their tendency towards wholesome life together than by the orthodoxy of their utterance." (p. 195) I shall make use of Day's findings without reproducing his line of thought.

287 D. Bonhoeffer, *Sanctorum Communio*, p. 32. "Nur am Du entspringt Ich, nur auf den Anspruch hin entsteht Verantwortung."

288 Cf. F. de Lange, *Individualisme*, p. 122.

289 Ibid., p. 29, 83.

290 Cf. E. Bethge, *Dietrich Bonhoeffer. Theologe, Christ, Zeitgenosse*, pp. 520, 981.

291 Ibid., p. 190.

292 Ibid., p. 87.
293 Th. Day, *Dietrich Bonhoeffer on Christian Community and Common Sense*, p. 1.
294 D. Bonhoeffer, *Sanctorum Communio*, p. 198.
295 Th. Day, *Dietrich Bonhoeffer on Christian Community and Common Sense*, p. 9.
296 D. Bonhoeffer, *Sanctorum Communio*, p. 89.
297 Ibid., p. 142.
298 Ibid., pp. 114-115. Cf. Th. Day, *Dietrich Bonhoeffer onChristian Community and Common Sense*, p. 21.
299 D. Bonhoeffer, *Widerstand und Ergebung*, p. 19.
300 Idem, *Sanctorum Communio*, p. 117ff.
301 Ibid., p. 99.
302 Idem, "Protestantismus ohne Reformation", *Gesammelte Schriften I*, p. 354.
303 Idem, *Ethik*, p. 89.
304 Idem, "Das Wesen der Kirche", *Gesammelte Schriften V*, p. 238.
305 Idem, *Akt und Sein*, p. 92.
306 Th. Day, *Dietrich Bonhoeffer on Christian Community and Common Sense*, p. 28.
307 Ibid., p. 47.
308 Luke 3:12; Acts 2:37. Cf. D. Bonhoeffer, *Gesammelte Schriften V*, p. 280.
309 Th. Day, *Dietrich Bonhoeffer on Christian Community and Common Sense*, p. 100.
310 Ibid., p. 105-106.
311 Ibid., p. 33.
312 D. Bonhoeffer, *Ethik*, p. 26ff. Cf. Day, *Dietrich Bonhoeffer on Christian Community and Common Sense*, pp. 47 and 139.
313 Ibid., p. 19.
314 E.g., D. Bonhoeffer, *Gesammelte Schriften III*, p. 52 (which is the same as *Gesammelte Schriften V*, p. 163, and *Barcelona, Berlin, Amerika 1928-1931. DBW 10*, p. 329).
315 Idem, *Gesammelte Schriften I*, p. 145.
316 Idem, *Sanctorum Communio*, p. 109-110.
317 Th. Day, *Dietrich Bonhoeffer on Christian Community and Common Sense*, p. 27.
318 Ibid., p. 26.
319 Ibid., p. 47.
320 D. Bonhoeffer, "Christologie", *Gesammelte Schriften III*, p. 193f.
321 Idem, *Ethik*, p. 94.
322 Ibid., p. 89.
323 Ibid., p. 219.
324 Th. Day, *Dietrich Bonhoeffer on Christian Community and Common Sense*, pp. 143, 146.
325 D. Bonhoeffer, *Sanctorum Communio*, p.170.
326 Idem, *Widerstand und Ergebung*, p. 415.
327 Th. Day, *Dietrich Bonhoeffer on Christian Community and Common Sense*, p. 202.
328 Ibid., p. 221.
329 Idem, *Sanctorum Communio*, p. 142.
330 Idem, "Wesen der Kirche", *Gesammelte Schriften V*, p. 230.
331 Idem, *Gesammelte Schriften III*, p. 286.

332 Idem, *Nachfolge*, pp. 277-278.
333 Th. Day, *Dietrich Bonhoeffer on Christian Community and Common Sense*, p. 25.
334 D. Bonhoeffer, *Widerstand und Ergebung*, pp. 415-416.
335 Ibid., pp. 331-334, 340f, 348. Cf. Th. Day, *Dietrich Bonhoeffer on Christian Community and Common Sense*, pp. 194f.
336 Cf. J. Moltmann, *Politische Theologie. Politische Ethik*, p. 142.
337 D. Bonhoeffer, *Ethik*, p. 364.
338 E. Bethge, *Dietrich Bonhoeffer*, p. 520.
339 Ibid., p. 23.
340 D. Bonhoeffer, *Gesammelte Schriften I*, p. 40.
341 Idem, Nachfolge, pp. 99f., 110ff.
342 Th. Day, "Conviviality and Common Sense", p. 218.
343 Ibid., p. 218.
344 Ibid., p. 224.
345 See D. Bonhoeffer, "Nach zehn Jahren. Rechenschaft an der Wende zum Jahr 1943", *Widerstand und Ergebung*, pp. 11-27, as well as E. Bethge, *Dietrich Bonhoeffer*, pp. 888-896.
346 D. Bonhoeffer, *Widerstand und Ergebung*, p. 24.
347 Ibid., p. 19.
348 Idem, "Der Blick von unten", *Gesammelte Schriften II*, p. 441, included in the English edition of the *Letters and Papers from Prison* at the conclusion of "After Ten Years".
349 E. Bethge, *Dietrich Bonhoeffer*, p. 994.
350 P. Lehmann, *Ethics in a Christian Context*, p. 45.
351 Ibid., p. 14.
352 Ibid., p. 14.
353 Ibid., p. 112.
354 Ibid., p. 90.
355 Ibid., p. 85.
356 See the study by N. Duff, *Humanization and the Politics of God. The Koinonia Ethics of Paul Lehmann*. Duff goes to some length to explicate the meaning of the assertion that God acts. See especially pp. 106, 112.
357 P. Lehmann, *Ethics in a Christian Context*, p. 49.
358 Ibid., p. 47.
359 Ibid., p. 72.
360 Ibid., p. 58.
361 Ibid., p. 101.
362 Ibid., p. 72.
363 Ibid., p. 131.
364 D. Bonhoeffer, *Ethik*, p. 319.
365 P. Lehmann, *Ethics in a Christian Context*, p. 74.
366 Ibid., p. 154ff. (Cf Duff, *Humanization and the Politics of God*, pp. 167ff.)
367 Ibid., p. 25.
368 Ibid., p. 58.
369 Ibid., p. 54.
370 N. Duff, *Humanization and the Politics of God*, p. 135. I am somewhat uncertain about F. de Lange's judgement in his book, *Individualisme* (pp. 78f., 83, 119, 122), regarding Lehmann's anti-individualism. While Lehmann is emphatic in his social interpretation in the face of an individualism understood as isolationalism, his concern for the maturity and integrity of human

individuals cannot be overlooked. The issue is one of context. Lehmann affirms integrity in and through interrelatedness. (*Ethics in a Christian Context*, p. 54) Thus while Lehmann's position is communitarian, it does not seem to be collectivist or hostile to individual integrity and responsibility. (See also B. Harvey, *Piety, Power and Politics*, pp. 144ff.)

371 P. Lehmann, *Ethics in a Christian Context*, p. 47.

372 Ibid., p. 131.

373 Ibid., p. 57.

374 Ibid., p. 75.

375 Ibid., p. 76.

376 Ibid., p. 77.

377 Ibid., p. 80.

378 Ibid., p. 55.

379 Ibid., p. 56.

380 Ibid., p. 54.

381 Ibid., pp. 50-51.

382 Ibid., pp. 326ff.

383 A thorough stud of conscience and its contextualization in Lehmann's theology has been provided by B. Harvey, *Piety, Power and Politics*. Harvey rightly points to the contextualization of conscience as the crucial issue. At the same time the concept remains elusive and problematic. I am more concerned with its suggestive function and with near synonyms than with establishing (or disestablishing) the concept itself.

384 P. Lehmann, *Ethics in a Christian Context*, p. 350.

385 Ibid., p. 353.

386 Ibid., p. 358.

387 Ibid., p. 359.

388 Ibid., p. 359.

389 Ibid., p. 360.

390 Ibid, p. 75, where Lehmann quotes Barth: "The problem of ethics is ... a great disturbance. How, indeed, can it be otherwise? For human behavior must inevitably be disturbed by the thought of God..." (*Der Römerbrief*, Munich 1929, p. 411).

391 P. Lehmann, *The Transfiguration of Politics: The Presence and Power of Jesus of Nazareth in and over Human Affairs*.

392 Cf. N. Duff, *Humanization and the Politics of God*, p. 176.

393 P. Lehmann, *The Transfiguration of Politics*, p. 58.

394 Ibid., pp. 75-76.

395 Ibid., p. 96f.

396 Ibid., p. 75.

397 Ibid., pp. 110, 235, 237.

398 Ibid., pp. 261-267.

399 Ibid., pp. 87-88, 240ff., 250ff.

400 Ibid., p. 107.

401 B. Harvey, *Piety, Power and Politics*, pp. 197, 200f.

402 P. Lehmann, *The Transfiguration of Politics*, p. 286. The concept of supplication and the quote given here are taken from a dissertation by P. Valliere, "M.M. Tareev: A Study in Russian Ethics and Mysticism", Colombia University 1973.

403 Ibid., p. 289.

404 S. Hauerwas, *The Peaceable Kingdom*. See the section entitled "On what I owe to whom". pp. xix-xxvi.

405 Ibid., p. xvi.

406 Ibid., p. xix. Hauerwas has in fact made an attempt to pull several strands together in his primer on Christian ethics, *The Peaceable Kingdom*. Also a systematic analysis is provided by J.M.L van Gerwen, *The Church in the Theological Ethics of Stanley Hauerwas*. I have some reservations about the attempt by Van Gerwen, a Belgian Catholic, to milk Hauerwas' particularist approach for purposes of more general, foundational considerations on ethics and/or ecclesiology. "It is my intuition that Hauerwas, while not intending to propose a general system or 'foundation' of ethics, has in fact proposed a very good one. One can debate whether the concepts of character, vision, narrative and community present only a so-called value-neutral conceptuality or meta-ethics, or if, indeed, they imply some moral imperatives. It is clear that ... Hauerwas, in the pursuit of his theological intentions, has developed an ethical vocabulary which is at least potentially applicable to communities other than the church. Furthermore, it appears to me that the author has come to his distinctively Christian ethic precisely through the prior study and application of those general ethical concepts." (p. 2) While it would seem true that Hauerwas has indeed developed ethical concepts and tools which might prove helpful beyond his own particular convictions or communities, it would also be helpful if Van Gerwen would be more specific about the distinction between concepts and vocabulary on the one hand and a foundation and/or system on the other.
I find more interesting R. Hütter's treatment of Hauerwas (and Barth) in *Evangelische Ethik als kirchliches Zeugnis*. While I find several matters bordering on my own understandings and concerns, Hütter's approach to church ethics is quite different from my own. Hütter seeks to relate ethics and ecclesiology in an understanding of the church as a witnessing community. While Hütter does seek to further develop Hauerwas' understanding of the non-violent character of Christian community, I am for the rest left with a feeling that Hütter's framework remains somewhat formal. And I am troubled by the attention paid to the notion of credibility (e.g., pp. 271, 279). I find the notion of credibility helpful in a heuristic sense but too ambiguous to provide substance to ethical identity. I wish also that he had worked out his comments on the next to last page regarding "true plurality" and a "meaningful diversity." (p. 284.)

407 S. Hauerwas, *The Peaceable Kingdom*, p. xxv.

408 Ibid., p.24.

409 Idem, *Christian Existence Today*, p. 101. Note the provocative title of this collection of essays which is a deliberate reference to Barth's *Theologische Existenz heute*. See p. 18. Hauerwas, like Barth, is concerned that theologians stick to their proper task and be unabashedly and distinctively Christian.

410 Idem, *A Community of Character*, p. 50.

411 Especially A. MacIntyre, *After Virtue. A Study in Moral Theory*. It is with a discussion of MacIntyre that R. Hütter begins his attempt to work out an ecclesial ethic. See *Evangelische Ethik als kirchliches Zeugnis*, pp. 2ff.

412 See for the following: S. Hauerwas and D. Burrell, "From System to Story: An Alternative Pattern for Rationality in Ethics", in S. Hauerwas/L. Gregory Jones, *Why Narrative?*, pp. 158-190.

413 Ibid., p. 175.

414 Ibid., p. 177.

415 Ibid., p. 1.
416 Ibid., p. 1.
417 Ibid., p. 24ff.
418 Ibid., p. 29f.
419 Compare the title of a collection of essays which Hauerwas has published with R. Bondi and D.B. Burrell, *Truthfulness and Tragedy. Further Investigations into Christian Ethics.*
420 S. Hauerwas, *A Community of Character*, p. 244.
421 Idem, *The Peaceable Kingdom*, pp. 30ff.
422 Idem, *The Peaceable Kingdom*, p. 33.
423 S. Hauerwas/D. Burrell, "From System to Story", p. 185ff, in S. Hauerwas/L.G. Jones, *Why Narrative?*.
424 Ibid., p. 185.
425 S. Hauerwas, *Truthfulness and Tragedy*, pp. 73-74.
426 Idem, *The Peaceable Kingdom*, p. 55.
427 Idem, *Character and the Christian Life*, pp. xxviiff. Hauerwas refers to G. Meilaender, "The Place of Ethics in the Theological Task", *Currents in Theology and Mission* 6 (1979) 199-200.
428 Hauerwas criticizes in this respect Bultmann and to a lesser degree Barth, although his criticism might in some respects also be applicable to Bonhoeffer. See *Character and the Christian Life*, chapter IV, pp. 129-178. The critique is extended as well to the the conceptions of situation-ethics and contextualism which similarly fail to account for the duration of the self and the substance of Christian ethics.
429 Ibid., pp. 2, 4. In a new introduction to *Character and the Christian Life*, from which the present quote is taken, Hauerwas restates his position and deems it a mistake to call 'command' or 'virtue' and 'character 'a metaphor. Instead he then borrows the metaphors which Meilaender juxtaposes, 'dialogue' and 'journey', to clarify what he had previously wanted to indicate with the notion of command versus that of virtue and character. See pp. xxvi-xxvii.
430 Ibid., pp. xxx, xxvii.
431 Ibid., p. 3.
432 Ibid., p. xxix. Similar is Hauerwas' perspective on the notions of sanctification and justification. On the one hand he can maintain that sanctification is a more determinative category than justification, as the former is more in keeping with the journey metaphor. Nevertheless he insists that both are "secondary theological notions; they are rules intended to remind us how the self is to be situated in order to hear and live the story of God as revealed through the life and death of Jesus of Nazareth." See pp. xxviii-xxix. See also *The Peaceable Kingdom*, p. 94.
433 Idem, *Character and the Christian Life*, p. 178.
434 Idem, *The Peaceable Kingdom*, p. 67.
435 Ibid., p. 67-68.
436 For the phrase "the enterprise of Christian ethics" see *The Peaceable Kingdom*, p. 29.
437 Ibid., p. 29.
438 Ibid., p. 72.
439 Ibid., p. 73.
440 Idem, *Against the Nations*, p. 114f.
441 Hauerwas is "content to assume that the Jesus we have in Scripture is the Jesus of the early church" for "he cannot be known abstracted from the disciples'

response." The story that is told of Jesus by his followers is primarily a witness to the significance of Jesus for their lives. Furthermore the form of the gospels is not only meant to display the life of Jesus, but to enable us to situate our lives in relation to his life.
This position of Hauerwas is not so much a critique of modern historical criticism with its questions about the Jesus of the gospels, but rather a critique of "ontological" Christologies which in response to the findings of modern criticism despair of knowing the historical Jesus and therefore postulate some claim on Jesus' nature and significance prior and somewhat incidental to the gospel portrayal. See *The Peaceable Kingdom*, pp. 72-75.

442 Ibid., p. xxiv, where Hauerwas briefly explicates his struggle with and indebtedness to J.H. Yoder. See e.g. from Yoder *The Politics of Jesus* and *The Priestly Kingdom*.

443 S. Hauerwas, *The Peaceable Kingdom*, p. 73.

444 See the chapter titled "Jesus: The Story of the Kingdom" in *A Community of Character*, pp. 36-52.

445 Idem., *Against the Nations*, p. 113.

446 Idem, *A Community of Chracter*, p. 45. The quotation from Barth was taken from *Church Dogmatics* II/2 (Edinburgh 1957), p. 1957. The description of Origen from "Commentary on Matthew", in *Ante-Nicene Fathers* (New York 1926), p. 298.

447 Ibid., p. 37.

448 To focus in this context on Bonhoeffer's explication of discipleship may be reductionistic. His more eschatological claims which he put in terms of worldliness, Christ-reality, the ultimate and the penultimate, etc., should perhaps also be considered. Nevertheless Bonhoeffer seems to lack the central emphasis on the context of the kingdom that Hauerwas explicates.

449 While Hauerwas appreciates Lehmann's influence on the context of Christian ethics as that which "God is doing in the world to make and keep human life human", he points out that Lehmann refuses to specify how life is kept human as that would foreclose God's grace. Thus the theological substance which Lehmann appears to provide dissipates, because he provides no continuity, no real story. See *Character and the Christian Life*, p.6. It is surprising to me that Hauerwas disregards the context of the koinonia by Lehmann. Granted, the koinonia remains a formal and underdeveloped category in Lehmann's description, but he refers to it emphatically and explicitly.

450 S. Hauerwas, *The Peaceable Kingdom*, p. 85.

451 Ibid., pp. 86-87.

452 Ibid., p. 85.

453 Ibid., p. 82.

454 Ibid., p. 94-95.

455 This is the issue in *Character and the Christian Life*.

456 S. Hauerwas, *The Peaceable Kingdom*, p. 95. I include the last sentence in the quotation because at this point I follow Hauerwas'own sequence in *The Peaceable Kingdom*. See chapter 5, "Jesus: The Presence of the Peaceable Kingdom", and chapter 6, "The Servant Community: Christian Social Ethics".

457 Idem, *Against the Nations*, "The Reality of the Kingdom", p. 112.

458 Ibid., p. 119.

459 Idem, *Christian Existence Today*, p. 61.

460 Ibid., p. v. Such is the title that Hauerwas gives to the first section of essays included in that book.

461 Ibid., p. 61.
462 Ibid., p. 101.
463 Idem, "The Moral Authority of Scripture," in: *Interpretation*, vol. 34, 1980, pp. 356.
464 Ibid., p. 362.
465 Ibid., p. 357.
466 Ibid., pp. 364-5.
467 Ibid., p. 367.
468 Idem, *A Community of Character*, p. 91.
469 Idem, *Christian Existence Today*, p. 102.
470 Idem, *Against the Nations*, p. 75-76.
471 Idem, *A Community of Character*, p. 191.
472 Idem, *Against the Nations*, p. 76.
473 Idem, *Christian Existence Today*, p. 181.
474 Quoted by Hauerwas in *Christian Existence Today*, pp. 12-13. Hauerwas refers to W. Brueggemann, "II Kings 18-19: The Legitimacy of a Sectarian Hermeneutic", *Horizons in Biblical Theology* 7, 1985, pp. 22-23.
475 S. Hauerwas, *Against the Nations*, p. 7.
476 Idem, *A Community of Character*, p. 93.
477 J.M.L. van Gerwen, *The Church in the Theological Ethics of Stanley Hauerwas*, p. 55.
478 Ibid., pp. 316-317, note 54 on p. 257.
479 F.O. Van Gennep, *De terugkeer van de verloren Vader*, esp. pp. 197-202.
480 S. Hauerwas, *A Community of Character*, p. 283, note 17, on p. 189. See also p. 68 where Hauerwas emphasizes that the community has a history and tradition which separate it from the world.
481 Ibid., p. 84.
482 Idem, *The Peaceable Kingdom*, p. 99.
483 Idem, *A Community of Character*, p. 93.
484 Idem, *Christian Existence Today*, p. 54.
485 Idem, *The Peaceable Kingdom*, p. 99, and *A Community of Character*, p. 74.
486 Idem, *The Peaceable Kingdom*, p. 100.
487 Idem, *A Community of Character*, p. 74.
488 Idem, *The Peaceable Kingdom*, p. 100, and *Christian Existence Today*, p. 105.
489 S. Hauerwas, *Christian Existence Today*, p. 12.
490 See, e.g., *Vision and Virtue*, p. 205, where Hauerwas is interpreting Yoder. It is not completely clear to what extent Hauerwas underwrites this way of putting things by Yoder.
491 S. Hauerwas, *The Peaceable Kingdom*, p. 60.
492 Ibid., p. 101.
493 Idem, *A Community of Character*, p. 108.
494 Idem, *Christian Existence Today*, p. 106.
495 See *The Peaceable Kingdom* where Hauerwas places the living of upright lives alongside word and sacrament as a sign of the church.
496 These views pervade Hauerwas' writings, but see e.g. *Character and the Christian Life*, pp. 33, 210.
497 Idem, *The Peaceable Kingdom*, p. 97.
498 Ibid., pp. 133-134.
499 Idem, *Community of Character*, p. 116.
500 Ibid., p. 107.
501 Idem, *The Peaceable Kingdom*, p. 16.

502 Idem, *Christian Existence Today*, pp. 53-54, 91.
503 Idem, *Against the Nations*, p. 57.
504 See especially the chapters "On Keeping Theological Ethics Imaginative", pp. 51-60, and "The Reality of the Kingdom: An Ecclesial Space for Peace", pp. 107-121, in *Against the Nations*. See also *The Peaceable Kingdom*, p. 128.
505 Idem, *Against the Nations*, p. 179.
506 See, e.g., "Salvation and Health: Why Medicine Needs the Church", in *Suffering Presence. Theological Reflections on Medicine, the Mentally Handicapped, and the Church*, pp. 63-83, and "Sex in Public: Toward a Christian Ethic of Sex", in *A Community of Character*, pp. 175-195.
507 Idem, *Suffering Presence*, pp. 159-217.
508 Idem, *The Peaceable Kingdom*, pp. 104-105.
509 Ibid., p. 114.
510 Idem, *After Christendom? How the Church Is to Behave If Freedom, Justice, and a Christian Nation Are Bad Ideas.*
511 Ibid., pp. 50ff. See also *The Peaceable Kingdom*, pp. 104-105, and *Against the Nations*, p. 119. I find these treatments too general and too suggestive.
512 Idem, *The Peaceable Kingdom*, pp. 104-105.
513 Idem, *Against the Nations*, p. 12.
514 Idem., *Vision and Virtue*, p. 214. It is in reference to the concept of responsibility that I would diverge from R. Hütter's attempt (*Evangelische Ethik als kirchliches Zeugnis*, pp. 220ff.) to employ H. Arendt's distinction between producing (*Herstellen*) and acting (*Handeln*). The former is violent because it serves a specific end or purpose. The latter is non-violent because it is open-ended. As I will argue below with the help of Dussel (and as can also be argued with the help of Bonhoeffer's views on responsibility), I think Christian praxis is correctly forceful in its concern with results and effects. Non-violent means are a form of participation in specific (non-violent) ends, not a rejection of power and the pursuit of ends.
515 S. Hauerwas, *The Peaceable Kingdom*, p. 113, and *Against the Nations*, p. 117.
516 Idem, *The Peaceable Kingdom*, p. 166.
517 Ibid., p.15.
518 Ibid., p. 17; *Christian Existence Today*, pp. 11, 91, 95; *A Community of Character*, p. 93.
519 Idem, *Christian Existence Today*, p. 258.
520 E. Dussel, *Ethics and Community*, p. 7.
521 "Liberation theology" has become a worldwide movement and a shared terminology of movements concerned with the liberation of the poor of Latin American, of minorities and women of North America and Europe, of the 'peoples' of Asia and Africa, etcetera. Its context can be 'Western', as in the case of European economic theologies, or decidedly non-Western, as in the case of indigenous African theologies. The term does not, therefore, refer to a uniform theological project. Yet without overlooking the variety and diversity of even a Latin American theology of liberation, one can, at least in that context, identify a shared starting point (the situation of mass poverty and oppression), a shared methodology (critical reflection on praxis), and a shared commitment (to liberation of the poor). In addition there seems to exist a general sense of conviviality among liberation theologians evident in their own self-description as well as in the contacts between them, so that it is legitimate to speak of "a theology of liberation". See e.g. *Concilium* 171 (1984/1),

entitled "Different Theologies, Common Responsibility: Babel or Pentecost". See also C.L. Nessan, *Orthopraxis or Heresy*, pp. 57 and 214ff. In the present chapter I will use the term primarily to refer to Latin American liberation theology as explicated by Dussel.

522 E. Dussel, "An Ethic of Liberation: Fundamental Hypotheses", in *Concilium* 172 (2/1984), p. 59. This essay appears in a somewhat revised form under the title "Liberation Ethics: Fundamental Hypotheses" as an appendix in *Ethics and Community*. See there p. 105.

523 Idem, *Ethics and Community*, p. 16.

524 Ibid. Dussel notes that the Greek title of Luke's apostolic history is 'Praxeis Apostolon'.

525 Ibid., pp. 7-10.

526 Ibid., p. 11.

527 Ibid., p. 13.

528 Ibid., p. 12.

529 See the analysis which Dussel provides in *Ethics and Community* in chapters on the ethics of work, an ethical critique of capital and dependence, transnationals, international finances, and arms commerce. Although the socio-economic critique which liberation theology presupposes and/or provides is not undisputed, I am generally convinced by Dussel's argument and I choose for my present purposes to refer to it and assume it rather than present it. I will not in this framework get into the particularities of the economic debate, however decisive that is. For a theological review of the matter, see Nessan, *Orthopraxis or Heresy*, in particular his treatment of poverty in Latin America and the dependency theory (pp. 19-39), as well as the responses in defense of democratic capitalism (pp. 238-255).

530 E. Dussel, *Ethics and Community*, pp. 22-24.

531 'Exteriority' is for Dussel more or less synonymous with transcendence, and he uses the term, in what I have read, primarily in this affirmative sense. In that sense it may be incorrect to speak of 'exteriorization' as a product of the system. To that end Dussel speaks of 'alterification' (*Ethics and Community*, p. 239) or 'alienation' ("An Ethic of Liberation"). Nevertheless I risk this dialectical interpretation in order to underline what I perceive to be the irony of the matter in question: The rejected of the world are the chosen of God, i.e., the poor are holy.

532 E. Dussel, "An Ethic of Liberation", p. 57.

533 Ibid.

534 Ibid.

535 Or: "inner transcendence". The phrase is from F. Hinkelammert, and Dussel refers to *The Ideological Weapons of Death: A Theological Critique of Capitalism*, Maryknoll 1986, p. 61.

536 E. Dussel, *Ethics in Community*, p. 95.

537 Ibid., p. 76.

538 Ibid., p. 95.

539 Ibid., p. 105.

540 A Jewish reading of the parable might choose to leave open the question whether the 'son of man' of the parable is to be identified with Jesus. Nevertheless, simply by telling the parable Jesus declares his solidarity and in that sense his identification with the poor.

541 S.W. Gray, *The Least of My Brothers*.

542 E. Dussel, "An Ethic of Liberation", p. 57.

543 Dussel, *Ethics and the Theology of Liberation*, p. 53. See also "An Ethic of Liberation", p. 59.
544 Ibid., p. 56.
545 Ibid., p. 124.
546 E. Dussel, *Ethics and Community*, pp. 52-53.
547 Ibid., pp. 68, 91, 211, etc.
548 Ibid., p. 84.
549 Ibid., pp. 54-55.
550 Ibid., p. 42.
551 Ibid.
552 E. Dussel, *Ethics and the Theology of Liberation*, p. 78.
553 E. Dussel, *A History of the Church in Latin America*, p. 242.
554 Ibid.
555 E. Dussel, *Ethics and Community*, p. 43.
556 Ibid., p. 45.
557 Ibid. See chapter 6 entitled "Sensibility, Justice, and Sacramentality", pp. 58-67.
558 Ibid., pp. 62-63.
559 Ibid., pp. 91-92.
560 E. Dussel, "Het brood van de viering", pp. 65-74.
561 Ibid., p. 65.
562 E. Dussel, *Ethics and the Theology of Liberation*, p. 99.
563 Idem, *Ethics and Community*, p. 15.
564 Ibid., p. 45.
565 See C.L. Nessan, *Orthopraxis or Heresy*, esp. pp. 371ff.
566 E. Dussel, *Ethics and the Theology of Liberation*, p. 89.
567 Idem, *A History of the Church in Latin America*, pp. 244, 252f.
568 Idem, *Ethics and the Theology of Liberation*, p. 59.
569 Ibid., p. 75.
570 Idem, "Het stromen en terugstromen van het evangelie", p. 83.
571 Idem, *Ethics and the Theology of Liberation*, p. 89-90.
572 Ibid., p. 63.
573 Idem, *Ethics and Community*, p. 97.
574 Idem, *Ethics and the Theology of Liberation*, p. 63.
575 Ibid., p. 69.
576 Ibid., pp. 69, 70, 76.
577 Ibid., p. 129.
578 Idem, *Ethics and Community*, p. 237.
579 Ibid.
580 Cf. *Ethics and the Theology of Liberation*, p. 129.
581 Idem, *A History of the Church in Latin America*, p. xviii.
582 Ibid., pp. 173-176.
583 I fear that both the church and political theology have generally been fascinated with the state, either in collaboration with it or in opposition to it. In some instances the state is an easy target, but I question whether it can meet the expectations we have of it with regard to solving social problems in general and the problem of violence in particular.
584 E. Dussel, *Ethics and Community*, pp. 89-90.
585 Ibid., p. 186.
586 Ibid., pp. 230, 232
587 Ibid., p. 82.

588 Ibid., p. 230.
589 Ibid., pp. 243, 238.
590 Ibid., p. 240.
591 Ibid., p. 86.
592 Ibid., p. 105.
593 Ibid., p. 80.
594 Ibid., pp. 79, 31.
595 Ibid., p. 222.
596 Ibid., p. 222.
597 Ibid., p. 52.
598 Ibid., p. 241. Cf. "An Ethic of Liberation: fundamental hypotheses", p. 58.
599 Ibid., p. 2.
600 Idem., *A History of the Church in Latin America*, p. 255.
601 Ibid., p. 240.
602 L. Boff, *Ecclesiogenesis*. The term *eclesiogênese* was coined, according to Boff, at a consultation of/on base communities at Vitória, Brazil, in 1975. See pp. 34f.
603 Ibid., especially pp. 34-37.
604 Ibid., pp. 10f., 19.
605 Ibid., pp. 6f, 28, 40.
606 Ibid., p. 4.
607 Ibid., p. 10.
608 Ibid., p. 35. See also the five points in which Boff summarizes a meeting in Itaici in 1981 (pp. 40-43): 1. Faith and the celebration of life are essential amidst the experienced struggles and dramas. 2. Reading the Bible leads to a raised social conciousness. 3. The main cause of misery is capitalism. 4. The strength for resistance and liberation is dependent on the interrelationships of the communities with popular movements. 5. A noble sense of politics as a quest for the common good of the whole people is being recovered. ("And what's politics but generating life, in justice and love?")
609 Ibid., p. 9.
610 Ibid., p. 5.
611 Ibid., pp. 17-18.
612 Ibid., p. 7.
613 Ibid., p. 23. Initially Boff identifies three understandings: 1. the priestly-episcopal-papal structure which yields not so much an ecclesiology as a 'parochiology'; 2. the word/sacrament structure which results in a prophetico-cultic picture of the church; and 3. the figure of the church on a journey with an accompanying historico-salvific vision.
614 E. Dussel, *A History of the Church in Latin America*, p. 242.
615 L. Boff, Ecclesiogenesis, pp. 56-58. Boff quotes E. Peterson, "Die Kirche aus Juden und Heiden", in *Theologische Traktate*, Munich 1957, pp. 411-429.
616 E. Schüssler Fiorenza, *Bread Not Stone*, p. 153 (note 21 from p. xvii).
617 Ibid., p. xiv.
618 Ibid., p. xiv.
619 Idem, *In Memory of Her,* pp. xxi, 10, 41.
620 Idem, Bread not Stone, pp. 32ff. and In Memory of Her, pp. 10, 35f, etc.
621 Idem, *In Memory of Her*, p. 10.
622 Ibid, p. 152.
623 Ibid., p. 36.
624 Ibid., p. 35.

625 Ibid., pp. 309, 31.
626 Idem, *Bread Not Stone*, p. 39.
627 Idem, *In Memory of Her*, p. 29., and *Bread Not Stone*, p. 85.
628 Idem, *In Memory of Her*, p. 35.
629 Idem, *Bread Not Stone*, p. 45.
630 Idem, *In Memory of Her*, p. xx.
631 Idem, *Bread Not Stone*, p. 13.
632 Idem, *In Memory of Her*, p. 30., and *Bread Not Stone*, p. 41.
633 Idem, *Bread Not Stone*, pp. 60, 88.
634 Ibid., p. xiv.
635 Ibid., p. 47.
636 Idem, *In Memory of Her*, pp. 31f., and *Bread Not Stone*, p. 60.
637 Idem, *Bread Not Stone*, p. 47.
638 Ibid., p. 39.
639 Ibid., p. 14.
640 Ibid., p. 59.
641 Idem, *In Memory of Her*, p. 31.
642 Ibid., pp. 130ff.
643 Ibid., pp. 118ff.
644 Ibid., p. 120.
645 Ibid., p. 130.
646 Ibid., pp. 129, 135f.
647 Ibid., p. 153.
648 Ibid., p. 138.
649 Ibid., p. 122.
650 Ibid., p. 140-142.
651 Ibid., p. 147.
652 Ibid., p. 215.
653 Ibid., p. 210.
654 Ibid., p. 192.
655 Ibid., pp. 90, 265.
656 Ibid., p. 175.
657 Ibid., p. 181.
658 Ibid., p. 169.
659 Ibid., p. 179.
660 Ibid., p. 184ff.
661 Ibid., p. 168.
662 Ibid., pp. 279, 180, 265.
663 Ibid., pp. 286f.
664 Ibid., pp. 251-270.
665 Ibid., p. 288.
666 Ibid., p. 319. See further 316-323.
667 Ibid., p. 326.
668 Idem, *Bread Not Stone*, p. 81.
669 Idem, *In Memory of Her,* p. 344.
670 Ibid., p. 345.
671 Ibid., p. 344.
672 Ibid., p. 347f.
673 E. Schüssler Fiorenza, "Patriarchale macht schept verdeeldheden", p. 18.
674 R. Radford Ruether, *Women-Church*.
675 Ibid., p. 3f.

676 Ibid., p. 58.
677 Ibid., p. 39.
678 Ibid., p. 62.
679 Ibid., p. 58.
680 Ibid., pp. 69, 72, 62.
681 E. Schüssler Fiorenza, *Bread Not Stone*, p. 7.
682 R. Radford Ruether, *Women-Church*, p. 76. Cf. L. Russel, *Church in the Round*, pp. 50ff.
683 E. Schüssler Fiorenza, "Patriarchale macht schept verdeeldheden", p. 37.
684 R. Radford Ruether, *Women-Church*, pp. 94f.
685 E. Schüssler Fiorenza, "Patriarchale macht schept verdeeldheden", pp. 37-38.
686 Ibid., p. 34.
687 R. Radford Ruether, *Women-Church*, p. 86.
688 E. Schüssler Fiorenza, "Patriarchale macht schept verdeeldheden", p. 39.
689 Ibid., p. 37.
690 L. Russel, *Church in the Round*, p. 113. I discovered Russel's book (dated 1993) at a late stage, when my manuscript had practically been completed. However, the proximity of my ecclesiology to hers led me to attempt to summarize some main themes and add them to my reviews.
691 Ibid., p. 83.
692 Ibid., p. 149.
693 Ibid., pp. 116f.
694 Ibid., p. 129.
695 Ibid.
696 Ibid., p. 197.
697 Ibid., p. 26. Russel refers to bell hooks, *Feminist Theory: From Margin to Center*, Boston 1984.
698 Ibid., pp. 175f.
699 Ibid., p. 135.
700 Ibid., p. 136.
701 Ibid., p. 161.
702 Ibid., p. 173.
703 Ibid., p. 137.
704 Ibid., p. 199.
705 Idem, *A Community of Character*, pp. 108ff, and *Christian Existence Today*, pp. 115ff.
706 Idem, *Christian Existence Today*, pp. 3ff.
707 For this insight I thank H.D. van Hoogstraten.
708 D. Bonhoeffer, *Sanctorum Communio*, p. 168.
709 S. Hauerwas, *Christian Existence Today*, pp. 3ff. See also *A Community of Character*, pp. 108ff.
710 Idem, *Christian Existence Today*, pp. 53, 101.
711 Ibid., p. 121.
712 Idem, *A Community of Character*, p. 109.
713 Idem, *Character and the Christian Life*, p. 205. Although Hauerwas makes these observations in reference to Christian character, I do not think his intent is individualistic. He is speaking of Christians as a people, so that I do not hesitate to apply these words to an understanding of the church as a social body.
714 P. Lehmann, *Ethics in a Christian Context*, p. 14. See chapter II.2. above.
715 S. Hauerwas, *Christian Existence Today*, pp. 12, 123-125.

716 Ibid., pp. 115ff.

717 A.J. Baart, "Om de kwaliteit van moreel beraad", in *Werkschrift Moreel Beraad in Kerken*, pp. 31-76.

718 H. Berkhof, *Christelijk Geloof*, p. 50.

719 Ibid., pp. 50-52.

720 F.O. van Gennep, *De terugkeer van de verloren Vader*, pp. 385f.

721 Ibid., p. 465ff.

722 G.H. ter Schegget in J.P. Heering, et al, *De gelijkenis van de verloren Vader*, p. 33.

723 Cf. the title of a recent book by J. Bishop, *Some Bodies. The Eucharist and Its Implications* (1992).

724 Jim Wallis, "Renewing the Heart of Faith. A Prophetic Convergence of the People of God".

725 This is implied in my understanding of the conciliar process for justice, peace, and the integrity of creation (JPIC). I only indicate the relation here, although I realize that it needs further development and explication. P. Valstar, e.g., points out how, in accordance with J. Moltmann, humankind may understand itself as a member of the community of creation. P. Valstar, "Schepping bij Moltmann", p. 56.

726 Quoted by M.G. Cartwright, "The Practice and Performance of Scripture", p. 39. The reference is to N. Lash, "Performing the Scriptures," in *Theology on the Way to Emmaus*, London 1986, p. 43.

727 S. Hauerwas speaks of "ascribing some sort of wholeness to the texts or set of texts." See "The Moral Authority of Scripture", p. 363.

728 M.G. Cartwright, "The Practice and Performance of Scripture", p. 36.

729 S.E. Fowl/L.G. Jones, *Reading in Communion*, p. 20.

730 Ibid., p. 47. Fowl and Jones propose that we work analogically. I think the notion of prototype illuminates how that works.

731 Ibid. Fowl and Jones emphasize that there is no substitute for practical wisdom. They also point out that scripture must be allowed to read us. They follow Bonhoeffer in insisting that we must read not just for ourselves, but also over-against ourselves.

732 Ibid., p. 156. Fowl and Jones borrow the description from Bonhoeffer. "The discipline of the secret [arcane discipline] is also important in Bonhoeffer's thought as a space where Christians can develop the habits and skills needed to discern who Christ is 'today', to articulate how Christ is taking form 'here and now'. Such discernment requires learning to read Scripture in communion with others in the Body of Christ, fully recognizing the polyphonic character of the Christ who is the centre of Scripture."

733 Ibid. See chapter 5 entitled "Listening to the Voices of Outsiders: Challenges to Our Interpretive Practices," pp. 110-130.

734 Ibid., p. 112.

735 G. H. ter Schegget, *Volmacht in onmacht*, p. 317.

736 S. Hauerwas, *Christian Existence Today*, p. 31.

737 E.J.P. Jansen, "Over integriteit en raakbaarheid", in M.A. Thung, ed., *Nieuwe mores leren*, p. 118.

738 A.J. Baart, "Om de kwaliteit van moreel beraad", pp. 31-76.

739 I. Clement, "Leerlingschap van gelijken onder gelijke leerlingen", pp. 63-82.

740 R. Bons-Storm/D. Vernooij, *Beweging in macht*, p. 7.

741 I owe this way of putting things to G.D.J. Dingemans.

742 C.B. Posthumus Meyjes raises the question of whether the church can be the church without the discipline of the observance of the Lord's day. See *Van ophouden weten*, p. 142. "Doing the sabbath" and/or observing the Lord's day as a confessional act resists the economic homogenization of time and the ensuing threat to social life. P. Valstar has pointed out to me as well how J. Moltmann considers the sabbath to be a second archetype of liberation. P. Valstar, "Schepping bij Moltmann", p. 18.

743 See E. Lange, *Die ökumenische Utopie*, p. 131, where it is pointed out that "People's conscience is more provincial than their consciousness."

744 F. de Lange, *Individualisme. Een partijdig onderzoek naar een omstreden denkwijze*. De Lange's book is quite provocative. He criticizes what he sees as a general tendency in theology to deduce from the basic sociality indicated in creation a normative sociality of being in community. He labels this a naturalistic fallacy, an example of arguing from reality to ethics. In turn, De Lange attempts to argue a "factual individuality" as an inescapable postulate of ethics. "In ethics an individuality is argued that religion posits. His responsibility makes a human an individual..." (p.125) I agree with De Lange's protest against the reduction of individualism to egoism as well as with his emphasis on subjectivity and individuality as conditions for responsibility. He correctly warns as well against the underhanded confusion of nature, creation, and sociality which arrives at a normative communitarianism.

A theological appeal to the biblical story of creation, however, can be understood in a different way. The story of creation is a way of narrating the qualified interrelatedness of human beings. It is not a description of the way things are in an ontological sense. It is a picturing of the original relatedness that Israel understood to lie at the root of God's calling and covenant. The label "naturalistic fallacy" is then inappropriate for the creation story does not refer to being in itself, but to being as known in (salvation) history. Similarly I assert the ethical reality of the church in terms of its historical being. That historical being is formed by and filled with value.

See more recently: F. de Lange, *Ieder voor zich? Individualisering, ethiek en christelijk geloof* (Kampen 1993). Regretfully this latter publication has not been included here.

745 Cf. K.H. Miskotte, "Das grosse Schisma," in *Theologische Opstellen*, pp. 98ff.

746 Cf. Psalm 122:6-9.

747 Cf. N. Duff, *Humanization and the Politics of God*, p. 62, with reference to P. Lehmann.

748 F.W. Marquardt, "Was heisst: Sich zum Christus bekennen?", in B. Klappert, et al, *Jesusbekenntnis und Christusnachfolge*, pp. 50ff.

749 K.H. Miskotte, *Theologische Opstellen*, especially "Het jodendom als vraag aan de kerk", pp. 89-97.

750 M. Walton, "Over het verschuiven van de ruimte in de kerk", p. 139-140.

751 G.H. ter Schegget, "In gesprek met Van Gennep", in J.P. Heering, et al, eds., *De gelijkenis van de verloren Vader*, pp. 32-33.

752 Cf. M. Walton, "Over het verschuiven van de ruimte van de kerk".

753 See F.O. van Gennep, *De terugkeer van de verloren Vader*.

754 E. Lange, *Die ökumenische Utopie*, p. 189.

755 See *Gemeente-zijn in de mondiale samenleving*, pp. 99-101.

756 J. Moltmann, *Politische Theologie. Politische Ethik*, p. 142.

757 See the discussion by C.L. Nessan, *Orthopraxis or Heresy*, p. 114ff.

758 Cf. A. Polhuis, "Over revolutie en geweld", p. 128.

759 S.E. Fowl/L.G. Jones, *Reading in Communion*, chapter 5, "Living and Dying in the Word: Dietrich Bonhoeffer as Performer of Scripture," especially the pages 157ff.

760 G.H. ter Schegget, *Volmacht in onmacht*, p. 149.

761 I thus take a slightly different position than J. Beumer, *Intimiteit en Solidariteit*, who argues that mysticism can serve as a bridge between dogmatics and ethics.

762 See the title of William D. Miller's history of the Catholic worker movement, *A Harsh and Dreadful Love*.

## BIBLIOGRAPHY


Aalders, P.F.Th., et al, "Geen Neutraliteit", *In de Waagschaal*, Nov. 24, 1973, pp. 22-23.

Abrecht, P./Koshy, N., eds., *Before It's Too Late. The Challenge of Nuclear Armament*, Geneva 1983.

Baart, A.J., "Om de kwaliteit van moreel beraad", *Werkschrift Moreel Beraad in Kerken*, Multidisciplinair Centrum voor Kerk en Samenleving, Driebergen 1990, pp. 22-30.

Barth, K., *Theologische Existenz heute!*, (ed. H. Stoevesandt) Munich 1984.

_______, *Eine Schweizer Stimme. 1938-1945*, Zurich 1983.

_______, *Kirchliche Dogmatik* III/4, Zurich 1951.

_______, *Texte zur Barmer Theologischen Erklärung*, (ed. M. Rohkrämer) Munich 1984.

Barth, M., *Das Mahl des Herrn. Gemeinschaft mit Israel, mit Christus und unter den Gästen*, Neukirchen-Vluyn 1987.

Baum, G., et al, *Een convocatie voor de vrede. Christelijke kerken zoeken samen een weg naar vrede, gerechtigheid en behoud van de schepping, Concilium* 1/1988.

Beek, A. van de, et al, *De zucht naar vrijheid. Ter Schegget doordacht*, Baarn 1992.

Beer, D. de, et al, *Het uur van de waarheid. Het 'Kairos-document' van Zuidafrikaanse christenen*, Baarn 1986.

Beker, J.C., *Paul the Apostle. The Triumph of God in Life and Thought*, Edinburgh 1980.

Berg, A. van den, *Churches Speak Out on Economic Issues. A Survey of Several Statements*, Geneva 1991.

Berkhof, H., et al, *Met de moed der hoop. Opstellen aangeboden aan Dr. C.F. Beyers Naudé*, Baarn 1985.

Bethge, E., *Dietrich Bonhoeffer. Theologe - Christ - Zeitgenosse*, Munich 1967/1970.

_______, *Am gegebenen Ort. Aufsätze und Reden 1970-1979*, Munich 1979.

_______, *Bekennen und Widerstehen. Aufsätze, Reden, Gespräche*, Munich 1984.

_______, *Erstes Gebot und Zeitgeschichte. Aufsätze und Reden 1980-1990*, Munich 1991.

_______, "Dietrich Bonhoeffer und die Juden", in E. Feil/I. Tödt, eds., *Konsequenzen. Dietrich Bonhoeffers Kirchenverständnis heute*, Munich 1980, pp. 171-214.

Beumer, J.J., *Intimiteit en Solidariteit. Over het evenwicht tussen dogmatiek, mystiek en ethiek*, Baarn 1993.

Bishop, J., *Some Bodies. The Eucharist and Its Implications*, Macon 1992.

Boff, L., *Ecclesiogenesis. Base Communities Reinvent the Church*, Maryknoll 1986.

_______, *Faith on the Edge. Religion and Marginalized Existence*, San Francisco 1989.

Boff, L./Elizondo, V., *La Iglesia Popular: Between Fear and Hope, Concilium* 176 (6/1984).

Bonhoeffer, D., *Gesammelte Schriften*, (ed. E. Bethge) vol. I-VI, Munich 1965-1974.

_______, *Sanctorum Communio. Eine dogmatische Untersuchung zur Soziologie der Kirche*, (ed. J. van Soosten) Dietrich Bonhoeffer Werke (DBW) 1, Munich 1986.

_______, *Akt und Sein. Transzendentalphilosophie und Ontologie in der systematischen Theologie*, (ed. H.-R. Reuter) DBW 2, Munich 1988.

_______, *Nachfolge*, (ed. M. Kuske/I. Tödt) DBW 4, Munich 1989.

_______, *Gemeinsames Leben/Das Gebetbuch der Bibel*, (ed. G.L. Müller/A. Schönherr) DBW 5, Munich 1987.

_______, *Ethik*, (ed. I. Tödt, et al) DBW 6, Munich 1992.
_______, *Jugend und Studium 1918-1927*, (ed. H. Pfeifer, et al) DBW 9, Munich 1986.
_______, *Barcelona, Berlin, Amerika 1928-1931*, (ed. R. Staats/H.C. von Hase) DBW 10, Munich 1991.
_______, *Widerstand und Ergebung*, (ed. E. Bethge), Munich 1970.
_______, *A Testament of Freedom. The Essential Writings of Dietrich Bonhoeffer*, edited by G.B. Kelley and F.B. Nelson, New York 1990.
Bonsen, J. et al, eds., *Nergenshuizen. Verhalen en utopieën voor de gemeente*, Gorinchem 1991.
Bons-Storm, R./Vernooij, D., eds., *Beweging in macht. Vrouwenkerk in Nederland?*, Kampen 1991.
Brown, R.M., *Kairos. Three Prophetic Challenges to the Church*, Grand Rapids 1990.
Bruin, J., *Kerkvernieuwing. Een praktisch-ecclesiologisch onderzoek naar de betekenis van 'Gemeenteopbouw' voor de Nederlandse Hervormde Kerk*, Zoetermeer 1992.
Carter, G., et al, *Bonhoeffer's Ethics. Old Europe and New Frontiers*, Kampen 1991.
Cartwright, M.G., *Practices, Politics and Performance: Towards a Communal Hermeneutic for Christian Ethics*, dissertation, Duke University 1988 (Ann Arbor: University Microfilms).
_______, "The Practice and Performance of Scripture: Grounding Christian Ethics in a Communal Hermeneutic", in: D.M. Yeager, ed., *The Annual of the Society of Christian Ethics*, Knoxville 1988.
*Christian Faith and the World Economy Today. A Study Document from the World Council of Churches*, Geneva 1992.
Clement, I., "Mensen als subject van strijd en van theologie", *Berichten van de Vereniging voor Theologie en Maatschappij* 2/2 (June 1986), pp. 13-16.
_______, "Leerlingschap van gelijken onder gelijke leerlingen", in R. Bons-Storm/D. Vernooij, eds., *Beweging in macht. Vrouwenkerk in Nederland?*, Kampen 1991, pp. 63-82.
Cloete, G.D./Smit, D.J., eds., *A Moment of Truth. The Confession of the Dutch Reformed Mission Church*, Grand Rapids 1984.
Day, Th., *Dietrich Bonhoeffer on Christian Community and Common Sense*, New York 1982.
_______, "Conviviality and Common Sense. The Meaning of Christian Community for Dietrich Bonhoeffer", in A. Klassen, ed., *A Bonhoeffer Legacy*, Grand Rapids 1981, pp. 213-236.
Dingemans, G.D.J., *Een huis om in te wonen. Schetsen en bouwstenen voor een Kerk en een Kerkorde van de toekomst*, The Hague 1987.
_______, *Als hoorder onder de hoorders. Hermeneutische homilitiek*, Kampen 1991.
Duchrow, U., *Conflict over the Ecumenical Movement*, Geneva 1981.
_______, *Weltwirtschaft heute - Ein Feld für Bekennende Kirche?*, Munich 1986.
Duff, N., *Humanization and the Politics of God. The Koinonia Ethics of Paul Lehmann*, Grand Rapids 1992.
Dulk, M. den, *...als twee die spreken. Een manier om de heiligingsleer van Karl Barth te lezen*, The Hague 1987.
_______, "De communicatieve structuur van het geweten", in A. van de Beek, et al, *De zucht naar vrijheid. Ter Schegget doordacht*, Baarn 1992, pp. 88-95.
Dussel, E., *Ethics and the Theology of Liberation*, Maryknoll 1978.

_______, *A History of the Church in Latin America*, Grand Rapids 1981.
_______, *Ethics and Community*, Maryknoll 1988.
_______, "Het brood van de viering", *Concilium* 1982/2, pp. 65-74.
_______, "An Ethic of Liberation: Fundamental Hypotheses", *Concilium* 172 (1984/2), pp. 54-63.
_______, "Het stromen en terugstromen van het evangelie", *Concilium* 1986/5, pp. 79-87.
*epd-Dokumentation*, Gemeinschaftswerk der evangelischen Publizistik, Frankfurt am Main.
Ellul, J., *The Presence of the Kingdom*, New York 1948/1967.
_______, *The Theological Foundation of Law*, New York 1960/1969.
_______, *Violence*, New York 1969.
Falcke, H., *Vom Gebot Christi, dass die Kirche uns die Waffe aus der Hand nimmt und den Krieg verbietet. Zum konziliaren Weg des Friedens. Ein Beitrag aus der DDR*, Stuttgart 1986.
_______, *Mit Gott Schritt halten. Reden und Aufsätze eines Theologen in der DDR aus zwanzig Jahren*, Berlin 1986.
Feil, E., *The Theology of Dietrich Bonhoeffer*, Philadelphia 1985.
_______, ed., *Verspieltes Erbe? Dietrich Bonhoeffer und der deutsche Nachkriegsprotestantismus*, Munich 1979.
Feil, E./Tödt, I., eds., *Konsequenzen. Dietrich Bonhoeffers Kirchenverständnis heute*, Munich 1980.
Flesseman-van Leer, E., *Wie toch is Jezus van Nazareth?*, The Hague 1985.
*Frieden wahren, fördern und erneuern. Eine Denkschrift der Evangelischen Kirche in Deutschland*, Gütersloh 1981.
Fowl, S.E./Jones, L.G., *Reading in Communion. Scripture and Ethics in Christian Life*, Grand Rapids 1991.
Fowl, S.E., "Could Horace Talk with the Hebrews? Translatability and Moral Disagreement in MacIntyre and Stout", *Journal of Religious Ethics* 19/1 (Spring 1991) pp. 1-20.
*Gemeente-zijn in de mondiale samenleving*, Netherlands Reformed Church, The Hague 1988.
Gennep, F.O. van, *Katholiciteit en pluraliteit*, Leiden 1980.
_______, *De terugkeer van de verloren Vader. Een theologisch essay over vaderschap en macht in cultuur en christendom*, Baarn 1989.
Gerwen, J.M.L. van, *The Church in the Theological Ethics of Stanley Hauerwas*, dissertation, Graduate Theological Union, Berkeley 1984 (Ann Arbor: University Microfilms).
Gollwitzer, H., *Von der Stellvertretung Gottes. Christlicher Glaube in der Erfahrung der Verborgenheit Gottes. Zum Gespräch mit Dorothee Sölle*, Munich 1967.
Goodall, N., ed., *The Uppsala Report*, World Council of Churches, Geneva 1968.
Gray, S.W., *The Least of My Brothers. Matthew 25:31-46. A History of Interpretation*, Atlanta 1989.
Gruchy, J.W. de, *Liberating Reformed Theology. A South African Contribution to an Ecumenical Debate*, Grand Rapids/Cape Town 1991.
Gruchy, J.W. de/Villa-Vicencio, Ch., eds., *Apartheid is a Heresy*, Grand Rapids 1983.
Guroian, V., "Bible and Ethics: An Ecclesial and Liturgical Interpretation", *Journal of Religious Ethics* 18/1 (1990), pp. 129-158.
Gutiérrez, G., *Theologie van de bevrijding*, Baarn 1974.
_______, "Talking about God", *Sojourners Magazine*, Feb. 1983, pp. 26-27.

Gutiérrez, G., et al, *Different Theologies, Common Responsibility: Babel or Pentecost?, Concilium* 171 (1/1984).
Harvey, B.A., *Piety, Power and Politics: Conscience as the Methodological Nexus for Christian Thought in the Theology of Paul Lehmann*, dissertation, Duke University 1987 (Ann Arbor: University Microfilms).
Hauerwas, S., *After Christendom? How the Church is to Behave if Freedom, Justice, and a Christian Nation Are Bad Ideas*, Nashville 1991.
_______, *Against the Nations. War and Survival in a Liberal Society*, Minneapolis 1985.
_______, *Character and the Christian Life. A Study in Theological Ethics*, San Antonio 1975/1985.
_______, *Christian Existence Today. Essays on Church, World and Living in Between*, Durham 1988.
_______, *A Community of Character*, Notre Dame 1981.
_______, *The Peaceable Kingdom*, Notre Dame 1983.
_______, *Suffering Presence. Theological Reflections on Medicine, the Mentally handicapped, and the Church*, Notre Dame 1989.
_______, with R. Bondi and D.B. Burrell, *Truthfulness and Tragedy. Further Investigations into Christian Ethics*, Notre Dame 1977.
_______, *Vision and Virtue. Essays in Christian Ethical Reflection*, Notre Dame 1981.
_______, "The Ethicist as Theologian", *The Christian Century* 92/15 (April 1975), pp. 408-412.
_______, "Review Essay of P. Lehmann, *The Transfiguration of Politics: The Presence and Power of Jesus of Nazareth in and over Human Affairs*", in: *Worldview* 18/12 (Dec. 1975), pp. 45-48.
_______, "The Moral Authority of Scripture: The Politics and Ethics of Remembering", Interpretation 34/4 (Oct. 1980), pp. 356-370.
Hauerwas, S./Jones, L.G., eds., *Why Narrative? Readings in Narrative Theology*, Grand Rapids 1989.
Hauerwas, S./MacIntyre, A., eds., *Revisions. Changing Perspectives in Moral Philosophy*, Notre Dame 1983.
Heering, G.J., *De zondeval van het christendom. Een studie over christendom, staat en oorlog*, Utrecht 1981[5], with an introduction bij J. de Graaf.
Heering, J.P., et al, *De gelijkenis van de verloren Vader*, Nijkerk 1991.
Hendriks, J., *Een vitale en aantrekkelijke gemeente. Model en methode van gemeenteopbouw*, Kampen 1990.
Hoedemaker, L.A., *Met Christus bij anderen. Opmerkingen over dialoog en apostolaat*, Baarn 1978.
_______, "Het schema van de wereld en het belijden van de kerk", *Wereld en Zending: "Verzuim en verwachting. Gelovig belijden in de wereldeconomie"*, 1988/4, pp. 346-352.
_______, "Moreel beraad en christelijk geloof", *Werkschrift Moreel Beraad in Kerken*, Multidisciplinair Centrum voor Kerk en Samenleving, Driebergen 1990, pp. 22-30.
Hoekendijk, J.C., *De kerk binnenste buiten*, (eds. L.A. Hoedemaker/P. Tijmes) Amsterdam 1964.
Huber, W., *Kirche*, Munich 1988.
Hunsinger, G., "Where the Battle Rages", *Dialog* 26/4, pp. 264-274.

_______, "Barth, Barmen and the Confessing Church Today", *Katallagete* 9/2 (Summer 1985), pp. 14-27. "Responses to [and from] Hunsinger" in *Katallagete* 10/1-3 (Fall 1987).
Hütter, R., *Evangelische Ethik als kirchliches Zeugnis. Interpretationen zu Schlüsselfragen theologischer Ethik in der Gegenwart*, Neukirchen-Vluyn 1993.
_______, "The Church: Midwife of History or Witness to the Eschaton?", *Journal of Religious Ethics 18/1 (1990), pp. 27-54.*
_______, "Ethik und Traditionen: Die Neo-Aristotelische Herausforderung in der philosophischen und theologischen Ethik der USA", *Verkündigung und Forschung* 35 (1990), pp. 61-84.
*In Christ - One Community in the Spirit*, Proceedings of the Sixth Assembly of the Lutheran World Federation (Dar es Salaam 1977), Geneva 1977.
Jeurissen, R., "Peace in the Ecumenical Movement", *Exchange* XVI/46 (April 1987), pp. 1-118.
Jones, J.A., *Preaching Ethics: Experimenting with a Lehmanian Approach*, dissertation 1987 (Ann Arbor:University Microfilms).
Jongh, J. de, *Verantwoordelijk...wat bedoel je?*, Zoetermeer 1992.
*Journal of Religious Ethics*, 20/2 (Fall 1992), essays by M. Walzer, J.H. Yoder, etc. on just war theory.
Jüngel, E., *Zum Wesen des Friedens. Frieden als Kategorie theologischer Anthropologie*, Munich 1983.
Kässmann, M., *Die Eucharistische Vision. Armut und Reichtum als Anfrage an die Einheit der Kirche in der Diskussion des ökumenischen Rates*, Munich/Mainz 1992.
Kelly, G.B./Nelson, F.B., eds., *A Testament of Freedom. The Essential Writings of Dietrich Bonhoeffer*, New York 1990.
Kerk en Vrede, "Uitnodiging tot belijden", Utrecht 1985.
Keshishian, A., *Conciliar Fellowship: A Common Goal*, Geneva 1992.
King, Jr., M.L., *A Testament of Hope: The essential writings and speeches of Martin Luther King, Jr.*, (ed. J.M. Washington) San Francisco 1986/1989.
*Kirchliches Jahrbuch der Evangelischen Kirche in Deutschland*, Gütersloh.
Klappert, B./Weidner, U., eds., *Schritte zum Frieden*, Wuppertal 1983.
Klappert, B., et al, *Jesusbekenntnis und Christusnachfolge*, Munich 1992.
Klassen, A.J., ed., *A Bonhoeffer Legacy. Essays in Understanding*, Grand Rapids 1981.
Koelega, D.G.A./Noordegraaf, H., *Visie en volharding. Naar een missionaire kerk die zich inzet voor een rechtvaardige en duurzame samenleving. Opstellen voor Mady A. Thung*, Multidisciplinair Centrum voor Kerk en Samenleving, Driebergen 1991.
Kraus, H.J., "We gaan naar een principieel pacifisme", *HN-Magazin, June 28, 1986, pp. 24-25.*
Krusche, G., *Bekenntnis und Weltverantwortung. Die Ekklesiologiestudie des Lutherischen Weltbundes. Ein Beitrag zur ökumenischen Sozialethik*, Berlin 1986.
Krusche, W., "Schuld und Vergebung - Der Grund christlichen Friedenshandelns" in: *epd-Dokumentation*, nr. 30a/1984, Frankfurt am Main.
Kuitert, H.M., *Everything is Politics, but Politics is not Everything*, Grand Rapids 1986.
Kuitert, H.M./Schillebeeckx, E., *Gesprek tussen twee vuren*, Baarn 1986.
Lamsma, S., "Over de roeping van de kerk in de moderne samenleving", unpublished paper.
Lange, E., *Die ökumenische Utopie oder Was bewegt die ökumenische Bewegung?*, Stuttgart 1972/1986.

Lange, F. de, *Een burger op z'n best. Dietrich Bonhoeffer*, Baarn 1986.
_______, *Individualisme. Een partijdig onderzoek naar een omstreden denkwijze*, Kampen 1989.
Lapide, P., *Jeder kommt zum Vater. Barmen und die Folgen*, Neukirchen-Vluyn 1984.
_______, "Bonhoeffer und das Judentum", in E. Feil, ed., *Verspieltes Erbe? Dietrich Bonhoeffer und der deutsche Nachkriegsprotestantismus*, Munich 1979.
Lehmann, P., *Ethics in a Christian Context*, New York 1963.
_______, *The Transfiguration of Politics: The Presence and Power of Jesus of Nazareth in and over Human Affairs*, New York 1975.
Lohfink, G., *Wie hat Jesus Gemeinde gewollt?*, Freiburg 1982/1983.
_______, *Wem gilt die Bergpredigt? Zur Glaubwürdigkeit des Christlichen*, Freiburg 1988/1993.
Lorenz, E., ed., *The Debate on Status Confessionis: Studies in Christian Political Theory*, Geneva 1983.
MacIntyre, A., *After Virtue. A Study in Moral Theory*, London 1985.
_______, *Whose Justice? Which Rationality?*, London 1988.
Marquardt, F.W., "Was heisst: Sich zum Christus bekennen?" in B. Klappert, et al, *Jesusbekenntnis und Christusnachfolge*, Munich 1992, pp. 47-64.
Maurin, P., *Easy Essays. Radical Christian Thought*, West Hamlin 1971.
Mehl, P.J., "In the Twilight of Modernity: MacIntyre and Mitchell on Moral Traditions and Their Assessment", *Journal of Religious Ethics* 19/1 (Spring 1991), pp. 21-54.
Meier, K., *Der Evangelische Kirchenkampf*, vol. 1, Halle 1976.
Meyer-Wilmes, H./Troch, L., eds., *Over hoeren, taarten en vrouwen die voorbijgaan. Macht en verschil in de vrouwenkerk*, Kampen 1992.
Mieth, D./Pohier, J., *Christian Ethics: Uniformity, Universality, Pluralism, Concilium* 150 (10/1981).
Míguez Bonino, J., *Toward a Christian Political Ethics*, Philadelphia 1983.
Miller, W.D., *A Harsh and Dreadful Love. Dorothy Day and the Catholic Worker Movement*, Garden City 1973.
Miskotte, K.H., *Theologische Opstellen*, Verzameld Werk 9, Kampen 1990.
Moltmann, J., *Kirche in der Kraft des Geistes. Ein Beitrag zur messianischen Ekklesiologie*, Munich 1989.
_______, *Politische Theologie - Politische Ethik*, Munich/Mainz 1984.
_______, ed., *Bekennende Kirche wagen. Barmen 1934-1984*, Munich 1984
Müller, C.R., *Dietrich Bonhoeffer's Kampf gegen die nationalsozialistische Verfolgung und Vernichtung der Juden*, Munich 1990.
Nessan, C.L., *Orthopraxis or Heresy. The North American Response to Latin American Liberation Theology*, Atlanta 1989.
Niemöller, W., *Kampf und Zeugnis der Bekennenden Kirche*, Bielefeld 1948.
_______, *Der Pfarrernotbund. Geschichte einer kämpfenden Bruderschaft*, Hamburg 1973.
Noordmans, O., *Zondaar en bedelaar*, Amsterdam 1946.
Nouwen, H.J.M., *The Road to Daybreak. A Spiritual Journey*, New York 1988.
*Pastorale brief over de kernbewapening*, Netherlands Reformed Church, The Hague 1981.
Polhuis, A., *Armen en Kernwapens. Een reaktie op de handreiking van de Generale Synode van de Nederlandse Hervormde Kerk*, Kerk en Vrede, undated.
_______, "Over revolutie en geweld", in A. van de Beek, et al, *De zucht naar vrijheid. Ter Schegget doordacht*, Baarn 1992, pp. 120-130.

_______, *Lotgenoten bondgenoten? Mogelijkheden van coalitievorming in oude stadswijken. Een bijdrage vanuit de kerk*, Zoetermeer 1994.
Posthumus Meyjes, C.B., *Van ophouden weten. De betekenis van het sabbatsgebod voor onze tijd*, The Hague 1992.
Radford Ruether, R., *Women-Church. Theology and Practice*, San Francisco 1986.
Rasmussen, L., with R. Bethge, *Dietrich Bonhoeffer - His Significance for North Americans*, Minneapolis 1990.
*Resources for Study of 'Christian Obedience in a Nuclear Age'*, Presbyterian Church U.S.A., Louisville 1988.
Russel, L., *Church in the Round. Feminist Interpretation of the Church*, Louisville 1993.
Schegget, G.H. ter, *Het beroep op de stad der toekomst. Ethiek van de revolutie*, Haarlem 1971.
_______, *Theologie en ideologie. Een aanzet tot verantwoordelijk theologiseren onder vervreemde maatschappelijke verhoudingen*, Baarn 1981.
_______, *Het gebed als hart van de ethiek*, Leiden 1982.
_______, *Het moreel van de gemeente. Essays over de ethiek van Paulus volgens Romeinen 12 en 13*, Baarn 1985.
_______, *Volmacht in onmacht. Over de roeping van de christelijke gemeente in de politiek*, Baarn 1988.
_______, "In gesprek met Van Gennep", in J.P. Heering, et al, *De gelijkenis van de verloren Vader*, Nijkerk 1991, pp. ___.
Schillebeeckx, E., *Als politiek niet alles is... Jezus in onze westerse cultuur*, Baarn 1986.
_______, *Mensen als verhaal van God*, Baarn 1989.
Schrage, W., *Ethik des Neuen Testaments*, Göttingen 1982.
Schüssler Fiorenza, E., *Bread Not Stone. The Challenge of Feminist Biblical Interpretation*, Boston 1984.
_______, *In Memory of Her. A Feminist Theological Reconstruction of Christian Origins*, New York 1983/1989.
_______, "Patriarchale macht schept verdeeldheden. Feministische verschillen geven ons kracht. De ethiek en politiek van bevrijding", in H. Meyer-Wilmes/L. Troch, eds., *Over hoeren, taarten en vrouwen die voorbijgaan. Macht en verschil in de vrouwenkerk*, Kampen 1992, pp. 13-46.
Schulze, H., *Theologische Sozialethik. Grundlegung, Methodik, Programmatik*, Gütersloh 1979.
Schulze, R., ed., *Barmen 1934-1984. Beiträge zur Diskussion um die Theologische Erklärung von Barmen*, Evangelical Church in the GDR, Berlin 1983.
Sobrino, J., "Het 'leergezag' van het volk van God in Latijns-Amerika", *Concilium* 1985/4, pp. 49-56.
Sölle, D., *Stellvertretung. Ein Kapitel Theologie nach dem "Tode Gottes"*, Stuttgart 1965.
Spijkerboer, A.A., "De 'status confessionis' en de politiek", in idem, ed. *Tussen uitdaging en traditie. Kerkelijk belijden in historisch en oecumenisch perspectief*, The Hague 1984, pp. 134-142.
"Status Confessionis and Church Unity - LWF Budapest 1984", *KISA-Report*, Uppsala 1984/2.
*Der status confessionis und die Einheit der Kirche*, Loccumer Protokolle 1/1983.
Stoll, K., *Status confessionis. Das Bekenntnis des Glaubens zu Jesus Christus im Zeitalter der atomaren Gefahr*, Hannover 1984.

Stringfellow, W., *An Ethic for Christians and Other Aliens in a Strange Land*, Waco 1973/1978.
_______, *Conscience and Obedience. The Politics of Romans 13 and Revelation 13 in Light of the Second Coming*, Waco 1978.
Thielicke, H., *Die Atomwaffe als Frage an die christliche Ethik*, Tübingen 1958.
Thung, M.A., ed., *Nieuwe Mores Leren*, The Hague 1986.
Touw, H.C., *Het verzet der hervormde kerk*, The Hague 1946.
Valstar, P., "Schepping bij Moltmann. Op zoek naar scheppingstheologische notities ten bate van het behoud van de schepping", unpublished paper.
Verdonk, W.E., *Ongehoord. Uit de nalatenschap van W.E. Verdonk*, (ed. A. Vos, et al) The Hague 1988.
"Verzuim en verwachting. Gelovig belijden in de wereldeconomie", topical issue of *Wereld en Zending* 1988/4.
Villa-Vicencio, Ch., *Between Christ and Caesar. Classic and Contemporary Texts on Church and State*, Grand Rapids 1986.
*Het vraagstuk van de kernwapenen*, Netherlands Reformed Church, The Hague 1963/1979.
Wallis, J., "Renewing the Heart of Faith. A Prophetic Convergence of the People of God", *Sojourners Magazine*, 22/2 (Feb./March 1993), pp. 10-14.
Walther, Chr., ed., *Der deutsche Protestantismus und die atomare Aufrüstung 1954-1961. Dokumente und Kommentare*, Munich 1981.
Walton, M.N., *Witness in Biblical Scholarship. A Survey of Recent Studies 1956-1980*, Leiden/Utrecht 1986.
_______, "The Evangelical Church in the GDR. A Church in Socialism", *Occasional Papers on Religion in Eastern Europe*, IV/5 (Oct. 1984).
_______, "Processus conciliationis et status confessionis. De samenspreking in de gemeente over haar identiteit", *In de Waagschaal*, 17/17 (Dec. 1988), pp. 7-10.
_______, "Over het verschuiven van de ruimte in de kerk", in A. van de Beek, et al, *De zucht naar vrijheid*, Baarn 1992, pp. 131-142.
*Werkschrift Moreel Beraad in Kerken. Een nadere begripsbepaling*, Multidisciplinair Centrum voor Kerk en Samenleving, Driebergen 1990.
*Wie geen doel heeft kan niet verdwalen. Gedichten*, Deventer 1992.
Wischnath, R., *Frieden als Bekenntnisfrage*, Güterloh 1984.
Wolf, E., ed., *Christusbekenntnis im Atomzeitalter?*, Munich 1959/1983.
Yoder, J.H., *The Politics of Jesus*, Grand Rapids 1972.
_______, *The Priestly Kingdom. Social Ethics as Gospel*, Notre Dame 1984.
Zeldenrust, H., ed., *De vrede belijden*, Kampen 1986.
Zijlstra, W., *Op zoek naar een nieuwe horizon. Handboek voor klinische pastorale vorming*, Nijkerk 1989.

## INDEX OF AUTHORS